Za početak prijateljstvo !

Ivica

12. 03. 2005

D1800137

Building Reliable Component-Based Software Systems

For a listing of recent titles in the *Artech House Computing Library,* turn to the back of this book.

Building Reliable Component-Based Software Systems

Ivica Crnkovic
Magnus Larsson

Editors

Artech House
Boston • London
www.artechhouse.com

Library of Congress Cataloging-in-Publication Data
Building reliable component-based software systems/Ivica Crnkovic, Magnus Larsson, editors.
p. cm.—(Artech House computing library)
Includes bibliographical references and index.
ISBN 1-58053-327-2 (alk. paper)
1. Component software—Reliability. 2. Software engineering.
I. Crnkovic, Ivica. II. Larsson, Magnus (Magnus Peter Henrik), 1969–
QA76.76.C66 B85   2002
005.1—dc21   2002021594

British Library Cataloguing in Publication Data
Building reliable component-based software systems. — (Artech House computing library)
1. Software engineering 2. Component software
I. Crnkovic, Ivica II. Larsson, Magnus
005.1
ISBN 1-58053-327-2

Cover design by Igor Valdman

© 2002 ARTECH HOUSE, INC.
685 Canton Street
Norwood, MA 02062

International Standard Book Number: 1-58053-327-2
Library of Congress Catalog Card Number: 2002021594

10 9 8 7 6 5 4 3 2 1

To Tea, Luka, and Gordana
—Ivica

To Emmy, Jacob, Ida, and Christina
—Magnus

Contents

Preface

This is a book about component-based software engineering (CBSE). CBSE is the emerging discipline of the development of software components and the development of systems incorporating such components. Component-based systems are built by assembling components developed independently of the systems. To assemble components, a proprietary code that connects the components is usually needed. This code is often referred to as "glue code." In an ideal world of components the assembly process would be smooth and simple. The effort required to obtain the glue code would be practically negligible; a system incorporating components would know everything about them—their operational interfaces and their nonfunctional properties and the components would be exactly what the system needs; in short, components could be assembled as easily as Lego blocks.

In the real world, the component-based development process is complex and often difficult; systems are built from preexisting components when appropriate and possible and by developing a new code specific to the particular system. The system may know about the syntax of the operational interfaces of the components, but not necessarily their other properties. Developing the glue code can be costly—it may take longer to develop the glue code than the components concerned. Software components are in fact much harder to assemble than Lego blocks. Constructing software systems from components "is more like having a bathtub full of Tinkertoy, Lego, Erector, Lincoln Log, Block City, and six other incompatible kits—picking out parts that fit specific functions and expecting them to fit together" (Mary

Shaw, "Architectural Issues in Software Reuse: It's Not Just the Functionality, It's the Packaging," Presentation at the Symposium on Software Reusability, SSR'95). CBSE tries to make the real world as close as possible to the ideal world of component-based development. We have a long way to go to achieve this goal.

In spite of many difficulties, the component-based approach has achieved remarkable success in many domains. A majority of the software programs we use everyday take advantage of component-based technologies. Many classes of software, however, take a rudimentary approach to component-based methods. For these classes of software the specification of "how" is at least as important as the specification of "what." Examples of these classes of systems are reliable systems; safety-, business-, or mission-critical systems (also known as dependable systems); and embedded systems. The general-purpose component technologies currently available cannot cope with the nonfunctional (or more correctly extrafunctional) requirements of such systems. These additional requirements call for new technologies, new methods, and the specific approach of CBSE. This book describes the basic principles and the trends in research and practice of CBSE with an emphasis on dependable systems.

Organization of This Book

The book is divided into parts, each of which explores a theme through the different chapters. Each part begins with a short introduction presenting its objective and an overview of the chapters. Although the parts and the chapters are relatively independent of each other, several principles apply to all. The first principle is *from general to specific*. The book begins with general parts related to software components, proceeds through topics such as processes related to CBSE, continues with domain-specific processes, and concludes with concrete case studies. The second principle is *from theoretical to practical issues*. Although the first chapters discuss theoretical topics such as component specifications, the last chapters give examples of the use of concrete component models. The third principle is *from simple to complex*. The first chapters discuss the elements of component-based development, the components, the middle parts describe systems built from components, and the final parts give complex examples of real component-based systems.

The book consists of seven parts:

- Part 1, *The Definition and Specification of Components*, gives an overall introduction to components and the basic terminology of component-based software engineering.

- Part 2, *Software Architecture and Components*, discusses different component models from the point of view of software architecture.

- Part 3, *Developing Software Components*, describes a component-based development process and certain methods for the successful design and specification of components.

- Part 4, *Using Software Components*, discusses problems related to component evaluation, integration, and testing.

- Part 5, *Software Product Lines*, provides an overview of software product-line architectures and gives a case study of a component model used in a product line.

- Part 6, *Real-Time Software Components*, discusses the principles and methods for building real-time, embedded, and safety-critical systems.

- Part 7, *Case Studies: CBD in Industrial Applications*, shows how the methods and theories described in the preceding parts of the book are implemented or utilized in concrete cases.

Who Should Read This Book?

This book is directed toward several reader categories. Software developers and engineers will find the theory behind existing component models. The case studies will provide useful information about challenges, pitfalls, and successes in the practical use of component-based technologies. Experienced developers will find useful technical details in the last part of the book, while inexperienced developers can learn about the principles of CBSE. Project and company managers will be interested in the process and organizational aspects of component-based development, either for developing components or systems, with a focus on the reuse of components.

The book includes topics related to current research and to the state of the art of CBSE. For this reason, it will be of interest to researchers, either those beginning research in this field or those already involved. Extensive lists of references in each chapter provide broad insight into current trends. Finally, the book is appropriate as a course book, primarily for graduate students or undergraduate students in the later years of their studies.

How to Use This Book

The different chapters have been written by different authors, experts in different areas. For this reason all chapters are relatively autonomous and can be read independently of each other. For a broader perspective of a topic, an entire part of interest can be read. This does not mean that the entire book shouldn't be read! It merely means that it is not necessary for the book to be read in the order in which it is organized. Those interested in basic principles and theories related to component models would be interested in the first parts, especially Chapters 1 through 5. As course literature, reading could begin with the first parts and a study of some of the chapters presenting case studies (i.e., Chapters 12, or 15 through 19). An experienced practitioner or researcher might be especially interested in these chapters. Chapters 2 and 6 through 10 are more theoretical in nature with many open questions and might therefore be of special interest to researchers and graduate students. Chapters 5, 11, 13, and 19 cover the component-based software life cycle and will be of special interest to project leaders or those working with development processes. Chapters 13 through 17 are related to real-time and dependable systems.

Web Site

The book's Web site, http://www.idt.mdh.se/cbse-book, includes a set of presentation slides and additional material to support the use of this book in teaching and personal study. Instructors may freely use and modify the presentation material.

Acknowledgments

Many people contributed to the development of this book. First, we wish to thank all of the authors. It was a wonderful experience to work with them, to read their contributions, and to discuss the book's overall objectives or particular ideas. We never met as a group but we made a great team. We are grateful to all the reviewers, known and unknown to us. Special gratitude goes to Heinz Schmidt, who reviewed the entire book and whose comments led invariably to its improvement. Students attending the CBSE course at Mälardalen University have analyzed, presented, and discussed different chapters and selected topics from the book. Their questions and comments were a positive contribution to its development. We wish to thank Victor

Miller who did a great job of reviewing all chapters and enhancing the writing style. We are particularly indebted to Tim Pitts, Ruth Harris, and Jill Hodgson Stoodley from Artech House for their enormous and continuous support during the writing and editing process.

Finally, we wish to express our gratitude to our families, to the children Tea and Luka, and Emmy, Jacob, and Ida, and to our wives, Gordana and Christina, for their unfailing patience, support, and love.

Ivica Crnkovic and Magnus Larsson
Västerås, Sweden
June 2002

Introduction

Ivica Crnkovic and Magnus Larsson

We are witnessing an enormous expansion in the use of software in business, industry, administration, research, and even in everyday life. Software is no longer used marginally in technical systems; instead it has become a central factor in many fields. Features based on software functionality, rather than other system characteristics, are becoming the most important factor in a competitive market. This trend increases the demands on software products such as enhanced usability, robustness, reliability, flexibility, adaptability, and simpler installation and deployment. As these demands are growing stronger, the complexity of processes that software manages is increasing along with the demand for the integration of processes from different areas. As a consequence, software programs are becoming increasingly large and complex. The main challenge for software developers today is to cope with complexity and to adapt quickly to change. Traditionally, software development addressed the challenges of increasing complexity and dependence on external software by focusing on one system at a time and on satisfying delivery deadline and budget requirements without considering the evolutionary needs of the system.

Focusing on one system at a time and neglecting forthcoming changes has led to a number of problems: the failure of the majority of projects to meet their deadline, budget, and quality requirements as well as the continued increase in costs associated with software maintenance.

One key to the solution of these problems is reusability. The idea of software reuse is not new. But, despite some successes, reusability has not become a driving force in software development. Many of the unsuccessful approaches to reuse did not satisfy the basic requirements of reusability [1]:

1. Reuse requires some modification of the object being reused.
2. Reuse must be integrated into specific software development.

In many approaches, reusability is not inherent in the development process. What can be reused and what cannot be reused is not precisely defined, and how the changes can be introduced in the reusable parts is not formalized. The rapidly emerging approach called component-based development (CBD) reestablishes the idea of reuse and introduces new elements. In CBD, software systems are built by assembling components already developed and prepared for integration. CBD has many advantages. These include more effective management of complexity, reduced time to market, increased productivity, improved quality, a greater degree of consistency, and a wider range of usability [2].

However, CBD has several disadvantages and risks that can jeopardize its success:

- *Time and effort required for development of components.* Among the factors that can discourage the development of reusable components is the increased time and effort required to build reusable units [3, 4].

- *Unclear and ambiguous requirements.* In general, requirements management is an important and complex phase in the development process, its main objective being to define consistent and complete component requirements. One of the major problems of software development in general comes from unclear, ambiguous, incomplete, and insufficient requirements specifications. Reusable components are, by definition, to be used in different applications, some of which may yet be unknown and the requirements of which cannot be predicted. This applies to both functional and nonfunctional requirements. This makes it more difficult to identify the requirements properly and hence to design and build components successfully [5, 6].

- *Conflict between usability and reusability.* To be widely reusable, a component must be sufficiently general, scalable, and adaptable; it will therefore be more complex (and thus more complicated to use) and more demanding of computing resources (and thus more expensive to use). A requirement for reusability may lead to another development approach, for example, a design on a more abstract level, which may reduce its ultimate flexibility and ability to be fine-tuned, but it will achieve greater simplicity [3, 4].

- *Component maintenance costs.* Although application maintenance costs can be lowered, component maintenance costs can be very high since the component must respond to the different requirements of different applications running in different environments, with different reliability requirements and perhaps requiring a different level of maintenance support [3].

- *Reliability and sensitivity to changes.* Because components and applications have separate life cycles and different kinds of requirements, there is some risk that a component will not completely satisfy the particular requirements of certain applications or that it may have characteristics not known to the application developer. When introducing changes at the application level (changes such as the updating of an operating system, the updating of other components, and changes in the application), developers face the risk that the change introduced will cause a system failure [7].

To enjoy the advantages and avoid the problems and risks of CBD, we need a systematic approach to CBD at the process and technology levels.

Component-Based Software Engineering

Both customers and suppliers have expected much from CBD, but their expectations have not always been fulfilled. Experience has shown that CBD requires a systematic approach to focus on the component aspects of software development [3]. Traditional software engineering disciplines must be adjusted to the new approach, and new procedures must be developed. Component-based software engineering (CBSE) has become recognized as a new subdiscipline of software engineering. The major goals of CBSE are as follows [8]:

- To provide support for the development of systems as assemblies of components;
- To support the development of components as reusable entities;

- To facilitate the maintenance and upgrading of systems by customizing and replacing their components.

The building of systems from components and the building of components for different systems require established methodologies and processes not only in relation to the development and maintenance aspects, but also to the entire component and system life cycle including organizational, marketing, legal, and other aspects [7, 9]. In addition to specific CBSE subjects such as component specification or composition and technologies, a number of software engineering disciplines and processes require specific methodologies for application in CBD. Many of these methodologies have not yet been established in practice, and some have not yet been theoretically sufficiently refined. The progress of software development in the near future will depend very much on the successful establishment of CBSE, a point that is recognized by both industry and academia.

Challenges of CBSE

It is obvious that CBD and CBSE are only in the starting phase of their expansion. CBD is recognized as a powerful new approach that will significantly improve—if not revolutionize—the development of software and software use in general. We can expect components and component-based services to be widely used by nonprogrammers when building their applications. Tools for building such applications by component assembly will be developed. Automatic updating of components over the Internet, already present in many applications today, will be a standard means of application improvement.

Another trend we have observed is the standardization of domain-specific components at the interface level. This will make it possible for developers to build applications and systems from components purchased from different vendors. The standardization of domain-specific components requires the standardization of domain-specific processes. Widespread work on standardization in different domains is already in progress. A typical example is the work of the OPC Foundation [10] on a standard interface to enable interoperability between automation/control applications, field systems/devices, and business/office applications. Support for the exchange of information between components, applications, and systems distributed over the Internet will be further developed. Current technologies such as

Extensible Markup Language (XML) [11] are already used to exchange information over the Internet.

CBSE is facing many challenges today, some of which are summarized here and developed further in different chapters of the book:

- *Component specification.* Although this problem has been addressed from the very beginning of development of component models, no consensus has been reached about what is a component and how it should be specified. Component specification is an important issue because the basic concepts of CBD rely on it and this book therefore pays much attention to this problem. Chapters 1, 2, and 6 discuss component specifications and other basic concepts of component technologies related to component specifications.

- *Component models.* Even though existing development models demonstrate powerful technologies, they have many ambiguous characteristics, they are incomplete, and they are difficult to use. The relations between system architecture and component models are not precisely defined. The basic principles of component models, their relations to software architectures, and descriptions of the most commonly used models are presented in Chapters 3 and 4.

- *Component-based software life cycle.* The life cycle of component-based software is becoming more complex because many phases are separated in unsynchronized activities. For example, the development of components may be completely independent of the development of systems using those components. The process of *engineering requirements* is much more complex because the possible candidate components usually lack one or more features that the system requires. In addition, even if some components are individually well suited to the system, it is not obvious that they function optimally in combination with others in the system. These constraints may require another approach in requirements engineering—an analysis of the feasibility of requirements in relation to the components available and the consequent modification of requirements. Because many uncertainties surround the process of component selection, a strategy is needed for managing risks in the component selection and evolution process [8, 12]. Similarly many questions remain in the late phases of component-based software life cycles. Because component-based systems include components with independent life cycles, the problem of system evolution becomes significantly more complex. Many different types of questions have not yet been solved. There are technical issues (Can a system be updated technically by replacing components?), administrative and organizational issues (Which components can be updated, which components should be or must be updated?), legal issues (Who is responsible for a system failure, the producer of the system or the producer of the component?), and so on. CBSE is a new approach and little experience has been gained regarding the maintainability of such systems. We face the risk that many such systems will be troublesome to maintain. The component-based system life cycle is discussed in Chapter 5.

- *Composition predictability.* Even if we assume that we can specify all of the relevant attributes of components, we do not necessarily know how these attributes will determine the corresponding attributes of systems of which they may become part. The ideal approach—to derive system attributes from component attributes—is still a subject of research. The questions remain: Is such derivation at all possible? Should we not concentrate on the determination of the attributes of component composites? [13]. Component evaluation and composition are discussed in detail in Chapters 8 and 9.

- *Trusted components and component certification.* Because the trend is to deliver components in binary form and the component development process is outside the control of component users, questions related to component trustworthiness become very important. One way of classifying components is to certify them. In spite of the common belief that certification means absolute trustworthiness, it in fact merely provides the results of tests performed and a description of the environment in which the tests were performed. Although certification is a standard procedure in many domains, it has not yet been established in software in general and especially not for software components [14, 15]. Chapter 10 elaborates on how trustworthiness can be achieved for software components.

- *Component configurations.* Complex systems may include many components, which, in turn, include other components. In many cases, compositions of components will be treated as components. As soon as we begin to work with complex structures, problems involving structural configurations appear. For example, two compositions may include the same component. Will such a component be treated as two different entities or will the system accept the component as a single instance, common to both compositions? What happens if different versions of a component are incorporated in two compositions? Which version will be selected? What happens if the different versions are not compatible? The problems of the dynamic updating of components are already known, but their solutions are still the subject of research [16, 17]. One way to handle such complex systems with many components is to make use of product line architectures [18, 19] to impose rules for component configurations. Chapter 11 presents the basis of such component configurations.

- *Tool support.* The purpose of software engineering is to provide practical solutions to practical problems, and the existence of appropriate tools is essential for successful CBSE performance. Development tools, such as Visual Basic, have proven to be extremely successful, but many other tools have yet to appear: component selection and evaluation tools, component repositories and tools for managing the repositories, component test tools, component-based design tools, run-time system analysis tools, component configuration tools, and so on. The objective of CBSE is to build systems from components simply and efficiently, and this can only be achieved with extensive tool support. Three chapters in this book, Chapters 12, 18, and 19, illustrate the necessity of using tools in the development and maintenance process.

- *Dependable systems and CBSE.* The use of CBD in safety-critical domains, real-time systems, and different process-control systems, in which the reliability requirements are particularly rigorous, is particularly challenging. A major problem with CBD is the limited possibility of ensuring the quality and other nonfunctional attributes of the components and thus our inability to guarantee specific system attributes. Several chapters of this book treat this problem, as specified in the following section.

Components in Reliable Systems

In many domains the CBD approach has been very successful. CBD, and software reuse in general, has been extensively used for many years in desktop environments and graphical and mathematical applications. The components used in these areas are, by their nature, precisely defined and they have intuitive functionality and interfaces. On the other hand, the extrafunctional characteristics and constraints are not of the highest priority. By extrafunctional characteristics we mean the component and system properties that determine an overall behavior, but cannot be expressed by functions and cannot be invoked and performed explicitly. Examples of extrafunctional properties include properties related to temporal constraints (execution time, latency, periodicity, deadlines, etc.) and then reliability, robustness, performance, safety, and security. In addition to these emergent system properties, we have properties related to the system life cycle: maintainability, usability, availability, adaptability, reusability, and so on. These properties are often referred to as nonfunctional properties.

Although component-based models deal successfully with functional attributes (although still being far from the ideal solutions), they provide no support for managing extrafunctional properties of systems or components.

CBSE faces two types of problems when dealing with extrafunctional properties. The first type, one common to all software development, is the fact that there are many and often imprecise definitions of these properties. The second, specific to component-based systems, is the difficulty of relating system properties to component properties. Let us take *reliability* as an example. An intuitive definition of the reliability of a system is the probability that a system will behave as intended. The formal definition of reliability is "the ability of a system or component to perform its required functions under stated conditions for a specified period of time" [20]. We should consider several points in this definition. To predict or calculate the reliability of a system correctly, we must state precisely the relevant conditions under which it is to apply. This definition does not apply to system behavior in unpredictable situations, but experience teaches us that problems most often occur when a system is exposed to unpredictable conditions. Uncertainty in the specification of conditions leads to uncertainty in any specification of system reliability. To include unpredictable (or predictable, but not "normal") conditions, we introduce the property of *robustness*. We distinguish between these two properties but cannot precisely define their relation. Other properties are also closely related to these two. The *availability* of a system is the probability that it will be up and running and able to provide useful service at any given time. *Trustworthiness* denotes a user's confidence that the system will behave as expected. There are systems in which the *safety* (i.e., the ability of the system to operate without catastrophic failure) and *security* (the ability of the system to protect itself against accidental or deliberate intrusion) are of main importance. In such systems, reliability, robustness, availability, and so forth must be very precisely specified. These systems are often designated as *dependable* [21].

The specific problems and challenges involved in CBD when dealing with extrafunctional properties are the determination of the relationship between component properties and system properties. Which properties should be considered when evaluating components, when composing them into assemblies, or when testing them? Can we predict the behavior of a system from the specifications of its components? Let us again consider reliability as an example. The first question that arises is how to define the reliability of a component. It depends on specified conditions, which might be only partially defined because these conditions are determined not only by the component itself but also by its deployment and run-time environment. The second question is how to predict the reliability of a system from the known reliabilities of its components. These questions are discussed in Chapters 8 and 9.

CBD usually reduces the development time and effort, but also the possibility of guaranteeing extrafunctional properties. For example, the main problem when using commercial components in safety-critical systems is the system designer's limited insight into the safety-critical properties of components. Increasing the number of test cases may decrease this uncertainty. We also need specific test methods to be applied to components. One way of performing tests is to use fault injection, which can reveal the consequences of failures in components to the rest of the system [22–24]. This and certain other methods are discussed in Chapter 10. Because, in general, the trustworthiness of commercial components is less than that of software developed in-house, we must perform as many tests as needed, but not more. If a component is extensively tested in one configuration, do we need to repeat all tests performed or can we assume some of the results of previous tests? Must we add new tests? This depends on the system requirements and on the system configuration. By studying changes in requirements, changes in the system environment and changes in the entire environment in which the system is performing, we can to some extent ascertain which test cases are already covered by the previous tests. This analysis is discussed in Chapter 14.

Component-based real-time systems (systems in which the correctness is also determined by time factors), and hence real-time components, must take into consideration timing constraints. Very often these systems are dependable systems (reliable, robust, safety critical, etc.). General-purpose component models do not provide real-time support. Many questions remain as to how to build component-based real-time systems: What is a real-time component, what are its properties, and how can a real-time component be specified? Chapter 13 discusses basic principles for modeling component-based systems. Chapters 16–19 illustrate, via different case studies, the possibilities of applying component-based principles and building real-time systems based on non-real-time component technologies.

References

[1] Basili, V. R., and H. D. Rombach, "Support for Comprehensive Reuse," *Software Engineering*, Vol. 6, No. 5, 1991, pp. 303–316.

[2] Brown, A. W., *Large-Scale Component-Based Development*, Upper Saddle River, NJ: Prentice Hall, 2000.

[3] Crnkovic, I., and M. Larsson, "A Case Study: Demands on Component-Based Development," *Proc. 22nd Int. Conf. Software Engineering*, Limerick, Ireland, ACM Press, 2000.

[4] Szyperski, C., *Component Software Beyond Object-Oriented Programming*, Reading, MA: Addison-Wesley, 1998, pp. 46–56.

[5] Maiden, N. A., and C. Ncube, "Acquiring COTS Software Selection Requirements," *IEEE Software*, Vol. 15, No. 2, 1998, pp. 46–56.

[6] Lamsweerde, A. V., "Requirements Engineering in the Year 00: A Research Perspective," *Proc. 22nd Int. Conf. Software Engineering*, Limerick, Ireland, ACM Press, 2000.

[7] Larsson, M., "Applying Configuration Management Techniques to Component-Based Systems," Licentiate Thesis Dissertation 2000-007, Department of Information Technology, Uppsala University, Uppsala, Sweden, 2000.

[8] Heineman, G. T., and W. T. Councill, *Component-Based Software Engineering, Putting the Pieces Together*, Reading, MA: Addison-Wesley, 2001.

[9] Takeshita, T., "Metrics and Risks of CBSE," *Proc. 5th Int. Symp. Software Tools and Technologies*, Pittsburg, PA, IEEE Computer Society, 1997.

[10] OPC Foundation, "OPC, OLE for Process Control," Report v1.0, OPC Standards Collection, 1998, http://opcfoundation.org.

[11] World Wide Web Consortium, "XML," http://www. w3c. org/XML/.

[12] Kotonya, G., and A. Rashid, "A Strategy for Managing Risks in Component-Based Software Development," *Proc. 27th Euromicro Conf. in the CBSE Workshop*, Warsaw, Poland, IEEE Computer Society, 2001.

[13] Wallnau, K. C., and J. Stafford, "Ensembles: Abstractions for a New Class of Design Problem," *Proc. 27th Euromicro Conf. in the CBSE Workshop*, Warsaw, Poland, IEEE Computer Society, 2001.

[14] Voas, J., and J. Payne, "Dependability Certification of Software Components," *J. Software Systems*, Vol. 52, 2000, pp. 165–172.

[15] Morris, J., et al., "Software Component Certification," *IEEE Computer*, Vol. 34, No. 9, 2001, pp. 30–36.

[16] Crnkovic, I., et al., *Object-Oriented Design Frameworks: Formal Specifications and Some Implementation Issues, in Databases and Information Systems*, Dordrecht: Kluwer Academic Publishers, 2001.

[17] Larsson, M., and I. Crnkovic, "New Challenges for Configuration Management," *Proc. 9th Symp. System Configuration Management*, Lecture Notes in Computer Science, No. 1675, Berlin, Springer Verlag, 1999.

[18] Bosch, J., *Design & Use of Software Architectures*, Reading, MA: Addison-Wesley, 2000.

[19] Bosch, J., "Product-Line Architectures in Industry: A Case Study," *Proc. 21st Int. Conf. Software Engineering*, Los Angeles, CA, ACM Press, 1999.

[20] *IEEE Standard Computer Dictionary: A Compilation of IEEE Standard*, New York: Institute of Electrical and Electronics Engineers, 1990.

[21] Sommerville, I., *Software Engineering*, Reading, MA: Addison-Wesley, 2001.

[22] Voas, J., and G. McGraw, *Software Fault Injection: Inoculating Programs Against Errors*, New York: John Wiley and Sons, 1998.

[23] Voas, J., "Discovering Unanticipated Software Output Modules," *The Annals of Software Engineering*, Vol. 11, No. 1, 2001, pp. 79–88.

[24] Besnard, J. F., S. J. Keene, and J. Voas, *Assuring COTS Products for Reliability and Safety Critical Systems*, Los Alamitos, CA: IEEE Computer Society, 1999.

Part 1:
The Definition and Specification
of Components

We have a general idea of what a component is, but in the software context, because what we know as components have so many varied forms, functions, and characteristics (as source code modules, parts of an architecture, parts of a design, and binary deployable executables), there are a correspondingly large number of definitions of a component. This part outlines different definitions of software components and other concepts related to component-based software development. A component has many different parts that must be specified for many different purposes and there is a consequent need for different specification techniques. It is not only the component that must be specified, the environment in which the component is intended to function must also be specified to prevent its misuse or unintended use. Functional, operational, quality, and design specifications are examples of different types of component specifications. The description of a component is not easy if it is not clear what a component is. Thus, a well-formulated and clearly understood definition of the component concept is needed.

The authors of the first chapter present the basic definitions of terms related to component specification and operation: interface, contract, framework, and pattern and the relations between them. A *component* is a reusable unit of deployment and composition that is accessed through an interface. An *interface* specifies the access points to a component. The component specification can be achieved through *contracts,* which make sure certain conditions hold true during the execution of a component within its environment. A *framework* describes a large unit of design with defined relationships between participants of the framework. The last term discussed is *patterns,* which define recurring solutions to recurring problems on a higher abstract level. Patterns enable reuse of the logical solutions and have proven very useful. The chapter describes these terms and discusses relations between them.

The second chapter describes various techniques for component specification. A component is specified by its interface, which must consist of a precise definition of the component's operations and context dependencies. In the existing component models the specification is focused on the syntactic aspects of the interface. The chapter also discusses other specification techniques that use Unified Modeling Language (UML) and the Object Constraint Language (OCL), in which a component implements a set of interfaces. Each interface consists of a set of operations with associated pre- and postconditions and invariants. The preconditions define which conditions must be satisfied before the operation begins, and the postconditions define which conditions will be valid after the execution of the operation. The invariants are the states that must remain valid during and after the execution of the operation. This type of specification gives more accurate information about component behavior. Finally the chapter discusses the extrafunctional characteristics of a component (for example, reliability) that are not covered by these types of specifications and which are matters of current research interest.

1

Basic Concepts in CBSE

Ivica Crnkovic, Brahim Hnich, Torsten Jonsson, and Zeynep Kiziltan

Introduction

It is very important to clarify some basic concepts frequently encountered in CBSE. Varying definitions of these concepts might cause confusion because CBSE is a young discipline. Many concepts have still not been completely explained or tested in practice, and as a consequence, their definitions remain imprecise. Different authors have different understandings of different concepts in different situations. In this chapter, general definitions of the concepts, together with their similarities and differences, are presented. For example, a clear distinction is made between a component and an object, and an obvious similarity is established between a framework and a contract.

CBSE is based on the concept of the component. Other terms, such as interface, contract, framework, and pattern, are thereby closely related to component-based software development. In this chapter we present an overview of these terms, their definitions, and the relationships among them. The terms and the different concepts related to them are used in later chapters of this book.

The following brief definitions of terms will be further discussed in subsequent sections. A *component* is a reusable unit of deployment and composition. A common view is that a component is closely related to an object

3

and that CBD is therefore an extension of object-oriented development. However, many factors, such as granularity, concepts of composition and deployment, and even the development processes, clearly distinguish components from objects. An *interface* specifies the access points to a component, and thus helps clients to understand the functionality and usage of a component. The interface is clearly separated from the implementation of a component. Strictly defined, an interface specifies the functional attributes of a component. A purely functional description of components is not enough.

The component specification can be achieved through *contracts,* which focus on the specification of conditions in which a component interacts with its environment. Although components may be of different sizes and very large components may be of interest, a set of components that plays a specific role is more often of interest than any one component. This leads us to frameworks. A *framework* describes a large unit of design, and defines the relationships within a certain group of potential participants. These participants may be components.

Finally, we discuss the relationships between components and patterns. *Patterns* define recurring solutions to recurring problems on a higher abstract level, and in this way enable their reuse. Patterns usually capture units of design that are small when compared with frameworks, because a framework encompasses several design patterns.

Components

Components are at the heart of CBSE, and we need a precise definition of a component in order to understand the basics of CBSE. We can find several definitions of a component in literature, most of which fail to give an intuitive definition of a component, but focus instead on the general aspects of a component. For example, in a Component Object Model (COM) technical overview from Microsoft, a component is defined as "a piece of compiled software, which is offering a service" [1]. Everyone agrees that a component is a piece of software, and it obviously offers a service but this definition is too broad because, for example, even compiled libraries (e.g., .o and .dll files) could be defined in this way.

In this section, we first clarify the notion of component by considering different but complementary definitions found in literature. In many cases, components are treated as objects and the main differences between components and objects are not clear. Thus, secondly, we will argue that components are not merely objects.

Different Component Definitions

Szyperski [2] defines a component precisely by enumerating the characteristic properties of a component: "A software component is a unit of composition with contractually specified interfaces and explicit context dependencies only. A software component can be deployed independently and is subject to composition by third party." The implication of these properties is as follows: For a component to be deployed independently, a clear distinction from its environment and other components is required. A component communicates with its environment through interfaces. Hence, a component must have clearly specified interfaces while the implementation must be encapsulated in the component and is not directly reachable from the environment. This is what makes a component a unit of third-party deployment.

The most important feature of a component is the separation of its interfaces from its implementation. This separation is different from those we can find in many programming languages (such as ADA or Modula-2) in which declaration is separated from implementation, or those in object-oriented programming languages in which class definitions are separated from class implementations. What distinguishes the concepts in CBSE from these concepts are requirements of integration of a component into an application. Component integration and deployment should be independent of the component development life cycle and there should be no need to recompile or relink the application when updating with a new component. Another important characteristic of a component is its visibility exclusively through its interface. An important implication of this is a need for a complete specification of a component including its functional interface, nonfunctional characteristics (performance, resources required, etc.), use cases, tests, and so forth. Unfortunately, the specification of a component is far from being complete. The current component-based technologies successfully manage functional interfaces only partially. Functional specifications are limited to syntactic lists of operations and attributes, and current technologies fall short of addressing the semantics of functional properties. Further, there is no satisfactory support for specification of nonfunctional properties.

D'Souza and Wills [3] define a component as a reusable part of software, which is independently developed and can be combined with other components to build larger units. It may be adapted but may not be modified. A component can be, for example, "compiled code" without a program source (so that it may not be modified) or part of a model or a design. Components are divided into two major types: general components and implementation components. General components are, for example, user-interface widgets dropped onto a canvas, C++ list templates, or class frameworks. Implementation components include any executable code, source code, interface specifications, or code templates.

Even though the reusability concept is familiar to us from object-oriented technologies, CBSE takes an approach to reusability that is different from conventional software reuse. Aoyama [4] explains this difference as follows: First, components can be composed at run time without the need for compilation. Second, a component detaches its interface from its implementation and conceals its implementation details, hence permitting composition without the need to know the component implementation details. The interface of a component should be standardized to enable reuse and allow components to interoperate in a predefined architecture.

Components are often understood in different ways in academia and in industry [5]. The academic view of a component is that it is a well-defined entity, often small and with easily understood functional and nonfunctional features. It is a black box because it has an explicit encapsulation boundary that restricts any external access. Industry follows this concept in general, and many domain-specific component models exist, some of them used as standards (for example, IEC 61131-3, described in Chapter 13), and some of them developed internally by companies (for example, Koala, described in Chapter 12; AspectObjects described in Chapters 17 and 18; or Object Modeler, discussed in Chapter 19). However, in many cases, industry sees a component as a large piece of software that is reusable and has a complex internal structure. It does not necessarily have well-understood interfaces, and it does not have an explicit encapsulation boundary preventing access to its internal entities. This is especially true for product-line architectures, in which different concepts and component models are used within the same systems [6].

There are many other definitions of components. These definitions begin with the consideration of CBSE from different viewpoints and they focus on different aspects of software engineering, for instance, different phases (in the design phase, components as reusable design parts; in the implementation phase, components confirmed to a specific component model, at run time, binary packages, distributed components), business aspects (business components, service components, COTS components), architectural issues (UML components), and so on.

What then is common to components? As previously defined, a component is a unit of composition, and it must be specified in such a way that it is possible to compose it with other components and integrate it into systems in a predictable way.

To be able to describe a component completely and to ensure its correct integration, maintenance, and updating, the component should consist of the following elements:

- A set of interfaces provided to, or required from, the environment. These interfaces are particularly for interaction with other components, rather than with a component infrastructure or traditional software entities (see Figure 4.1).
- An executable code, which can be coupled to the code of other components via interfaces.

To improve the component quality, the following elements can be included in the specification of a component:

- The specification of nonfunctional characteristics, which are provided and required;
- The validation code, which confirms a proposed connection to another component;
- Additional information, which includes documents related to the fulfilling of specification requirements, design information, and use cases.

Obviously, certain problems are inevitable in CBSE. A typical difficulty is deciding how to deal with nonfunctional aspects of communication, cooperation, and coordination included in a component architecture. In the same way as components themselves, these nonfunctional properties should be possible to compose and easy to control. A clear separation of nonfunctional requirements gives a component more context independence, and possibly permits reuse of the component across a wide range of contexts. Another serious problem is the *syntactic* fragile base class problem, which arises due to the incompatibility of different versions of a component. This problem should not be confused with the *semantic* fragile base class problem. If client components dependent on a component rely on a particular behavior of the objects in a component but are unaware of updates that change the inner workings of the component, the client components' function may cease, perhaps causing a system failure. This is designated the semantic fragile base class problem.

Objects and Components

The terms *object* and *component* are often thought to be synonymous or very similar. Szyperski and Pfister [7] view a component as a collection of objects, in which the objects cooperate with each other and are intertwined tightly. The boundary between a component and other components or objects is specified, and the interaction of the component (and thus its objects) across the boundary is implemented through the component interface while the inner granularity of a component (i.e., its objects) is hidden. Objects within a single component have access to each other's implementation. However, access to the implementation of an object from outside the component must be prevented.

Instead of containing classes or objects, a component could contain traditional procedures, global (static) variables, and can thus be realized by using not only an object-oriented approach but also functional programming or an assembly language approach. Similar to the inheritance relation between objects, a component can have an import relation with another component. A superclass of a class need not be in the same component as the class itself. If a class in a component has a superclass in another component, the inheritance relation between these classes occurs at the boundary between the components [8].

D'Souza and Wills [3] discuss the differences between and similarities of objects and components. An important question is whether a class is a component or not. If a class were packaged together with the explicitly defined interfaces that it requires and implements, then this class would be a component. An application programming interface (API) is a specification, written in a programming language, of the properties of a module on which clients may depend [9]. The API of a component is available in the form of one or more interface constructs (e.g., Java interfaces or abstract virtual classes in C++). In the same way as classes, components may be associated with other classes. If these classes themselves have a fully defined API, the resulting set of classes is designated a *component composition*. The differences between a component and a class are discussed further in Chapter 7.

The following are other important distinctions between objects and components [3]:

- Components often use persistent storage whereas objects have local state.

- Components have a more extensive set of intercommunication mechanisms than objects, which usually use the messaging mechanism.

- Components are often larger units of granularity than objects and have complex actions at their interfaces.

We can conclude that the object-oriented approach and CBSE have many similarities, but a clear distinction exists between the two approaches. They are, however, not conflicting; on the contrary, object-oriented analysis, design, and development constitute a set of technology and methods naturally used in CBSE.

Interfaces

An interface of a component can be defined as a specification of its access point [2]. The clients access the services provided by the component using these points. If a component has multiple access points, each of which represents a different service offered by the component, then the component is expected to have multiple interfaces.

It is important to note that an interface offers no implementation of any of its operations. Instead, it merely names a collection of operations and provides only the descriptions and the protocols of these operations. This separation makes it possible to (1) replace the implementation part without changing the interface, and in this way improve system performance without rebuilding the system; and (2) add new interfaces (and implementations) without changing the existing implementation, and in this way improve the component adaptability.

Clients customize components by means of interfaces because an interface is the only visible part. Ideally, in an interface, each operation's semantics must be specified because this is important to both the implementers of the interface and clients using the interface. However, this is often not the case. In most of the existing component models, the interface defines only the syntax (e.g., types of inputs and outputs) and gives very little information about what the component does.

Interfaces defined in standard component technologies can express functional properties. Functional properties include a signature part in which the operations provided by a component are described, and a behavior part, in which the behavior of the component is specified. Bergner et al. [10] point out that most description techniques for interfaces such as *interface definition language* (IDL) [11] are only concerned with the signature part. Such interface description techniques, however, are not sufficiently well equipped to express extrafunctional properties (for example, quality attributes such as accuracy, availability, latency, security) [9].

We can distinguish two kinds of interfaces. Components can export and import interfaces to and from environments that may include other components. An exported interface describes the services provided by a component to the environment, whereas an imported interface specifies the services required by a component from the environment. The general approach to interfaces is traditionally syntactic [12]. However, the realization of the semantic issues related to context dependencies (i.e., specification of the deployment environment and run-time environment) and interaction has indicated the need for a contract that clearly specifies the behavior of a component (see the "Contracts" section) [13].

Different versions of an interface may cause problems. Szyperski [2] notes that the traditional way of coping with different versions of an interface is to assign major and minor numbers to the versions. However, this approach assumes that the versions of a component evolve at a single source. For controlling different versions, some systems freeze the interfaces once they are published and never change them again. COM takes this approach by freezing the current interface and creating new interfaces, thus supporting multiple interfaces for the different versions of an interface. This, however, leads to a sudden increase in the number of new interfaces, which in practice describe the same component.

Contracts

Most techniques for describing interfaces such as IDL [11] are only concerned with the signature part, in which the operations provided by a component are described, and thus fail to address the overall behavior of the component. A more accurate specification of a component's behavior can be achieved through contracts. As mentioned by Meyer [14], a contract lists the global constraints that the component will maintain (the invariant). For each operation within the component, a contract also lists the constraints that need to be met by the client (the precondition) and those the component promises to establish in return (the postcondition). The precondition, the invariant, and the postcondition constitute the specification of a component's behavior. For instance, contracts are used in the design of Eiffel [15] (for object-oriented software development), the unified modeling language (UML) [16], and so on.

Beyond the specification of the behavior of a single component, contracts can also be used to specify interactions among groups of components. However, they are employed in a slightly different manner. A contract specifies the interactions among components, in terms of:

- The set of participating components;

- The role of each component through its contractual obligations, such as type obligations, which require the component to support certain variables and an interface, and causal obligations, which require the component to perform an ordered sequence of actions, including sending messages to the other components;

- The invariant to be maintained by the components;

- The specification of the methods that instantiate the contract.

Note that components not only provide other components with services but also require them from yet other components. This is valid for both functional and nonfunctional requirements. Hence, the contractual obligations for components differ significantly from only preconditions and postconditions of the methods provided by a component.

The use of contracts to specify interactions among components led to the design of contract languages such as that introduced by Helm et al. [17] and extended by Holland [18]. Note that according to Helm et al., the participants are assumed to be objects, but because components are reusable units they may also participate in a contract. In a contract language, the contract is used to explicitly specify the set of participating components. A contract also lists the services to be provided by the participating components. By properly choosing the components and the methods to be used, the components work together in a contract to achieve a particular objective or to maintain some invariant. Each component, in such a group, provides some of the required functionality and communicates with the other members of the group.

Using contracts to specify the behavior of interacting components supports the reuse and refinement of larger grained software components based on behavior. First, contracts permit the software developer to isolate and specify explicitly, at a high level of abstraction, the roles of different components in a particular context. Second, different contracts make it possible to modify and extend the role of every participant independently. Finally, new contracts can be defined by associating different participants with different roles.

The total behavior of a component may be quite complex because it may participate in many contracts. Furthermore, contracts specify the conditions in which components interact with other components in terms of preconditions and postconditions on operations. The preconditions specify what characteristics the environment must meet so that the operations of the contract can guarantee the postconditions. Simple preconditions/postconditions on operations establish *partial correctness,* whereas to achieve *total correctness,* termination is required. Because contracts are designed to represent message-passing protocols between components, they are imperative in nature and therefore difficult to express in a declarative form.

Note also that contracts and interfaces are quite different concepts. Whereas an interface is a collection of operations that specifies a service provided by a component, a contract specifies the behavioral aspects of a component or the interaction between different components.

Patterns

An architect named Christopher Alexander first introduced a new concept of patterns during the late 1970s [19]. In this context, a pattern defines a recurring solution to a recurring problem. Gamma et al. [20] further refined this definition by specifying the characteristics of a pattern and its objectives. Patterns capture nonobvious solutions, not just abstract principles or strategies, in an indirect manner, as distinct from many other problem-solving techniques (such as software design paradigms or methods) that derive solutions from principles. The solutions should be proven to solve the problem rather than being theories or speculations. Patterns describe relationships between deeper system structures and mechanisms and not only independent modules. Finally, human factors are a part of patterns. A design pattern can be employed in the design and documentation of a component. A component, as a reusable entity, can be seen as an implementation of some design pattern. Design patterns can be used to describe the low-level implementation details of the behavior and structure of the components, or the relationships between the components in the context of a particular programming language.

Patterns can be classified in three major categories depending on the level of abstraction on which they are used when documenting a software solution or design. At the highest level of abstraction, *architectural patterns* deal with the global properties and architecture of a system composed of large-scale components. Architectural patterns capture the overall structure and organization of a software system, and encode high-level tactics, which describe the set of participating subsystems, specify their roles, and express the relationships between them. At a lower level of abstraction, *design patterns* refine the structure and the behavior of the subsystems as well as the components of a software system, and the relationships that exist among them. They encode microarchitectures of subsystems and components for a general design problem within a particular context, which describes the structure and behavior of the subsystems and components as well as the communication among them. At the lowest level of abstraction, *idioms* are low-level patterns that are dependent on the chosen paradigm and the programming language used.

Patterns have been applied to the design of many object-oriented systems, and are considered to be reusable microarchitectures that contribute to an overall system architecture. However, the use of design patterns is not without problems. The first problem is that the knowledge encoded in the design pattern is unstructured knowledge that contains many ambiguities because of the informal description of solutions. Two further major challenges related to patterns face the pattern community. The first is concerned with the validation of the conformation of a particular implementation with the specification of a given pattern. The second challenge is concerned with the refinement (also known as specialization) of design patterns, that is, whether one pattern refines (is a special case of) another.

The relationship between components and design patterns can be viewed as follows. Design patterns are widely used in the process of designing component-based systems in which the reusable units must be identified. The use of design patterns makes it easier for us to recognize those reusable parts and either find them in the form of preexisting components or develop them as reusable units. Design patterns can be used to describe the behavior of the inner parts of a component, and thus can be used to develop components. Furthermore, design patterns can also be used to describe a component composition when designing an assembly or a framework that associates several components.

Frameworks

CBSE means that we build software by "putting pieces together." In such an environment it is essential that a context exists in which the pieces can be used. Frameworks are a means of providing such contexts. So what exactly is a framework and how do we use it in CBSE?

Previous attempts to define frameworks have been approached from different points of view and at different levels of detail. For instance, a framework may be seen as a reusable design of a system in which the design consists of the representation of abstract classes and the interaction of different instances of these. At another level the framework is simply "a skeleton of an application which can be customized by an application developer" [21]. Jacobson et al. define framework in relation to the term architecture: "A microarchitecture which provides an incomplete template for systems within a specific domain…" [22].

One way of using the term framework centers on the idea that the design efforts, when building computer systems, may have abstract results that can be reused in other situations. A framework is then used to describe something that is not only usable in the current specific situation, but after some modification, in any similar (or isomorphic) situation. This modification may take place during execution or during design time and is called an instantiation of the framework. It is also often stated that the framework is defined for a class of problems within a certain domain or problem area.

Frameworks are closely related to patterns. They define a certain group of participants and the relations among them that could be reused in any isomorphic situation. Szyperski [1] finds that they, in comparison with patterns, describe a larger unit of design and that they are more specialized than patterns. A typical, and often used framework is the Smalltalk Model-View-Controller (MVC) framework, which defines a setting in which a model (the information to be handled) is presented through a view, and a controller manages the user manipulations. Frameworks are also suitable units for sharing and reusing architectures.

A distinction can be made between different types of frameworks. The MVC framework is an example of what are called low-level application frameworks but general/business frameworks and component frameworks are also available. While the term framework in general describes a typical and reusable situation at a model level [3], a *component framework* describes a "circuit board" with empty slots into which components can be inserted to create a working instance. Typically, components are dynamically inserted at run time. An example of such a framework is the Blackbox Component

Framework (BCF) from Oberon Microsystems, the OpenDoc referred to by Szyperski. Tkach and Puttick [23] define three different types of frameworks. Their definition conflicts in some ways with the preceding definitions. They see three types or levels of frameworks: (1) technical frameworks, (2) industrial frameworks, and (3) application frameworks. The first is similar to that which we termed application frameworks and of which the MVC framework is an example. The other two represent two levels of model frameworks, the first at an industrial level, biased toward a certain business area, while the second is biased toward certain types of application domains such as certain business problems.

Another example of a component framework is the Visual Basic development environment from Microsoft. Forms are built by adding components (controls) to a form, which was originally empty (the circuit board). The developer, through a programming language (Basic), then adds variants to the component behavior. This is done through an interface of messages and events that are exchanged between components. The form itself is also considered a component. The framework is built around the structures of a typical Windows application. Visual Basic is built around the COM model, which is a component model. Visual Basic is an example of a commercially available component platform biased toward the user interface side of applications [24]. Such component models (COM, EJB, etc.) are also referred to as component frameworks. Frameworks within certain component models are further described in Chapter 4, where a component framework is defined as a set of formalisms used to describe certain aspects of components, the services provided by the component model, the run-time infrastructure, and a number of predefined components.

The two concepts of component models and component frameworks are sometimes intermixed. The question of how to distinguish them is discussed by Bachman et al. [9]. A component model defines a set of standards and conventions used by the component developer, whereas a component framework is a support infrastructure for the component model.

The key contribution of frameworks is that they force components to perform their tasks via mechanisms controlled by the framework, thus enforcing the observance of architectural principles. Even if frameworks are defined formally or semiformally as described here, there seems to be a limit to what they can express. The invariant section does not describe in detail the behavior of the participating components. It is therefore difficult to describe formally the behavior with which a component participating in the framework must conform, even if a section with preconditions and postconditions exists. To meet this limitation, contracts, as discussed by Helm et al. [16], extend the definitions of frameworks to also include formal behavioral definitions of the participating components.

Frameworks provide a solution for a powerful context in which the participating components can be effectively assembled. The problem of making correct assemblies and evaluating them is discussed in Chapters 8 and 9. A way to enhance the effectiveness of frameworks through the use of roles and collaborations is described in Chapter 7. Frameworks used here are object-oriented frameworks that are somewhat different from component frameworks. Object-oriented frameworks are more abstract—they are partial designs and implementations for applications in a particular domain. The framework is responsible for handling the often complex interactions and the components must only fulfill their roles in the framework.

Relations Between Concepts

It is interesting to study the relations between some of the concepts in the previous section. Bachman et al. [9] depict the relations in a very illustrative way, as we show in Figure. 1.1. In this "component pattern" a component implements one or more interfaces. The component satisfies certain obligations specified by a contract. A component-based system is based on

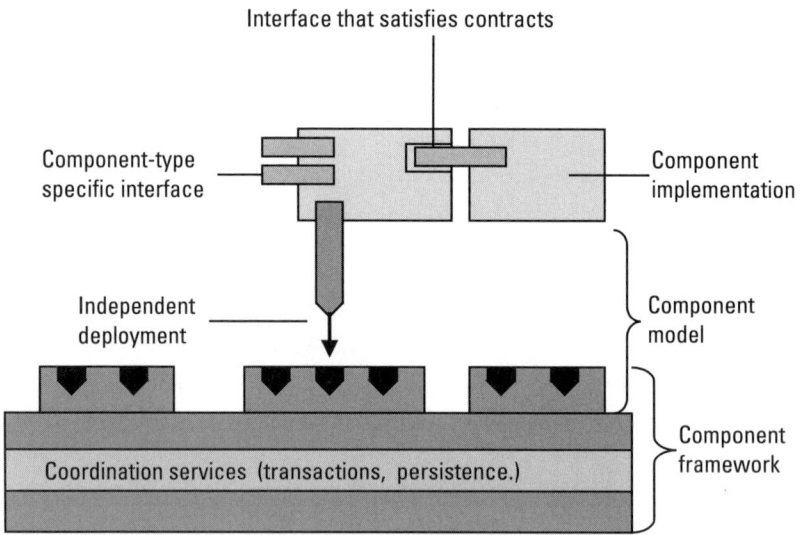

Figure 1.1 The concepts of a component-based system.

components of particular types, each of which plays a specialized role in a system and is described by an interface. A component model is the set of component types, their interfaces, and, additionally, a specification of the allowable patterns of interaction among component types. A component framework provides a variety of deployment and run-time services to support the component model.

In particular, we can study three relationships that exist between frameworks and components, frameworks and contracts, and finally frameworks and patterns.

Frameworks and Components

By the definition of frameworks as described earlier, a framework can be seen as a circuit board (component framework) in which empty positions are waiting for the insertion of components (here used as "slot fillers"). The framework (the circuit board) is instantiated by filling in the empty slots. Requirements are specified to indicate to what the components must conform to be able to function as intended in the circuit. In the notion of formal frameworks, we have seen that the behavior of the framework can be specified in terms of the preconditions and postconditions of the framework, invariants, and instantiations, as well as which components are to participate and the static relations between them. Two remaining problems are to formalize the connection among components and to specify in more detail which interfaces the components should have to the surrounding frameworks (i.e., to the other components).

The open slots could be filled with atomic components or with other frameworks, which in turn could be compositions of other components. The same formalism and languages as described by Lau and Ornaghi [25] are used to define both frameworks and components. However, note that only interfaces and relations between components are described. The internal details of the specification (the implementation) are still concealed within the component and should remain so. Component frameworks are thus filled with components and instantiated in this way. As a framework is instantiated with components it will itself become a new component available for usage in new frameworks.

Component models and their framework implementations, which are different to some extent, are discussed in further detail in Chapter 4, where a number of well-known component models such as COM, DCOM, CCM, Java Beans, and .NET are described.

Frameworks and Contracts

Contracts, as described by Helm, and frameworks may at first sight seem to be similar concepts because they both describe situations in which groups of participants interact with each other. In the contract case they are referred to as participants and in the framework case they are shown as open slots. However, notable differences exist between contracts and frameworks. Frameworks focus on the overall properties of component compositions giving the general and standard rules within the composition that all components must follow. Contracts give specifications for relationships between concrete components, and these specifications may be different for components, within one composition.

Components are added to the framework in an instantiation of it, resulting in an application. Once in the framework the component will be used by other components (the clients). The syntactical, behavioral, synchronizational, and quantitative requirements of this communication are then explicitly defined in contracts [26].

Frameworks and Patterns

Johnson employed design patterns both in the design and the documentation of frameworks [27]. It is important to realize that design patterns and frameworks are distinct concepts having different natures. Design patterns are of a logical nature, representing knowledge of and experience gained with software, whereas frameworks are of a physical nature, and are executable software used in either the design or the run-time phase. The relationship between frameworks and design patterns is a mutual relation: Frameworks are the physical realization of one or more design patterns; patterns are the instructions for implementing those solutions.

Gamma et al. [20] summarize the major differences between design patterns and frameworks. The first difference is the level of abstraction of frameworks and design patterns. Design patterns are more abstract than frameworks. The implication of this difference is that frameworks are implemented in a programming language and represent reusable pieces of code that can not only be studied, but can also be executed. On the other hand, design patterns need to be implemented each time they are used, but they encode more knowledge about the trade-offs and consequences of the design. The second difference is that design patterns are smaller architectural elements than frameworks. A typical framework contains several design patterns but a pattern never contains several frameworks. The last difference is the level of specialization of frameworks and design patterns.

Frameworks are more specialized and are employed in a particular application domain, whereas design patterns can be used in any kind of application.

Conclusion

In the previous sections, we have seen that many different concepts, definitions, and specifications lie behind attempts to manage CBD successfully. Most of these concepts are presently in the research stage and first attempts are being made to utilize them successfully. They are still immature, not completely explained, and in many cases difficult to understand. The main objective of CBSE is to obtain a more efficient development with shorter development times and better quality products. This requires clear concepts and simple methods. Because the basic concepts and all of their details have not yet reached that level, we must ask who must be familiar with them, why, and when? Component specifications are essential for component users who are focused on the component features, functional and nonfunctional. It is important for users to become familiar with them and to learn to use them easily and correctly. Component developers provide component specifications, so they must be able to understand the basic concepts related to component specifications and they must be able to implement them. The contract, as an extension of the interface specification, will be of special interest in particular domains dealing with systems with specific requirements, such as real-time systems, safety-critical systems, or systems with other constraints.

The main purpose of frameworks is to support the process of component composition. Consequently, developers, both of components and of systems using components, must be able to utilize framework support. They may not need to know the theoretical principles behind the support, but they must be able to use its functions. Component developers must obey the rules and formats specified by the framework to develop and to specify the component, whereas component users will use frameworks to compose systems from components in a more efficient and accurate way. The framework tools play a crucial role—as is well-known in practice. (The popularity of Visual Basic does not originate from the language itself, but from the user-friendly framework environment.)

Patterns give an abstract and more general view of a function, procedure, or similar item, which can be implemented in the form of systems or components. For this reason they are interesting to designers. System designers can recognize and identify the reusable parts of the system with the help of patterns. Component designers will use patterns in the design process to design components more efficiently. Typically, specific patterns already exist or are being developed in different domains. The same patterns can be used for different kinds of components, providing the same functionality but containing different nonfunctional attributes. Alternatively, patterns can be used for the specific nonfunctional attributes.

Experience shows us that although the different basic concepts and terms of CBSE are used by different people and in different phases of system or component life cycles, a general understanding of them is very important for successful CBD.

Summary

In this chapter, we have introduced the basic concepts of CBSE, summarized as follows. A component is a reusable unit of deployment and composition that has no persistent state. It can be composed at run time, with no need for compilation and its implementation details, but it cannot be modified. The specification of the services provided by a component is the role of interfaces, which are useful in the processes of customization and composition of components. Design patterns can be used to describe the low-level implementation details of the behavior and structure of components, or the relationships between the components in the context of a particular programming language. Contracts or frameworks can be used to permit the construction and reuse of larger grained software components. Frameworks constitute a group of participants and specify relations and the interactions between them that could be reused in any isomorphic situation. Contracts and frameworks may at first look quite similar, but there are notable differences. A framework defines a set of rules for different services (e.g., transaction, persistence, and deployment) and an infrastructure of the component model. Contracts are used for specification of a component and the concrete interaction between components—and in this sense it is a different form of framework. A component can be implemented in different component models, and they will utilize different internal mechanisms of framework services, but all the implementations may have the same interface or the same contract.

Patterns are also often used in combination with frameworks in that they define smaller parts of a system than frameworks define. However, the main difference between frameworks and patterns are that frameworks concretely describe a set of rules and services, whereas patterns describe behavior in a more abstract way. A framework can be constructed using several patterns. The CBSE terms will be used later in this book in different contexts and sometimes in different ways, but in general their use follows the definitions discussed in this chapter.

References

[1] Microsoft "The Component Object Model Specification," Report Vol. 99, Microsoft Standards, Redmond, WA: Microsoft, 1996.

[2] Szyperski, C., *Component Software—Beyond Object-Oriented Programming*, Reading, MA: Addison-Wesley, 1998.

[3] D'Souza, D., and A. C. Wills, *Objects, Components and Frameworks: The Catalysis Approach*, Reading, MA: Addison-Wesley, 1998.

[4] Aoyama, M., "New Age of Software Development: How Component-Based Software Engineering Changes the Way of Software Development," *Proc. 1st Workshop on Component Based Software Engineering*, 1998.

[5] Bosch J., "Component Evolution in Product-Line Architectures," *Proc. Int. Workshop on Component-Based Software Engineering*, Los Angeles, CA, 1999.

[6] Crnkovic, I., and M. Larsson, "A Case Study: Demands on Component-Based Development," *Proc. 22nd Int. Conf. Software Engineering*, Limerick, Ireland, ACM Press, 2000.

[7] Szyperski C. and Pfister C., "Why Objects Are Not Enough," *Proc. Int. Component Users Conference*, Munich, Germany, SIGS, 1996.

[8] Szyperski, C., "Components vs. Objects vs. Component Objects," *Proc. Object Oriented Programming*, Munich, Germany, 1999.

[9] Bachman, F., et al., "Technical Concepts of Component-Based Software Engineering," Report CMU/SEI-2000-TR-008, Software Engineering Institute, Carnegie Mellon University, 2000.

[10] Bergner, K., A. Rausch, and M. Sihling, "Componentware—The Big Picture," *Proc. Int. Workshop on Component-Based Engineering*, Kyoto, Japan, 1999, http://www.sei.cmu.edu/ cbs/icse99.

[11] Gudgin, M., *Essential IDL: Interface Design for COM*, Reading, MA: Addison-Wesley, 2001.

[12] Lycett, M., and R. J. Paul, "Component-Based Development: Dealing with Non-Functional Aspects of Architecture," *Proc. ECOOP*, Bryssels, Belgium, Springer, 1998.

[13] Ólafsson, A., and D. Bryan, "On the Need for 'Required Interfaces' of Components," *Proc. Special Issues in Object-Oriented Programming: Workshop Reader of the 10th*

European Conference on Object-Oriented Programming, ECCOP '96, Linz, Austria, Springer, 1998.

[14] Meyer, B., "Applying Design by Contracts," *IEEE Computer,* Vol. 25, No. 10, 1992, pp. 40–51.

[15] Meyer, B., *Eiffel: The Language,* Upper Saddle River, NJ: Prentice Hall, 1992.

[16] Fowler, M., and K. Scott, *UML Distilled—Applying the Standard Object Modelling Language,* Reading, MA: Addison-Wesley, 1997.

[17] Helm, R., I. Holland, and D. Gangopadadhyay, "Contracts: Specifying Behavioral Compositions in Object Oriented Systems," *Proc. Conf. Object Oriented Programming: Systems, Languages and Application,* Ottawa, Canada, AMC Press, 1990.

[18] Holland, I., "Specifying Reusable Components Using Contracts," *Proc. ECOOP,* Utrecht, The Netherlands, Springer, 1992.

[19] Alexander, C., *The Timeless Way of Building,* Oxford, UK: Oxford University Press, 1979.

[20] Gamma, E., et al., *Design Patterns, Elements of Reusable Object-Oriented Software,* Reading, MA: Addison-Wesley, 1995, pp. 39–42.

[21] Johnson, R. E., "Frameworks = (Components + Patterns)," *Communications of the ACM,* Vol. 40, No. 10, 1997.

[22] Jacobson, I., M. L. Griss, and P. Jonsson, *Software Reuse, Architecture, Process and Organization for Business Success,* Reading, MA: Addison-Wesley and ACM Press, 1997.

[23] Tkach, D., and R. Puttick, *Object Technology in Application Development,* Reading, MA: Addison-Wesley, 1996.

[24] Maurer, P. M., "Components: What If They Gave a Revolution and Nobody Came?" *IEEE Computer,* Vol. 33, Issue 6, 2000, pp. 28–34.

[25] Lau, K.-K., and M. Ornaghi, "OOD Frameworks in Component-Based Software Development in Computational Logic," *Proc. LOPSTR'98,* Lecture Notes in Computer Science, No. 1559, Berlin, Springer Verlag, 1999.

[26] Beugnard, A., "Making Components Contract Aware," *IEEE Computer,* Vol. 32, Issue 7, 1999, pp. 38–43.

[27] Johnson, R. E., "Documenting Frameworks Using Patterns," *Proc. OOPSLA,* New York, ACM Press, 2001.

2

Specification of Software Components

Frank Lüders, Kung-Kiu Lau, and Shui-Ming Ho

Introduction

In its simplest form a software component contains some code (that can be executed on certain platforms) and an interface that provides (the only) access to the component. The code represents the operations that the component will perform when invoked. The interface tells the component user everything he needs to know in order to deploy the component. Components can of course be deployed in many different contexts. Ideally, components should be black boxes, to enable users to (re)use them without needing to know the details of their inner structure. In other words, the interface of a component should provide all of the information needed by its users. Moreover, this information should be the only information they need. Consequently, the interface of a component should be the only point of access to the component. Therefore, it should contain all of the information that users need to know about the component's operations (that is, what its code enables it to do) and its context dependencies (that is, how and where the component can be deployed). The code, on the other hand, should be completely inaccessible (and invisible) if a component is to be used as a black box.

The specification of a component is therefore the specification of its interface. This must consist of a precise definition of the component's operations and context dependencies and nothing else. Typically, the operations and context dependencies will contain the parameters of the component.

The specification of a component is useful to both component users and component developers. For users, the specification provides a definition of its interface, namely, its operations and context dependencies. Because it is only the interface that is visible to users, its specification must be precise and complete. For developers, the specification of a component also provides an abstract definition of its internal structure. Although this should be invisible to users, it is useful to developers (and maintainers), at least as documentation of the component.

In this chapter, we discuss the specification of software components. We identify all features that should be present in an idealized component, indicate how they should be specified, and show how they are specified using current component specification techniques.

Current Component Specification Techniques

The specifications of components used in practical software development today are limited primarily to what we will call syntactic specifications. This form of specification includes the specifications used with technologies such as COM [1], the Object Management Group's Common Object Request Broker Architecture (CORBA) [2], and Sun's JavaBeans [3]. The first two of these use different dialects of the IDL, whereas the third uses the Java programming language to specify component interfaces. In this section, COM is mainly used to illustrate the concepts of syntactic specification of software components.

First, we take a closer look at the relationships between components and interfaces. A component provides the implementation of a set of named interfaces, or types, each interface being a set of named operations. Each operation has zero or more input and output parameters and a syntactic specification associates a type with each of these. Many notations also permit a return value to be associated with each operation, but for simplicity we do not distinguish between return values and output parameters. In some specification techniques it is also possible to specify that a component requires some interfaces, which must be implemented by other components. The interfaces provided and required by a component are often called the incoming and outgoing interfaces of the component, respectively.

Figure 2.1 is a UML class diagram [4] showing the concepts discussed above and the relationships between them. Note that instances of the classes shown on the diagram will be entities such as components and interfaces, which can themselves be instantiated. The model is therefore a UML metamodel, which can be instantiated to produce other models. It is worth noting that this model allows an interface to be implemented by several different components, and an operation to be part of several different interfaces. This independence of interfaces from the component implementations is an essential feature of most component specification techniques. The possibility of an operation being part of several interfaces is necessary to allow inheritance, or subtyping, between interfaces. The model also allows parameters to be simultaneously input and output parameters.

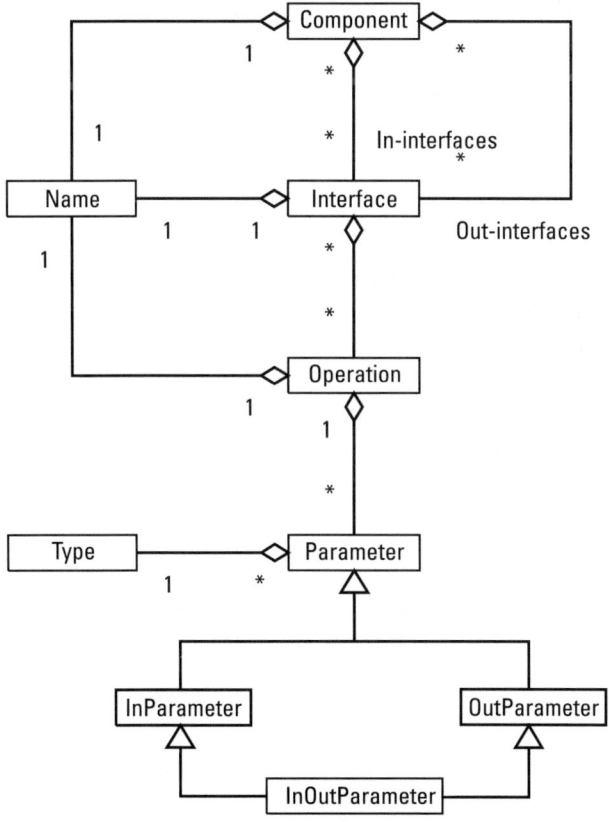

Figure 2.1 UML metamodel of the concepts used in the syntactic specification of software components.

The model presented in Figure 2.1 is intended to be a generic representation of the relationships between components, interfaces, and operations. In practice, these relationships vary between specification techniques. For example, one can distinguish between object-oriented specifications and what might be called procedural specifications. In this chapter we consider only object-oriented specifications that are used by current technologies. This leads to no loss of generality, because procedural specification can be seen as a special case of object-oriented specification. Subtle differences are seen in the precise nature of the relationship between a component and its interfaces in different object-oriented specification techniques. In COM, for example, a component implements a set of classes, each of which implements a set of interfaces. The statement that a component implements a set of interfaces thus holds by association. In more traditional object-oriented specification techniques, a component is itself a class that has exactly one interface. The statement that a component implements a set of interfaces still holds, because this interface can include, or be a subtype of, several other interfaces.

As an example of a syntactic specification, we now consider the specification of a COM component. Below we provide a slight simplification of what might be the contents of an IDL file. First, two interfaces are specified, including a total of three operations that provide the functionality of a simple spell checker. Both interfaces inherit from the standard COM interface IUnknown. (All COM interfaces except IUnknown must inherit directly or indirectly from IUnknown. See [1] for more information about the particulars of COM.) All operations return a value of type HRESULT, which is commonly used in COM to indicate success or failure. A component is then specified (called a *library* in COM specifications), thus implementing one COM class, which in turn implements the two interfaces previously specified. This component has no outgoing interfaces.

```
interface ISpellCheck : IUnknown
{
  HRESULT check([in] BSTR *word, [out] bool *correct);
};

interface ICustomSpellCheck : IUnknown
{
  HRESULT add([in] BSTR *word);
  HRESULT remove([in] BSTR *word);
};

library SpellCheckerLib
{
```

```
coclass SpellChecker
{
    [default] interface ISpellCheck;
    interface ICustomSpellCheck;
};
};
```

Relating this specification to the model above, there is one instance of Component, which is associated with two instances of Interface. Taking a closer look at the first interface, it is associated with a single instance of Operation, which is itself associated with one instance of InParameter and two instances of OutParameter, representing the two named parameters and the return value. The information that can be obtained from a component specification such as the above is limited to what operations the component provides and the number and types of their parameters. In particular, there is no information about the effect of invoking the operations, except for what might be guessed from the names of operations and parameters. Thus, the primary uses of such specifications are type checking of client code and as a base for interoperability between independently developed components and applications. Different component technologies have different ways of ensuring such interoperability. For example, COM specifies the binary format of interfaces, whereas CORBA defines a mapping from IDL to a number of programming languages.

An important aspect of interface specifications is how they relate to substitution and evolution of components. Evolution can be seen as a special case of substitution in which a newer version of a component is substituted for an older version. Substituting a component *Y* for a component *X* is said to be safe if all systems that work with *X* will also work with *Y*. From a syntactic viewpoint, a component can safely be replaced if the new component implements at least the same interfaces as the older components, or, in traditional object-oriented terminology, if the interface of the new component is a subtype of the interface of the old component. For substitution to be safe, however, there are also constraints on the way that the semantics of operations can be changed, as we will see in the next section.

Specifying the Semantics of Components

Although syntactic specifications of components are the only form of specifications in widespread use, it is widely acknowledged that semantic information about a component's operations is necessary to use the component effectively. Examples of such information are the combinations of parameter values an operation accepts, an operation's possible error codes, and constraints on the order in which operations are invoked. In fact, current component technologies assume that the user of a component is able to make use of such semantic information. For instance, COM dictates that the error codes produced by an operation are immutable; that is, changing these is equivalent to changing the interface. These technologies do not, however, support the specification of such information. In the example with COM, there is no way to include information about an operation's possible error codes in the specification.

Several techniques for designing component-based systems that include semantic specifications are provided in the literature. In this section, we examine the specification technique presented in [5], which uses UML and the Object Constraint Language (OCL) [6] to write component specifications. OCL is included in the UML specification. Another well-known method that uses the same notations is Catalysis [7]. The concepts used for specification of components in these techniques can be seen as an extension of the generic model of syntactic specification presented in the previous section. Thus, a component implements a set of interfaces, each of which consists of a set of operations. In addition, a set of preconditions and postconditions is associated with each operation. Preconditions are assertions that the component assumes to be fulfilled before an operation is invoked. Postconditions are assertions that the component guarantees will hold just after an operation has been invoked, provided the operation's preconditions were true when it was invoked. In this form of specification, nothing is said about what happens if an operation is invoked while any of its preconditions are not fulfilled. Note that the idea of pre- and postconditions is not a novel feature of component-based software development, and it is used in a variety of software development techniques, such as the Vienna Development Method [8] and Design by Contract [9].

Naturally, an operation's pre- and postconditions will often depend on the state maintained by the component. Therefore, the notion of an interface is extended to include a model of that part of a component's state that may affect or be affected by the operations in the interface. Now, a precondition is, in general, a predicate over the operation's input parameters and this state, while a postcondition is a predicate over both input and output parameters as well as the state just before the invocation and just after. Furthermore, a set of invariants may be associated with an interface. An invariant is a predicate over the interface's state model that will always hold. Finally, the component specification may include a set of inter-interface conditions, which are predicates over the state models of all of the component's interfaces.

The concepts introduced here and the relationships among them are shown on the UML class diagram of Figure 2.2 and as an example in Figure 2.3. For the sake of readability, the classes Name, Type, and InOut-Parameter are not shown, because they have no direct relationships with the newly introduced classes. Note that this model allows the same state to be associated with several interfaces. Often, the state models of different interfaces of a component will overlap rather than be identical. This relationship cannot be expressed in the model because we cannot make any assumptions about the structure of state models. Note also how each postcondition is associated with both input and output parameters and two instances of the state model, representing the state before and after an invocation.

In the model presented in Figure 2.2, a partial model of the state of a component is associated with each interface, to allow the semantics of an

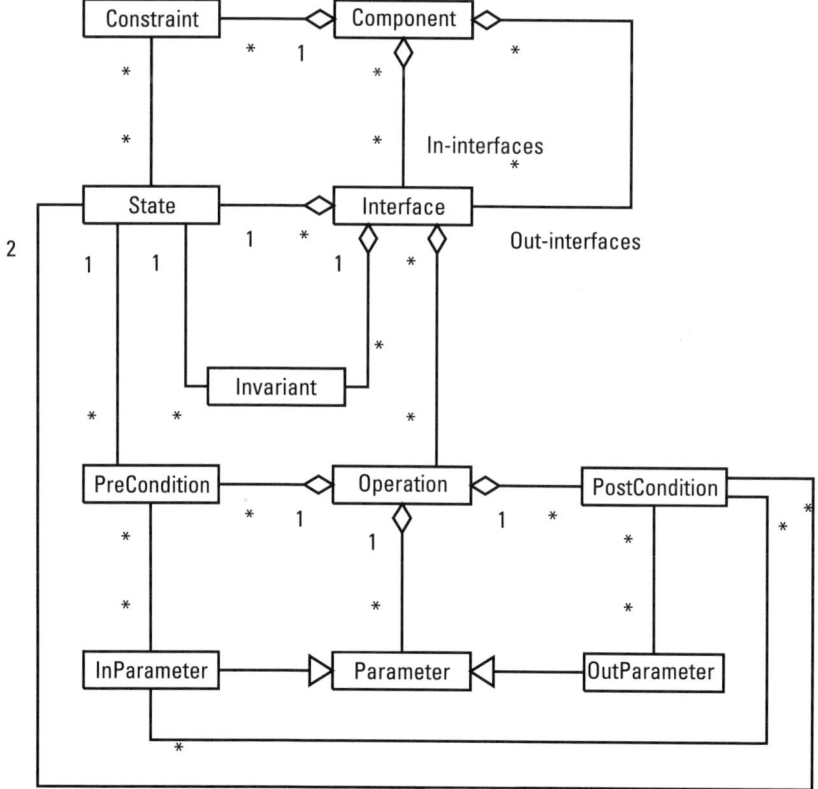

Figure 2.2 UML metamodel of the concepts used in semantic specification of software components.

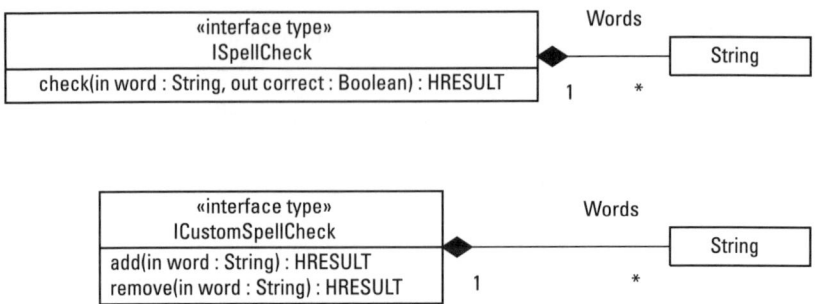

Figure 2.3 Example interface specification diagram.

interface's operations to be specified. The reader should note that this is not intended to specify how a state should be represented within the component. Although state models in component specifications should above all be kept simple, the actual representation used in the component's implementation will usually be subject to efficiency considerations, depending on the programming language and other factors. It is also worth mentioning that the model is valid for procedural as well as object-oriented specification techniques.

Before discussing the ramifications of this model any further, we now consider an example specification using the technique of [5]. Figure 2.3 is an example of an interface specification diagram. It shows the two interfaces introduced in the previous section as classes with the <<interface type>> stereotype. Thus, all information in the syntactic interface specifications is included here. The state models of the interfaces are also shown. A state model generally takes the form of one or more classes having at least one composition relationship with the interface to which the state belongs. The special stereotype <<interface type>> is used instead of the standard <<interface>> because the standard <<interface>> would not allow the state models to be associated with the interfaces in this way.

The interface specification diagram is only a part of the complete interface specifications. The pre- and postconditions that specify the semantics of the operations as well as any invariants on the state model are specified separately in OCL. Below is a specification of the three operations of the two interfaces above. There are no invariants on the state models in this example.

```
context ISpellCheck:: check(in word : String, out correct :
        Boolean) : HRESULT
    pre:
```

```
      word <> ""
   post:
      SUCCEEDED(result) implies correct =
         words->includes (word)

   context ICustomSpellCheck::add(in word : String) : HRESULT
   pre:
      word <> ""
   post:
      SUCCEEDED(result) implies  words =
         words@pre->including(word)

   context ICustomSpellCheck::remove(in word : String) :
    HRESULT
   pre:
      word <> ""
   post:
      SUCCEEDED(result) implies words =
         words@pre-> excluding(word)
```

The precondition of the first operation states that if it is invoked with an input parameter that is not the empty string, the postcondition will hold when the operation returns. The postcondition states that if the return value indicates that the invocation was successful, then the value of the output parameter is true if `word` was a member of the set of words and false otherwise. The specifications of the two last operations illustrate how postconditions can refer to the state before the invocation using the `@pre suffix`. This specification technique uses the convention that if part of an interface's state is not mentioned in a postcondition, then that part of the state is unchanged by the operation. Thus, `words = words@pre` is an implicit postcondition of the first operation. All specifications refer to an output parameter called result, which represents the return value of the operations. The function `SUCCEEDED` is used in COM to determine whether a return value of type `HRESULT` indicates success or failure.

Like interface specification diagrams, component specification diagrams are used to specify which interfaces components provide and require. Figure 2.4 is an example of such a diagram, specifying a component that provides the two interfaces specified above. The component is represented by a

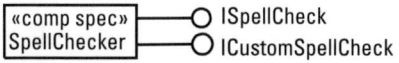

Figure 2.4 Example of a component specification diagram.

class with stereotype <<comp spec>> to emphasize that it represents a component specification. UML also has a standard component concept, which is commonly used to represent a file that contains the implementation of a set of concrete classes.

The component specification is completed by the specification of its inter-interface constraints. The component in this example has one such constraint, specifying that the sets of words in the state models of the two interfaces must be the same. This constraint relates the operations of the separate interfaces to each other, such that invocations of add or remove affect subsequent invocations of check. The constraint is formulated in OCL as follows:

```
context SpellChecker
ISpellCheck::words = ICustomSpellCheck::words
```

An important property of the model presented in Figure 2.2 is that state models and operation semantics are associated with interfaces rather than with a component. This means that the semantics is part of the interface specification. Consequently, a component cannot be said to implement an interface if it implements operations with the same signatures as the interface's operations but with different semantics. Note that the terminology varies in the literature on this point, because interfaces are sometimes seen as purely syntactic entities. In such cases, specifications that also include semantics are often called contracts. UML, for instance, defines an interface to be a class with only abstract operations and it can have no state associated with it.

Although the main uses of syntactic specifications are for type checking and ensuring interoperability, the utility of semantic specifications is potentially much larger. The most obvious use is perhaps for tool support for component developers as well as developers of component-based applications. For the benefit of component developers, one can imagine an automatic testing tool that verifies all operations produce the correct postconditions when their preconditions are satisfied. For this to work, the tool must be able to obtain information about a component's current state. A component could easily be equipped with special operations for this purpose that would not need to be included in the final release. Similarly, for application developers, one can imagine a tool that generates assertions for checking that an operation's preconditions are satisfied before the operation is invoked. These assertions could either query a component about its current state, if this is possible, or maintain a state model of its own. The last technique has a requirement, however, that other clients cannot affect the state maintained by a component, since the state model must be kept synchronized with the actual state. Such assertions would typically not be included in a final release either.

With the notion of an interface specification that include semantics, the concept of substitution introduced in the previous section can now be extended to cover semantics. Clearly, if a component Y implements all (semantically specified) interfaces implemented by another component X, then Y can be safely substituted for X. This condition is not necessary, however, for substitution to be safe. What is necessary is that a client that satisfies the preconditions specified for X must always satisfy the preconditions specified for Y, and that a client that can rely on the postconditions ensured by X can also be ensured it can rely on Y. This means that Y must implement operations with the same signatures as the operations of X, and with pre- and postconditions that ensure the condition above. More specifically, if X implements an operation O, where pre(O) is the conjunction of its preconditions and post(O) the conjunction of its postconditions, Y must implement an operation O' with the same signature such that pre(O') implies pre(O) and post(O) implies post(O'). In other words, the interfaces implemented by Y can have weaker preconditions and stronger postconditions than the interfaces implemented by X. It follows from this that the state models used for specifying the interfaces of X and Y need not be identical. This condition for semantically safe substitution of components is an application of Liskov's principle of substitution [10]. Note that the above discussion is only valid for sequential systems. For multithreaded components or components that are invoked by concurrently active clients, the concept of safe substitution must be extended as discussed in [11]. Finally, note that a client can still malfunction after a component substitution, even if the components fulfill semantic specifications that satisfy the condition specified above. This can happen, for instance, if the designers of the client and the new component have made conflicting assumptions about the overall architecture of the system. The term *architectural mismatch* has been coined to describe such situations [12].

The component specification diagram in Figure 2.4 shows how we can indicate which interfaces are offered by a component. In this example, we indicated that the spell checker offered the interfaces ISpellCheck and ICustomSpellCheck and used the constraint

```
ISpellCheck::words = ICustomSpellCheck::words
```

to specify that the interfaces act on the same information model. We could, however, extend such diagrams to indicate the interfaces on which a component depends. This is illustrated in Figure 2.5.

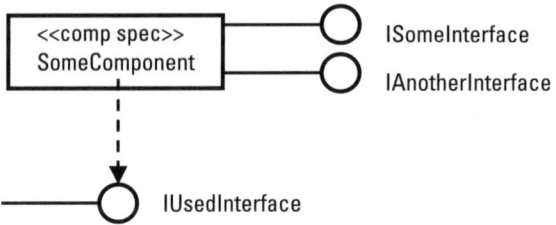

Figure 2.5 Component specification showing an interface dependency.

We can also specify realization contracts using collaboration interaction diagrams. For example, in Figure 2.6 we state that whenever the operation op1 is called, a component supporting this operation must invoke the operation op2 in some other component. Component specification diagrams and collaboration interaction diagrams may therefore be used to define behavioral dependencies.

Specifying Extrafunctional Properties of Components

The specification of extrafunctional properties of software components has recently become a subject of interest, mainly within the software architecture community. In [13], it is argued that the specification of architectural components is not properly addressed by conventional software doctrines. Architectural components are components of greater complexity than algorithms and data structures. Software components, as defined above, generally belong to this class. Conventional software doctrine is the view that software

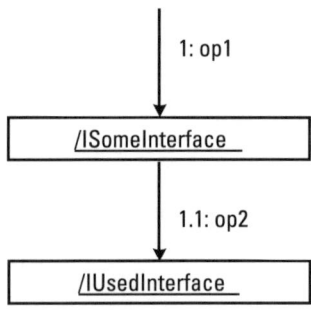

Figure 2.6 Collaboration interaction diagrams.

specifications must be sufficient and complete (that is, provide everything a user needs to know and may rely on in using the software), *static* (written once and frozen), and *homogeneous* (written in a single notation).

To use an architectural component successfully, information about more than just its functionality is required. This additional information includes structural properties, governing how a component can be composed with other components; extrafunctional properties, such as performance, capacity, and environmental assumptions; and family properties, specifying relationships among similar or related components. It is not realistic to expect specifications to be complete with respect to all such properties, due to the great effort this would require. (Nor is it realistic to expect that the developer of a component could anticipate all aspects of the component in which its user might be interested.) Because we cannot expect software components to be delivered with specifications that are sufficient and complete, and because developers are likely to discover new kinds of dependencies as they attempt to use independently developed components together, specifications should be extensible. Specifications should also be heterogeneous, since the diversity of properties that might be of interest is unlikely to be suitably captured by a single notation.

The concept of credentials is proposed in [13] as a basis for specifications that satisfy the requirements outlined above. A credential is a triple <Attribute, Value, Credibility>, where Attribute is a description of a property of a component, Value a measure of that property, and Credibility a description of how the measure has been obtained. A specification technique based on credentials must include a set of registered attributes, along with notations for specifying their value and credibility, and provisions for adding new attributes. A technique could specify some attributes as required and others as optional. The concept has been partially implemented in the architecture description language UniCon [14], which allows an extendable list of <Attribute, Value> pairs to be associated with a component. The self-describing components of Microsoft's new .NET platform [15] include a concept of attributes in which a component developer can associate attribute values with a component and define new attributes by subclassing an existing attribute class. Attributes are part of a component's metadata, which can be programmatically inspected, and is therefore suitable for use with automated development tools.

The concept of credentials has been incorporated in an approach to building systems from preexisting components; this approach is called *Ensemble* [16] and it focuses on the decisions that designers must make, in particular when faced with a choice between competing technologies, competing products within a technology, or competing components within a product. In Ensemble, a set of credentials may be associated with a single technology, product, or component, or with a group of such elements. In addition, a variation of credentials is introduced to handle measures of properties that are needed but have not yet been obtained. These are called postulates and can be described as credentials where the credibility is replaced by a plan for obtaining the measure. The credential triple is thus extended with a flag isPostulate.

Returning our focus to the specification of single components, we now extend the ideas of Ensemble to allow a set of credentials to be associated with a component, an interface, or an operation. A UML metamodel with the concepts of syntactic specification augmented with credentials is shown in Figure 2.7. The class Name and the subclasses of Parameter have been omitted for brevity. Note that the concept of credentials is complementary to the specification of a component's functionality and completely orthogonal to the concepts introduced for semantic specifications. Because the specification of extrafunctional properties of software components is still an open area

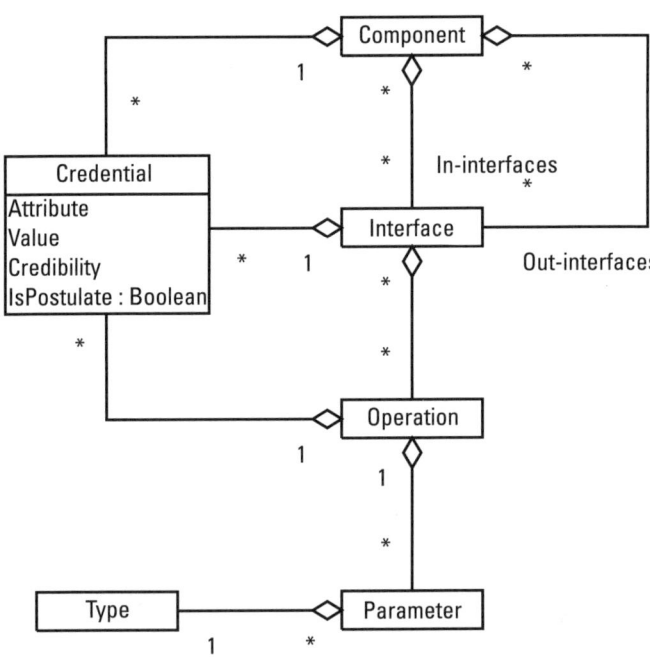

Figure 2.7 UML metamodel of concepts used to specify extrafunctional properties of software components.

of research, it would probably be premature to proclaim this to be a generic model.

Because the extrafunctional properties that may be included in a component specification can be of very different natures, we cannot formulate a general concept of safe substitution for components that includes changes of such properties. A set of extrafunctional properties, which can all be expressed as cost specifications, is studied in [17] where it is shown that, depending on the chosen property, weakening, strengthening, or equivalence is required for substitution to be safe.

Summary

A component has two parts: an interface and some code. The interface is the only point of access to the component, and it should ideally contain all of the information that users need to know about the component's operations: what it does and how and where the component can be deployed, that'is, its context dependencies. The code, on the other hand, should be completely inaccessible (and invisible). The specification of a component therefore must consist of a precise definition of the component's operations and context dependencies. In current practice, component specification techniques specify components only syntactically. The use of UML and OCL to specify components represents a step toward semantic specifications. Specification of extrafunctional properties of components is still an open area of research, and it is uncertain what impact it will have on the future of software component specification.

References

[1]   Microsoft, "The Component Object Model Specification," Report v0.99, Microsoft Standards, Redmond, WA: Microsoft, 1996.

[2]   OMG, "The Common Object Request Broker: Architecture and Specification," Report v2.4, OMG Standards Collection, OMG, 2000.

[3]   Sun Microsystems, "JavaBeans 1.01 Specification," http://java.sun.com/beans.

[4]   OMG, "OMG Unified Modeling Language Specification," Report v1.3, OMG, June 1999.

[5]   Cheesman, J., and J. Daniels, *UML Components—A Simple Process for Specifying Component-Based Software*, Reading, MA: Addison-Wesley, 2000.

[6] Warmer, J., and A. Kleppe, *The Object Constraint Language*, Reading, MA: Addison-Wesley, 1999.

[7] D'Souza, D., and A. C. Wills, *Objects, Components and Frameworks: The Catalysis Approach*, Reading, MA: Addison-Wesley, 1998.

[8] Jones, C. B., *Systematic Software Development Using VDM*, Upper Saddle River, NJ: Prentice Hall, 1990.

[9] Meyer, B., *Object-Oriented Software Construction*, Upper Saddle River, NJ: Prentice Hall, 1997.

[10] Liskov, B., "Data Abstraction and Hierarchy," *Addendum to Proc. OOPSLA'87*, Orlando, FL, SIGPLAN Notices, 1987.

[11] Schmidt, H., and J. Chen, "Reasoning About Concurrent Objects," *Proc. Asia-Pacific Software Engineering Conf.*, Brisbane, Australia, IEEE Computer Society, 1995.

[12] Garlan, D., R. Allen, and J. Ockerbloom, "Architectural Mismatch: Why Reuse Is So Hard," *IEEE Software*, Vol. 12, No. 6, 1995, pp. 17–26.

[13] Shaw, M., "Truth vs Knowledge: The Difference Between What a Component Does and What We Know It Does," *Proc. 8th Int. Workshop Software Specification and Design*, Schloss Velen, Germany, IEEE Computer Society, 1996.

[14] Shaw, M., et al., "Abstractions for Software Architecture and Tools to Support Them," *IEEE Trans. on Software Engineering*, Vol. 21, No. 24, 1995, pp. 314–335.

[15] Conrad, J., et al., *Introducing .NET*, Wrox Press, 2000.

[16] Wallnau, K. C., and J. Stafford, "Ensembles: Abstractions for a New Class of Design Problem," *Proc. 27th Euromicro Conf.*, Warsaw, Poland, IEEE Computer Society, 2001.

[17] Schmidt, H., and W. Zimmerman, "A Complexity Calculus for Object-Oriented Programs," *Object-Oriented Systems*, Vol. 1, No. 2, 1994, pp. 117–148.

Part 2:
Software Architecture and Components

Software architecture and components are closely related. All software systems have an architecture that can be viewed in terms of the decomposition of the system into components, connectors, and attachments representing units of system functionality and their potential run-time interactions. The placing of constraints on their interactions permits the assembly of groups of component and connector types into families of systems designated architectural styles. Patterns of interaction can support reasoning with respect to certain system-related quality attributes such as modifiability, reliability, and confidentiality.

Traditionally, software architecture is focused on in the early design phase when the overall structure of the system is designed to satisfy functional and nonfunctional requirements. In monolithic applications, the architecture specified in the design process is concealed at execution time in one block of executable code. Component technologies focus on composition and deployment, closer to or at execution time. In a component-based system, the architecture remains recognizable during application or system execution, with the system still consisting of clearly separated components. The system architecture thus remains an important factor during the execution phase. CBSE embraces the total life cycles of components and component-based systems and all procedures involved in such life cycles. It is therefore of interest to consider the similarities and differences between software architecture and CBD. The aim of this chapter is to show components and component-based systems from a software architecture point of view.

Chapter 3 provides a bird's-eye view of software architecture and relates this subject, with particular reference to architectural style, the development of component frameworks, the analysis of component-based systems for functional and extrafunctional correctness, and to the more general problem of creating systems from software components.

Chapter 4 presents a survey of several component models (Java Beans, the CORBA component model, the .NET component model, and the Open Service Gateway Initiative component model) from the software architecture point of view. The main characteristics of architectural definition languages are described first and are subsequently used in descriptions of component models. In addition to the main characteristics of each component model, the following component forms are presented: the interface of a component, the implementation of a component, component assembly, and component packaging and deployment.

3

Architecting Component-Based Systems

Jan Bosch and Judith A. Stafford

Introduction

For decades, the software engineering community has identified the reuse of existing software as the most promising approach to addressing certain problems. Although the reuse of software has been rather successful in some areas, if we ignore the reuse of functionality provided by operating systems, database management systems, graphical user interfaces and Web servers, and domain-specific software, reuse has been considerably limited.

With the emergence of explicit software architecture design, a highly promising approach to software architecture-driven reuse has evolved. The architecture defines the components of a software system as well as their interactions and can be used to analyze its quality attributes. What, then, is software architecture? Consider this frequently cited definition [1]: "The software architecture of a program or computing system is the structure or structures of the system, which comprise software components [and connectors], the externally visible properties of those components [and connectors] and the relationships among them." Thus, it is clear that software architecture and software components are two sides of the same coin (i.e., the software architecture defines the components that make up the system), but on the other hand, the properties and functionality of the components define the overall system functionality and behavior. Consequently, even though the focus of this book is on CBD, software architecture is included as a topic because it represents an integral part of any component-based software system.

The remainder of this chapter is organized as follows. In the next section, we discuss the various roles that software architecture might play during software development. Then, we present a generic process for the design of software architectures. The subsequent sections discuss the notion of component frameworks and architecture-driven component development, respectively. Finally, we summarize the chapter.

Role of Software Architecture

In the introduction to this chapter, we introduced the notion of software architecture as a key success factor for component-based software development. The software architecture plays many important roles during the development and evolution of component-based software systems. Typically, we identify three main uses for the software architecture: assessment and evaluation, configuration management, and dynamic software architectures. Each of these is discussed in more detail next.

Assessment and Evaluation

Software architecture captures the earliest design decisions concerning a software system. The earliest design decisions made are the hardest and most expensive to change once the software system has been developed. It is, therefore, very important to determine whether the designed software architecture accurately balances the—typically conflicting—requirements from the different stakeholders (i.e., all persons or departments that have a stake in the system). In addition, both the software architect and the stakeholders are very interested in determining that a system built based on a certain software architecture will fulfill not only its functional, but also its quality requirements. Because one of the driving forces with respect to software architecture is that the software architecture constrains the quality attributes, the software architecture is a suitable artifact for assessing correctness with respect to the quality requirements. Next we discuss three types of assessment or evaluation: stakeholder-based evaluation, expert-based assessment, and quality-attribute assessment.

The purpose of stakeholder-based assessment is to determine whether the trade-offs between requirements in the software architecture match the actual stakeholder priorities for these requirements. The software architect may have decided to prioritize a requirement from stakeholder A over a requirement from stakeholder B. However, during the assessment, it may be discovered that the priority of the requirement for stakeholder B is much higher than the priority for stakeholder A. Stakeholder-based assessment allows the stakeholders and the software architect to evaluate the architecture for such mistakes. The most well-known stakeholder-based assessment method is probably SAAM [2], which has evolved into the recently documented Architecture Trade-off Analysis Method (ATAM)[1] [3].

Expert-based assessment is similar to stakeholder-based assessment. However, in the case of expert-based assessment, a team of experienced architects and designers assesses the software architecture designed by the project team to determine whether a system built based on this architecture will fulfill its functional and quality requirements.

Whereas stakeholder- and expert-based assessment qualitatively assess the software architecture for all its requirements, quality-attribute-oriented assessment aims to provide a quantitative prediction of one quality attribute (e.g., maintainability, performance, reliability, or security). For instance, in [4] an approach is discussed for predicting the required maintenance effort for a system built based on the assessed software architecture, the maintenance profile, the expected number of change requests, and the average productivity of software engineers. The maintenance profile captures the most likely change scenarios for which the architecture should be optimized. Based on this maintenance profile, the impact of each change scenario on the software architecture can be determined. Based on the impact analysis and the data mentioned earlier, one could predict the required maintenance effort. Other techniques exist for other quality attributes; for example, see Alonso et al. [5] for assessing real-time behavior.

Configuration Management

A second use of software architecture can be found in the context of software product lines. During product derivation, the product architecture is derived

---

1. Registered servicemark by Carnegie/Mellon University.

from the product-line architecture and subsequently populated with selected and configured product-line components. Also in single-product contexts, especially if the product is highly configurable, the software architecture is frequently used as a means to manage the configuration of the product.

As mentioned earlier, the first-class representation of the software architecture is used in increasingly later phases of the life cycle, for instance, configuration management and to manage run-time structure (e.g., dynamic software architectures).

Dynamic Software Architectures

The third and final use of software architecture is currently in an experimental phase, but is evolving rapidly. Here the software architecture is kept as a first-class entity for the operation of the system. This is typically referred to as *dynamic software architecture* because the architecture is used to aid in modifying the system during its operation. Possible modifications range from replacing components to reorganizing the software architecture in response to changed quality requirements for the system. Because it is generally accepted that the architecture constrains the quality attributes of the system and the most important quality requirements should drive the design of the software architecture, the logical consequence is that if the quality requirements of the system change dynamically (e.g., because of changes in the context of the system), the software architecture should reorganize itself in response to these changes.

Note that in this case, the first-class representation of the software architecture is kept even during run time. This is, of course, what component-based systems are all about. The main difference is that component-based systems are typically configured and bound at compile time, whereas we here discuss the notion of run time and dynamic system (re)configuration.

Designing Software Architectures

In this chapter, we have discussed the importance and uses of software architecture. However, to this point we have assumed the software architecture to be present, but the artifact, of course, needs to be designed. In this section, we discuss the typical process used when designing a software architecture. The discussion is based on [6].

Architecture Design Process

The architecture design process can be viewed as a function that takes a requirement specification as input and generates an architectural design as output. However, this function is not an automated process and considerable effort and creativity from the involved software architects is required. In Figure 3.1, the main phases in software architecture design are presented graphically.

The design process starts with functionality-based design (i.e., a design of the software architecture based on the functional requirements specified in the requirement documents). Although software engineers generally will not design a system without concern for reliability or reusability, the quality requirements are not explicitly addressed at this stage. Functionality-based

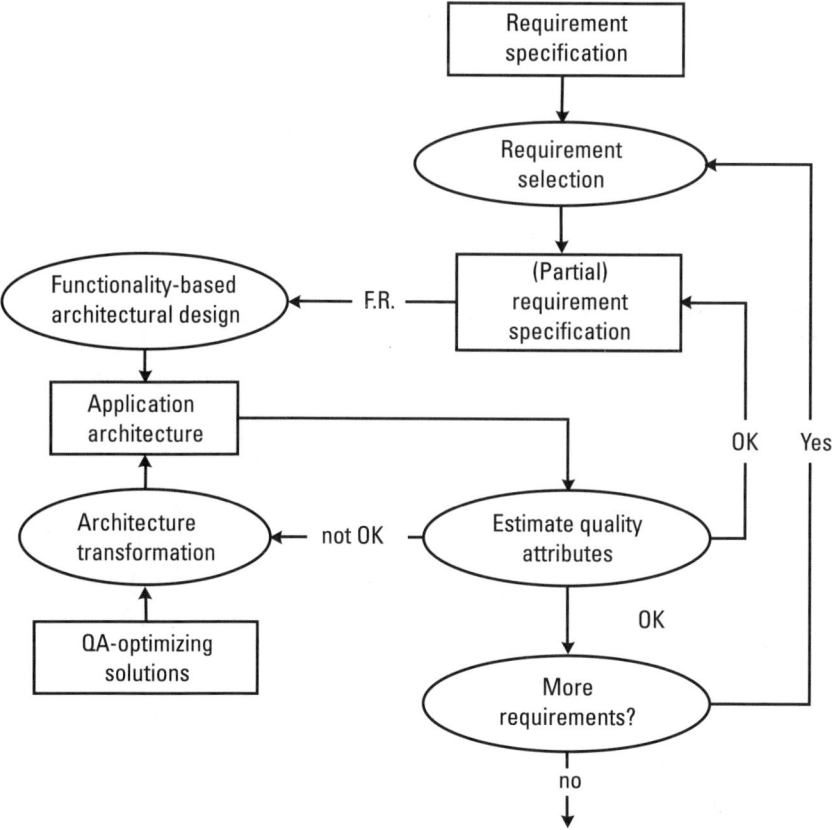

Figure 3.1 General software architecture design process.

design consists of four steps: (1) defining the boundaries and context of the system, (2) identification of archetypes, (3) decomposition of the system into its main components, and (4) the first validation of the architecture by describing a number of system instances.

The second phase is the assessment of the quality attributes of software architecture in relation to the quality requirements. Each quality attribute is given an estimate in using a qualitative or quantitative assessment technique. As discussed in the previous section, several techniques are available for assessing quality attributes including scenario-based assessment [3, 6], simulation [7], static analysis [8], metrics-based models [5], and expert-based assessment [6]. Typically, scenario profiles are used to specify the semantics of quality attributes. If all estimated quality attributes are as good or better than required, the architectural design process is completed. Otherwise, the third phase of software architecture design is entered: architecture transformation.

The third phase of the software architecture design process is concerned with selecting design solutions to improve the quality attributes while preserving the domain functionality captured by the software architecture. Each set of so-called "transformations" (one or more) results in a new version of the software architecture. This design is again evaluated and the same process is repeated, if necessary, until all quality requirements are fulfilled or until the software engineer decides that no feasible solution exists. In that case, the software architect needs to renegotiate the requirements with the customer. The transformations (i.e., quality attribute optimizing solutions) generally improve one or more quality attributes while affecting others negatively.

As shown in Figure 3.2, transformations can be organized according to two dimensions: the scope of impact and the type of transformation. At each location in the two-dimensional space, one can identify a transformation category. For each architectural design decision, one can identify at least five possible structural effects: (1) adding, splitting, or merging one or more components, (2) functionality added to the existing components, (3) behavior superimposed on existing component functionality, (4) additional design rules, and (5) additional design constraints. We refer to the next section and to [6] for a more complete discussion of the topic.

Architectural Styles

The study of software architecture has revealed that certain structures recur and are used to solve specific types of problems. These structures can be

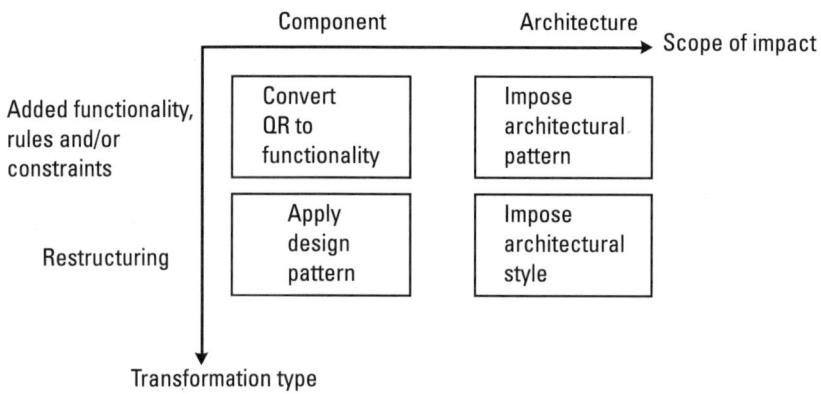

Figure 3.2 Architecture transformation categories.

identified in terms of the types of components and connectors that comprise them and the patterns of interactions among the components and connectors. Several of these structures have been identified and classified as architectural styles. We describe three architectural styles below and follow these descriptions with a brief discussion of the relationship between architectural styles and system quality attributes.

Pipe-and-Filter Architecture

The pipe-and-filter architectural style has only one component and one connector type. The component type is the filter and the connector type is the pipe. Their interactions are constrained in such a way that pipes receive streams of data from filters and deliver these streams to other filters. Additional constraints can be added to pipe-and-filter styles that define the numbers of filters that can provide input to, or receive output from, a pipe at a given time. Programs written using the pipe feature of the UNIX operating system are examples of the use of the pipe-and-filter architectural style.

Blackboard Architecture

The component types of the blackboard style are repositories and data processing components that use the repository. The data processing elements interact with the repository by scanning the repository for required inputs, and by writing to the repository when appropriate. Interaction among repository users is implicit in their shared use of the data values stored in the repository.

Object-Oriented Architecture

The component type of the object-oriented style is the object and the connector type is the synchronous message passing, or procedure call. Objects have state and methods for manipulating that state. The methods are invoked synchronously via the connectors. An object may or may not be aware of the identity of the object to be invoked before requesting a service.

Architectural styles can be specialized in various ways in order to further constrain interactions associated with the components and connectors to support meeting specific quality-related goals. For instance, the pipe-and-filter style might be specialized to disallow cycles, thus improving maintainability.

System-level quality attributes can often be predicted based on the observation of certain architectural styles in a system's architecture. The positive or negative relationship between architectural styles and quality attributes is generally determined by the degree of concurrency supported by the style, the degree to which components can be directly interconnected, and the degree to which data shared by components and management of component interactions is centralized. Table 3.1 contains a summary of the relationship between the architectural styles described above and five quality attributes that are often of concern to system developers. In the table, a plus sign in a cell indicates that the style naming the row has a positive impact on the quality attribute that names the column. A minus sign indicates a negative relationship. When both types of signs appear in a cell, the style can have both positive and negative effects.

In some cases it is possible to moderate the degree to which a quality attribute is affected by using a variant of the style. It is also possible for a particular variant of a style to have both positive and negative effects on a given quality attribute. Again, using the pipe-and-filter style as an example, the style can affect performance positively because it naturally allows for the concurrent operation of filters. However, it can also have a negative effect because a large amount of data manipulation may be required. And, what is

Table 3.1
Architectural Styles and Their Affinity to Quality Attributes

Architecture	Performance	Maintainability	Reliability	Safety	Security
Pipes and filters	+ −	+ −	−	−	+
Blackboard	−	+	+ −	−	+ −
Object-oriented	+ −	+ −	+ −	+	+ −

good for one quality attribute is not necessarily good for another. The blackboard style is not a good style to use if you are building a safety-critical part of a system because of the large amount of data-sharing among components. Use of the blackboard style allows bad data to be immediately read by all components attached to the blackboard. This same characteristic of the blackboard style that leads to potential safety problems because of centrally located data, however, makes it easier to monitor data access and thereby can have a positive impact on security. See [6] for more details on the relationship between architectural styles and quality attributes.

Architecture-Driven Component Development

Once the architecture of the system has been detailed in terms of its components and connectors, it is time to embody these architectural elements. The styles used to design the architecture might suggest the use of a specific component framework (e.g., CORBA, EJB) or set of frameworks for implementation. Implementation components, that is, components that can be executed, are developed or selected to fulfill the requirements assigned to the architectural components, which define the components' specifications. As we said in the "Role of Software Architecture" section of this chapter, the quality of the system is, in part, a function of the properties of the components that comprise it. The goal for the embodiment phase of design is to either build or select components and connectors that possess the quality attributes identified during the architecting phase of development. Only when this is the case can architecture-based analysis be relied on to predict correctly the quality of the component assembly.

Three types of components may be available to embody architectural components: *custom-built components,* components developed, or commissioned, by an organization for a specific purpose; *reusable components,* components already owned by the organization; and *commercial components,* components developed to be sold in a marketplace by vendors. The type of project and the culture of the development organization may restrict choice among these but it is likely that some decision will need to be made about the most appropriate source of components for a project. Determining the quality attributes associated with components of each of these types presents a different problem for developers. In the remainder of the section we discuss issues related to determining component properties. Issues related to component composition and integration are addressed in Chapter 9.

Custom Components

As is the case with any type of custom development, the costs are high in terms of both time and money, but the results are likely to meet the needs of the project commissioner. In the particular case of software development, custom component development is most likely to pay off in cases of software that is very unusual, safety critical, or highly secure. Benefits to be gained include the fact that components can be created to precisely meet the specification of the architectural components, thereby providing assurance that the component assembly will, in fact, possess the quality attributes it was designed around.

Preexisting Components

The two main classes of preexisting components are reusable components and commercial components. Components that are being reused provide different challenges for the architect than do those that are being purchased from commercial vendors.

Up to this point in the discussion we have assumed that the architect retains control over all aspects of design. It is more often the case that the design is constrained by a variety of factors. For instance, a business decision may have been made to reuse certain aspects of a system that is already in place; a marketing decision may have been made to use a specific technology; the organization might have prior experience using a certain component framework or a set of communication mechanisms and services to support component integration; or time-to-market requirements might encourage the use of commercial components.

Regardless of the reason, designing a system around preexisting components and component frameworks over which the designer has little control is a fundamentally different problem from custom design as described in previous sections. In this case, the requirements to use specific components and component frameworks drive the architecture. Components are generally not mutable, thus solutions to this design problem center on adapting component interactions rather than on adapting components themselves.

Reusable Components

Developers consider many breeds of components to be reusable. These can exist on a wide scale of reusability within any organization. On one end of the scale they might be components that were custom designed by the organization for a certain purpose and they perform a task the way that the developer required, but were not designed with reuse in mind. They must be adapted in order to be integrated into the new environment. Also, they must be analyzed to produce sufficient information to determine how the components will actually compose. In most cases, designers will need to create adapters, often referred to as glue code, to modify these types of components so they can be used in the new context.

At the other end of the scale are components developed with reuse in mind. These may be in the form of parameterized components that can readily be used in a variety of settings and with a variety of property values and interdependencies explicitly stated. Clearly, ease of integration and composition will depend on the level of reusability of the components. Product-line development exemplifies the use of preplanned reusable components. Product lines are described in Chapter 11.

Commercial Components

The use of commercial components impacts the design process in profound ways that often reflect other problems rather than design difficulty. Commercial components introduce a large degree of uncertainty into the design process. Market demands impact component selection in ways that go beyond the lack of visibility; commercial components tend to be complex, idiosyncratic, and unstable—complex because market demands require constant feature expansion; idiosyncratic because differentiation, rather than standardization, is rewarded in the marketplace; and unstable because the pressures of the marketplace never let up. When these issues are considered in addition to issues of software privacy and requirements of commercial developers, one wonders if there is any potential for a true marketplace of commercial components. These issues are addressed more fully in Chapter 8.

It is easy to see that consideration of the types of components to be used in a system must be of concern to the architect and adjustments in scheduling and range of acceptable quality must be made as early as possible with regard to the types of components that are likely to be used to assemble the system.

Component-Driven Architecture Development

When a software architect must design a software architecture that needs to use preexisting components, additional constraints are placed on the architect. The introduction of component frameworks to system assembly is analogous to the advent of structured programming. In the early days of program analysis, programmers recognized that unconstrained use of control flow constructs resulted in programs that were difficult, if not impossible, to analyze; restricting control-flow paths provided measurable improvement in program readability and static analysis. Component frameworks impose restriction on component interactions. Because component frameworks have typically been defined to support certain quality attributes, limitations on the types of interactions supported by a framework may constrain the architectural styles that can be used to design the system.

When designing on the basis of preexisting components, the architect might not be allowed access to the source code of the components. Design freedom is limited to component selection and the way the selected components are integrated. This restricted freedom magnifies the importance of managing and controlling component integration. A component's API does not normally provide enough information to indicate how the component will actually behave when used in a given environment. This difficulty raises issues related to understanding and verifying both the functional and extra-functional properties of the components so that the unexpected mismatches among components are avoided and overall system quality can be accurately predicted.

When custom components are developed into requirements, these requirements become the requirements specification for the component. Verification of component properties is required for developers to be confident that a system will behave as its architect predicted it would. Issues related to the measurement and verification of components is a relatively new area of research [9]. Only when these objectives have been met will it be possible to predictably select components that embody architecture.

As mentioned earlier, the types of components that a system is composed of influence the architecture of the system. This is because the existence of preexisting or commercial components reduces the architect's control over the final product. In a like manner, the framework into which components are to be plugged influences the architecture of the system and, in fact, influences the process by which the system is designed. If one views an operating system as a customizable framework, the constraints on the architect are high when developing to a specific framework, but they decrease as other types of frameworks are allowed to coexist in the system.

Different development processes are required when building systems depending on the degree to which the components are preexisting, perhaps commercial, and the frameworks are prescribed. Various development approaches have been suggested and documented in books. The greatest amount of design freedom is retained when building systems with custom components to be deployed into an operating system, and the least amount of freedom is obtained when using commercial components and deploying them in a predetermined component framework such as EJB or CORBA.

Current trends in component-based design point toward an increased focus on this type of development primarily because it enforces a structured approach to CBD that is expected to result in similar benefits to those reaped through the application of structured programming techniques to computer programs.

The theory is that more reliable systems can be produced more quickly and at less expense due to the restrictions on design freedom. At first glance, and as stated in the previous section, the cost of moving in this direction will be to sacrifice the ability to optimize components and connectors in order to produce precisely the system that is desired. If this statement is true, then it seems we will not be able to bridge the gap between architecture and components. We are not as pessimistic about the state of things as it may seem. In fact, we can imagine a commerce in components similar to what exists for most other engineering disciplines. As an example, the development of commerce in plumbing components resulted when plumbing standards supported ease of installation and repair of plumbing fixtures and other parts. Not many years ago in the United States there was no agreement as to how far from the wall a toilet drain should be placed. The toilet needed to be chosen before an architect could design a bathroom. Today a drain is centered 15 inches from the wall. Thus, the plumbing and floor can be installed before the actual toilet is purchased or even chosen. Reaching for a similar goal seems reasonable for software engineering today. As is the case with plumbing, designers will need to deal with legacy systems for years and the desire to build custom systems will never die out completely. However, given an increase in domain- or application-specific component models that describe standards for components and a framework for providing services and constraining interactions, component-driven architectural design will follow.

Summary

Software architecture is a key enabler for CBSE. Components and software architecture form two sides of the same coin: Software architecture defines the components that make up the system as well as the interactions among them, whereas the properties and functionality of the components define the overall system behavior.

Software architecture plays multiple roles during the development and evolution of component-based systems. First, the software architecture may be used for stakeholder-, expert-, or quality-attribute-based assessment. Second, the software architecture may be used for configuration management. One can identify this especially in the context of software product lines. Finally, software architecture can be used to dynamically reorganize the system at run time (i.e., dynamic software architectures).

Design of software architectures consists of three main phases. The first phase is functionality-based architectural design, which is the process of designing a domain model based on the functional requirements only. The second phase is software architecture assessment during which the software architecture is evaluated with respect to the driving quality requirements. Finally, architecture transformation is concerned with improving the quality attributes of the software architecture through imposing an architectural pattern, using a design pattern, or by converting a quality requirement to functionality.

Once the software architecture has been defined, the components that make up the system need to be developed or selected. One can identify three categories of software components: custom, reused, and commercial components. Custom components are developed specifically for the system at hand. Reused components are typically developed within the organization, but were present before the design of the software architecture. Commercial components are developed by an external organization and typically purchased through an intermediary. Preexisting components typically need to be integrated into the system through the use of glue code.

Finally, we discussed the extreme case of systems development based on the use of preexisting components (i.e., component-driven architectural design). In this case, software architecting is primarily concerned with identifying means for optimizing the interactions among the given components.

References

[1]   Bass, L., P. Clements, and R. Kazman, *Software Architecture in Practice,* Reading, MA: Addison-Wesley, 1998.

[2]   Kazman, R., et al., "SAAM: A Method for Analyzing the Properties of Software Architectures," *Proc. 16th Int. Conf. Software Engineering,* ACM Press, 1994.

[3]   Clements, P., R. Kazman, and M. Klein, *Evaluating Software Architectures: Methods and Case Studies,* Reading, MA: Addison-Wesley, 2000.

[4]   Bengtsson, P., and J. Bosch, "Architecture Level Prediction of Software Maintenance," *Proc. 3rd European Conf. Software Maintenance and Reengineering—CSMR'99,* Los Alamitos, CA, IEEE Computer Society, 1999.

[5]   Alonso, A., M. Garcia-Valls, and J. A. de la Puente, "Assessment of Timing Properties of Family Products," *Proc. 2nd Int. ESPRIT ARES Workshop on Development and Evolution of Software Architectures for Product Families,* Lecture Notes in Computer Science, No. 1429, Berlin, Springer Verlag, 1998.

[6]   Bosch, J., *Design & Use of Software Architectures,* Reading, MA: Addison-Wesley, 2000.

[7]   Luckham, D. C., et al., "Specification and Analysis of System Architecture Using Rapide," *IEEE Trans. on Software Engineering,* Special Issue on Software Architecture, Vol. 21, Issue 4, 1995, pp. 336–354.

[8]   Shaw, M., and D. Garlan, *Software Architecture: Perspectives on an Emerging Discipline,* Upper Saddle River, NJ: Prentice Hall, 1996.

[9]   Hissam, S. A., J. Stafford, and K. C. Wallnau, "Packaging Predictable Assembly," in *Proc. of the First International IFIP/ACM Working Conference on Component Deployment,* Berlin, Germany, 2002.

4

Component Models and Technology

Jacky Estublier and Jean-Marie Favre

Introduction

The many definitions of what a component is—and what it is not—often try to define a component in opposition either to object-oriented programming languages or to architecture description languages (ADLs). This chapter does not intend to provide yet another definition, but tries to clarify the situation showing the models of the different component technologies currently available in the industry: JavaBeans [1] , COM+ [2], CCM [3, 4], .NET [5, 6], and the Open Service Gateway Initiative (OSGI) [7].

A difficulty is that industrial component technologies focus on practical problems and are described in technical terms, thus providing many implementation details and making it difficult for users to understand concepts and principles. Available documentation is either oriented toward decision makers and provides mostly marketing arguments, or it is oriented toward programmers or tool implementers and includes pieces of code and complex API specifications.

The ADL community, by contrast, has tried primarily to establish high-level concepts and principles and has produced many research papers. A large amount of work has been dedicated to the analysis and comparison of the different features proposed by the various ADLs [8].

Whereas component technologies focus on the last phases of the life cycle, that is, on implementation, deployment, and execution, ADLs focus on the early stages, mainly on design. Indeed, comparing component technologies and ADLs is difficult because they do not address the same problems and they are not described at the same level of abstraction. It is useful, however, because they share the component concept and their scope is complementary.

The goal of this chapter is to describe component technology in the same terms as ADLs at the same abstraction level. Of course, this chapter does not intend to provide in-depth coverage or present the different facets of these technologies. We shall try instead to identify the component model underlying each component technology. This allows us to identify similarities and differences, both between the various component technologies and between ADLs and current component technologies.

The remainder of this chapter is organized as follows. In the next section, we provide a short historical perspective showing where component technology has its roots. Then we present a broad overview of the main features provided and introduce the notation used in this chapter. The next section briefly introduces Acme as a representative of the main concepts typically found in ADLs. The subsequent sections briefly present industrial component technology, namely, Sun's JavaBeans, OMG's CORBA Component Model (CCM), Microsoft's .NET, and OSGI. Finally, the chapter is summarized.

A Short Historical Perspective

Programming languages, apart from their linguistic aspect, can be seen from either the run-time point of view (run-time support while executing the program) or from the design and reuse perspective (designing new programs and reusing existing programs). The first perspective provides transparent support during program execution, dynamic loaders and binary interoperability being examples of the (extrafunctional) properties added to a program by run-time support. The second perspective, reuse and design, leads to more abstract concepts such as classes, inheritance, and polymorphisms and to methods and notation like UML.

To a large extent, component-based technology is the logical continuation of the first perspective (introspection capability and run-time support), whereas ADLs are the logical follow-up of the second (design and reuse). Take the example of dynamic loading. The association of the language run-time support with the operating system, and the addition of a limited form of introspection to executables (a table of symbols with their offset), is sufficient to provide new properties for applications (incremental loading, module substitution, partial recompilation, portability, etc.) without any change in the application source code.

It is the development of this idea that is the basis for component-based technology: By relying on the component framework, it is possible to transparently provide new services and remove information from source code. These goals can only be reached by improving source code introspection or by defining new formalisms. Indeed, the approach was used to (1) explicitly define components and their interactions with other components (to perform static connection checking and automate connection control), (2) explicitly define their implementation from native code and interactions with other "native" code (to dynamically instantiate and control instance life cycle), and (3) explicitly define components (extrafunctional) properties and services (to delegate their realization to the component framework). Indeed these three goals were addressed, more or less simultaneously, by different groups, and ended up in different systems.

Component Interface and Connections

ADL

The ADL community focused on the definition of a component, its interface, and relationships with other components. ADLs primarily address the issues related to the early phases of software engineering: design and analysis. They identify a number of concepts such as architecture, configurations, connectors, bindings, properties, hierarchical models, style, static analysis, and behavior (see Chapter 3). Simultaneously, but on a different abstraction level, industrial component technology addresses similar issues, emphasizing more pragmatic aspects.

Improving Code Independence

The compilation techniques used in classic languages like C and C++ are such that even a simple change in a program could result in dramatic recompilations that increase development costs and reduce reusability. The idea of improving code independence was to improve the independence of "programs," relying on the definition of explicit "interfaces" and on a simple interaction protocol (e.g., asking for a "connection" to an interface).

COM falls into this category. It proposes an improved binary interoperability convention and a few composition techniques: *containment* and *aggregation*. Dassault Systèmes' component model improved the composition technique with *extensions* and *delegation* (see Chapter 19).

Simplifying Composition

JavaBeans focuses on increasing composition capabilities and reuse. The system is based on considerably extended introspection capabilities and on many programming conventions. The result is that beans are highly reusable and can be easily composed, statically or dynamically. Specific assembly tools have been developed, for example, Net Bean [9].

Performing Services Transparently

Performing Distribution

The goal here was to provide a way to realize distributed applications almost transparently. The remote procedure call (RPC) is the ancestor of this very successful line of work. CORBA Object Request Broker (ORB) extended the approach with object-oriented (OO) and language heterogeneity. COM+ relies on RPC.

In these approaches, introspection requires "full" knowledge of the interfaces, which are provided in the IDL and processed by a compiler. Run-time support requires more resources, the ORB itself being only one of the required run-time components.

Generalizing Services

The goal here was to generalize the big success of distribution support on a number of other extrafunctional properties. This produced a proliferation of "services" (see CORBA services [10] and MTS specification) including transaction and persistency. The complexity of each service, and, much worse, of their combination, led to their encapsulation under the concept of *container* (EJB). The container is an abstraction for the set of services to be applied to a component.

The CCM, adding among other things language heterogeneity, generalized the approach.

Here introspection is more demanding, and the description of the services to apply to a component requires specific formalism(s). The container is an abstraction for the set of services to apply to a component, and its implementation is a mixture of run-time interpreters (code introspection and container information), of objects generated when compiling the container description (stubs, skeletons, etc.), and of general run-time services (ORB, DBs, etc.).

In an abstract way, in these approaches, a component is a box. The box itself is the container that describes and controls the access and properties of its content; and the content is the "functional" or executable code of the component. The box manages the content but the content ignores the box. These approaches emphasize the distinction between the box itself (described in a number of specialized formalisms), and the content (described in classic programming languages, object-oriented or not). The box describes how to manage the content at execution.

Notation and Plan

A component model specifies, at an abstract level, the standards and conventions imposed on software engineers who develop and use components. Compliance with a component model is one of the properties that distinguishes components from other software entities.

In this chapter we call a component framework the set of (1) the formalisms used to describe some aspects of components; (2) a number of tools, including the above formalisms, compilers, design tools and others; (3) the run-time infrastructure that interprets part of the above formalism and enforces specific properties; and (4) a number of predefined components and libraries.

Though imprecise, industrial component models often make assumptions about important steps in an implicit product life cycle. Table 4.1 gives a rough picture of the major steps that could be identified.

In the following discussion, we look at different industrial component models. For each model we will provide the intended goal of the model and describe it from different aspects: (1) interface and assembly, (2) implementation, (3) framework, and (4) the life cycle.

Table 4.1
Majors Steps in CBD Life Cycle

Aspect	Phase	Actor
Interface	Definition	Designer
Assembly	Assembly	Architect
Implementation	Implementation	Developer
Life cycle	Packaging, deployment	Administrator
Framework, run-time support	Execution	End user

For the purpose of this chapter, we will use a simple graphical formalism, in which a component is a gray box (Figure 4.1). The closed box is used to represent the interface of the component and the concepts provided to model the interaction points of the component with the external world. In all ADLs, as well as in most component models, the unique (meta) entity is the component, and interaction points are only relationships between components. We will instead identify three classes of "entities," the components (gray), the run-time component framework (black), and the other users programs (white). We emphasize the relationship of a component with (1) the other components (left and right), (2) the component run-time framework (bottom), and (3) the usual programs that are no components (top).

Acme ADL

Many architecture description languages have been proposed, sometimes to satisfy the needs of different application domains. Different surveys have been published (e.g., [8]). Although there is little consensus about what exactly an ADL is, there is agreement about what the set of core concepts could be, at least regarding the structural aspect of architectural description. Acme is an architectural description language [11] that incorporates these concepts. In this section, we give a very brief description of Acme in order to present typical ADL concepts. Acme is a second-generation ADL that focuses on the definition of a core set of concepts related to the structural aspects of software architecture in order to make it possible to exchange descriptions between independently developed ADLs. Acme is a generic

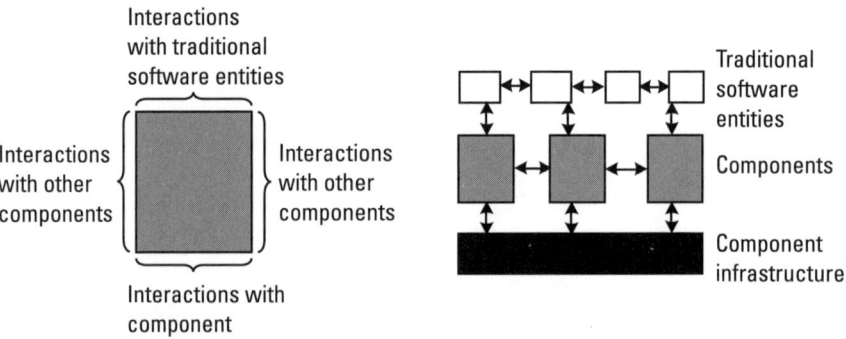

Figure 4.1 Component interactions.

ADL that can be used to describe more specific concepts by specializing the core concepts.

Just like other ADLs, Acme concentrates on the design and evaluation of software architecture, emphasizing the notation used as illustrated by the following statement: "An important problem for component-based systems engineering is finding appropriate notations to describe those systems. Good notations make it possible to document component-based design clearly, reason about their properties, and automate their analysis and system generation" [11]. Acme is made of a textual and a graphical notation. In this chapter, we use a very similar graphical notation as an aid to compare the major concepts of ADLs and component models.

A system is described as a graph of components and connectors as shown in Figure 4.2.

Components and Ports

Components represent the computational elements and data stores of a system. There are no restrictions on the size of a component. A component can be as small as a button in a graphical user interface or as large as a Web server. For large and complex components, it is essential to be able to hide their internal structures. The interface of a component, that is, its external view, is described as a set of ports. The ports are the points of interaction between a component and its environment.

Connectors and Roles

Connectors represent interactions between components. Like components, connectors can be of arbitrary complexity. This notion makes it possible to represent, in a unified way, simple concepts such as a method call as well as complex and abstract connections such as an SQL connection between a

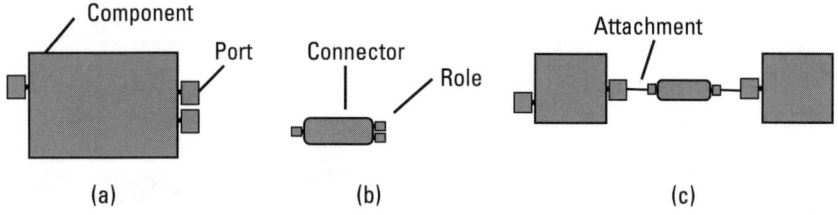

Figure 4.2 Components, ports, connectors, roles, systems, and attachments in (a) a component interface, (b) a connector interface, and (c) a very simple system.

client and a database server. Indeed, making a connector a first-class entity is one of the important features of many ADLs. Because a connector can be rather complex, it is important to be able to describe its interface independently from its internal structure. The interface of a connector is defined as a set of *roles*. A role is to a connector what a port is to a component, that is, its interaction points. Many simple connectors are binary. For instance, a method call is a connector with two roles, the caller and the callee; a pipe has a writer and a reader; an event channel has an emitter and a receiver, and so forth. Simple arrows could be seen as suitable notation for binary connectors but this is just a matter of graphical notation.

Systems and Attachments

Acme makes it possible to describe components and connectors separately, but the goal is to describe a complete system as an assembly of components and connectors. The structure of a system is specified by a set of components, a set of connectors, and a set of attachments. An *attachment* links a component port to a connector role. Connections between components are thus modeled as a component–port–role–connector–role–component sequence. This may seem unnecessarily complex, but it is needed to model complex systems. In particular, it allows us to reason about connectors in isolation, which is possible only if connector interfaces are explicitly defined.

Representations and Bindings

The concepts presented above make it possible to describe how a system is made of components and connectors, giving an overall view of this system, an example of which is shown in Figure 4.3. To support top-down design of

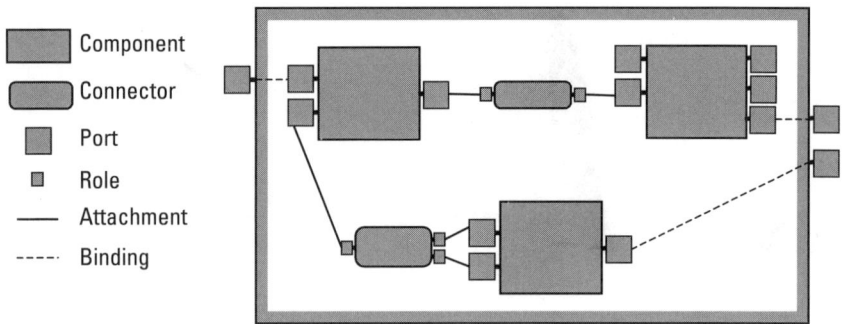

Figure 4.3 Representation of a system.

software architectures, a refinement feature is needed. One or more component representations can be associated with a component interface. A component representation is made of a system and a set of bindings. Each *binding* links an internal port to an external port. A component can thus be decomposed hierarchically. Connectors can also be decomposed in a similar way. One important aspect of this approach is that the same formalism is used at each level of decomposition.

Properties, Constraints, Types, and Styles

The concepts introduced can be used to describe the structural aspect of software architecture. To improve the description of components, connectors, and systems, each ADL offers additional information to define, for instance, component behavior, protocols of interaction, and functional and extrafunctional properties. Instead of defining a fixed set of features, Acme makes it possible to annotate each entity with an arbitrary set of *properties*. Acme also includes a constraint language based on first-order predicate logic. One or more *constraints* can be attached to any architectural entity. This includes simple constraints defining the range of values an attribute can take, the number of connections accepted by a component, but also sophisticated constraints to control the topology of a system.

Acme also provides a facility for defining new types, including types of properties, types of components, types of connectors, and types of ports. Types are not expressed in terms of the structure of the elements they characterize; they also include constraints that must be satisfied by the elements. One interesting feature of Acme is that it enables us to define the style of architecture, that is, the type of system.

Discussion

Acme defines a relatively small set of clearly identified concepts commonly found in other ADLs and can be considered as a typical ADL. Acme does not contain all of the features found in all ADLs, but its generality and focus on structural aspects makes it particularly interesting in a comparison with typical industrial component models.

Indeed, industrial component models concentrate on a subset of the concepts described above and largely ignore advanced features such as behavior specification. Finally Acme, in the same way as other ADLs, emphasizes the notation and design of new systems but does not provide substantial help for implementation software or dealing with existing pieces of code, which explains why it is unlikely that Acme, and other existing ADLs, will be widely used by software engineers in industry.

JavaBeans Component Model

The JavaBeans component model was proposed by Sun in 1997, as the first integration of the notion of a component on top of the Java language: A *bean* is a component.[1] The main quality of this component model is its simplicity—at least when compared to other industrial component models: The whole specification of the JavaBeans model is a 114-page document [1], which can be compared to, say, 1,172 pages for the CCM specification [4]. The scope of this component model is quite limited and it does not scale up to large CBD. Despite its limitations this component model has been widely used and is influential and popular in the Java community; more than a dozen books have been written on it.

Key Features

One of the factors explaining the success of JavaBeans is the Bean Box, a tool delivered with the specification to demonstrate the feasibility of an appealing idea. The first sentence of the specification is, "The goal of the JavaBeans APIs is to define a software component model for Java, so that third party ISVs can create and ship Java components that can be composed together into applications by end users" [1]. The visual assembly or composition of existing components is at the origin of the JavaBean component model: "A JavaBean is a reusable software component that can be manipulated visually in a builder tool" [1]. The reader is invited to contrast this definition with the others provided in this book. JavaBean was designed for the construction of graphical user interfaces (GUIs). Customization of components plays an essential role in JavaBean.

An interesting aspect of this component model is the importance given to the various contexts in which a component can be considered. "First a bean must be capable of running inside a builder tool. Second, each bean must be usable at run-time within the generated application" [1]. JavaBeans is one of the few models in which the component is explicitly tailored to

---

1. Sun later released a second distinct component model, namely, Enterprise JavaBeans (EJB). These two models are fairly distinct and should not be confused because their names are misleading. EJB is very complex and is similar to CORBA's CCM.

interact in two different contexts: at composition time, within the builder tool, and at execution time, in the run-time environment. This feature illustrates the fact that component models can take into account the collaboration between components and different contexts, not only execution.

Interface of a Component

A bean can be described from an external view as a set of ports though this terminology is not used in JavaBeans. This model defines four types of ports: methods, properties, event sources, and event sinks called listeners. In Figure 4.4, we introduce a graphical notation to ease the understanding of the model. Other component models will also be described in a similar way.

The notion of *property* can be used both to parameterize the component at composition time (as described above) or as a regular attribute (in the object orientation sense of the term) during run time. From a client point of view, three main operations are associated with a property: getting the value of a property, setting a new value, and editing the property. This last operation is the one used typically by the builder tool to support the customization of the component. A "bound property" can generate an event whenever it changes its values. A "constrained property" is a property that can be modified only if no other components reject the proposed change after a validation protocol.

The notion of method is directly bound to the notion of method in the Java programming language. From the client point of view, calling the method is the only operation associated with ports.

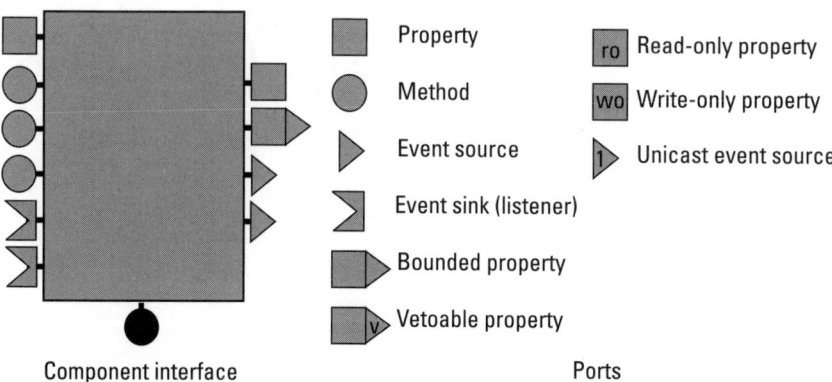

Figure 4.4 Interface of a bean component.

Event-based communication is also allowed and plays a major role in this model. *Event sources* generate events of a certain type, while *event sinks* receive events. Multicast event sources can be connected to an arbitrary number of event sinks, while unicast only supports one sink at the most. From a client point of view, the only operations supported by the event sources are the connection and disconnection of an event sink.

Implementation of a Component

The information described in the previous section represents the interface of a component; nothing else is visible from other components. Most bean components are implemented by a simple Java object, the object being encapsulated in the component [Figure 4.5(a)]. Mapping between object methods and component ports is implicit thanks to the use of naming conventions. Sometimes more sophisticated implementations are required as suggested in Figure 4.5(b):

- *Wrapping a legacy object.* It is possible to wrap an existing object that cannot be changed and does not follow the standard naming convention. This wrapping is done through a set of explicit bindings between object methods and component ports.

- *Multiple-objects implementation.* A component may encapsulate a collection of objects collaborating in the realization of the component.

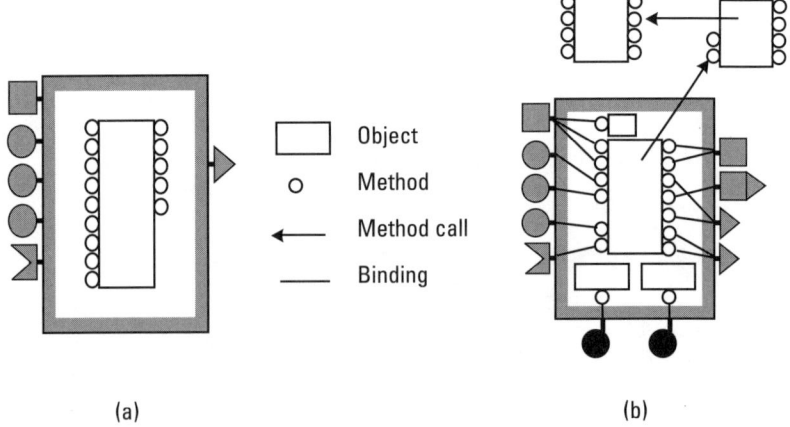

(a)   (b)

Figure 4.5 Implementations of bean components: (a) simple implementation and (b) more complex implementation.

These objects are shown inside the component in Figure 4.5(b). In particular, additional objects can be attached to the core functionality of the component to support its extrafunctional aspects such as the customization service; for instance, a property editor of a given property, as shown in the figure in the top-left corner, or a "customizer" as shown in the bottom part.

- *Dependency on traditional entities.* A bean object may call another object outside the component boundary and it thus depends on objects outside of it.

The implementation of a component is described here from a conceptual point of view. A component is built by grouping different objects and binding them to the components ports. From a technical point of view, this is achieved by means of nontrivial APIs.

Components Assembly

Although assembly is one of the key features of JavaBeans, this component model does not provide any specific solution. Instead, the component model has been designed to support different ways of assembling components: "Some builder tools may operate entirely visually, allowing the direct plugging together of JavaBeans. Other builders may enable users to conveniently write Java classes that interact with and control a set of beans. Other builders may provide a simple scripting language to allow easy high-level scripting of a set of beans" [1].

The JavaBeans distribution includes a toy prototype, the Bean Box, to illustrate the notion of interactive and visual assembly of beans components. This approach has been successfully integrated in various commercial programming environments such as Sun's Net Beans, IBM's Visual Age, and Borland's JBuilder. Whatever the builder used, from a conceptual point of view, a bean assembly can be seen as a graph of components as suggested in Figure 4.6(a).

Nevertheless, it is important to stress that JavaBeans neither specifies an assembly language nor the kind of connections that can be used to connect components. Obviously event sources can be directly connected to event sinks, but the range of connections available depends on the assembly tool. For instance, the Bean Box supports only connections between event sinks and methods with no arguments. Commercial builder tools allow the user to

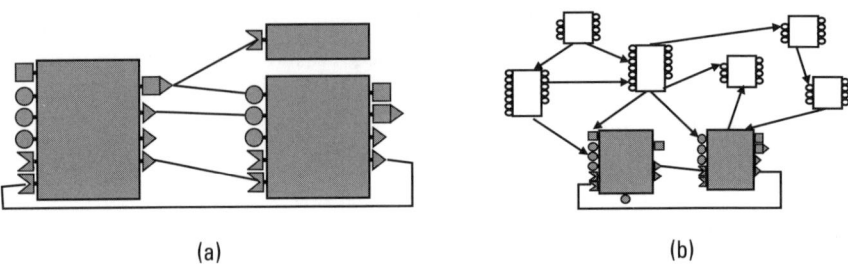

Figure 4.6 Bean-based systems: (a) component-based assembly and (b) heterogeneous assembly.

express much more sophisticated connections and generate code behind the scene when necessary.

Although these tools have proven useful in the construction of GUIs, currently most existing systems combine component-based and traditional technology [Figure 4.6(b)]. This smooth integration has been planned: "Note that while beans are primarily targeted at builder tools they are also entirely usable by human programmers. All the key APIs, such as events, properties, and persistence, have been designed to work well both for human programmers and for builder tools" [1].

Packaging and Deployment

JavaBeans define a model for packaging components into archives. When the archive is loaded into a builder tool, all packaged beans will be added to the directory of available components.

Packaging is required in practice because most bean components depend on resources (e.g., icons and configuration files) and on other Java classes. To avoid duplication of items shared by different beans, it is therefore better to package all of these items together. To handle packaging issues, the JavaBeans definition includes the definition of dependency relationships between the package items.

The customization code associated with a component may be potentially quite large. For example, if a component includes a "wizard customizer" guiding a user through a series of choices, then the customization code can be more complex than the component itself. It is therefore important to be able to eliminate this code if necessary. Each package item can be marked "Design Only," so that they can be removed in a final application.

COM, DCOM, MTS, and COM+

These technologies come from Microsoft.[2] COM (1995) is typical of early attempts to increase program independence and allow programming language heterogeneity, but for C/C++ like languages, in a centralized context, and on Windows platforms. COM relies on binary interoperability conventions and on interfaces. DCOM extends COM with distribution, and MTS extends DCOM with persistency and transaction services. Together they constitute COM+, which is discussed here.

Interfaces and Assembly

A COM interface is seen as a C++ virtual class and takes the form of a list of data and function declarations without associated code.[3] The binary convention is based on the C++ technique to support polymorphism: a double indirection for the access to the interface elements (see Figure 4.7). COM does not provide an assembly language; it instead provides a simple protocol that COM objects can use to dynamically discover or create objects and interfaces. All interfaces are descendants of the `IUnknown` interface, which defines the basic functions: `QueryInterface`, `AddRef`, and `Release`.

Implementation

A COM object is a piece of binary code that can be written in any programming language as long as the compiler generates code following the binary interoperability convention. These objects can be packaged in executables or DLL dynamic libraries that contain the minimum information (introspection) required for dynamic link and COM object identification.

COM supports two composition techniques: *containment* and *aggregation*. Containment is the operation by which a COM object contains other COM object(s). The outer object declares some of the inner object interfaces. The implementation of these interfaces is simply a call (delegation) to the same function of the inner object. Of course, clients see a single object (the outer one) as implementing all interfaces.

Aggregation is more complex. The outer object can expose interfaces of the inner object as if the outer object implemented them, but without the

---

2. Microsoft terminology is very obscure; these "definitions" come from [2].

3. An interface can be declared using C++ alone, or using the MIDL language, an extension of OSF DCE IDL; MIDL is required only for DCOM.

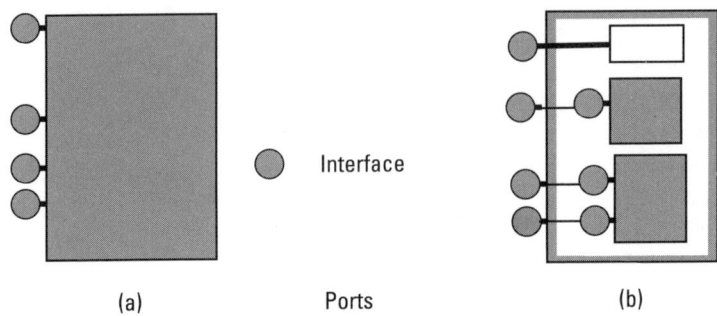

Figure 4.7 COM interface: (a) component interface and (b) component implementation.

need to implement them (it avoids the call indirection). Unfortunately, the process of aggregation requires the source code of both the inner and outer objects to be changed so as to handle the IUnknown interface properly.

Framework

The COM framework consists of standard interfaces (IUnknown, IDispatch, etc.) and a simple run time that interprets, in collaboration with the dynamic library run time, the calls for creating COM objects, returning interface handles, and managing the reference count for releasing objects. Fortunately, the COM framework proposes a set of tools, like Visual Studio, that vastly simplifies the implementation of COM objects; indeed many COM programmers ignore the COM component model.

DCOM (Distributed COM, 1996) extends COM with distribution, based on the DCE RPC mechanism. The component model is unchanged, but the framework is extended. The MIDL language and compiler are required for interface definition; the introspection capability is much enhanced by means of *type libraries*.

MTS (Microsoft Transaction Server, 1997) extends DCOM with the container approach, already presented in CCM, to produce COM+ (1999). MTS introduced the distributed transactional approach and added services, similar to those of CORBA.

Life Cycle

COM and COM+ are strictly execution-time and binary component models. No life-cycle issues are explicitly supported. The .NET component model is a departure from this approach, as described later in this chapter.

CCM

The CCM is the most recent and complete component specification from OMG[4]. It has been designed on the basis of the accumulated experience using CORBA service, JavaBeans, and EJB.

Like many component models, CCM focuses on the developer who builds applications by assembling available parts, but also explicitly the component designer, assembler, and deployer. The major goal behind the CCM specification was to provide a solution to the complexity reached by CORBA and its services: "CORBA's flexibility gives the developer a myriad of choices, and requires a vast number of details to be specified. The complexity is simply too high to be able to do so efficiently and quickly" [4]. The choice was to define a component model generalizing the standard defined by EJB, in which the number of details to be specified and the risk of inconsistent mixtures are vastly reduced. CCM focus is "a server-side component model for building and deploying CORBA applications" [4].

One of the advantages of CCM is its effort to "integrate" many of the facets involved in software engineering. As a consequence, a software application is described in different formalisms along two dimensions: the time dimension (the life cycle, from design to deployment) and the abstract dimension (from abstractions to implementation). Altogether, this makes a rather complex specification. As of early 2002, no complete implementation of CCM had been accomplished.

For CCM, a component is "a self-contained unit of software code consisting of its own data and logic, with well-defined connections or interfaces exposed for communication. It is designed for repeated use in developing applications, either with or without customization"[4].

Interface and Assembly

The external view of a component is an extension of the traditional CORBA IDL language; a component interface is made of ports divided into these pieces (Figure 4.8):

- *Facets,* which are distinct named interfaces provided by the component for client interaction;

---

4. First draft: October 1999; first revision: November 2001.

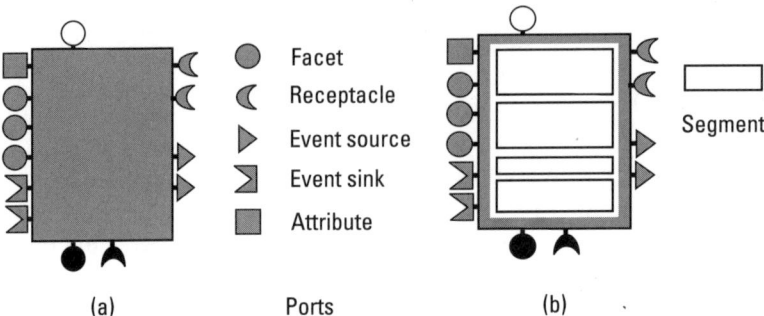

Figure 4.8 CORBA component interface: (a) component interface and (b) component implementation.

- *Receptacles,* which are named connection points that describe the component's ability to use a reference supplied by some external agent;

- *Event sources,* which are named connection points that emit events of a specified type to one or more interested event consumers, or to an event channel;

- *Event sinks,* which are named connection points into which events of a specified type may be pushed;

- *Attributes* are named values, exposed through accessor and mutator operations. Attributes are primarily intended for use in component configuration, although they may be used in a variety of other ways [4].

CCM considers ports as named and typed *variables* (most models consider only interfaces, i.e., a type), thus different facets of the same component can have the same type. Components are typed and can inherit (simple inheritance) from other components (i.e., it inherits its interface).

Homes are component factories that manage a component instance life cycle: creation, initialization, destruction, and retrieval of (persistent) component instances. Homes are also typed and can inherit from other home types. A home type can manage only one component type, but a component type can have different home types. Homes are defined independently from components, which allow component life-cycle management to be changed without changing the component definition.

CCM uses the term *navigation* to describe the framework operations that can be called by a component to dynamically discover and connect to other components and ports.

Assemblies

CCM simply defines the concept of connection as "an object reference"; thus CCM, like all other industrial component models, does not provide a connector concept. Nevertheless, components are connected by linking facets to receptacles and event sources to event sinks. Connections are binaries and oriented, but the same port can handle multiple connections.

Connections can be explicitly described (in the assembly descriptor, an XML file) and established by the CCM framework at initialization. A component assembly describes the initial configuration of the application (i.e., which components make up the assembly), how those components are partitioned, and how they are connected to each other. The assembly does not address architecture evolution during execution.

It is interesting to note that the CCM specification explicitly refers to the Rapide ADL: "The provides and uses statements in this submission are similar to the Interface Connection Architecture implemented in Rapide [12] and discussed in [13]. The Rapide Interface Connection Architecture applies provides and requires statements to individual functions in a class declaration ... the difference being that we specify dependencies with respect to interfaces rather that individual methods" [4].

Implementation of a Component

The implementation of a component is a set of *segments* or executors. Segments are executable code written in any programming language, implementing at least one port. Segments are loaded only when required. No (segment) composition operators are defined. Nothing prevents a segment from calling conventional programs; conversely, the concept of "equivalent interface" was defined to turn a program into a component and to make a component appear as a classic program.

Because implementation is always a set of executable code, the CCM model is not hierarchical. The same applies to homes which are directly bound to executors.

CCM proposes a Component Implementation Definition Language (CIDL) that describes the segments, the associated home executor, the type of storage, and the class of container (see discussion of containers). Different implementations can be associated with the same (abstract) component.

Framework: The Container Approach

Like CORBA, MTS, and EJB, CCM emphasizes the fact that many services can be made available to components without having to change that component's source code. This approach increases component reusability, reduces complexity, and significantly improves maintainability. These reasons are at the origin of the many CORBA services; unfortunately, the multiplication of services has (re)introduced a level of complexity incompatible with widespread use of that technology.

Like EJB, CORBA components use a container to implement component access to system services using common design patterns gleaned from experience in building business applications using object technology and CORBA services. Containers are defined in terms of how they use the underlying CORBA infrastructure and thus are capable of handling services like transactions, security, events, persistence, life-cycle services, and so on. Components are free to use CORBA services directly (component-managed service), but CCM emphasizes container-managed service (i.e., the container managing services automatically); the component code itself ignores the associated services. To do so, the container intercepts communications between components and calls, if needed, framework services. In Figure 4.9, the container is represented as the part of the run-time framework located between the ports and the component implementation. Components may have to implement callback operations defined by the framework if they need to manage their own persistent state.

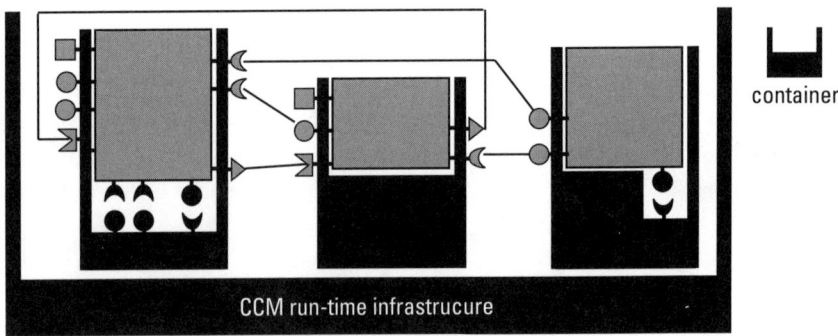

container

CCM run-time infrastrucure

Figure 4.9 CCM run-time framework.

Life Cycle

A package descriptor is a file, in XML, describing a set of files and descriptors, including the component assembly descriptor. CMM does not define the set of formalisms from which this XML file is produced; thus the CCM specification does not describe the actual packaging and deployment. Vendors, in the future, should provide assembly, packaging, and deployment design tools, whose purpose will be to help users in the design and specification of these topics, as well as deployment tools, which, by interpreting the information found in the packaging, assembly, and component implementation descriptors, will perform actual deployment and assembly.

CCM is the best effort to date to gather the advances made in different fields, to include a wide spectrum of life-cycle activities, while still claiming efficiency and heterogeneity capabilities, but the whole does not provide the feeling of being as "simple" as claimed.

.NET Component Model

.NET [5], the latest component model from Microsoft, represents a discontinuity—it no longer relies on COM, because binary interoperability is too limited. .NET relies instead on language interoperability and introspection. To do so, .NET defines an internal language Microsoft Intermediate Language (MSIL), which is very similar to Java Byte Code and its interpreter with introspection capabilities: the Common Language Runtime (CLR), which is very similar to a Java Virtual Machine.

Interfaces and Assembly

.NET represents the programming language approach for component programming. It means that the program contains the information related to the relationships with other "components," and that the compiler is responsible for generating the information needed at execution. This (proprietary) approach contrasts with the Object Management Group (OMG) (open) approach where separate formalisms (and files) are used to indicate component-related information, with languages and compilers being unchanged.

What most resembles a component is an assembly. The *manifest* is the component descriptor. It gathers in a single place all information about an assembly: exported and imported methods and events, code, metadata, and resources.

Because of the programming language approach, the corresponding programming language, C#, which is very similar to Java, includes some features of a component model: (first-class) events and extensible metadata information. The compiler not only produces MSIL byte code but also generates, in the *manifest*, the interface description of the component (called assembly), in the form of a list of import and export types. There is no explicit concept of connection but rather the traditional list of imported and exported resources. .NET relies on a specific dynamic linker to realize the connections, during execution, between the provided and required resources.

Implementation

A component (assembly) consists of *modules*, which are traditional executable files or dynamic link libraries (DLLs). Following the programming language approach, the list of modules composing an assembly is provided in the compiler command line when compiling the main module. The compiler thus generates the manifest in the same file as the main module executable. Modules are loaded only when required. Modules cannot be assemblies, thus the .NET model is not hierarchical. Figure 4.10 shows the .NET interface and component implementation.

Framework

.NET relies on the traditional programming approach in which the framework is seen as the language run-time support: "The .NET Runtime is designed to give first-class support for modern component-based programming—directly in the Runtime" [6]. Extrafunctional aspects such as distribution, security, confidentiality, and version control are delegated at

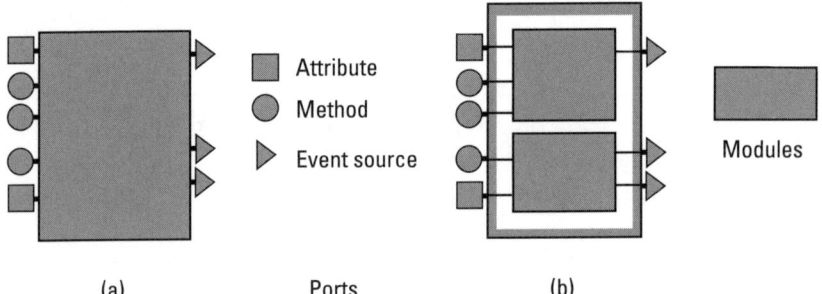

Figure 4.10   .NET component (a) interface and (b) implementation.

execution to the operating system and loader (see the life-cycle section below). Transaction control relies on Microsoft Transaction Server (MTS).

Life Cycle

Unlike when using traditional DLLs, the .NET model includes visibility control, which allows assemblies (and their modules) to be local to an application, and thus different DLLs with the same name can run simultaneously. Further, each assembly keeps track of versioning information about itself and about the assemblies it depends on, provided either in the form of attributes in the code source or as command-line switches when building the manifest.

Version control is delegated to the dynamic loader, which selects the "right" version, local or distant, based on the assembly's version information and on a set of default rules. Both at the machine-wide level and at each applications level, the default rules can be altered using XML configuration files.

These features significantly improve application packaging and deployment control (with respect to traditional Windows application deployment). The early life-cycle phases (design, analysis) appear not to have received corresponding attention to date.

The OSGI Component Model

The OSGI was founded in 1999 with the mission of creating "open specifications for the delivery of multiple services over wide area networks to local networks and devices" [7]. The OSGI emphasis is on a lightweight framework that can be executed in low-memory devices. Actually, the OSGI targets products such as set-top boxes, cable modems, routers, consumer electronics, and so on. The OSGI relies on Java to ensure portability on different hardware. An important characteristic of this technology is that it has been tailored to support dynamic evolution of the system architecture. Components can be downloaded, updated, and removed dynamically, without even stopping the system. Moreover, the OSGI allows for remote administration of the system via the network.

Two Levels of Components

The OSGI is based on two main concepts that can be interpreted as components: bundles and services. "Developers should design an application as a set of bundles that contain services, with each service implementing a segment of the overall functionality. These bundles are then downloaded on demand" [7]. The term *component* is used alternatively for each concept in the specification.

While some authors define components as a unit of composition and as a unit of deployment, these two concepts can be distinguished in the OSGI. A *service* is a unit of composition; a *system* is a set of cooperating services that are connected. A *bundle* is a unit of deployment that groups a set of services that can be deployed as a unit. The following discussion centers on bundle components because the OSGI provides many more features at this level than at the level of service components. Indeed, a service component is merely defined as an implementation and as a set of interfaces.

Interface of a Bundle Component

A bundle packages a set of software entities that collectively form a piece of software. These entities may depend on entities packaged in other bundles, therefore creating dependencies between bundles. The OSGI manages these dependencies. From an external point of view, the interface of a bundle could be represented as shown in Figure 4.11. As suggested in the figure, a bundle uses three kinds of ports to express its interactions, (1) with traditional technology, (2) with others components, and (3) with the run-time environment.

First, the OSGI clearly recognizes the importance of handling traditional technology. In particular, a bundle may require and provide one or more Java packages. It declares this information statically by means of appropriate ports depicted on the topside of the interface.

Second, bundles manage dynamic connections between services. At any time, and for any reason, a bundle may display or remove a service interface. Similarly, at any time, and for any reason, a bundle may require or release the use of a service interface. Service interfaces can therefore be attached and detached dynamically on the left and right sides.

Third, bundles can interact with the run-time environment through the ports depicted on the bottom side. Bundles may listen to events published by the framework such as the insertion of a new component in a system or the publication of a new service. In this way bundles can take appropriate action as the architecture evolves.

Assembly of Bundle Components

Most ADLs and component models are based on the notion of static assembly: The set of participating components is known and components are connected by a human to form a valid system. The OSGI is based on a radically

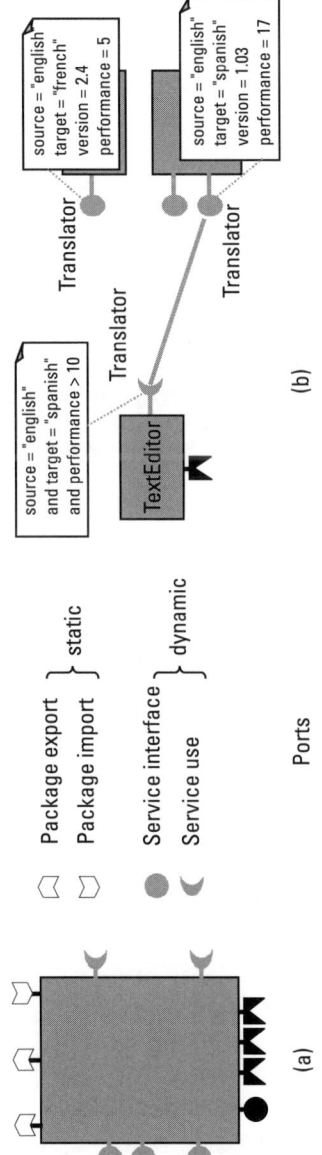

Figure 4.11 (a) Interface of a bundle component and (b) dynamic connection.

different approach. A system is an evolving set of bundle components. Components can connect to each other dynamically based on their own decisions. Components cannot assume that the interfaces they use will be available at all times since the component displaying these interfaces may be uninstalled or may decide to remove this interface from their ports. This means that components may have some knowledge about how to connect and disconnect.

The process of dynamic connection is illustrated in Figure 4.12. When a bundle component publishes a service interface, it can attach to it a set of properties describing its characteristics. When a component requires an interface for its use, it will select one via a query expression based on these properties. The destination of a connection is never given explicitly. The result of the query depends on the actual state of the system. This contrasts with the traditional approach in which each connection statically links ports of identified components. At a given point in time, an OSGI system may look like that shown in Figure 4.12.

The set of connections between components (in the middle of the figure) evolves dynamically. This flexibility also has its counterpart. Once a connection is established with a bundle, there is no guarantee that the service will remain available. Each bundle component must listen to events generated by the OSGI run-time environment and must take appropriate action as the system evolves. These connections are displayed in the bottom of the figure. On the top of the figure, the connections between Java packages are shown. The framework automatically creates these connections on the basis

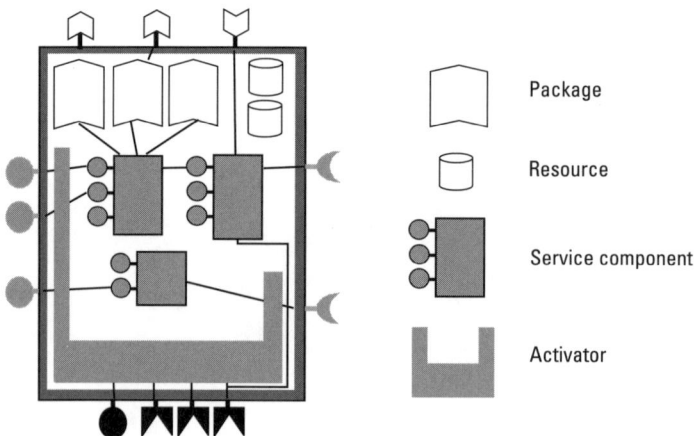

Figure 4.12 Implementation of a bundle component.

of the information provided in the bundle interface. Various bundles may provide the same package but in different versions. In this case, the framework will ensure that only one will be selected on the basis of the preference expressed by the bundles requiring the packages and on a set of default rules specified by the OSGI. A bundle cannot be activated until all of the packages it imports are present in a system.

Implementation of a Bundle Component

The section above described a bundle from an external point of view. Actually, from a concrete point of view, a bundle is represented as a JAR archive containing (1) service components, (2) Java packages, and (3) other resources files such as configuration files and images (Figure 4.12).

The set of entities contained in a bundle component can be connected to form a running system. If a bundle provides an "activator" object, the framework will call this object to activate and passivate the bundle. The entities contained in the bundle are not visible from outside as long as the bundle does not export them. They are independent from the rest of the system as long as they do not require a service provided by another bundle.

One wonders then if every service component must handle the complexity of dealing with the dynamic apparition and retirement of external services. The OSGI specification does not provide any information with respect to this question, but in some situations it is possible to regroup this behavior in a piece of code providing a default value when a connection cannot be resolved or when a resolved connection later becomes unavailable. In this case, communication with the outside of the bundle can be made totally transparent to the internal components; the connection manager can be seen as a container providing a connection service. This method does not prevent individual components from registering directly with framework events if they want to achieve a specific behavior.

Summary

The following briefly summarizes the main differences among the presented component models, along our four dimensions.

Interface

Although interfaces appear to be similar, a number of differences exist in the concept and in the way they are defined. In the programming language approach, JavaBeans and .NET, the structure is a language one: virtual classes (.NET) or interfaces (Java), and the compiler are in charge of generating the required information. In EJB and COM, an interface corresponds to a set of methods; it is a type. In CCM, ports are typed variables but in all cases interfaces are described in a separate formalism.

In ADLs, interfaces and ports are carefully designed but abstract concepts. The connector, as a first-class concept, is typical of ADLs. Connectors may have ports, are typed, can inherit, and can be associated with potentially complex behavior. Connections and necessary connectors do not yet exist in today's industrial component models.

Assembly

JavaBeans is original in that assembly is a step directly supported by the framework. Beans can include code that helps in customizing and assembling components. EJB and COM do not provide specific features. CCM makes explicit and automates the initial connections, .NET relies on the dynamic loader, and the OSGI focuses on the dynamic discovery of services.

In ADLs, assemblies (often called configurations) and the analysis of their properties are important facets, but assembly is seen from a static point of view, during design.

Implementation

Surprisingly, all models are flat, but most models consider a component as a set of executables: segments (CCM), modules (.NET), and classes. From this point of view, components provide a higher level of structuring and packaging than programming languages. In all models, components are seen as a composition unit; in many cases they are also seen as the packaging and deployment unit.

In all models, component implementations can call the usual programs, which are not components. In ADLs, all models are hierarchical, but the relationship with executables is seldom considered.

Framework

In the language approach, the operating system and loaders perform most of the work in a transparent way. In JavaBeans and COM no added formalism is required, but added (extrafunctional) services are not provided either. In .NET the loader has been extended to provide distribution, security, deployment, and versioning services, but attributes and configuration files are required. In MTS, EJB, and CCM, the container concepts make explicit a set of services, described in a specific formalism, and supported at execution by the framework.

In most models the infrastructure is limited to the run time, JavaBeans shows that the infrastructure can provide support to the assembly phase, but the same idea can be extended to all phases: design, deployment, and so on. In ADLs, this aspect is not explicitly addressed. Extrafunctional properties, such as distribution and transaction, and the way they can be implemented are not usually considered important.

Conclusion

The major differences between ADLs and component technologies are seen in their focus. Component technology addresses primarily execution and technological issues, including interoperability, heterogeneity, distribution, efficiency, fast life cycle, deployment, and multiprogrammer development. In component technologies, pragmatism and realism require that an application is always a mixture of components (which satisfy the model and protocols) and of the usual programs (classes and procedures). The component support system manages the former and simply ignores the latter.[5, 6] ADLs make the hypothesis that all system parts are components.

Component technology often makes the distinction between the component model specification (e.g., CORBA) and the implementation of the standards (many companies, such as Visigenic and Iona, market their CORBA implementations), the in-house developed component, and the components available in the marketplace. ADLs do not make these distinctions. Component technology emphasizes the relationships with operating systems and the run-time support, not ADLs. Conversely, component technologies do not have a hierarchical model, propose very limited formalisms, do not propose any connector concept, have no design formalism, and do not propose any analysis tool. To say the least, there is room for improvement.

Component-based technologies and ADLs are the logical results of evolution from the previous generation of software engineering technology.

---

5. Which makes difficult, or useless, many of the analyses ADL systems can perform.

6. The OSGI is one of the very few exceptions, see the section on the OSGI component technology.

Thus drawing a definitive boundary between them is difficult and irrelevant. Trying to contrast ADLs and component-based technology is also irrelevant since, initially, the former focused on early life-cycle phases (analysis and design) while the latter focused on the execution phase and its technological issues. Their natural fate is to be merged to provide next-generation software engineering environments, tools, techniques, and methods.

References

[1] Sun Microsystems, "JavaBeans 1.01 Specification," http://java.sun.com/beans.

[2] Eddon, G., and H. Eddon, *Inside COM+ Base Services,* Redmond, WA: Microsoft Press, 2000.

[3] Marvie, R., and P. Merle, "CORBA Component Model: Discussion and Use with Open CCM," Techincal report Laboratoire d'Informatique Fondamentale de Lille Université des Sciences et Techniques de Lille, Lille, France, Jan. 2001.

[4] OMG, "CORBA Components," Report ORBOS/99-02-01, OBJECT MANAGE-MENT GROUP, 1998, http://www.omg.org.

[5] Microsoft, .NET, http://www.microsoft.com/net/.

[6] Microsoft, *"Microsoft Development Network (MSDN),"* http://msdn.microsoft.com.

[7] OSGI, "OSGI Service Gateway Specification," Release 1.0, http://www.osgi.org.

[8] Medividovic, N., and R N. Taylor, "A Classification and Comparison Framework for Software Architecture Description Languages," *IEEE Trans. on Software Engineering,* Vol. 26, No. 1, 2000, pp. 70–93.

[9] NET Beans, "NetBeans, an Open Source, Modular IDE," http://www.netbeans.org.

[10] OMG, "CORBA Services: Common Object Services Specification," Object Management Group, 1997, http://www.omg.org.

[11] Garlan, D., R. T. Monroe, and D. Wile "ACME: Architectural Description of Component-Based Systems," *Foundations of Component-Based Systems,* G. T. Leavens and M. Sitarman, Eds., Cambridge, UK: Cambridge University Press, 2000.

[12] Stanford University, "The Stanford Rapide Project," http://poset.stanford.edu/rapide/.

[13] Luckham, D. C., et al., "Specification and Analysis of System Architecture Using Rapide," *IEEE Trans. on Software Engineering,* Special Issue on Software Architecture, 1995, pp. 336–354.

Part 3:
Developing Software Components

In a component-based development process we distinguish development of components from development of systems. When developing component-based systems, we focus on identification of reusable entities and selection of components that fulfill system requirements. When developing components our focus is on reusability. Components are developed as reusable entities to be used in many products. For this reason they must be general enough but also sufficiently specific to be easily identified, understood, and used.

Components communicate with their environment only through the interface, so it is the interface that provides all of the information needed and it is only the interface that provides this information. For this reason it is natural that component development is interface-focused. One of the main challenges of component development is to design an appropriate interface. Two chapters in this part address this challenge. One chapter discusses the component-based development process.

Chapter 5 discusses the component-based system life cycle. The development process is separated into two processes—component development and system development; components can be developed independently of systems. The processes, however, have many interaction points. Component requirements are related to system requirements and an absence of their influence on each other may cause severe problems in designing both systems and components. The maintenance phases are strongly related. One way of minimizing the problems related to incompatibilities between these processes is to follow standards. However, the standards in component-based development are not well defined because the processes and technologies are still not stable.

Chapter 6 shows that syntactic descriptions alone cannot ensure the semantic integrity of a component. Two dimensions of CBSE are presented where semantics play an important role. One dimension encompasses five levels of formalism in describing component semantics. The other dimension covers three phases in the life of a component, in which each phase requires certain semantic considerations. Based on these two dimensions, the taxonomy for component semantics is discussed. For safety-, mission-, or business-critical applications, formal semantics may be necessary, but are hardly necessary for the noncritical domains.

Chapter 7 demonstrates how interfaces can be divided into smaller modeling roles. Role-based component engineering extends the traditional object orientation component paradigm and provides more natural support for modeling component collaborations. The idea of role-based components is to split the public interface into smaller interfaces that represent different roles. Users of a component can communicate with the component through the smaller role interfaces instead of using the full interface. The use of roles makes it possible to have multiple views of one class. These role perspectives are more cohesive than the total class interface. The chapter discusses the usefulness of the role-based approach and the development methods for role-based components.

5

CBD Process

Benneth Christiansson, Lars Jakobsson, and Ivica Crnkovic

Introduction

Traditional software development can be considered to lie between two extremes. At one extreme is the custom design of a solution tailored to the exact requirements of a single customer; at the other is the development of standard application packages based on the general requirements of an entire customer segment [1]. Custom design has the advantage of supporting the customer's own business practices and, if these are unique, providing him with an advantage over his competitors [2].

The disadvantages of custom design are the high cost of development and the usual long time to market, although it is assumed that the potential profits to be gained by using the system are expected to more than pay for the costs of its development. Another disadvantage is the uncertain capability of the new system to communicate with other existing and future software systems [1]. These disadvantages do not apply to standard application packages but these have their own disadvantages. One is the possible need to reorganize habitual business practices to adapt to a newly acquired standard application package. Another disadvantage is that competitors may acquire and use the same standard application package and thereby neutralize a competitive lead. Another drawback with the use of a standard application package is the difficulty of adapting such a package to possible future changes in the company's own business practices [3].

These two alternatives should be considered as extremes and, in practice, most software development projects consist of a combination of the two alternatives. Typically, a development organization will focus on its core business, developing those parts in which they have a competitive advantage and not spending efforts on those parts that are not relevant to their primary business interest. For example, a company developing industrial automation systems will concentrate on functions directly related to industrial processes, but will buy rather than develop general graphics packages, compilers, or other general-purpose components. The reuse of software components from earlier projects is likely to increase the productivity and thereby the cost efficiency of development projects. According to some experience, reuse of software packages is already profitable if reused at least three times [4]. Reuse of internally built components and reuse of the same software architecture is the main idea of software product-line architectures. Product-line architectures are described in detail in Chapter 11. It may also be possible to purchase commercial off-the-shelf (COTS) software from different vendors.

A focus on the reuse of existing components on the one hand and the production of reusable units on the other introduces new elements in the software development process. This chapter describes the component-based software life cycle.

In the next section we give an overview of generic software engineering processes and development life-cycle models. Then, we motivate a need for recognition of different processes when developing components and when building systems or applications from components. Finally, we describe these processes, reviewing their procedures and highlighting the parts that are specific for CBD.

Software Process Models

A software system can be considered from a life-cycle point of view. This means that the system is observed from the first notion of its existence to its operation and management. Several different approaches to the development life cycle are considered below. The different approaches are all based on the same activities [5], described in Table 5.1, and vary only in the way they are performed. We will briefly look at different life-cycle models and describe their basic characteristics.

Table 5.1
Generic Life-Cycle Activities

Activity	Description
Requirements analysis and system specification	The system's services, constraints, and goals are established. They are then defined in detail and serve as a system specification.
System and software design	Software design involves identifying and describing the fundamental software system abstractions and their relationships. An overall system architecture is established. A detailed design follows the overall design.
Implementation and unit testing	The formalization of the design in an executable way, which can be composed of smaller units. The units are verified to meet their specifications.
Integration, system verification, and validation	The system units are integrated; the complete system is verified, validated, and delivered to the customer.
Operation support and maintenance	A system in operation requires continuous support and maintenance.
Disposal	A disposal activity, often forgotten in life-cycle models, includes the phasing out of the system, with possible replacement by another system or a complete termination.

The Sequential Model

The sequential model (for example, a waterfall model) follows a systematic, sequential approach that begins at the system level and progresses successively from analysis to settlement. Each activity is regarded as concluded before the next activity begins (Figure 5.1). The output from one activity is the input to the next.

This approach to software development is the oldest and the most widely used. It rests on the notion that it is possible to define and describe all system requirements and software features beforehand, or at least very early in the development process. Many major problems in software engineering arise from the fact that it is difficult for the customer to state all requirements explicitly. A sequential model requires a complete specification of requirements and there can be difficulty in accommodating the natural uncertainty that exists at the beginning of many projects.

It is also difficult to add or change requirements during the development because, once performed, activities are regarded as completed. In practice, requirements will change and new features will be called for and a

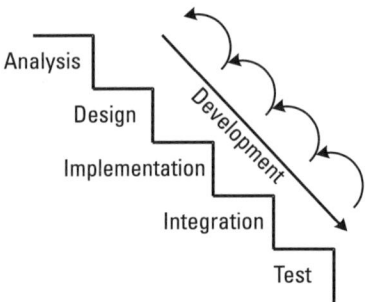

Figure 5.1 The sequential model.

purely sequential approach to software development can be difficult and in many cases unsatisfactory. Another problem sometimes encountered when a sequential model is applied is the late response to the customer. A working version of the software will not be available until late in the system development process and a major misunderstanding, if undetected until the working program is reviewed, can be disastrous.

The sequential model has an important place in software engineering. It provides a template into which methods for analysis, design, implementation, integration, verification, validation, and maintenance can be placed. Although in practice it is never used in its pure (and rather naïve) form, the sequential model has remained the most influential software development process model. For example, the waterfall model in combination with prototyping, or the V-model [6], has been extensively used for entire life cycles or as a part of other models, covering particular phases of the entire process model.

Evolutionary Development

The basic principle of evolutionary development is to develop a system gradually in many repetitive stages, increasing the knowledge of the system requirements and system functionality at each stage and exposing the results to user comments [6]. This model reduces the risk of only detecting critical and costly problems in later phases of the development. It also enables better management of changes of requirements appearing during the development process. One disadvantage of the evolutionary approach is the increased difficulty of project coordination and evaluation. It can, for example, be difficult to determine the exact number of iterations beforehand, and new iterations may be added as requirements change or evolve.

Iterative Approach

The iterative approach [see Figure 5.2(a)] to software development is based on the sequential model supplemented with the possibility of returning to previous activities. Each iteration addresses the full system and increases the functionality of system parts. This approach permits further refinement of system requirements, which increases the possibilities of managing low-level requirements, and requirements related to technologies (in general, those requirements that tend to change more often). One specific disadvantage of using this approach is the inability to predict the feasibility of the final implementation.

Incremental Model

The incremental model combines elements of the sequential model (applied repetitively) with the iterative approach. As Figure 5.2(b) shows, the incremental model applies the sequential model in stages as calendar time progresses. Each sequence produces a deliverable "increment" of the software with new functionality added to the system [4, 7, 8].

When the incremental model is used, the first increment is often the core of the software system. Basic requirements are addressed but many supplementary features remain undelivered. As a result of the use and/or evaluation of the core software, a plan is developed for the next increment. The plan proposes the modification of the core software to satisfy requirements more effectively and the delivery of additional features and functionality. This process is repeated following the delivery of each increment, until the complete software system has been developed.

The incremental model is particularly useful for handling changes in requirements. Early increments can be implemented to satisfy current requirements and new and altered requirements can be addressed in later increments. If the core software is well received, the next increment can be added according to the plan. Increments can also be planned to manage technical risks.

Prototyping Model

The evolutionary model for software development is based on the creation of a prototype very early in development activities. The prototype is a preliminary, or intentionally incomplete or scaled-down, version of the complete system. As shown in Figure 5.2(c), the prototype is then gradually improved and developed until it meets a level of acceptability decided on by the user.

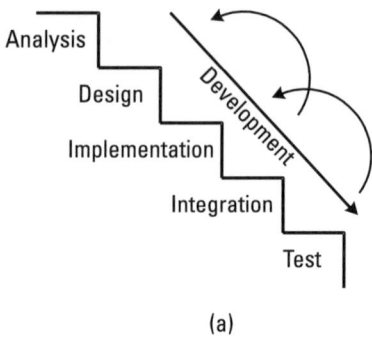

(a)

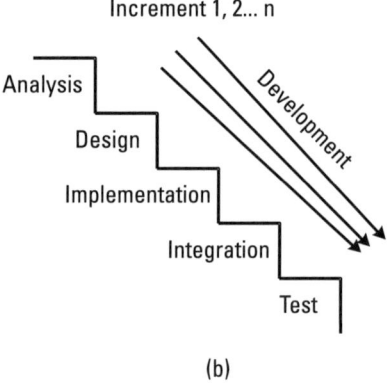

(b)

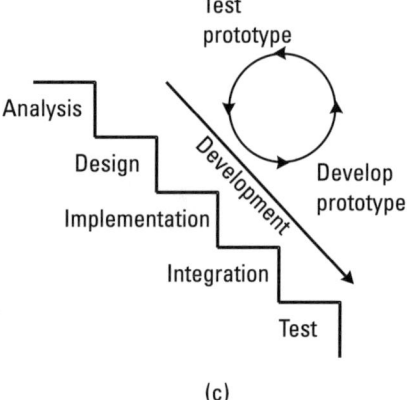

(c)

Figure 5.2 (a) Iterative, (b) incremental, and (c) prototype evolutionary model.

Iteration is used to tune the prototype to satisfy the needs of the customer. The developer is able at the same time to determine what measures need to be taken. When these changes are made, the prototype becomes the new system.

This approach can be hazardous when the entire system rests on an initial software core that may be just barely usable. It may be too slow, too large, or too awkward to use, or all three. The solution to this problem is to use a slightly different approach, *throw-away prototyping,* in which the prototype serves merely as a mechanism for identifying software requirements. When the requirements are captured, the prototype functions purely as a model with respect to requirements and features for the real software development task, which will then begin from scratch.

In his famous spiral model [9], Boehm has combined iterative, incremental, and evolutionary procedures in a model in which activities are performed several times in an iterative manner, beginning with a base functionality and addressing in each loop the following issues: objective setting, risk assessment and reduction, development and validation, and planning for the next loop. The iteration can be concluded when a complete working software system has been developed.

Unified Process

Jacobson et al. [10] have developed a systems development process designated the Unified Process (UP), optimized for object-oriented and component-based systems. The UP is an iterative incremental development process consisting of four phases (Figure 5.3):

1. *Inception,* the first phase in which the system is described in a formalized way, providing a base for further development;
2. *Elaboration,* the phase in which the system architecture is defined and created;
3. *Construction,* the development of completely new products, with reuse capabilities;
4. *Transition,* the work of delivering the product to the customer. This phase includes the installation of the system and the training of its users.

Several iterations of core workflows occur during these phases: requirements, analysis, design, implementation, and test. These workflows occur in

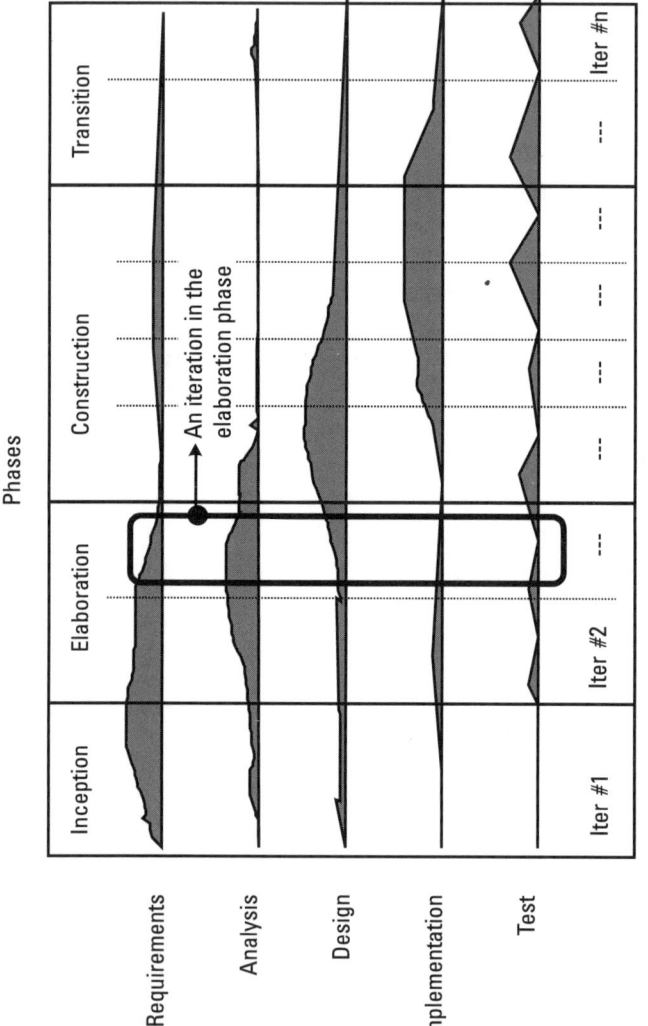

Figure 5.3 The four phases of UP and its workflows.

each of the four phases of inception, elaboration, construction, and transition. This is the iterative part of UP. The incremental part is based on the fact that successful iterations will result in the release of a system. As an iterative/incremental model, UP has the advantages of both incremental and iterative models but also inherits the disadvantages of both the iterative and incremental approaches.

CBD

Reuse Approach

CBD originates from reuse. The reuse approach is not new. Significant research work was performed during the 1980s and 1990s [4, 11], the main goal of which was to develop systematic approaches to the effective reuse of experience gained previously. The reuse approach makes the following assumptions [11]:

- All experience can be reused;
- Reuse typically requires some modification of objects being reused;
- Reuse must be integrated into the specific software development;
- Analysis is necessary to determine when, and if, reuse is appropriate.

Although they may seem obvious, many approaches to reuse did not succeed because these assumptions were not fulfilled. For example, the modification of objects for reuse could require more effort than the development of a comparable object from scratch. Similarly, if the reuse principle is not integrated in the development process, it is probable that the reuse opportunities will not be utilized (for example, developers may experience problems when trying to identify reusable entities or will be motivated to try to find them).

Which of these principles are acquired by CBD? To answer this question, let us first define what we assume by reuse: For given requirements r for an object x, we propose the reuse of the already existing object x_k. The reuse procedure includes identification of a set of objects $x_1, x_2, \ldots, x_m$ as candidates, selection of one of these, and, if required, its modification to translate x_k to x' which is as close to x as possible. The object x can be of any type—a system architecture, an overall design, design pattern, infrastructure, or different types of components or services.

The first reuse principle (reuse of all experience) is integrated in CBSE. We reuse system architecture determined by the component models (which we also reuse), we reuse component frameworks, and finally we reuse the components that provide particular services. The modification principle is also to a large extent determined by the component model; because a component is specified by its interface and the source of the implementation is, in principle, not available, there is less risk of performing uncontrolled modifications. The reuse approach is inherent to component technologies and CBD; it is much easier to use components as reusable entities, which have precisely defined operational interfaces, than other entities in a non-CBD. The last principle (analysis if and when reuse is appropriate) is not part of component-based technologies, and it must be built into the development process model. Later in this chapter we will see that such analysis occurs in the system design and maintenance phase, as well as in the component evaluation phase.

Separation of Development Processes

CBSE addresses challenges and problems similar to those encountered elsewhere in software engineering. Many of the methods, tools, and principles of software engineering used in other types of system will be used in the same or a similar way in CBSE. There is, however, one difference: CBSE specifically focuses on questions related to components and in that sense it distinguishes the process of component development from that of system development with components. There is a difference in requirements and business ideas in these two cases and different approaches are necessary. Components are built to be used and reused in many applications, some of which might not yet exist and might require use of the components in some possibly unforeseen way. A component must be well specified, easy to understand, sufficiently general, easy to adapt, easy to deliver and deploy, and easy to replace.

The component interface must be as simple as possible and when used strictly separated (both physically and logically) from its implementation. Marketing factors play an important role, because development costs must be recovered from future earnings, this being especially true for COTS software. System development with components is focused on the identification of reusable entities and relations between them, beginning from the system requirements and from the availability of components already existing [12, 13]. Much implementation effort in system development will no longer be necessary but the effort required in dealing with components, locating them, selecting those most appropriate, testing them, and so on, will increase [14].

We not only recognize different activities in the two processes, but also find that many of these activities can be performed independently of each other. In reality, the processes are already separate because many components are developed by third parties, independently of system development. Even components being developed internally in an organization that uses these very same components are often treated as separate entities developed separately.

However, even if we separate the processes, they remain dependent on each other to a certain degree. A component is assumed to be an integrated part of a larger application or system, but its component life cycle may not be compatible with the life cycles of many applications and systems.

CBD: The Consumer Perspective

Typically a component consumer selects a component (according to particular criteria) and then uses it in a software system. But several aspects of this process must be addressed to ensure the correctness of component selection with respect to both behavior and impact on the system as a whole.

The component life cycle must be considered in relation to the life cycle of the system as a whole. For example, component maintenance and operation support may be essential for successful system operation. Will the component producer be able to deliver a new component version when this is required? How will changes in a component in the system affect the behavior of another component? Will the component be compatible with newer versions of the surrounding systems and applications? The question of operation support may even be of importance to the end user. If a system fails due to a component failure (or due to unpredictable behavior of component compositions), who is responsible for the failure and who is responsible for the support—the system producer or the component producer? These questions are not related to the attributes of the component (neither functional nor extrafunctional), but belong to the development and maintenance processes, and relationships between the producers and consumers.

Component Development: The Producer Perspective

The basic prerequisite for the success of the component-based approach is the existence of a developed component market. Because the development of reusable components requires significantly more effort than the development of special-purpose software, it is essential that a component be reused as much as possible. For this reason the producer of a component must have in mind what is required of the component from both his point of view (for example, the business goal, component functionality, maintenance policy) and that of the consumer (the type of application and system in which the component will be used, the requirements of the system, and the life expectancy of relevant systems).

As mentioned above, the maintenance requirements of components and systems are not necessarily compatible. It is therefore important when selecting components for their maintenance requirements to be synchronous with those of the system in which they are to be incorporated. In many cases, component producer and consumer have no direct contact, and it is important that both be aware of the maintenance and support policy of the other.

We can recognize two different types of disposal of component-based systems. One is initiated by consumers when they conclude that the component no longer provides the support of the system it was intended to provide or that the system no longer needs the component. The other type occurs when a component becomes obsolete and the producer ceases component maintenance and operation support. The most likely reason for disposal in this case would be the production of a new, more effective component with the same, similar, or extended functionality, but it is also possible that the producer is not able to continue with support or maintenance. The consumer should have a fair chance to upgrade or at least have time to obtain a replacement for the old component (if necessary). This is of interest to both producer and consumer who should, ideally, arrive at a compromise with respect to the life cycles of their different products. However, it is not obvious that this will happen. A component producer can disappear from the market or can change its business goals. For this reason the consumer should always have in mind an alternative solution, such as the replacement of the component with another developed internally or by another producer.

Component-Based Software Life Cycle

In this section we consider the component-based system development process. Because we have mentioned that we distinguish between two processes—building systems with components and building components—we shall discuss these processes separately. In many real situations they will be combined, and maybe even not distinguished as separate activities. However, the separation of the processes is a particular characteristic of the component-based approach and to gain its advantages, the means of managing the separation should be available.

Development with Components

The development of systems as an assembly of components is similar to the development of non-component-based systems. There is, however, a crucial difference in a component-based system development process. The emphasis is not on the implementation of the system designed, but on the reuse of pre-existing components. This approach has many obvious advantages but also a number of disadvantages. It is first necessary to find reusable units that will meet the requirements specified and will be compliant with the system design. Secondly, the amount of extra effort required to use reusable units instead of units dedicated to a particular purpose must be determined. How much performance overhead can be tolerated? A further question is related to trustworthiness: How far can we trust component specifications (if we have any)? How can we test these components? We address these and other questions related to the component-based approach by studying system life-cycle activities. We will see that we need to include new procedures related to component management.

Requirements Analysis and Definition

The analysis activity involves identifying and describing the requirements to be satisfied by the system. In this activity, the system boundaries should be defined and clearly specified. Using a component-based approach, an analysis will also include specifications of the components that are to collaborate to provide the system functionality. To be able to do this, the domain or system architecture that will permit component collaboration must be defined. In CBD, the analysis is an activity with three tasks. The first task is the capture of the system requirements and the definition of the system boundaries. The second task is the definition of the system architecture to permit component collaboration, and the third task is the definition of component requirements to permit the selection or development of the required components.

The approach described above is an optimistic and an idealized view of the process. It assumes that the component requirements can be precisely defined and that it is possible to find components that satisfy these requirements. In reality, we experience several problems [15]. It is not easy to derive component requirements from system requirements and we must accept that they may be (as requirements often are) inconsistent, insufficient, and not precisely defined. The process of finding components to meet these requirements may be even more difficult. We can be almost certain that we will not find any component that exactly satisfies the requirements.

The next problem that we will meet is the problem of incompatible component assemblies; even if we find components that meet the component requirements defined, it is not at all certain that they will interact as intended when assembled. Very often, when beginning from specific requirements, we find that none of the components meets the requirements and the only way to continue with the system development process is to develop a new component. This return to traditional development means that the benefits of reuse are lost in the case of this particular component. In reality, the process of design and even requirements engineering will be combined with component selection and the evaluation process. Experiences from COTS-based development projects at NASA show that which COTS software is selected drives the requirements to at least some extent [14]. In some cases new functionality was discovered in a COTS that was useful although not originally planned.

Component Selection and Evaluation

To perform a search for suitable components and make their identification possible, the components must be specified, preferably in a standardized manner. Again, this may often not be the case. The component specifications will include precisely defined functional interfaces, while other attributes will be specified informally and imprecisely (no method is developed for this) if specified at all. The components selected must therefore be evaluated. The process of evaluation will include several aspects (see Chapter 8) of both a technical and nontechnical nature. Technical aspects of evaluation include integration, validation, and verification. Examples of nontechnical issues include the marketing position of the component supplier, maintenance support provided, and alternative solutions.

An important method that decreases the risk of selecting a "wrong" component is to identify several component candidates, investigate these, reject those not compliant with the main requirements, continue with the evaluation of the reduced number of candidate components, if necessary refine the requirements, and repeat the evaluation process. This process is known as *procurement-oriented requirements engineering* [16]. An example of selection is the choice between an internal and an external component. One scenario is to search for an internally developed component and, if nothing suitable is found, to continue by searching for an external component [17].

An internal component need not be chosen simply because it is internal and thereby has certain evident advantages. Other criteria, such as time to market, production and maintenance costs, and quality, may favor the selection of an external component.

Finally, in many cases, it may be more relevant to evaluate a set of components composed as an assembly than to evaluate a component. The availability of assemblies is more common than might be expected. Some assemblies may be purchased as functional packages that disintegrate into several components when deployed. Another example of such an assembly is a set of components that, when integrated together, constitutes a functional unit. In such cases, it is necessary to evaluate the assembly; evaluation of the individual components is not sufficient. This implies that an investigation of the integration procedure may be part of an evaluation.

If a component is selected that only partly fulfills the specification on which the selection is based, two immediate alternatives are available: either the component is adapted to the particular specification, or the specification is adapted to the component. The latter alternative may be considered radical, but there are advocates who will point out the advantages of this approach [18]. A third possibility is the development of a new component. From the system development point of view, this is a bad choice, if this activity was not planned for at the beginning of the development process. The consequence of such a decision would require additional resources and development time.

System Design

System design activity typically begins with the system specification and the definition of the system architecture and continues from there. In traditional development, the design of the system architecture is the result of the system requirements, and the design process continues with a set of sequences of refinements (for example, iterations) from the initial assumptions to the final design goal. In contrast with traditional development, many decisions related to the system design will be a consequence of the component model selected.

The initial architecture will be a result of both the overall requirements and the choice of component model. The component model defines the collaboration between the components and provides the infrastructure supporting this collaboration. The more service provided by the component framework (i.e., by a particular component model), the less effort required for component and hence system development. Thus, the choice of component model is very important.

Although many domains will use standard and de facto standard component models, within particular domains with specific requirements, the specific component models providing particular services will be used, and even internally developed. Chapters 12, 14, and 19 discuss the necessity of domain-specific component models and then the costs for their development. Chapters 16 and 17 discuss cases in the particular domains that use a standard component model and add new properties to them by designing and standardizing the system architecture and framework. The design activity is very much determined by the component selection procedure. This procedure begins with the selection of component candidates and continues with consideration of the feasibility of different combinations of these. Consequently the design activity will not be a sequence of refinements of the starting assumptions, but will require a more dynamic and exploratory and, consequently, evolutionary approach: The goal will be to find the most appropriate and feasible combination of the component candidates. In this way the results of the design activity may be less predictable, but on the other hand, components will automatically introduce many solutions on the design detail level [19–21].

System Implementation

In an ideal CBD process, the implementation by coding will be reduced to the creation of the "glue code" and to component adaptation. Note that if the components selected are not appropriate or an inappropriate model is used, or if the components are not well understood, the costs of glue code and component adaptation may be greater than that of the development of the components themselves! The effort for the development of glue code is usually less than 50% of the total development effort, but effort per line of glue code is about three times the effort per line of the application's code [22]. Note also that it may still be necessary to design and implement some components—those that are business critical or unique to a specific solution and those that require refinement to fit into a given solution.

System Integration

Integration is the composition of the implemented and selected components to constitute the software system. The integration process should not require great resources, because it is based on the system architecture and the use of deployment standards defined by the component framework and by the communication standard for component collaboration [19]. This is, however, valid only for syntactic and partially semantic integration. Several other aspects need to be taken into consideration: component adaptation, reconfigurations of assemblies, and emerging properties of assemblies integrated into the system.

- *Component adaptation.* In many cases a component must be adjusted to system requirements. This adjustment can be achieved in different ways. In some cases it will be enough to specify the component's parameters; in others, a wrapper that will manage the component's inputs and outputs must be developed, and in some cases even a new component that will control particular components and will guarantee the fulfillment of the system requirements must be added to the system.

- *Reconfigurations of assemblies.* Different assemblies (or composite components) can include common basic components. By introducing assemblies into the system, conflicts between the basic components can develop. It may happen, for example, that assemblies include different versions of the same basic component. In such a case a mechanism for reconfiguring assemblies must exist, either supported by the component framework, or used manually. This case is discussed in the "System Operation Support and Maintenance" section of this chapter.

- *Emerging properties.* An important fact is that it is not possible to discover all the effects of a component until the integration is performed. For this reason it is necessary to include test procedures as a part of the integration, both for component assemblies and the entire system.

Finally, one of the characteristics of many component-based systems is the ability to dynamically integrate components without interrupting system execution. This means that the integration activity in CBD is present in several phases of the component-based system life cycle.

Verification and Validation

This last step before system delivery is similar to the corresponding procedures in a traditional development process. The system must be verified and validated. These terms can be easily confused although there is a clear distinction between them. Verification is a process that determines whether the system meets its specified functional and nonfunctional requirements. A validation process should ensure that the system meets customer expectations. Or as succinctly expressed by Boehm [23]:

- Validation: Are we building the right product?
- Verification: Are we building the product right?

Within validation and verification, two techniques can be used [5]: *software inspection* (analyzing and checking systems artifacts such as requirements specification, design documentation, and source code), and *software testing* (executing the system implemented with test data and examining outputs and system behavior).

To successfully perform testing, we must know what is to be tested, how to perform the test, and what the system is expected to accomplish. In a traditional system development process, this implies that the specifications from the analysis and design activities are used to define test cases. A problem in obtaining the necessary test cases is that the analysis results must be translated into concrete tests during the implementation activity, both on the module and on the system level. In CBD we distinguish validation and verification of components from validation and verification of systems; we must perform comprehensive initial test and inspection activities before using a component.

- *Component validation and verification.* After a component is selected, it should be tested to check that it functions in accordance with its specification. Tests may also be conducted to achieve a better understanding and knowledge of a given component. In Chapter 4 we have seen that evaluation of a component alone (which includes verification) is not sufficient, and that component assemblies must be tested. Similarly, when a component is dynamically integrated in a system, we must ensure the correct operational behavior of the system, even with failure of the component. To achieve this, we can incorporate in the system different mechanisms such as wrappers [24], which detect component run-time failure and prevent its propagation to the system. We can see that test activities that are similar to integration activities are distributed over different phases of the system life cycle and are not strictly connected to the overall system verification. We should also note that the component validation is strongly related to system validation, because the role of validation is to check out the overall system characteristics.
- *System verification and validation.* The system verification and validation process is similar to the processes for non-component-based systems. The difference is that the implications of the processes may

be different—new component requirements may emerge and it may happen that the selected components cannot meet the new requirements. This may include severe problems especially in COTS-based development. To decrease the risk of a selection of a nonsatisfactory component, the component validation in relation to system validation should be performed in the component evaluation phase.

System Operation Support and Maintenance

The purpose of the operational support and maintenance of component-based systems is the same as that of monolithic, non-component-based systems, but the procedures might be different. One characteristic of component-based systems is the existence of components even at run time, which makes it possible to improve and maintain the system by updating components or by adding new components to the system. This makes faster and more flexible improvement possible—it is no longer necessary to rebuild a system to improve it. In a developed component market it also gives end users the opportunity to select components from different vendors. On the other hand, maintenance procedures can be more complicated, because it is not necessarily clear who is supporting the system—the system vendor or the component vendors.

Another serious and, unfortunately, common problem may appear when a component is replaced with a different component or with a new version of the same component. It is not unusual for a component to be used by several other components, and the new version turns out to be compliant with one, but not with another [25]. The same problem may appear when we install a component package (seen from the system point of view as one component, but consisting of several subcomponents) which replaces a common subcomponent. An example of this inconsistent integration is shown in Figure 5.4. Product P version $V2$ (P_{v2}) uses component A version $V2$ and component B version $V2$ (A_{v2} and B_{v2}). At the same time, component A_{v2} uses component version B_{v1}, an older version. Integration in a system of different versions of the same component may cause unpredictable behavior of the system.

System Development Process

From the previous discussion we have seen that the CBD process includes a number of procedures related to component management. The process consists of parallel tracks in which the basic architecture and its environment are being developed and managed concurrently with both the development of

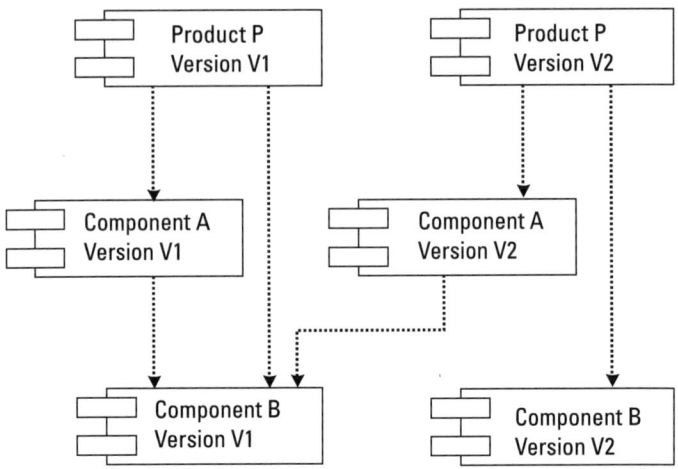

Figure 5.4 An example of inconsistent component integration.

applications consisting of components and the evaluation of the actual components. These concurrent processes can all be characterized as evolutionary (for example, as a combination of an incremental model and an iterative approach) because many activities overlap each other and are strongly related. One strategy is to adapt the Unified Process [10]. The concept is quite simple; instead of producing the complete system as a single, monolithic release, the approach is to build up the complete functionality of the system by deliberately developing the system as a series of smaller increments, or releases. These releases can be at the architectural, application, or component level [26].

The entire system development process is illustrated in Figure 5.5. Of course, there may be a third parallel process—component development. This process is discussed next.

Component Development

The component development process is in many respects similar to system development: Requirements must be captured, analyzed, and defined and the component must be designed, implemented, verified, validated, and delivered [5, 27, 28]. When building a new component the developers will reuse other components and will use procedures similar to those for component evaluation for system development. Some significant differences exist,

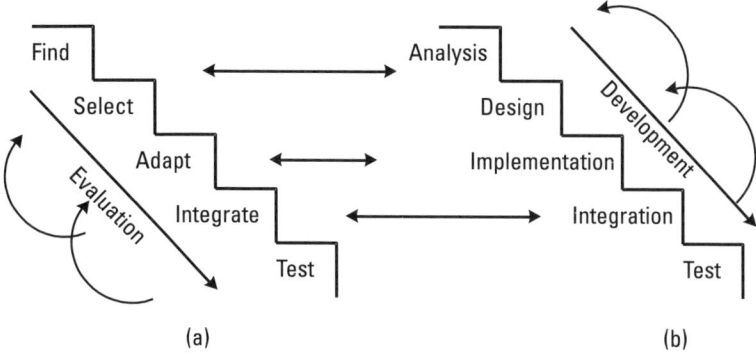

Figure 5.5 CBD process: (a) component evaluation and (b) system development.

however. Components are built to be part of something else. They are intended for reuse in different products, many of them yet to be designed. The consequences of these facts are as follows:

- Managing requirements is more difficult.
- Greater effort is needed to develop reusable units.
- A precise component specification is required.

Component Requirements Analysis and Definition

The main problems of requirements analysis are even more evident when analyzing component requirements. The requirements may be unclear, incomplete, inconsistent, and even unknown. The development of reusable components would be easier if requirements remained constant during the time of component and system development. As a result of new requirements for the system, old or new requirements for the components will emerge. The more reusable a component is, the more demands are placed on it. A number of the requirements of different systems may be the same or very similar, but this is not necessarily the case; new systems may generate completely new requirements.

To satisfy these requirements, the components must be updated rapidly and the new versions must be released more frequently than the systems in which they are incorporated. The component evolution process is more dynamic in the early stage of the component's life cycle. At that stage, the components are less general and cannot respond to the new requirements of the products without being changed. In later stages, their generality and adaptability increase, and the impact of the system requirements becomes less significant. In this period, systems benefit from the combinatorial and synergic effects of component reuse. In the last stage of its life, the components are becoming out of date until they finally become obsolete for different reasons, such as the introduction of new techniques, new development and run-time platforms, new development paradigms, and new standards.

We also face the risk that the initial component cohesion will degenerate when many changes are introduced, in turn requiring more effort. This process is illustrated in Figure 5.6. The number of demands on a common component increases faster in the beginning, stabilizes in the period $[t_0 - t_1]$, and increases again when the component features become inadequate.

Designing for Reusability

For a component to be reusable, it must be designed in a more general way than a component tailored for a unique situation. Components intended to be reused require adaptability. This will increase the size and complexity of the components. At the same time, they must be concrete and simple enough to serve a particular requirement in an efficient way. This requires much more design and development effort. Developing a reusable component requires three to four times more resources than developing a component that serves a particular purpose [1]. Selling the component to many consumers will pay for these additional efforts, but the producer must investigate the market and consider the possible risks of not getting a return on the investment.

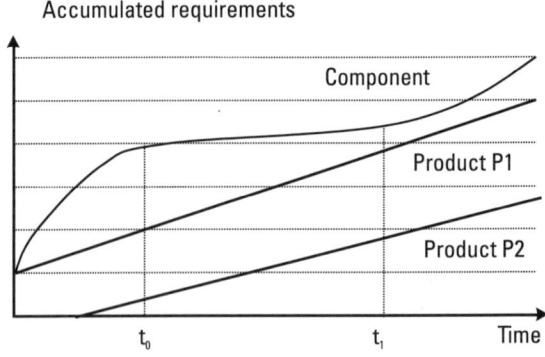

Figure 5.6 Accumulated component requirements.

Component Specification

Because the objective is to reuse components as much as possible, and because a producer is, in principle, not the same as the consumer, it is important for the component to be clearly and properly specified. This is especially true if the component is delivered in a binary form. The consumer must be able to understand the component specification. This is where the importance of using a standardized mode of expression for component specification is evident [17]. We have already discussed the component specification problem in Chapters 1 and 2.

The components must also be trustworthy. One way of making components trustworthy is to certify them. In spite of the common belief that certification means absolute trustworthiness, it in fact only gives the results of tests performed and a description of the environment in which the tests were performed. Although certification is a standard procedure in many domains, it is not yet established in software in general and especially not for software components [29, 30].

Summary

In this chapter we have discussed a CBD process in relation to traditional software development. In a CBD process we distinguish development of components from development of systems using components. While the component development process is focused on building reusable units, the system development process concentrates on the reuse of components and their evaluation and integration.

These processes are often performed independently of each other. This on the one hand has many advantages, such as shorter time to market and encouragement of the use of standard solutions, but on the other suffers from many problems such as difficulty understanding and predicting component behavior and increased uncertainty regarding maintenance and operational support. Achieving a proper balance between the independence of and collaboration between the processes remains a challenge for researchers and practitioners.

References

[1]   Szyperski, C., *Component Software Beyond Object-Oriented Programming*, Reading, MA: Addison-Wesley, 1998.

[2] Casanve, C., "Business-Object Architectures and Standards," *Proc. Data Access Corporation,* Miami, FL, 1995.

[3] Steel, J., "Component Technology Part I An IDC White Paper," *Proc. Int. Data Corporation,* London, 1996.

[4] Basili, V. R., and G. Caldiera, "Identifying and Qualifying Reusable Software Components," *IEEE Computer,* Vol. 24, Issue 2, 1991, pp. 61–70.

[5] Sommerville, I., *Software Engineering,* Reading, MA: Addison-Wesley, 2001.

[6] Pfleeger, S. L., *Software Engineering, Theory and Practice,* Upper Saddle River, NJ: Prentice-Hall, 2001.

[7] Selby, R., V. R. Basili, and T. Baker, "Cleanroom Software Development: An Empirical Evaluation," *IEEE Trans. on Software Engineering,* Vol. 13, No. 9, 1987, pp. 1027–1037.

[8] Basili, V. R., "Software Development: A Paradigm for the Future," *Proc. 13th Annual Int. Computer Software and Application Conf.,* Orlando, FL, 1989, pp. 471–485.

[9] Boehm, B., "Spiral Development: Experience, Principles and Refinements," Special Report CMU/SEI-2000-SR-008, Software Engineering Institute, Carnegie Mellon University, 2000.

[10] Jacobson, I., G. Booch, and J. Rumbaugh, *The Unified Software Development Process,* Reading, MA: Addison-Wesley-Longman, 1999.

[11] Basili, V. R., and H. D. Rombach, "Support for Comprehensive Reuse," *Software Engineering Journal,* Vol. 6, September 1991, pp. 301–318.

[12] Bass, L., P. Clements, and R. Kazman, *Software Architecture in Practice,* Reading, MA: Addison-Wesley, 1998.

[13] Garlan, D., R. Allen, and J. Ockerbloom, "Architectural Mismatch: Why Reuse Is So Hard," *IEEE Software,* Vol. 12, No. 6, 1995, pp. 17–26.

[14] Morisio, M., et al., "Investigating and Improving a COTS-Based Software Development Process," *Proc. 22nd Int. Conf. on Software Engineering,* Limerick, Ireland, ACM Press, 2000.

[15] Wallnau, K. C., S. A. Hissam, and R. C. Seacord, *Building Systems from Commercial Components,* Reading, MA: Addison-Wesley, 2001.

[16] Heineman, G. T., and W. T. Councill, *Component-Based Software Engineering, Putting the Pieces Together,* Reading, MA: Addison-Wesley, 2001.

[17] Christiansson, B., "Component-Based Systems Development—A Shortcut or the Longest Way Around?" *On Methods for System Development in Professional Organizations,* A. G. Nilsson and J. S. Pettersson, Eds., Studentlitteratur, 2001.

[18] Vidger, N. R., W. M. Gentleman, and J. Dean, *COTS Software Integration: State of the Art,* Ottawa, Canada: National Research Council of Canada, 1996.

[19] Pressman, R. S., *Software Engineering—A Practitioner's Approach*, New York: McGraw-Hill International Ltd., 2000.

[20] McClure, C., *Software Reuse Techniques*, Upper Saddle River, NJ: Prentice-Hall 1997.

[21] Leach, R., *Software Reuse Methods, Models and Costs*, New York: McGraw-Hill, 1997.

[22] Basili, V. R., and B. Boehm, "COTS-Based Systems Top 10 List," *IEEE Computer*, May 2001, pp. 91–95.

[23] Boehm, B., "COCOMO II Model Definition Manual," Los Angeles, CA: Science Department, University of Southern California, 1997.

[24] Popov, P., et al., "On Systematic Design of Protectors for Employing OTS Items," *Proc. 27th Euromicro Conf.*, Warsaw, Poland, IEEE Computer Society, 2001.

[25] Crnkovic, I., and M. Larsson, "A Case Study: Demands on Component-Based Development," *Proc. 22nd Int. Conf. Software Engineering*, Limerick, Ireland, ACM Press, 2000.

[26] Jacobson, I., M. L. Griss, and P. Jonsson, *Software Reuse, Architecture, Process and Organization for Business Success*, Reading, MA: Addison-Wesley and ACM Press, 1997.

[27] Carrano, F. M., *Data Abstraction and Problem Solving with C++*, Reading, MA: Addison-Wesley-Longman, 1995.

[28] Meyer, B., *Object-Oriented Software Construction*, Upper Saddle River, NJ: Prentice-Hall, 1997.

[29] Voas, J., and J. Payne, "Dependability Certification of Software Components," *J. of Software Systems*, Vol. 52, 2000, pp. 165–172.

[30] Morris, J., et al., "Software Component Certification," *IEEE Computer*, Vol. 34, No. 9, 2001, pp. 30–36.

6

Semantic Integrity in CBD

Eivind J. Nordby and Martin Blom

Introduction

As seen in previous chapters, a component has certain characteristics that set it apart from other software. The requirement of separate deployability is perhaps the single characteristic that distinguishes components most from other software [1–3]. This property allows a component to be dropped into a system and put to work [4]. For this to work, the interfaces provided by the component to the surroundings and those required by the component from the surroundings need to be specified [5]. Because the source code of the component is generally not available for evaluation or reference, it is important that the specifications be as useful and readable as possible.

The specification of an interface is partly syntactic, partly semantic. Informally, the syntax of an interface is its form or arrangement, as opposed to its semantics, which is its interpretation [6]. The syntax can be described for instance using an IDL for CORBA or COM or by a Java interface.[1] The semantic component properties, the focus of this chapter, are expressed using invariants for the component as a whole and contracts expressed through pre- and postconditions, for each operation. This is more fully described in [7] and in Part 1 of this book. A component specification should include both functional and nonfunctional aspects, for instance, synchronization and quality of service. Some of these aspects may be included in the invariants and the interface contracts whereas others have to be handled by other mechanisms.

This chapter presents some areas of concern for component semantics and a structural framework for the management of the semantic specifications of a component with a focus on semantic integrity. The *semantic integrity* of a software system is the degree to which its semantic properties are preserved. The term can be explained by stating that each part of the system should respect the intended purpose of all the other parts. It is essential for any stable system that its semantic integrity be maintained. This requires each part to be clearly described and the description to remain valid as the part evolves. If the semantic integrity is violated, the system will enter an unstable state, which eventually will lead to some kind of malfunction. Defining a contract for each operation and then following it exactly is essential in order to maintain the semantic integrity of component-based systems.

The next section presents some component issues where semantics play an important role. The issues discussed are specification levels, weak and strong contracts, and required and provided interfaces. The section after that presents five levels of formalism for the specification of component semantics and relates them to current specification techniques. The levels are characterized by no semantics, intuitive semantics, structured semantics, executable semantics, and formal semantics. The section after that highlights three phases in the life of a component and investigates the semantic issues that characterize each phase. The phases are the creation phase, the use phase, and the maintenance phase. The levels of formalism and the life-cycle phases are then combined into a taxonomy that can be used to identify different approaches to semantic specifications.

General Issues of Semantic Concern

This section discusses three general component issues that affect the semantic integrity of a system: specification levels, weak and strong contracts, and

---

1. The purist will object that data typing is semantics, so an IDL specification is concerned about semantics, not only syntax. True, but programming language semantics is not concerned with the application area of the component, which is what this chapter is about, so it will be treated as syntax here.

required and provided interfaces. A fourth issue, the versioning problem, is mentioned with maintenance in the section on life-cycle phases.

Specification Levels

The properties to be specified for a component may be divided into four levels: syntax, behavior, synchronization, and quality of service [8]. Level 1 includes specifications on the programming language level, which is covered by earlier parts of this book and is not dealt with further in this chapter. Level 2 relates to contracts [7] and is the main focus of this chapter. Level 3 describes the dependencies between services provided by a component, such as sequence, parallelism, or shuffle. Some techniques to manage these issues are discussed in [7–9] and are not pursued in this chapter. However, the structural framework presented supports this level. The same applies for level 4, which deals with quality of service, for instance, maximum and average response delay, precision of the result, and throughput for data streams [10].

Weak and Strong Contracts

The semantics of an operation are described with a contract. The precondition specifies the required entry conditions for activating the operation and the postcondition specifies the exit conditions guaranteed by the operation at the end of its execution, provided the precondition was satisfied at its entry. The outcome when the precondition was not satisfied is explicitly left undefined [7].

When an operation can only succeed under specific conditions, these conditions are included in the precondition, and the postcondition merely needs to specify the outcome in those well-defined situations. This may be called a *strong contract* [11]. However, in CBD, components that are directly accessible to human users should not have preconditions because humans cannot be expected to check conditions at all times. Instead, such a component should be capable of filtering out invalid uses in order to meet the preconditions of the internal components it uses [12]. The postcondition for such user-interface components will then specify the outcome of the invalid uses, which are filtered out as well. Such contracts may be called *weak contracts*. A component with strong contracts may be replaced by one with corresponding weak contracts without affecting its clients [13]. Architectures with front-end components with weak contracts and back-end components with strong contracts are common, as for instance in [14]. By making the distinction between strong and weak contracts explicit, one may profit more easily from their properties.

Required and Provided Interfaces

To be composable solely on the basis of its specification, a component needs to be equipped with explicit declarations of required as well as provided properties, such as functionality, synchronization, and quality [1]. A component can be used in a given architectural environment only if its required properties are satisfied by the suppliers in the environment and its provided properties satisfy the requirements from the clients in the environment. From a contractual point of view, a supplier interface S satisfies the demands from a client environment C if the contracts required by C are the same as or stronger than those provided by S [11, 15]. This matching must be done for a component's required as well as provided interfaces. In the rest of this chapter, the fact that a component is playing a dual role as both client and supplier is not stressed, because both the required and the provided interfaces are covered by the general considerations. The focus of the presentation will be on provided interfaces, because that is what a component designer can manipulate most easily.

Levels of Formalism for Semantic Specifications

A component can be described with different levels of formalism. Different environments and developer preferences as well as the maturity of the developers influence the choice of level of formalism. The semantic awareness of component designers varies as does their ability and willingness to formalize the semantic specification. During a literature survey [16], five levels of formalism of semantic issues were identified. These are used in structuring this chapter and are also used in the taxonomy in the last section. The levels of formalism can be defined, in increasing order of formalism, by the key phrases "no semantics," "intuitive semantics," "structured semantics," "executable semantics," and "formal semantics." For each level, we give an example of an operation using the techniques available at that level. Based on practical experience, the descriptions given are believed to be representative for the different levels of formalism. The operation of the example is part of the supplied interface of the component.

An Example

A complete semantic description of a component should include both an overall description, showing its general properties and component invariants, and a specification for each public operation. In this presentation, however, we will use a running example with a focus on an individual operation rather than on an entire component.

The example is a component controlling the access to random access file of a record type R. This file access component will be called Random-Access. It may be used, for instance, by a database management system to access the physical file structure. The physical file controlled by the component contains records of a fixed size, and the access to the file is by record number, counted from zero. We assume that the file is continuous, so that all records up to and including a current maximum number, called the high water mark, are in use. The component defines operations for adding and removing records to and from the physical file, for querying the current high water mark, and for retrieving and updating a particular record.

In our example, we will assume that the file is already populated and concentrate on the component operation getRecord to retrieve a given record. The precondition for this interface contract is that the single input parameter of the operation is the number of the record concerned, which must exist in the file. The postcondition is that the result of the operation is the required data record of type R. If an unrecoverable system error occurs, such as a disk read error or some other file system error, the operation indicates a failure, so this part of the contract is weak. However, no indication will be provided about possibly unsatisfied preconditions, for example, a request for a record number that is too high. This strong part of the contract simply assumes that this does not happen [12].

In the remainder of this section, this example operation is described for each of the five levels of formalism. Where relevant, we will use Java as the specification and implementation language, with the obvious assumptions about class, operation, and type names.

No Semantics

The focus for a component at the "no semantics" level is exclusively on the syntactic parts of the interfaces, represented by CORBA or COM IDL, Java interfaces, or similar IDLs. They represent the minimum level of specification needed to connect components. Operations are not explained, except that the names used may be chosen to be as self-explanatory as possible. We have only included this level for the sake of completeness, because it is not concerned with semantics at all. The interpretation is left to the reader's intuition. The definition of the operation getRecord may be defined as in Example 6.1.

Nothing is said about when number is a legal parameter, the interpretation of number or the resulting R object, or the cases in which an IOException is thrown. There is plenty of room for free guesses. Most would agree that with this level of semantic specification, a commercial software component would not be trustworthy [1].

Intuitive Semantics

By "intuitive semantics" we mean plain text, unstructured descriptions and comments about a component and its parts, as illustrated in Example 6.2. The description has no particular structure and no guidelines are provided to determine the kind of information it should contain or how the information should be presented. Lacking such structure for the specification, the designer of the component must rely on his or her intuition and experience when describing its semantic properties.

The description in Example 6.2 has two serious drawbacks. First, the description does not give the conditions for using the operation correctly. Second, this kind of description is unstructured and the information it contains is scattered and arbitrary. Both of these factors make this kind of description difficult to use.

An investigation of a number of software engineering projects showed that the semantic aspects were largely based on intuitive reasoning of the same kind as in Example 6.2 [17]. We believe that a large portion of the non-critical software being developed today falls into this category, that is, that

```
public R getRecord (int number)
        throws IOException
```

Example 6.1 A purely syntactic specification of getRecord.

```
The operation getRecord retrieves a record by its number, returning the record
requested. If an error occurs, such as disk read error or file system error, the I/O
error is returned.
```

Example 6.2 An intuitive specification of getRecord.

the semantics are mentioned and intuitively described, but without structure and consistency. Compared with what we have seen elsewhere, Example 6.2 shows a reasonably good intuitive description. The next level of formalism may be a step forward for designers at this level [1].

Structured Semantics

Structured semantics are produced by designers and engineers who are highly aware of the semantic implications and requirements of their components, but who are reluctant to express the specifications in a too formal way. Extra cost and competence requirements on present and future users of the specification are examples of valid reasons for such a choice, as is the fact that many requirements are hard to formalize. The semantics are presented in a structured way but need not be in accordance with any particular syntax or formalism. In Example 6.3, the semantic conditions are expressed as plain-text contracts [7, 18] that can be inserted as comments in the design documentation, in the interface descriptions, or in the code itself. The major focus for structures semantics is on a conscious, structured approach to semantic questions without being too focused on the formalities or executable test mechanisms. One way to structure the information is to begin with a short description of the operation and its parameters, followed by the relevant preconditions and postconditions, as in Example 6.3. The postcondition is only specified for cases in which the precondition is satisfied.

This structured description is easier to read than the intuitive description in Example 6.2, even if it may contain the same information. The fact that the same structure applies to the specification of all the operations also reduces the risk of leaving out important information. It is, however, necessary for the designer to understand the implication of the different parts of the specification. Case studies have shown that pre- and postconditions were

---

`getRecord` returns a record identified by its number.
Parameters:
number: the number of the record to retrieve, counted from zero
Precondition: number >=0 and number<= the high water mark
Postcondition: the record with the given number is returned, unless a file system error occurs, in which case a file system error is reported and the value returned is undefined.

Example 6.3 A structured specification of getRecord.

sometimes used in specifications but that their implications were not understood, so that the conditions set up were meaningless or even incorrect [17].

A structured approach without formal requirements may be a useful improvement from a purely intuitive handling of semantics [19]. It supports two major aspects of the development process. First, formulating the semantics in a structured, textual form stimulates extra thinking and favors a better design. Second, the structured documentation makes reading and understanding the specification easier for client programmers as well as for component implementers. This kind of specification can also handle nonexecutable conditions [20], which set a limit to the applicability of the next level of formalism, the executable semantics.

Executable Semantics

By "executable semantics" we mean that semantic aspects are expressed in a way that can be executed and controlled by the system during run time. As such, the executable specification for an operation is included in the implementation of the component. It must therefore be expressed using some executable syntax in the implementation language. The specification of getRecord for Java may, for instance, be expressed as in Example 6.4. We assume that hwm() returns the current high water mark, result is an implicitly declared variable representing the result of the function, and record() is a primitive function returning a record from the file. The contract in the example says that, provided the number is between zero and hwm, the requested record is returned unless an irrecoverable I/O error occurs, which is signaled through an exception. The contract does not state the result if the number is not in the required interval. That situation corresponds to a coding error and a violation of the semantic integrity of the system. It is not covered by the strong contract used. An I/O error, on the other hand, corresponds to a failure outside the control of the software and must be captured in a weak contract.

---

getRecord returns a record identified by its number.
Parameters:
number: the number of the record to retrieve, counted from zero
Precondition: (0 <= number) && (number <= hwm())
Postcondition: throw IOException || (result == record (number))

Example 6.4 An executable specification of getRecord.

With this formalism, assertions can be used to express preconditions and postconditions and to test them during run time. The most obvious candidate to test is the precondition. Bertrand Meyer is a strong advocate of this approach, which is integrated in the Eiffel language [21]. Another example is Biscotti, an extension of Java that enhances Java remote method invocation interfaces with Eiffel-style preconditions, postconditions, and invariants [22]. A third example is OCL [23], a specification language developed within the framework of UML where conditions are compiled into executable statements. Other examples include Jass [24], iContract [25], Guerreiro's approach [26], and jContractor [27]. The execution of the assertions should not add functionality to the component; instead they serve to detect possible violations of the conditions defined. We stress that these assertions serve to detect coding errors and should not try to handle or compensate for them [7]. Because these assertions might not be turned on at all times, the behavior of the software system should not be affected by whether or not they are actually executed. In fact, OCL only defines inquiry operations without side effects. OCL statements cannot be used for data processing or for corrective actions. What to do when an assertion does not hold is a robustness issue and not a correctness issue. A broken assertion is a sign of a coding error and a violation of the semantic integrity. It is not discussed in this chapter, which focuses on how to avoid violating the semantic integrity, not on how to repair it once it is broken.

For the purpose of our example, we will assume that the System class in Java contains an assert method that can be used to execute the assertions. It takes one Boolean argument. If the value of the argument is true, the method returns without any visible effect. If the value of the argument is false, the method terminates the program, possibly leaving some suitable tracing information to help detect the offending code. For debugging purposes, the component itself may then use the executable precondition to trap offending calls, as shown in Example 6.5 [12].

```
public R getRecord (int number) throws IOException
{
    System.assert((0 <= number && (number <= hwm())));
    // the implementation of the method
}
```

Example 6.5 Use of an executable precondition in a supplier component to trap offending calls.

It may be worth mentioning again that this assertion is not a mechanism for *handling* errors, only for *detecting* them. If the logical expression (0 <= number) && (number <= hwm()) has the value false, then the method System.assert does not return. Instead, because this condition identifies a situation in which the outcome of a call to getRecord is not defined, the program is typically terminated. This is especially useful for detecting errors early during the development and testing of client systems [11].

The client code may also take advantage of the executable assertions by checking the precondition before the call, as in Example 6.6. We assume that the client has a variable theFile of class RandomAccess and a variable record of class R.

In addition to the benefits for design and documentation given by the structured semantics approach, the executable specification supports the efforts to maintain semantic integrity by early error detection and removal. However, this benefit is limited by the fact that not all conditions can be expressed in an executable way. This is illustrated by the postcondition in Example 6.4, where the fact that an exception may be thrown is only expressed as a comment.

Formal Semantics

With formal semantics, programs can be proven to have consistent and sound semantics [28–30]. Formal specification languages such as VDM, Z, and λ are well-known. We will use Z to express the formal specification of getRecord. The concept for the Z description is taken from [31] but modified to suit our purpose. For further details regarding the meaning of terms and symbols used, the reader is referred to literature on Z, for example, [31–33].

The visible state of the random access component is defined in a state schema called RandomAccess, shown in Example 6.7. The term *records*

```
if ((0 <= number) && (number <= theFile.hwm()))
{
   try {
record = theFile.getRecord(number);
   // record == the record requested
   }
   catch (IOException e)
   { /* unrecoverable IO error */ }
}
```

Example 6.6 Use of executable semantics in a client component to ensure a correct call.

```
┌─ RandomAccess ─────────────────────┐
│ records: N → R                     │
│ hwm: N                             │
├────────────────────────────────────┤
│ ∀i:0..hwm × {records (i)} ≠ ∅      │
└────────────────────────────────────┘
```

Example 6.7 Z state schema for the random access file.

represents all the records in the file and *R* is the record data type. The variable *hwm* (for high water mark) shows how much of the file is in use.

The formula $\forall i:0..hwm \times \{records(i)\} \neq \emptyset$ in the lower part of the schema expresses the invariant for the component, which is that all the records from number zero up to and including the high water mark are in use; that is, the file has no "holes."

The file operation is defined as a state schema called `getRecord`, shown in Example 6.8.

The upper part specifies the parameters of the inquiry and the lower part expresses its pre- and postconditions. In agreement with the contract used, no return value is defined if the precondition *number* ≤ *hwm* is not satisfied. Similarly, also in accordance with the contract, the return value of record is undefined if a file system error occurs, so no record value is specified for that case.

A formal approach is valuable for security-critical applications. Büchi [34] argues that such an approach will simplify the process of formal reasoning of components and make it easier to compose components based on their contracts. However, the rigid formalism restricts the application of their

```
┌─ getRecord ────────────────────────┐
│ Ξ RandomAccess                     │
│ number?: N                         │
│ record!: R                         │
│ status!: {OK, FileSystemError}     │
├────────────────────────────────────┤
│ number? ≤ hwm                      │
│ ((status! = OK) ∧ record! = records (number?))∨ │
│ (status! = FileSystemError)        │
└────────────────────────────────────┘
```

Example 6.8 Z schema for the operation getRecord.

proposed ideas to environments in which the overhead of formal methods can be tolerated. The major part of the component market may find the formal approach too costly or too difficult to access.

Phases in a Component's Life

During its lifetime, a component passes through different phases. This section considers their creation phase, use phase, and maintenance phase from a semantic point of view. The creation phase of a component includes its design and implementation, both for the initial creation and for subsequent additions of new functionality. This phase corresponds roughly to the traditional development cycle. The use phase includes all regular use, both initial use and reuse. The maintenance phase includes all changes to the existing functionality after release, including versioning.

All of these phases may recur in no particular order, except for the initial creation phase. In particular, use and maintenance of a component are often closely related. As a component is being used, problems and deficiencies are detected and corrected. For the following discussion on semantic considerations, it is assumed that the operation getRecord is specified with the structured contract of Example 6.3.

Creation Phase

The first creation phase begins when the need for a component is identified. Further creation phases frequently occur later during the component's life, when new functionality is identified and added to the component. During the creation phase, the semantic focus is on design and implementation.

The design of a component defines its required and provided functional and nonfunctional characteristics. We have already stressed how semantic integrity depends on good semantic specifications and that a syntactic description is not enough. The semantic part of the design includes invariants for the component, and required and provided contracts with pre- and postconditions for each operation. Implementation details should be kept out of this description.

Normally, the client programmer will not see any code for the interfaces provided by the component, nor will the component designer see the code for the required interfaces, so the semantic description must express all information needed by the user about the component and its required and provided interfaces. Even if the code were available to the developer, it could only show what the current implementation happens to be and not the purpose of the operation. This becomes evident in the maintenance phase when the code is modified, as described below. Any client program based on the current implementation instead of on the specification will be endangered by any such modification.

Once designed, the component should be implemented. The contracts and invariants should be implemented in a consistent way. Because the code will not, and should not, be available to the client programmer, no new conditions should be introduced during implementation without also being reflected in the design specification.

Use Phase

A component enters the use phase when it is used as a service provider by some client software. The main semantic issue for the client programmer is to determine the semantic specification of the component and to use it accordingly. If a contract required by the client is the same as or stronger than a contract provided by the component, the operation may be used directly [11, 15]. In other cases, it will be necessary to create an adapting shell around the component, where the interface defined by the shell is being better adapted to the client requirements than the component itself [35].

A component is sometimes developed for use in a particular context and is normally used in this context first. At the same time, one objective in designing components is to produce reusable software, with the component developer not needing to know much about the different contexts in which it will be possible to use the component. In both cases, the rules for use are the same. To ensure the semantic integrity of the system, the component should only be used as defined in its semantic specification; therefore, the specification must be complete and consistent. If the description is unstructured and intuitive, interpretation problems easily arise and trial and error might be the only way to determine how the component behaves.

Testing is sometimes advocated as the major quality assurance mechanism for components [36]. If the component to be used is not adequately described, testing may be the only practical approach, although very resource consuming. However, basing the use of a component on its empirical behavior may cause problems during maintenance of the component, as discussed next. Sometimes, as in the case of the French rocket Ariane 5 [37, 38], testing is explicitly excluded because of the high costs. In any case, the use of testing does not contradict the usefulness of thorough planning and a thorough description of the semantic aspects of a component. On the contrary, such a description can reduce the number of errors and thereby speed up the testing process.

Maintenance Phase

Maintenance is the work performed on a component after its deployment in order to correct errors, to improve performance or other properties, or to adapt it to changes in the environment [39]. The main semantic issue here is to maintain backward compatibility and to detect when it is discontinued. Addition of new functionality is not classified as maintenance, but is treated as if in the creation phase.

Because the component is identified externally by its semantic descriptions only, any modification of the component that respects these is unproblematic. It is, however, important to check that a modification does not in fact violate the description.

If the contract of an operation is changed to put changed demands on the clients, problems may arise. A change in a component is sometimes harmless to client systems, and sometimes harmful. Liskov's substitutability principle [13] can be applied to determine which effect it will have. It implies that a change is safe if the client cannot observe it. If the new contract is weaker than the original, so as to demand less from the clients, no problems arise, since all existing clients already conform to the new specification [11, 15]. Otherwise, existing clients conforming to the first contract may suddenly violate the modified contract although the clients themselves have not changed. The modified operation should be recognized as being different, for instance, with a new interface definition. This versioning issue is a serious source of problems when components are replaced [2].

A Taxonomy for Component Semantics

We now suggest a two-dimensional taxonomy for component semantics. One dimension encompasses the five levels of formalism and the other the three phases of a component's life. This taxonomy may serve as a reference when components and component issues are discussed and presented. A recent survey of the state of the art in semantic management of components is also summarized and related to the taxonomy.

To find out how semantic aspects are managed in the software engineering community, a literature survey was conducted during Spring 2000 [16]. The survey was updated with the latest references in November 2001 and included a large number of journals and conference proceedings. Out of the articles searched and examined, we judged 37 publications to be relevant for our purposes. Figure 6.1 shows how these publications are related to the taxonomy. Each reference in the survey is represented by an asterisk and some of the references appear more than once. Each reference is related as truthfully as possible to the taxonomy according to its main approach to semantics. Of course, because the survey focuses on semantic management, it did not include publications in the "No semantics" column.

The limited number of references found during the survey may be an indication that semantic issues are not actively discussed in component contexts. It was also found that authors have very different approaches to the semantic aspects when discussing components. However, consensus has been reached that there is a need for semantic descriptions of components and that this need is not covered by the interface description languages as they stand.

Two interesting conclusions can be drawn from the distribution of the publications shown in Figure 6.1. The first is that most of the publications dealing with component semantics are found in the area of executable semantics. This reflects a general view that exact semantics cannot be efficiently expressed in plain text [23]. However, our experience is that the state of the art among practitioners is mostly at the intuitive level. For practitioners who find themselves at this level, the structured level may be a first step toward a more organized approach to semantics. The structured approach gives good support to the design process itself as well as to the documentation, both of which are crucial factors for components, without requiring too

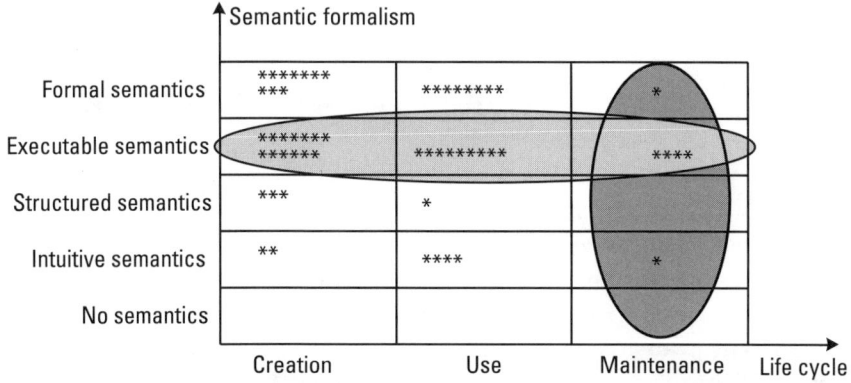

Figure 6.1 A literature survey related to the proposed taxonomy for component semantics.

much formalism. It may be applied even if the conditions in the contract are not executable.

The other interesting observation from the diagram is that there is little discussion of component maintenance issues. This lack of discussion is a serious threat to the long-term stability of any component-based system. We believe that it would be possible to establish a sound practice for component maintenance by applying Liskov's principle of substitutability [13] to components with descriptions at the structured level of formalism or above. Using this principle will help to avoid the problem which arises when a new release of a component compromises the stability of complete systems.

Summary

In this chapter, we have presented some important semantic component issues, how semantic properties of components can be described with different levels of formalism, and the importance of semantic integrity in the different phases in a component's life. Finally a two-dimensional taxonomy for component semantics was presented along with the results of a recent literature survey that shows how semantic aspects are handled in current research.

One dimension in the taxonomy encompasses five levels of formalism in describing component semantics, where the level chosen for a particular project depends on the application domain and the degree of experience of the designers. The other dimension covers three phases in a component's life, in which each phase requires certain semantic considerations. The taxonomy allows a designer to position himself with respect to his semantic awareness and to increase this awareness. The majority of the publications in the survey focused on intuitive or executable semantics in the creation and use stages. Few publications discuss the semantic issues involved in maintenance and even fewer discuss structured semantics.

Component developers who find themselves at the level of intuitive semantics can benefit from applying structured semantics for improved design and documentation. Executable semantics add the potential for dynamic error detection. For critical and semicritical applications, formal semantics may be necessary, but are hardly motivated for the noncritical market. The main point is that, to maintain semantic integrity, the specification of required and provided properties should be complete and understandable, not only by the component developers, but also by the users of the component and by those maintaining it. For the component market in particular, an increased focus on semantics during maintenance should reduce the number of problems experienced in this area today.

References

[1] Szyperski, C., "Components and Contracts," *Software Development Magazine*, Vol. 8, No. 5, 2000.

[2] Szyperski, C., "Greetings from DLL Hell," *Software Development Magazine*, Vol. 7, No. 10, 1999.

[3] Douglas, B. P., "Components, States and Interfaces, Oh My!" *Software Development Magazine*, Vol. 4, 2000.

[4] Szyperski, C., "Point, Counterpoint," *Software Development Magazine*, Vol. 8, No. 2, 2000.

[5] Szyperski, C., *Component Software—Beyond Object-Oriented Programming*, Reading, MA: Addison-Wesley, 1998.

[6] Aho, A., R. Sethi, and J. Ullman, *Compilers—Principles, Techniques and Tools*, Reading, MA: Addison-Wesley, 1986.

[7] Meyer, B., *Object-Oriented Software Construction*, Upper Saddle River, NJ: Prentice-Hall, 1997.

[8] Beugnard, A. et al., "Making Components Contract Aware," *IEEE Computer*, Vol. 32, Issue 7, 1999, pp. 38–45.

[9] Watkins, D., "Using Interface Definition Languages to Support Path Expressions and Programming by Contract," *Proc. Tools 26: Technology of Object-Oriented Languages and Systems*, Los Alamitos, CA, IEEE Computer Society, 1998.

[10] Preiss, O., A. Wegmann, and J. Wong, "On Quality Attribute Based Software Engineering," *Proc. EUROMICRO 2001 CBSE Workshop*, Warsaw, Poland, IEEE Computer Society, 2001.

[11] Nordby, E., M. Blom, and A. Brunström, "On the Relation Between Design Contracts and Errors, A Software Development Strategy," *Proc. 9th IEEE Conf. and Workshops on Engineering of Computer-Based Systems*, Lund, Sweden, IEEE Computer Society, 2002.

[12] Meyer, B., "The Significance of dot-NET," *Software Development Magazine*, Vol. 11, 2000.

[13] Liskov, B., "Data Abstraction and Hierarchy," *Addendum to Proc. OOPSLA'87*, Orlando, FL, ACM Press, 1987.

[14] Bhagat, S., and R. K. Joshi, "Behavioral Contracts for COM Components," *Proc. Information System Technology and Its Applications—ISTA 2001*, Lecture Notes in Informatics, 2001.

[15] Nordby, E., and M. Blom, "Semantic Integrity of Switching Sections with Contracts: Discussion of a Case Study," *Informatica*, Vol. 10, No. 2, 1999, pp. 203–218.

[16] Blom, M., and E. Nordby, "Semantic Integrity in Component Based Development," Internal report on CBSE, Mälardalen University, Västerås, Sweden, 2000.

[17] Blom, M., et al., "Using Quality Criteria in Programming Industry: A Case Study," *Proc. European Software Day, Euromicro 98*, 1998.

[18] D'Souza, D., and A. C. Wills, *Objects, Components and Frameworks: The Catalysis Approach*, Reading, MA: Addison-Wesley, 1998.

[19] Meyer, B., Contracts for Components, "Interface Definition Languages As We Know Them Today Are Doomed," *Software Development Magazine*, Vol. 7, 2000.

[20] Kotula, J., "Source Code Documentation: An Engineering Deliverable," *Proc. TOOLS-34*, Santa Barbara, CA, IEEE Computer Society, 2000.

[21] Meyer, B., *Eiffel: The Language*, Upper Saddle River, NJ: Prentice-Hall, 1992.

[22] Cicalese, C. D. T., and S. Rotenstreich, "Behavioral Specification of Distributed Software Component Interfaces," *IEEE Computer*, Vol. 32, Issue 7, 1999, pp. 46–53.

[23] Warmer, J., and A. Kleppe, *The Object Constraint Language*, Reading, MA: Addison-Wesley, 1999.

[24] Bartetzko, D., et al., "Jass—Java with Assertions," *Proc. Workshop on Runtime Verification, 2001,* held in conjunction with *13th Conf. Computer Aided Verification*, Paris, France, Elsevier Science, 2001.

[25] Kramer, R., "iContract—The Java Design by Contract Tool," *Proc. Technology of Object-Oriented Languages—TOOLS26*, Los Alamitos, CA, IEEE Computer Society, 1998.

[26] Guerreiro, P., "Another Mediocre Assertion Mechanism for C++," *Proc. Technology of Object-Oriented Languages—TOOLS33*, Los Alamitos, CA, IEEE Computer Society, 2002.

[27] Karaorman, M., U. Hölze, and J. Bruno, "jContractor: A Reflective Java Library to Support Design by Contract," *Proc. Metal-Level Architectures and Reflection*, Lecture Notes in Computer Science, No. 1616, Berlin, Springer Verlag, 1999.

[28] Findler, R. B., and M. Felleisen, "Contract Soundness for Object-Oriented Languages," *Proc. OOPSLA2001*, Tampa Bay, FL, AMC Press, 2001.

[29] Miao, H., C. Yu, and L. Li, "A Formalized Abstract Component Object Model Z-COM," *Proc. TOOLS36*, Xian, China, IEEE Computer Society, 2000.

[30] Reussner, R. H., "Enhanced Component Interfaces to Support Dynamic Adaption and Extension," *Proc. 34th Hawaii Int. Conf. System Sciences*, Hawaii, IEEE Computer Society, 2001.

[31] Spivey, J. M., *The Z Notation, A Reference Manual*, Upper Saddle River, NJ: Prentice-Hall, 1992.

[32] Potter, B., J. Sinclair, and D. Till, *An Introduction to Formal Specification and Z*, Upper Saddle River, NJ: Prentice-Hall, 1991.

[33] Diller, A., *Z, An Introduction to Formal Methods*, New York: John Wiley & Sons, 1995.

[34] Büchi, M., and E. Sekerinski, "Formal Methods for Component Software: The Refinement Calculus Perspective," *Proc. 2nd Int. Workshop on Component-Oriented Programming—WCOP'97*, 1997.

[35] Edwards, S. H., B. W. Weide, and J. Hollingsworth, "A Framework for Detecting Interface Violations in Component-Based Software," *Proc. Fifth Int. Conf. Software Reuse*, Victoria, Canada, IEEE Computer Society, 1998.

[36] Weyuker, E. J., Testing Component-Based Software: A Cautionary Tale, *IEEE Software*, Vol. 15, Issue 5, 1998, pp. 54–59.

[37] Le Lann, G., "An Analysis of the Ariane 5 Flight 501 Failure—A System Engineering Perspective," *Proc. 4th Int. Conf. Engineering of Computer-Based Systems*, Los Alamitos, CA, IEEE Computer Society, 1997.

[38] Inquiry Board, "ARIANE 5—Flight 501 Failure," Inquiry Board report.

[39] IEEE, "IEEE Standard for Software Maintenance," Report IEEE Std 1219-1998, 1998.

7

Role-Based Component Engineering

Jilles van Gurp and Jan Bosch

Introduction

COTS components have been a long-standing software engineering dream [1]. Several technologies have tried to fulfill this dream but most of them, so far, have failed despite some successes (such as Visual Basic components). From time to time, a promising new technique appears. The most successful technique to date has been OO, but even this technique has failed to deliver truly reusable COTS components. In this chapter we investigate a promising extension of OO called *role-based component engineering*. Role-based component engineering extends the traditional OO component paradigm to provide a more natural support for modeling component collaborations.

The idea of role-based components is that the public interface is split into smaller interfaces that model different roles. Users of a component can communicate with the component through the smaller role interfaces instead of using the full interface. In this chapter we examine why roles are useful, discuss methods and techniques for using them, and discuss how they can be used to make better OO frameworks.

Four different definitions of a component are given in [2] and a number of definitions have been discussed elsewhere in this book. This indicates that it is difficult to get the software community as a whole to agree on a single definition. Rather than continuing this discussion here, we will focus on aspects of object-oriented components that are relevant to role-based component engineering (for a more elaborate discussion of these concepts, see [3]):

- *The interface.* The interface of a component defines the syntax of how to use a component. The semantics of the interface are usually implicit, despite efforts to provide semantics in various languages (e.g., Eiffel [4]).

- *The size or granularity.* One purpose of using components is to extend reusability, so the larger the component the more code is reused. A second purpose of components is to improve flexibility but as Szyperski noted, there is a conflict between small components and flexibility on the one hand and large components and usability on the other ("maximizing reusability minimizes usability") [5].

- *Encapsulation.* The main motivation behind software components, however, is to achieve the same as has been achieved in electronics: pluggable components. To achieve this, a clear separation must exist between the externally visible behavior of a component and its internal implementation. The latter must be encapsulated by the component. This feature is also referred to as information hiding or black-box behavior and is generally considered to be an important feature of the OO paradigm.

- *Composition mechanisms.* A component is used by connecting it to other components, thus creating a system based on multiple components. Components can be plugged together in many ways. These range from something as simple as a method call to more complex mechanisms such as pipes and filters or event mechanisms. Currently, three component models dominate: COM, CORBA, and JavaBeans. These models provide a general architecture for plumbing components. All three allow for method calls (synchronous calls) and event mechanisms (asynchronous calls).

The concept of roles is based on the notion that components may have several different uses in a system. These different uses of a component in a system are dependent on the different roles a component can play in the various component collaborations in the system. The idea of role-based components is that the public interface is separated into smaller interfaces, which model these different roles. Users of a component can communicate with the component through the smaller role interfaces instead of through the full interface. The main advantage of this is that by limiting the communication between two components by providing a smaller interface, the communication becomes more specific. Because of the smaller interfaces the communication also becomes easier to generalize (i.e., to apply to a wider range of components). These two properties make the components both more versatile and reusable.

This is particularly important when component collaborations (i.e., archetypal behavior of interacting components) are to be modeled. Traditionally, the full interface of a component is considered when modeling component collaborations. Because of this, the conceptual generality of a collaboration is lost in the design as the lowest level at which modeling can be performed is the class interface. This means that collaborations are always defined in terms of classes and the only way for components to share an interface (i.e., to be part of the same collaboration) is to inherit from a common base class. In some cases, multiple inheritance can be applied to inherit from multiple base classes, but this is generally considered to be a bad practice. By introducing roles, these collaborations can be modeled at a much more finely grained level.

If, for example, we analyze a simple GUI button, we observe that it has several capabilities. It can be drawn on the screen, it has dimensions (height, width), it produces an event when clicked, it has a label, it may display a tool tip, and so forth. If we next analyze a text label, we find that it shares most of its capabilities with the button but sends no event when it is clicked.

The OO approach to modeling these components would be to define a common base class to expose an interface, which then accommodates the common capabilities. This approach has severe limitations when modeling collaborations because in a particular collaboration, usually only one particular capability of a component is of interest. A button, for instance, could be used to trigger some operation in another component (i.e., the operation is executed when a user clicks the button). When using OO techniques, this must be modeled at the class level. Even though only the event-producing capability of the button is relevant in this particular collaboration, all other capabilities are also involved because the button is referred to as a whole.

Roles radically change this because roles make it possible to involve only the relevant part of the interface. The button in the example above, for instance, could implement a role named EventSource. In the collaboration, a component with the role EventSource would be connected to another component implementing the role EventTarget. Similarly, the ability to display text could be captured in a separate DisplayText interface that also applies to text labels, for example. This way of describing the collaboration is more specific and more general—more specific because only the relevant part of the interface is involved and more general because any component that supports that role can be part of the collaboration.

This idea has been incorporated into the OORam [6] method, which is discussed later in this chapter. The term *role model* will be used to refer to a collaboration of components implementing specific roles. Role models can be composed and extended to create new role models and role models can be mapped to component designs. Note that multiple roles could be mapped to a single component, even if these roles are part of one role model. In the example given above, a button component could be both an EventSource and an EventTarget. This means that it is possible to model a component collaborating with itself. Of course, this is not particularly useful in this example but it does show the expressiveness of roles as opposed to full class interfaces.

From the above comments, we can conclude that there is no need to place many constraints on the component aspects discussed earlier, in discussing role-based component engineering. Role-based components can support multiple, typically small interfaces. The size of the component is not significant. Because multiple, functionally different components will support the same role interface, it is not desirable to take the implementation of a component into account when addressing it through one of its role interfaces.

The relation between a role and a component, which supports that role, should be seen as an "is-a" relation. The relations between roles can be both "is-a" and "has-a" relations. Although hybrid components are possible (components that are only partly role-oriented), it is, in principle, not necessary to have component-to-component relations in the source code. Typically, references to other components will be typed using the role interfaces rather than component classes.

The goal of this chapter is to study role-based component engineering from several different perspectives. In the following sections we will first advocate the use of roles by using existing metrics for object-oriented systems. Several techniques that make it possible to use roles in both design and implementation are then discussed and, finally, we discuss the use of roles in object-oriented frameworks.

Encouraging the Use of Roles

In this section we argue that using roles as outlined in the introduction improves an OO system in such a way that some of the metrics typically used to assess the software quality of an OO system will improve.

Chidamber and Kemerer [7] describe a metric suite for object-oriented systems. The suite consists of six different types of metrics which together make it possible to perform measurements on OO systems. The metrics are based on so-called viewpoints, gained by interviewing a number of expert designers. On the basis of these viewpoints, Kemerer and Chidamber presented the following definition of good design: "good software design practice calls for minimizing coupling and maximizing cohesiveness" [7].

Cohesiveness is defined in terms of method similarity. Two methods are similar if the union of the sets of class variables they use is substantial. A class with a high degree of method similarity is considered to be highly cohesive. A class with a high degree of cohesiveness has methods that operate primarily on the same properties in that class. A class with a low degree of cohesiveness has methods that operate on distinct sets; that is, there are different, more or less independent sets of functionality in that class.

Coupling between two classes is defined as follows: "Any evidence of a method of one object using methods or instance variables of another object constitutes coupling" [7]. A design with a high degree of coupling is more complex than a design with a low degree of coupling. Based on this notion, Lieberherr et al. [8] created the law of Demeter, which states that the sending of messages should be limited to the following: argument classes (i.e., any class that is passed as an argument to the method that performs the call or self) and instance variables. Applied to role-based component engineering, this rule becomes even stricter; the sending of messages should be limited to argument roles and instance variables (also typed using roles).

The use of roles makes it possible to have multiple views of one class. These role perspectives are more cohesive than the total class interface since they are limited to a subset of the class interface. The correct use of roles ensures that object references are typed using the roles rather than the classes. This means that connections between the classes are more specific and more general at the same time—more specific because they have a smaller interface, and more general because the notion of a role is more abstract than the notion of a class. Although roles do nothing to reduce the number of relations between classes, it is now possible to group the relations in interactions between different roles, which makes them more manageable.

Based on these notions of coupling and cohesiveness, Kemerer and Chidamber created six metrics [7]:

1. *Weighted methods per class (WMC)*. This metric reflects the notion that a complex class (i.e., a class with many methods and properties) has a larger influence on its subclasses than a small class. The

potential reuse of a class with a high WMC is limited, however, because such a class is application-specific and will typically need considerable adaptation. A high WMC also has consequences with respect to the time and resources needed to develop and maintain a class.

2. *Depth of inheritance tree (DIT)*. This metric reflects the notion that a deep inheritance hierarchy constitutes a more complex design. Classes deep in the hierarchy will inherit and override much behavior from classes higher in the hierarchy, which makes it difficult to predict their behavior.

3. *Number of children (NOC)*. This metric reflects the notion that classes with many subclasses are important classes in a design. While many subclasses indicate that much code is reused through inheritance, it may also be an indicator of lack of cohesiveness in such a class.

4. *Coupling between object classes (CBO)*. This metric reflects the fact that excessive coupling inhibits reuse and that limiting the number of relations between classes helps to increase their reuse potential.

5. *Response for a class (RFC)*. This metric measures the number of methods that can be executed in response to a message. The larger this number is, the more complex the class. In a class hierarchy, the lower classes have a higher RFC than higher classes since they can also respond to calls to inherited methods. A higher average RFC for a system indicates that implementation of methods is scattered throughout the class hierarchy.

6. *Lack of cohesiveness in methods (LCOM)*. This metric reflects the notion that noncohesive classes should probably be separated into two classes (to promote encapsulation) and that classes with a low degree of cohesiveness are more complex.

The most important effect of introducing roles into a system is that relations between components are no longer expressed in terms of classes but in terms of roles. The effect of this transformation can be evaluated by studying its effects on the different metrics:

1. *WMC*. Roles model only a small part of a class interface. The amount of WMC of a role is typically less than that of a class.

Components are accessed using the role interfaces. A smaller part of the interface must be understood than when the same component is addressed using its full interface.

2. *DIT.* The DIT value will increase since inheritance is the mechanism for imposing roles on a component. Note, however, that roles only define the interface, not the implementation. Thus while the DIT increases, the distribution of implementation throughout the inheritance hierarchy is not affected.

3. *NOC.* Because role interfaces are typically located at the top of the hierarchy, the NOC metric will typically be high. In a conventional class hierarchy, a high NOC for a class expresses that that class is important in the hierarchy (and probably has a low cohesiveness value). Similarly, roles with a high NOC are important and have a high cohesiveness value.

4. *CBO.* The CBO metric will decrease because implementation dependencies can be avoided by only referring to role interfaces rather than by using classes as types.

5. *RFC.* Because roles do not provide any implementation, the RFC value will not increase in implementation classes. It may even decrease because class inheritance will be necessary to inherit implementation only, interfaces are no longer necessary.

6. *LCOM.* Roles typically are very cohesive in the sense that the methods for a particular role are closely related and roles will thus, typically, have a lower LCOM value.

Based on the analysis of these six metrics it is safe to conclude the following:

- Roles reduce complexity (improvement in CBO, RFC, and LCOM metrics) in the lower half of the inheritance hierarchy because inter-component relations are moved to a more abstract level. This is convenient because this is generally the part of the system where most of the implementation resides.

- Roles increase complexity in the upper half of the inheritance hierarchy (higher DIT and NOC values). This is also advantageous because it is now possible to express design concepts that were previously hard-coded in the lower layers of the inheritance hierarchy on a higher, more abstract level.

Role Technology

The use of roles during both design and implementation is discussed in this section. Several modeling techniques and the use of roles in two common OO languages (Java and C++) are studied.

Using Roles at the Design Level

Though roles provide a powerful means of modeling component collaborations, the common modeling languages (e.g., UML [9] and OMT) do not treat them as first-class entities. Fowler and Scott [10] suggest the use of the UML refinement relation to model interfaces. Although this technique is suitable for modeling simple interfaces it is not very suitable for modeling more complex role models.

In a recent document [11], the shortcomings of UML in representing component collaborations are discussed. Reenskaug defines collaboration as follows: "A Collaboration describes how a number of objects work together for a common purpose. There are two aspects. The structural aspect is a description of the responsibilities of each object in the context of the overall purpose of the collaboration; and also the links that connect the objects into a communication whole. The dynamic aspect is a description of how stimuli flow between the objects to achieve the common purpose..." [11].

It is essential that collaborations model the interaction of objects participating in the collaboration. In UML, a class diagram models the relations between classes. According to the UML 1.3 specification a class is defined as follows: "A class is the descriptor for a set of objects with similar structure, behavior, and relationships..." [9]. As distinct from a class, an object in a collaboration has an identity. UML also provides the possibility of modeling object collaborations (object diagram) but Reenskaug argues that these are too specific to model the more general role models he uses in OORam, which is introduced in his book *Working with Objects* [6]. Using a UML object diagram, it is possible to express how a specific object interacts with another specific object. This diagram applies, however, only to those two objects.

In [11] Reenskaug proposes an extension to UML that provides a more general way to express object collaborations without the disadvantage of being too general (class diagrams) or too specific (object diagrams). Essentially, Reenskaug uses what he calls *ClassifierRoles* to denote the position an object holds in an object structure. Note that there is an important difference when modeling roles as interfaces only. Reenskaug's ClassifierRoles retain object identity, whereas an interface has no object identity. Because of this it is possible to specify a relation between ClassifierRoles without explicitly specifying the identity of the objects and without giving up the notion of object identity completely, as in a class diagram. In principle, a single object can interact with itself and still be represented by two ClassifierRoles in the collaboration.

Reenskaug defines ClassifierRoles as follows: "a named slot for an object participating in a specification level Collaboration. Object behavior is represented by its participation in the overall behavior of the Collaboration. Object identity is preserved through this constraint: 'In an instance of a collaboration, each ClassifierRole maps onto at most one object' " [11].

Catalysis [12] is a very extensive methodology based on UML, which offers a different approach to using roles in the design phase. Catalysis uses the concepts of frameworks to model component interactions, treating roles in a manner unlike that of OORam. It includes a notion of types and type models. A type corresponds to a role and a type model describes typical collaborations between objects of that type (i.e., the performance of a role in the collaboration). New type models can be composed from those existing. Type models can then be used to create components and frameworks. Unlike OORam's RoleClassifier, a type has no identity. It classifies a set of objects in the same way as a class but unlike a class it provides no implementation. This minor difference is the most important between the two notations apart from naming and methodology issues (both approaches include a development methodology).

UML in its default form is not sufficiently expressive to express the concepts Catalysis and OORam use. The UML metamodel, however, is extensible and both Catalysis and OORam use this to role-enable UML.

Using Roles at the Implementation Level

After a system has been designed, it must be implemented. Implementation languages are typically on a lower abstraction level than the design. This means that in the process of translating a design to an implementation, some design information is lost (e.g., constraints such as cardinalities on aggregation relations). Relations between classes in UML are commonly translated to pointers and references when a UML class diagram is implemented in, for example, C++. This information loss is inevitable but can become a problem if it becomes necessary to recover the design from the source code (for example, for maintenance).

With roles, a similar loss of information occurs. In the worst case, roles are translated into classes, which means that one class contains the methods and properties of multiple roles. It is not possible to distinguish between the roles on the implementation level. Fortunately, languages such as Java and C++ can both be used to represent roles as first-class entities (even if, in the case of C++, some simple tricks are required).

Native support for interfaces is provided in Java. More importantly, interface extension and multiple inheritance of interfaces are supported. Because of this, it is possible to create new interfaces by extending those existing and one class may implement more than one interface. This makes Java very suitable for supporting role-based component engineering, since it is easy to map the design level roles to implementation level interfaces.

The advantage of expressing roles in this way is that references to other classes can be typed using the interfaces. Many errors can be prevented by using type checking during compilation. In the case of Java, these types can also be used during run time (i.e., two components that were developed separately but implement roles from a particular role model can be plugged together at run time). The run-time environment will use the type information to permit only legal connections between components.

A problem with Java is that objects must often be cast in order to get the correct role interface to an object. A common example is the collection classes in Java, which by default return object references that need to be cast before they can be used. C++ does not have this problem since in C++, templates can often be used to address this. A similar solution in the form of a Java language extension is currently planned in an upcoming version of Sun's JDK [13].

C++ has no language construct for interfaces. Typically, the interface of a class is defined in a header file. A header file consists of a preprocessor and declarations. The contents are typically mixed with the source code at compile time. This means that the implied "is-a" relation is not enforced at compile time. Fortunately it is possible, as in Java, to simulate interfaces. Interfaces can be simulated by using abstract classes containing only virtual methods without implementation. Because C++ supports multiple inheritance, these abstract classes can be combined as in Java. This style of programming is often referred to as using *mixing classes*. Unfortunately, the use of virtual methods (unlike Java interfaces) has a performance impact on each call to such methods, which may make this way of implementing roles less feasible in some situations.

Roles can also be mapped to IDL interfaces, which make it possible to use multiple languages (even those not object oriented) in one system. An important side effect of using component frameworks such as CORBA, COM, or JavaBeans is that in order to write components for them, IDL interfaces must be defined and in order to use components, these IDL interfaces must be used. Adopting a role-oriented approach is therefore quite natural in such an environment.

As an example, consider the JButton class in the Swing framework commonly used for GUI applications in Java. According to the API documentation, this class implements the following Java interfaces: Accessible, ImageObserver, ItemSelectable, MenuContainer, Serializable, SwingConstants. These interfaces can be seen as roles, which this class can play in various collaborations. The Serializable interface, for example, makes it possible to write objects of the JButton class to a binary stream. How this is done is class specific. However, the object responsible for writing other objects to a binary stream can handle any object of a class implementing the Serializable interface, regardless of its implementation.

A problem is that many roles are associated with a more or less default implementation, slightly different for each class. However, imposing such default implementation on a component together with a role is difficult. Some approaches (e.g., the framelet approach discussed below) attempt to address this issue. An approach, which appears to be gaining ground currently is the aspect-oriented, programming approach suggested by Kiczalez et al. [14]. In this approach program fragments can be combined with an existing piece of software, resulting in a new software system that has the program fragments included in the appropriate locations in the original program. However, these approaches have not yet evolved beyond the research state and adequate solutions for superimposing [15] behavior associated with roles on components are lacking.

Frameworks and Roles

Why roles are useful and how they can be used during design and implementation was described earlier. In this section we argue that using roles together with object-oriented frameworks is useful. Object-oriented frameworks are partial designs and implementations for applications in a particular domain [16].

By using a framework, the repeated reimplementation of the same behavior is avoided and much of the complexity of the interactions between objects can be hidden by the framework. An example of this is the *Hollywood principle* ("don't call us, we'll call you") often used in frameworks.

Developers write components that are called by the framework. The framework is then responsible for handling the often complex interactions, whereas the component developer has only to make sure that the component can fulfill its role in the framework.

Most frameworks begin at a small scale, as a few classes and interfaces generalized from a few applications in the domain [17]. At this stage the framework is difficult to use because it has hardly any reusable code and the framework design changes frequently. Inheritance is the technique usually used to enhance such frameworks for use in an application. As the framework evolves, custom components, which permit frequent usage of the framework, are added. Instead of inheriting from abstract classes, a developer can now use predefined components, which can be composed using the aggregation mechanism.

Black-Box and White-Box Frameworks

The relations between different elements in a framework are shown in Figure 7.1. The following elements are shown in this figure:

- *Design documents.* The design of a framework can consist of class diagrams (or other diagrams), written text, or merely an idea in the developer's head.

- *Role interfaces.* Interfaces describe the external behavior of classes. Java includes a language construct for this. Abstract classes can be used in C++ to emulate interfaces. The use of header files is not sufficient because these are not involved by the compiler in the type checking process. (The importance of type checking when using interfaces was also argued by Pree and Koskimies [18].) Interfaces can be used to model the different roles in a system (for example, the roles in a design pattern). A role represents a small group of interrelated method interfaces.

- *Abstract classes.* An abstract class is an incomplete implementation of one or more interfaces. It can be used to define behavior common to a group of components implementing a group of interfaces.

- *Components.* As noted before, the term *component* is a somewhat overloaded term and its definition requires care. In this chapter, the only difference between a component and a class is that the API of a component is available in the form of one or more interface

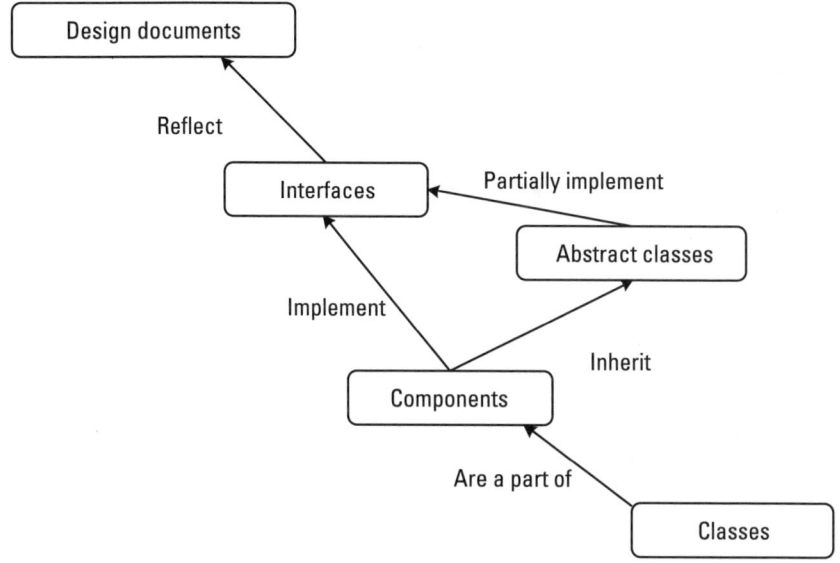

Figure 7.1 Framework elements.

constructs (e.g., Java interfaces or abstract virtual classes in C++). In the same way as classes, components can be associated with other classes. In Figure 7.1, we attempted to illustrate this by the "are a part of" arrow between classes and components. If these classes themselves have a fully defined API, we denote the resulting set of classes as a *component composition.* Our definition of a component is influenced by Szypersi's views on this subject [5] (see also Chapter 1). However, in this definition, Szyperski considers components in general, whereas we limit ourselves to object-oriented components. Consequently, in order to conform with this definition, an OO component can be nothing else than a single class (unit of composition) with an explicit API and certain associated classes that are used internally only.

- *Classes.* Classes are at the lowest level in a framework. Classes differ from components only in the fact that their public API is not represented in the interfaces of a framework. Typically, classes are used internally by components to delegate functionality to. A framework user will not see those classes since he or she deals only with components.

The elements in Figure 7.1 are connected by labeled arrows, which indicate the relations between these elements. Interfaces together with the abstract classes are usually called the *white-box framework*. The white-box framework is used to create concrete classes. Some of these classes are components (because they implement interfaces from the white-box framework). The components together with the collaborating classes are called the *black-box framework*.

The main difference between a black-box framework and a white-box framework is that in order to use a white-box framework, a developer must extend classes and implement interfaces [17]. A black-box framework, on the other hand, consists of components and classes that can be instantiated and configured by developers. The components and classes in black-box frameworks are usually instances of elements in white-box frameworks. Composition and configuration of components in a black-box framework can be supported by tools and are much easier for developers to perform than composition and configuration in a white-box framework.

A Model for Frameworks

The decomposition of frameworks into framework elements in the previous section permits us to specify the appearance of an ideal framework. In this section we do so by specifying the general structure of a framework and comparing this with some existing ideas on this topic.

In [16], it is revealed that multiple frameworks, covering several subdomains of the application, are often used in the development of an application and that a number of problems surround the use of multiple frameworks in an application:

- *Composition of framework control.* Frameworks are often assumed to be in control of the application. When two such frameworks are composed, synchronizing their functionality may be a difficult task.

- *Composition with legacy code.* Legacy code must often be wrapped by the frameworks to avoid reimplementing existing code.

- *Framework gap.* The frameworks provided often do not cover the full application domain. In such cases, a choice must be made between extending one of the frameworks with new functionality, creating a new framework for the desired functionality, or implementing the functionality in the glue code (i.e., in an ad hoc, nonreusable fashion).

- *Overlap of framework functionality.* The opposite problem may also occur if the frameworks provided overlap in functionality.

These problems can be avoided to some extent by following certain guidelines and by adhering to the model we present in this section.

We suggest that rather than specifying multiple frameworks, developers should instead focus on specifying a common set of roles based on the component collaborations identified in the design phase. This set of roles can then be used to specify implementation in the form of abstract classes, components, and implementation classes. Whenever possible, roles should be used rather than a custom interface. Role interfaces should be defined to be highly cohesive (i.e., the elements of the interface should be related to each other) and small and general enough to satisfy all of the needs of the components that use them (i.e., it should not be necessary to create variants of an interface with duplicated parts).

Subsequently, components should use these roles as types for any delegation to other components and to fully encapsulate any internal classes. Not following this rule reduces the reusability of the components because this causes implementation dependencies (i.e., component *A* depends on a specific implementation, namely, component *B*).

This way of developing frameworks addresses, to some extent, the problems identified in [16]. Because role interfaces do not provide implementations, the problem of composition of framework control is avoided although, of course, it may affect component implementations. However, the smaller role interfaces should provide developers with the possibility of either avoiding or solving such problems.

The problem of legacy code can be addressed by specifying wrappers for legacy components, which implement interfaces from the white-box framework. Because the other components (if implemented without creating implementation dependencies) can interact with any implementation of the appropriate role interfaces, they will also be able to interact with the wrapped legacy components. Framework gap can be addressed by specifying additional role interfaces in the white-box framework. Whenever possible, existing role interfaces should be reused. Finally, the most difficult problem to address is the resolving of framework overlap. One option may be to create wrapper components, which implement roles from both interfaces, but in many cases this may only be a partial solution.

The use of roles in combination with frameworks has been suggested before. In [18] the notion of *framelets* is introduced. A framelet is a very small framework (typically no more than 10 classes) with a clearly defined interface. The general idea behind framelets is to have many, highly adaptable small entities that can be easily composed into applications. Although the concept of a framelet is an important step beyond the traditional monolithic view of a framework, we consider the framelet concept to have one important deficiency: It does not take into account the fact that there are components whose scope is larger than one framelet.

As Reenskaug showed in [6], one component may implement roles from more than one role model. A framelet can be considered an implementation of one role model only. Rather than the Pree and Koskimies [18] view of a framelet as a component, we prefer a wider definition of a component, which may involve more than one role model or framelet as in [6].

Another related technology is Catalysis, which was also discussed earlier in this chapter. Catalysis strongly focuses on the precise specification of interfaces. The Catalysis approach would be very suitable for implementing frameworks in the fashion we describe in this chapter. Note, however, that Catalysis is a design-level approach whereas our approach can, and should, also be applied at implementation time.

Dealing with Coupling

From previous research with frameworks in our research group we have learned that a major problem in using and maintaining frameworks are the many dependencies between classes and components. More *coupling* between components means higher maintenance costs (McCabe's cyclomatic complexity [19], the law of Demeter [8]). We have already argued in the section on encouraging the use of roles that the use of role interfaces minimizes coupling and maximizes cohesiveness.

In this section we outline a few strategies for minimizing coupling. Several techniques permit two classes to work together. What these techniques have in common is that for component X to use component Y, X will need a reference to Y. The techniques differ in the way this reference is obtained. The following techniques can be used to retrieve a reference:

1. *Y is created by X and then discarded.* This is the least flexible way of obtaining a reference. The type of the reference (i.e., a specific class) to Y is compiled into a class specifying X but X cannot use a different type of Y without editing the source code of X' class.

2. *Y is a property of X.* This is a more flexible approach because the property holding a reference to *Y* can be changed at run time.

3. *Y is passed to X as a parameter of some method.* This is even more flexible because the responsibility of obtaining a reference no longer lies in the *X'* class.

4. *Y is retrieved by requesting it from a third object.* This third object can, for example, be a factory or a repository. This technique delegates the responsibility of retrieving the reference to *Y* to a third object.

A special case of technique 3 is the delegated event mechanism such as that in Java [20]. Such event mechanisms are based on the observer pattern [21]. Essentially, this mechanism is a combination of the second and the third techniques. *Y* is first registered as being interested in a certain event originating from *X.* This is done using technique 3. *Y* is passed to *X* as a parameter of one of *X*'s methods and *X* stores the reference to *Y* in one of its properties. Later, when an event occurs, *X* calls *Y* by retrieving the previously stored reference. Components notify other components of certain events and those components respond to this notification by executing one of their methods. Consequently the event is decoupled from the response of the receiving components. This coupling procedure is referred to as *loose coupling*.

Regardless of how the reference is obtained, two types of dependencies are seen between components:

1. *Implementation dependencies.* The references used in the relations between components are typed using concrete classes or abstract classes.

2. *Interface dependencies.* The references used in the relations between components are typed using only interfaces. This means that, in principle, the component's implementation can be changed (as long as the required interfaces are preserved). It also means that any component using a component with a particular interface can use any other component implementing that interface. This means, in combination with dynamic linking, that even future components, which implement the interface, can be used.

The disadvantage of implementation dependencies is that it is more difficult to replace the objects to which the component delegates. The new object must be of the same class or a subclass of the original object. When interface dependencies are used, the object can be replaced with any other object implementing the same interface. Interface dependencies are thus more flexible and should always be preferred to implementation dependencies.

In the model presented in this section, all components implement interfaces from role models. Consequently, it is not necessary to use implementation dependencies in the implementation of these components. Using this mechanism is therefore an important step towards producing more flexible software.

Summary

Roles and frameworks are already combined in many programming environments (e.g., Sun's JavaBeans and Microsoft's COM). In this chapter we have argued why this is useful, how it can be performed during both design and implementation, and how the idea of roles complements the notion of frameworks.

We first looked for a motivation for role-based component engineering in the form of a discussion of OO metrics. From this discussion we learned that these metrics generally improve when roles are used. By using roles, complexity is moved to a higher level in the inheritance hierarchy. This leads to a higher level of abstraction and makes the component relations more explicit (because roles are generally more cohesive than classes) while reducing coupling since implementation dependencies can be eliminated.

We then considered how roles could be incorporated in both design and implementation and found that UML in itself is too limited but can be extended in many ways (Catalysis and OORam) to support the role paradigm. Roles can also be supported on the implementation level. This is particularly easy in a language such as Java but can also be supported in C++ if the inconvenience of having extra virtual method calls can be accepted.

We then discussed how roles can help in the structuring of frameworks. By providing a common set of role models (either OORam-style role models or Catalysis-type models), interoperability between frameworks is improved and common framework integration problems can be addressed.

References

[1]   McIlroy, M. D., "Mass Produced Software Components," *Proc. Report on Software Engineering Conf.*, NATO Science Committee, 1968.

[2] Brown, A. W., and K. C. Wallnau, "The Current State of CBSE," *Proc. Asia Pacific Software Engineering Conf., Workshop on Software Architecture and Components,* Los Alamitos, CA, IEEE Computer Society, 1999.

[3] van Gurp, J., and J. Bosch, "Design, Implementation and Evolution of Object Oriented Frameworks: Concepts & Guidelines," *Software Practice & Experience,* Vol. 33, No. 3, 2001, pp. 277–300.

[4] Meyer, B., *Eiffel: The Language,* Upper Saddle River, NJ: Prentice-Hall, 1992.

[5] Szyperski, C., *Component Software Beyond Object-Oriented Programming,* Reading, MA: Addison-Wesley, 1998.

[6] Reenskaug, T., *Working with Objects,* Manning Publications, 1996.

[7] Chidamber, S. R., and C. G. Kemerer, "A Metrics Suite for Object Oriented Design," *IEEE Trans. on Software Engineering,* Vol. 20, No. 6, 1994, pp. 267–271.

[8] Lieberherr, K., I. Holland, and A. Riel, "Object-Oriented Programming: An Objective Sense of Style," *Proc. OOPSLA Conf.,* San Diego, CA, ACM Press, 1988.

[9] OMG, "OMG Unified Modeling Language Specification," Report version 1.3, OMG, June 1999.

[10] Fowler, M., and K. Scott, *UML Distilled—Applying the Standard Object Modelling Language,* Reading, MA: Addison-Wesley, 1997.

[11] Reenskaug, T., "UML Collaboration Semantics—A Green Paper, http://www.ifi.uio .no/~trygver/documents.

[12] D'Souza, D., and A. C. Wills, *Objects, Components and Frameworks: The Catalysis Approach,* Reading, MA: Addison-Wesley, 1998.

[13] JavaSoft, "Add Generic Types to the Java Programming Language," http://jcp.org/jsr/ detail/014.jsp.

[14] Kiczalez, G., et al., "Aspect Oriented Programming," *Proc. ECOOP,* Jyväskylä, Finland, Springer, 1997.

[15] Bosch, J., "Superimposition: A Component Adaptation Technique," *J. Information and Software Technology,* Vol. 5, No. 5, 1999 pp. 257–273.

[16] Bosch, J., et al., "Object Oriented Frameworks—Problems & Experiences," in *Object-Oriented Application Frameworks,* M. E. Fayad, D. C. Schmidt, and R. E. Johnson, Eds., New York: John Wiley & Sons, 1999.

[17] Roberts, D., and R. Johnson, *Patterns for Evolving Frameworks,* Reading, MA: Addison-Wesley, 1998.

[18] Pree, W., and K. Koskimies, "Rearchitecting Legacy Systems—Concepts and Case Study," *Proc. First Working IFIP Conf. on Software Architecture—WICSA'99,* San Antonio, TX, Kluwer Academic Publishers, 1999.

[19] McCabe, T. J., "A Complexity Measure," *IEEE Trans on Software Engineering*, Vol. 2, 1976.

[20] Sun Microsystems, "JavaBeans 1.01 Specification," http://java.sun.com/beans.

[21] Gamma, E., et al., *Design Patterns, Elements of Reusable Object-Oriented Software*, Reading, MA: Addison-Wesley, 1995.

Part 4:
Using Software Components

The main advantage of component-based system development is the reuse of components when building applications. Instead of developing a new system ab initio, components already existing are assembled to give the required result. Systems are being increasingly constructed using off-the-shelf software components but this is not a straightforward procedure. To incorporate a component in a system successfully, a procedure of *selection, composition,* and *integration,* and, finally, *test* and *verification* must be followed. One of the basic difficulties is to obtain predictability. Can we predict the behavior of a component in a system environment by simply knowing the behavior of the component itself and the rules of composition?

This part discusses the procedures involved in the use of software components: component evaluation, component assembly and integration, and testing of component-based systems.

Chapter 8 argues against strongly entrenched misconceptions about component evaluation. Where COTS components are to be used, there will probably be several competing components from which to choose, and so, naturally, a component selection decision is required. This has led to a pernicious myth in software engineering literature and in practice: that component selection implies the necessity of a formal process for component evaluation. A consequence of this myth is the emergence of numerous component evaluation techniques that have little connection with, or relevance to, current component-based design process. The authors demonstrate that while components must be selected, it is assemblies of components that must be evaluated. Component selection is thus only one part of a design procedure, the objective of which is to select sets of components that work together as required in an assembly.

Chapter 9 describes the process of component composition and integration. While software system composition and component integration may be viewed as synonyms, they distinguish the two terms in order to elevate the process of composition, which not only involves integration, or "wiring" components together to create an assembly, but also the unification of the assembly into a composed system. Failures associated with integration led to the development of component standards and frameworks (e.g., EJB and CORBA) to support integration through the imposition of constraints on component form and interaction mechanisms. However many difficulties can be encountered when building assemblies that result from mismatch assumptions that lie deeper than the information available in syntactic component interfaces.

The chapter describes the use of analysis to identify and eliminate potential problems. Similar analysis techniques can also be used to assess the properties of assemblies so that the assemblies can, themselves, be used as components. The chapter concludes with a presentation of a possible solution in which systems are composed from well-understood preexisting components in such a way that the composed system does what it is supposed to, correctly, and as specified by the system commissioners.

In the last chapter of this part, Chapter 10, the authors discuss the problem of system reliability and other nonfunctional characteristics when using components. Even if trustworthy components are integrated, the resulting system itself need not be trustworthy. As shown in Chapter 8, it is not sufficient to evaluate just the component but instead the assembly or system must be evaluated. This chapter stresses the same point by describing how components must be tested in the system environment to ensure system reliability. The author proposes the use of *interface propagation analysis* (IPA), which propagates the corrupted states through the interfaces that connect COTS software components with other types of components. Inverted operational profile testing, in conjunction with IPA, is an effective means of increasing the a priori knowledge of the reliability of a system.

8

Dispelling the Myth of Component Evaluation

Kurt Wallnau and Judith A. Stafford

Introduction

Software systems have become increasingly dependent on software components supplied by the commercial marketplace, or what we will call COTS software components. Given this, it is of no little concern to understand what, if any, effect commercial software components have on software engineering practices. There is certainly no shortage of opinion regarding this question. In this chapter we critically examine the widely held opinion that rigorous component evaluation is an essential element of CBSE practice. We refer to this opinion as the myth of component evaluation.

Before turning to the main argument we must introduce some terminology:

- *Components* are independently deployed software implementations. *Commercial components* are components that are supported by vendors motivated profit by incentives.

- *Assemblies* are aggregations of components that provide integrated behavior. Assemblies may be acquired "off the shelf," for example,

Web browsers and HTTP servers; but more often they are the product of a design activity.

- *Selection* decisions arise when there are clearly identifiable alternatives among discrete choices. Choosing one component over another involves selection.

- *Evaluation* is the formalized process of quantifying human judgment by assigning value to choices. All selection decisions, for example, whether or not to read this chapter, involve assigning value to choices; evaluation makes this process formal, explicit, and quantifiable.

The myth of component evaluation is based on the reasonable supposition that a system is only as good as its components. That is, while it might be possible for us to construct systems of poor quality from high-quality components, it is unlikely to be the case that we can construct systems of high quality from poor-quality components. More formally, this supposition can be expressed as a logical argument:

- If the quality of software components (in some way) determines the quality of the composed system,
- Then CBSE must provide techniques to reliably and repeatedly select high-quality components.

It is difficult to disagree with either the premise or its conclusion—the first seems true, and the second seems to follow. In fact, we accept this argument, which we call the argument for component selection, as entirely plausible and, for all practical purposes, valid.

However, although we accept the argument for component selection, we utterly reject the validity of the argument that invariably (it seems) follows. This new argument, the argument for component evaluation, uses the previously established conclusion as its premise, and from this draws a new (but, suspect) conclusion:

- If CBSE must provide techniques to reliably and repeatedly select high-quality components,
- Then component evaluation is a distinguished CBSE activity, with distinguished workflows and techniques.

After all, what could be more reasonable than to assume that we must first evaluate what we must select? That this argument has many adherents can be seen from the literature on so-called "component evaluation practice" [1–6]. Many techniques have been defined for building and using models, called *multiple-criteria decision aids,* to evaluate components against explicit norms, or criteria, and to select components that best satisfy these norms. Multiple-criteria decision aids are mathematical models of decisions and have been used in business, public policy, social sciences, and elsewhere to help decision makers obtain insight into critical decisions.

We do not take issue with the usefulness of multiple-criteria decision aids; in fact, we will show later in this chapter how these decision aids can be used to select components. Rather, we reject the myth that component evaluation is a distinguished CBSE activity. Although it may seem paradoxical at first, the need for component evaluation, as that notion is reflected in the literature, does not follow from the need to select high-quality components.

In this chapter we replace naïve component evaluation with a far more general, and effective, notion: assembly evaluation. That is, COTS components do not merely determine (in some way) the qualities of an assembly. Commercial components also determine the design of the assemblies in which they operate. Therefore, a designer is not confronted with a set of component alternatives, but rather with a set of design alternatives. Each such design alternative is an expression of one or more underlying component selection decisions. It is not the components that must be evaluated, but their assemblies.

As we will show in this chapter, the shift in focus from component evaluation to assembly evaluation is not merely a rhetorical device, but is rather a real and necessary consequence of the current state of commercial software component technology. Moreover, this shift in focus also has profound implications on the design process. In our judgment and experience, the design process that emerges from this shift in emphasis is intellectually rigorous, and better reflects the design processes that arise in the actual practice of CBSE.

In this chapter we first describe an abstract model for multiple-criteria decision aids and instantiate this abstract model in the familiar form of a multiple-attribute utility model. We then demonstrate why multiple-criteria aids are insufficient for evaluating commercial software components, and why we must focus our attention instead on evaluating design alternatives, called assemblies. We next turn our attention to the implications of this shift in emphasis on the design process itself. We discuss the relationship between assembly evaluation and design search; this discussion establishes a practical link between component selection and the design process. This, in turn, reestablishes the role of multiple-criteria decision aids in both moderating the design search and in selecting from among the design alternatives (i.e., assemblies) that emerge from this search. We then summarize the main points and build a bridge to a later discussion of component composition.

Multiple-Criteria Evaluation

A considerable literature is associated with *multiple-criteria* decision theory.[1] In this discussion we focus our attention on decision aids for solving decision problems involving a fixed (and usually small) number of alternatives, a class of decision problem often referred to as selection problems.[2] Still, the literature is vast even within the confines of multiple-criteria selection aids, and there is no hope of providing a comprehensive overview of this topic. Nonetheless, a particular genus of decision aid has emerged in software engineering literature, and within this genus a variety of species have been concretely (if not formally) defined and applied. We first describe the genus, and then one particularly successful species. Our purpose in describing both genus and species is to provide the reader with some facility in understanding the general concepts that lie beneath multiple-criteria selection aids, and how these concepts are realized in practical settings.

Genus: Preference Structure-Based Evaluation

The following description is an adaptation of an excellent overview of the topic provided by Morisio and Tsoukias [5]. Their concern was to describe a generic process framework within which a unique species of decision aids could be custom made for particular selection problems. Our concern is merely to extract the main features held in common by these species of decision aid:

1. Also frequently called multiple-objective and multiple-criteria decision making.

2. In contrast, optimization problems involve an uncountable number of alternatives, with each alternative defined as a specific configuration of variables and their values. An example of an optimization problem is choosing a setting on a graphic equalizer (a piece of audio equipment).

1. *A preference structure.* This is the model of the decision—for example, the factors that govern the decision and judgments about these factors.

2. *An aggregation technique.* This is the tool that generates interpretations of the model—for example, classifying or ranking alternatives.

A preference structure emerges from the integration of a set of evaluation attributes, their measures and measurement scales, and a preference relation. We discuss each in turn. We only briefly touch on aggregation techniques, since the species of decision aids found in practice are essentially indistinguishable in their aggregation techniques.

Evaluation Attributes

The result of a selection decision is an outcome. Sometimes the correlation of decision and outcome is so strong that the distinction might seem trivial: The outcome of choosing between chicken and fish for dinner is that we eat a chicken or fish dinner. Sometimes, however, the correlation is not as clear: The outcome of choosing a course of university study is, for example, future opportunities in our careers and for self-fulfillment. Evaluation attributes describe qualities that, in some way, distinguish the "goodness" of these outcomes. It is worth emphasizing that the attributes are essentially descriptive of the qualities of outcomes; they are only incidentally descriptive of the qualities of the options themselves. Consider Figure 8.1, which describes evaluation attributes for a hypothetical component selection decision.

Evaluation attributes are conventionally defined hierarchically, although there is no need to do so. The root of the hierarchy refers to the outcome, and the attributes are qualities that influence the outcome. Basic

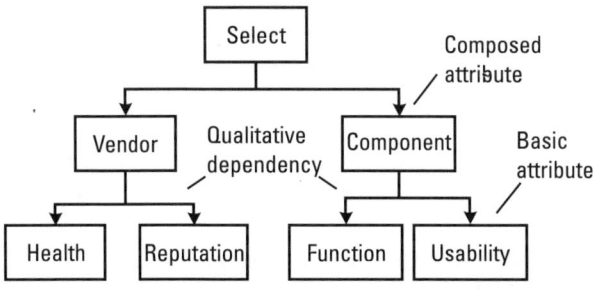

Figure 8.1 Evaluation attributes.

attributes are found at the frontier of the hierarchy; they are basic because they are not decomposed. These are the observable qualities. Composed attributes are found in the interior of the hierarchy. A composed attribute qualitatively comprises other composed attributes or basic attributes. Because the composition is qualitative, it expresses human judgment.[3]

Measures and Measurement Scales

One of the qualities we require of decision aids, when they are applied to engineering decisions, is repeatability. That is, the fact that evaluation attributes are qualitatively composed, or express judgment, does not imply that decisions based on these attributes are nonrepeatable. The basis for repeatability lies in measurement. Consider Figure 8.2, which is based on the previous illustration. Each basic attribute has been assigned a measurement.

We can measure the functionality of a component by counting the number of distinct menu items; we can also compute a usability measure on the basis of the number of observed usability features, such as the "infinite undo" feature. Basic attributes defined by empirical measures are called, oddly enough, *measured attributes*. Although these measures may not be particularly meaningful, they must be repeatable. By virtue of this repeatability, these measures are said to express something essential about a component (i.e., about its "essence"); we therefore say that measured attributes enable essential judgments. In contrast, the measures associated with a vendor are based on judgment, and are therefore nonrepeatable. For example, we might ask system administrators if the component vendor has a good reputation for product support.[4] Depending on which administrator we ask, we may get entirely different answers. Unmeasured attributes lead to nonrepeatable judgments.

Each measurement has a *measurement scale*. For example, the number of menu items and the usability index would probably be expressed using a nominal scale. Performance measures, for example, latency, might be

---

3. In this context, attribute composition is, by definition, qualitative, not quantitative. A composed attribute consisting only of quantitative dependencies would, in effect, be a basic attribute possessing an observable, though aggregate, quality. For example, volume might be quantitatively composed from height, width, and depth, but volume would itself be a basic attribute.

4. We wish to be clear that it is certainly possible to enable essential judgments for vendor health and reputation. In a practical vein, there is a trade-off among measurement rigor, cost of measurement, accuracy of measurement, predictive qualities of the measurement, and the criticality of the decision.

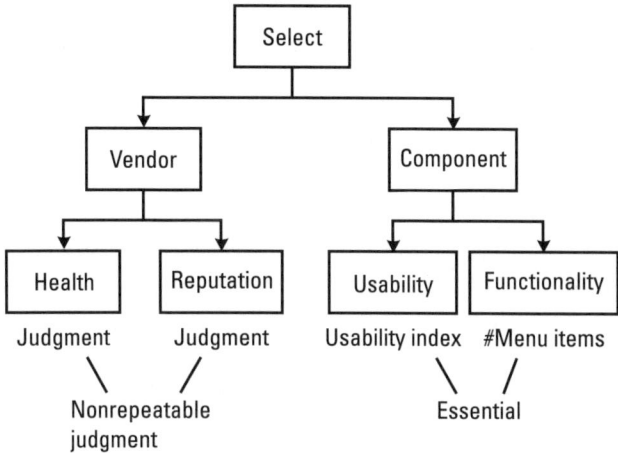

Figure 8.2 Evaluation attributes revisited.

expressed in a ratio scale. We will not dwell on the topic of measurement scales other than to observe that a failure to consider the effect of scale type on operations performed on, and interpretations of, measures can seriously compromise the effectiveness of a decision aid. Kontio describes clearly the issues involved in selecting appropriate measurement scales for multiple-criteria evaluation [3].

Preference Relation

We now leave the realm of measurement and enter into the realm of formalized judgment. The basis for formalized judgment is the preference relation, S. We use the notation $S(x, y)$ to denote $(x, y) \in S$. Informally, $S(x, y)$ states that x is preferred to y. Examined more closely, S can be constructed from three more primitive relations:

1. $P(x, y)$, *strict preference*, states that x is strictly preferred to y.
2. $I(x, y)$, *indifference*, states that neither x nor y is preferred.
3. $R(x, y)$, *incomparability*, states that x and y are incomparable.

For example, we might define a preference relation $S(x, y) = P(x, y) \cup I(x, y)$ to mean that with respect to preference, two components are related to one another either through strict preference or through indifference.

Preference Structure

A preference structure emerges when we express preference relations in terms of attributes. In the following, we define the set of attributes to be G, and use $g \in G$ to denote a particular evaluation attribute. Informally, we wish to know whether one component is preferred to another with respect to some particular attribute. If we could answer this question for each attribute, we would have a basis for making repeatable selection decisions. Clearly, it is advantageous to restrict G to only measured attributes if our ultimate objective is repeatability; however, this restriction is not strictly required by this genus or the many kindred species of decision aids.

Here we part company with Morisio and Tsoukias only in our formalization of this idea. We do so by redefining preference as a ternary relation constructed from three primitive relations:

1. $P(x, y, g)$, strict preference: x is strictly preferred to y with respect to g,

2. $I(x, y, g)$, indifference: neither x nor y is preferred with respect to g, and

3. $R(x, y, g)$, incomparability: x and y are incomparable with respect to g,

where x and y are components and g is either a measured or unmeasured attribute.

We can now explore ways of quantifying the judgment expressed by the preference structure. For example, if g is a measured attribute, we might treat it as a function whose domain is components that possess that measurable attribute, and whose codomain is the measurement scale associated with the attribute measure. If the measurement scale is numeric (for example, nominal or ratio scale), we might define a preference structure:

$$S(x, y, g) = P(x, y, g) \cup I(x, y, g)$$
$$P(x, y, g) \leftrightarrow g(x) - g(y) \geq k$$
$$I(x, y, g) \leftrightarrow |g(x) - g(y)| < k$$

for some arbitrary sensitivity threshold k, with $\leftrightarrow$ denoting "if and only if." That is, x is preferred to y with respect to g if it outperforms y by at least k units of performance in the scale of g, x and y are indistinguishable (that is, indifferent) if the difference in their performance does not exceed threshold k.

In the more general case, where g is either an unmeasured attribute, or is a measured attribute lacking a numeric measurement scale (e.g., g is of ordinal scale), we can define a further transform function t for the measurement scale of g. That is, we merely replace each occurrence of $g(x)$ with $t(g(x))$ in the above definition of $S(x, y, g)$. In fact, we need not stop here. We can also introduce a substitution rate r_x, sometimes known as a weight or priority, for example, $r(t(g(x)))$. As we will soon see, this is precisely the approach taken in multiple-attribute utility evaluation.

Incidentally, the role of the incomparability relation, $R(x, y, g)$ should now be clear. In cases where only one of x and y possess an attribute g, and where the existence of this attribute is not itself a preference judgment, x and y are, strictly speaking, incomparable. Oddly enough, this aspect of evaluation is usually ignored in component evaluation literature.

Aggregation

It should be clear that the preference relation that emerges from even a moderately complex selection decision could be quite large, given the combinatorial behavior of a preference structure. For example, if we let $|S|$ denote the cardinality of preference structure, that is, the set of triples $S(x, y, g)$ constructed for a particular evaluation, then:

$$|S| = \frac{m \times n!}{2 \times (n - 2)!} \qquad (8.1)$$

for n components and m attributes. So, for $n = 5$ components and $m = 20$ attributes, $|S| = 200$, which is quite a lot of data. An aggregation technique produces an overall, or aggregate preference, for a preference structure, and provides concise roll-up views of different aspects of a decision model. Many aggregation techniques are available, and the decision of which to use depends on the kinds of information we wish to extract from the preference structure. An aggregation technique that generates a total ordering of components in S may be different than one that partitions S into the singleton set "best" and the remainder set "rest." A small hint of the ingenuity possible can be seen in Roy's "outranking" approach and the associated decision aids [7].

Despite this variety, the overwhelming majority of documented component evaluation methods employs only simple variants of the aggregation technique used in the multiple-attribute utility approach to evaluation. We turn to this next.

Species: Multiple-Attribute Utility Evaluation

Although some might disagree, we assert that most industrial and academically published component evaluation methods are local variations of the multiple-attribute utility species [1, 3, 4]. The simplest way to describe this species is through its formulaic expression, in which each evaluation attribute $g_k \in G$ is defined as the triple (w_k, u_k, g_k):

$$U_x = \sum w_k \times u_k \left(g_k(x) \right) \qquad (8.2)$$

where U_x denotes the overall utility of component x, u_k denotes a transform function that maps the scale of attribute measure g_k to a universal utility scale u_k, and w_k denotes the substitution rate for g_k. As we will illustrate below, U is usually taken to be a simple interval scale, although a ratio scale is occasionally found. Equation (8.2) aggregates the performance of a component with respect to all of its evaluation attributes and produces an overall, aggregate measure of utility for that component.

The overall aggregation function, that is, the aggregation function over the entire preference structure, is a simple matter of "more is better." The preference structure most frequently associated with multiple-attribute utility is as follows:[5]

$$S(x, y, g) = P(x, y, g) \cup I(x, y, g) \qquad (8.2a)$$

$$P(x, y, g) \leftrightarrow U_x > U_y \qquad (8.2b)$$

$$I(x, y, g) \leftrightarrow U_x = U_y \qquad (8.2c)$$

which states that x is preferred to y if it has a higher utility, and x and y are indifferent if they have the same utility.

We should mention that there is no magic in defining utility functions, although there may be some art (see the fine monograph by Edwards and Newman [8]). Consider Figure 8.3, which illustrates a simple linear utility transform function for usability on the left, and a bilinear transform function

---

5. We are guilty here of oversimplifying the simplification. Not all multiple-attribute utility approaches employ such a simple scheme of aggregation. The analytic hierarchy process (AHP) requires pair-wise comparisons, leading to a complex aggregation process alluded to in (8.1), as discussed earlier.

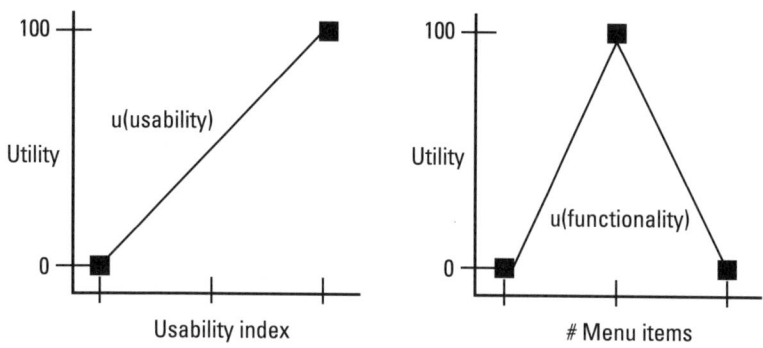

Figure 8.3 Simple utility transform functions.

for functionality on the right (which reflects the judgment that more is not always better). For nonmeasured attributes we simply express component performance directly in utility scale.

As can be seen in Figure 8.3, there has been a steep drop-off in complexity from the general concepts of multiple-criteria evaluation in the genus to multiple-attribute utility species. For example, in place of many pair-wise comparisons, each component can be independently evaluated. The resulting simplicity is no doubt part of the appeal of multiple-attribute utility approaches to evaluation. There are, however, many pitfalls lurking in this simplicity. Among the assumptions underlying the validity of the multiple-attribute utility approach are independence of evaluation attributes, independence of selection decisions, and feasibility of all selection options. In practical settings, all of these assumptions (and others as well) will almost certainly be violated.

We might make an effort to expand on these pitfalls and give tips on how to avoid them. Ultimately, however, that would be missing the key point. And that point is that the problem lies not with multiple-criteria evaluation, but with the notion that component evaluation is itself fundamentally and irretrievably flawed. We now substantiate this claim, and then set matters right.

Exploding the Myth of Component Evaluation

We must now demonstrate that while component selection is an important activity in the design process, component evaluation is not. We emphasize again that by evaluation we mean a formal, explicit, and quantifiable assignment of value to choices. In the following argument, we assume that candidate components have found their way into a design decision-making process. Clearly, for this to be so there must have been some earlier selection decisions; and, naturally, some evaluative process governed these selections. What we argue against is the assumption that these "evaluative processes" are, of necessity, formal, explicit, and quantifiable. Instead, we argue that whatever formal decision processes are at work would be more productively applied to assemblies of components rather than individual components.

What follows is a logical argument that, while falling short of being demonstrable, is certainly highly plausible. It conforms to our direct experience working on large-scale industrial projects, and to our post mortem assessments of successful and unsuccessful industrial projects; in each of these projects, the use of commercial software components was a significant element of the system under development. To make this argument, we will introduce several conceptual distinctions and the graphical and notational devices to represent them.

Components, Assemblies, Properties, and Determinants

To begin, consider a simpler-than-real-world situation consisting entirely of commercial software components and the systems assembled from these components. In this world, the components exist prior to a development activity, the system exists after development is complete. Now, we know that one system will interact with other systems. It is often convenient to represent this idea through hierarchical abstraction, that is, as systems, subsystems, sub-subsystems, and so forth.[6] Because the scope of a system, or its relative position in a hierarchy of systems, is not material to what follows, we will use the term *assembly* in place of *system*. That is, commercial components are assembled into assemblies.

We know that assemblies, once they exist, will exhibit a variety of properties: functionality, reliability, usability, and so forth. We know that commercial components also exhibit properties: functionality, reliability, usability, and so forth. Because assemblies do not exist independent of their constituent components, we can be sure that the properties of an assembly are determined, in some way, by the properties of the components

---

6. In this view a "system of systems" is a system comprising a collection of systems, each of which plays the role of a subsystem.

themselves. Although this observation seems quite obvious, is it surprising that its consequences have not been fully understood (or, at least, reflected) in the literature on component evaluation.

The situation as we have described it is depicted in Figure 8.4. Assembly A, depicted as a dashed box, comprises components C_1 and C_2, depicted as solid boxes. The assembly possesses a set of properties P_A, and C_1 and C_2 possess sets of properties P_1 and P_2, respectively. We said above that P_A is determined, in some way, by P_1 and P_2. This vague notion is expressed by the equation $P_A = D(P_1, P_2)$.[7]

Dispensing with Inconsequential Component Evaluation

We can now inquire, informally, about how strongly correlated P_A is with P_1 and P_2. If the correlation is exceedingly weak, then the selection of C_1 in favor of some other components that might have played the same role in A can be made without too much regard for P_A. That is, we could decouple the selection decision for C_1 from other decisions pertinent to the development of A. We could, in this case, evaluate these competing components using multiple-attribute utility evaluation. This is, however, a logical absurdity. To say that P_1 is only weakly determinant of P_A is to say that the selection of C_1 is not of significant consequence to the design of A. If this is so, it makes no sense to use rigorous evaluation technologies such as those described above for inconsequential selection decisions. In fact, many such largely inconsequential selection decisions arise in practice, for example, selection of a

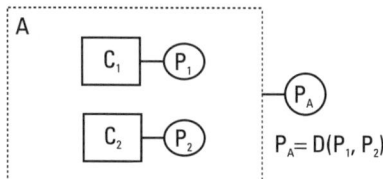

Figure 8.4 Assembly properties determined by component properties.

---

7. It might be argued that P_A is not wholly determined by P_1 and P_2, but may be determined by other factors as well. In particular, some $p \in P_A$ may be determined by an interaction between C_1 and C_2, for example, "p = A can deadlock." This is a subtle point best deferred to a later discussion of component composition. Whether P_A is wholly determined by P_1 and P_2 or is determined by P_1 and P_2 and other factors is immaterial to the present discussion, because in both cases, P_1 and P_2 play a role in determining P_A.

graphical user interface control. In these situations the investment in rigorous and repeatable evaluation would be senseless.

What remains, then, are situations in which the correlation between P_A and P_1 (and P_2) is sufficiently strong to be of interest to the designer of A, and it is for these situations that the value of repeatable, formal component evaluation should be manifest. To see why this is not the case, we must introduce a distinction that is often ignored in evaluation literature: an abstract interface versus a concrete (or "real") interface.

Distinguishing Abstract from Concrete Interfaces

In Figure 8.4, P_1 and P_2 denote the properties of components. These properties constitute, in effect, the interfaces of these components. Here we are going beyond the conventional idea of interface as "API" (application programming interface); we use the term *interface* to encompass the visible properties of P_1 and P_2 that may determine P_A. In our use of the term, the API of a component is just one property (or set of properties) of that component.

When we specify evaluation attributes, we are, in effect, defining an abstract interface; it is an interface of a hypothetical exemplar of the class of component being selected. This exemplar interface defines the norms that must be satisfied by real components, and our evaluation activity quantifies the degree to which a component satisfies the norms set by its exemplar.

The situation as we now have it is depicted in Figure 8.5, in which C_2 is not shown to simplify the presentation. The premise of component evaluation is that P_A can be predicted on the basis of P_{E1} and P_{E2}, the norms established by hypothetical exemplars. That is, the specification of P_{E1} and P_{E2} is germane to the design of A, and all that is required is that we demonstrate that selected components satisfy these norms. Because this is just what we do when we evaluate components, then it would seem that component evaluation is instrumental in the design of A. This is the heart of the myth of component evaluation.

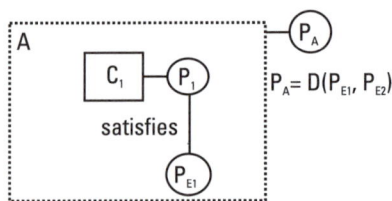

Figure 8.5 Satisfaction of normative abstract interface.

This notion of evaluation breaks down for two reasons, either of which would be sufficient to demonstrate the fallacy of component evaluation and, in addition, demonstrate the need for assembly evaluation in place of component evaluation. So that the myth of component evaluation is fully exploded, however, we elaborate both reasons: The first concerns the impact of partial rather than complete satisfaction of exemplar interfaces, and the second concerns the inherent incompleteness of exemplar interfaces.

Partial Satisfaction of Evaluation Attributes

As noted, P_{EI} defines an ideal interface. The task of evaluation is to select the component that best satisfies this ideal. We can assume, therefore, that in Figure 8.5, C_1 was selected from among its competitors because it came closest to satisfying P_{EI}. To come close to a norm is not the same as equaling the norm.[8]

In both theory and practice, then, an inevitable variance exists between the norms specified by an abstract interface (the evaluation attributes) and the concrete interface of candidate components. Satisfaction is not, therefore, an "all or nothing" affair—it is not merely a matter of acceptance testing. Therefore, a more accurate representation of satisfaction is depicted in Figure 8.6, which shows satisfaction as a condition of variance between a concrete interface and its abstract counterpart.

Under the circumstances of Figure 8.6, it is hardly reasonable to expect P_A to be determined by P_{EI} and P_{E2} alone. Instead, it is determined by P_{EI} and P_{E2}, and also the variance of P_1 and P_2 from these ideals. Because each candidate will, in general, exhibit a different variance, we must expect the assembly properties to likewise vary. It is plain, then, that the selection of a component will influence the properties of the assembly—and will in effect result in a unique assembly for each possible component selection decision. In this situation, we cannot select a component without first selecting the assembly; or, more correctly, assembly selection supplants component selection. The problem of component selection, and therefore component evaluation, has been shifted to assembly selection, and therefore assembly evaluation.

---

8. If a component is required to absolutely satisfy some evaluation attribute, then that attribute imposes a feasibility requirement on the component. Such attributes impose necessary conditions, not preference conditions, on components. As can be seen by examining (8.1), there is no place for necessary conditions in multiple-attribute utility evaluation. (For example, what is the substitution rate of a necessity?)

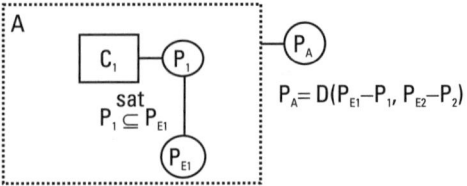

Figure 8.6 Accommodating variance from evaluation norms.

Fundamental Exemplar Incompleteness

In practice, we will find that the concrete interface of a component will include properties not found in any abstraction of that interface. It is widely understood that "formal" interface specification languages lack the abstractions to describe all of the properties that may appear in a concrete interface and that may be determinant of an assembly property (e.g., reliability, performance, resource consumption, and so forth). Beyond that, we have time and again discovered that component properties that we have been taught as computer scientists to regard as "implementation details," and therefore sublingual to specifications, have in fact found expression (usually unhappy expression) in the properties of their assemblies. Implementation details such as "uses kernel threads instead of application threads" have been known to cause assemblies to fail [9]. Whether such properties reflect implementation details or not is arguable; what is not arguable is that they appear, by virtue of their impact on assemblies, in the concrete interface of a component. This lamentable situation is depicted in Figure 8.7.

In Figure 8.7, we have (artificially) partitioned the concrete interface of C_1 into to sets: P_1, the properties which correspond to the exemplar, and P_{H1}, those which will be visible and determinant of P_A but that are not found in

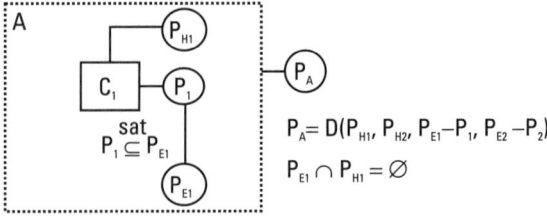

Figure 8.7 The inevitability of hidden properties.

P_{EI}. We say this situation is lamentable because the state of the art in software component technology, to say nothing of the state of the practice in the commercial component marketplace, is such that P_{HI} can be a large set. Moreover, P_{HI} is usually hidden from view until an unexpected emergent property in P_A highlights its existence. It is preposterous to ignore these properties simply because we lack the language to express them or the foresight to anticipate them. And this is precisely what the myth of component evaluation would have us do.

It is apparent from a study of function D in Figure 8.7 that we can no longer sustain the idea that components can be selected independently of assembly selection and that, in fact, a more reasonable approach is to evaluate assemblies and treat component selection as a "side effect" of the design process. Moreover, the presence of a hidden concrete interface (P_{HI}) provides clues as to the nature of this design process. We turn to this next.

Assembly Evaluation and Search

Having taken the trouble to dispel the myth of component evaluation, we should be careful to replace it with something authentic. Ignoring for the moment the existence of the hidden interface, we might be inclined to conclude that we need simply to shift the focus from component evaluation to assembly evaluation. That is, in place of hypothetical component exemplars and their abstract interfaces, we specify hypothetical assembly exemplars with their abstract interfaces. Unfortunately, things are not so simple, because assemblies may be, and most likely will be, composed into higher level assemblies. Thus, what appears as an assembly at one level of abstraction will be a component at another. If we are not careful, we will simply reintroduce the myth of component evaluation elsewhere in a new form.

This is more obvious when we consider the hidden interface. What this interface represents, in fact, is the set of unknown but potentially determinant properties of a component. From the designer's point of view, another name for this might be the *risk potential* of a component. The risk potential of an assembly based on that component is, of course, positively correlated with the magnitude of the hidden interface of that component. This is an important clue that leads us to conclude that the evaluation of assemblies will be linked, in some way, to evaluating the magnitude of the hidden interface—that is, to evaluating the risk presented by a component and therefore to an assembly on which it is based.

How can the magnitude of the hidden interface be assessed? Consider that the hidden interface consists of both known unknowns, that is, known risks, and unknown unknowns, or unknown risks. A known risk might be an unanticipated performance problem with a component; the property is known and is of itself not a risk, but its mitigation may be uncertain, and this uncertainty presents the risk. An unknown risk is what the performance problem was prior to its discovery. It is obviously problematic to assess the magnitude of a hidden interface (that is, the nature of unknown unknowns) beyond this simple rule of thumb: Complex components will probably have larger hidden interfaces than simple components.

Therefore, the criteria for selecting an assembly (and its components) cannot be the magnitude of the hidden interface. We must adopt a more dynamic view of assembly evaluation—one that accommodates the process of discovering the hidden interface. In brief, we must find a way to incorporate assembly evaluation into a discovery process. To that end, it is worthwhile to ponder the following quotation from the essay "The Science of Design" by Herbert Simon, a man who knew a thing or two about design [10]:

> Design procedures in the real world do not merely assemble problem solutions from components but must search for appropriate assemblies. In carrying out such a search, it is often efficient to divide one's eggs among a number of baskets—that is, not to follow out one line until it succeeds completely or fails definitively, but to begin to explore several tentative paths, continuing to pursue a few that look most promising at a given moment. If one of the active paths begins to look less promising, it may be replaced by another that had previously been assigned a lower priority.

If we believe Simon, and if we accept the logic of the argument just presented, we are led to the conclusion that assembly evaluation involves at least two aspects. In one aspect, we view the assembly as a point of departure for further design exploration. We evaluate this aspect of assemblies in terms of the value (in terms of reducing risk, for example) that we assign to the search that will follow from that point. In another aspect, we view the assembly as a destination, perhaps a design, or a prototype, or a full-fledged implementation. We evaluate this aspect of assemblies in the more familiar terms of satisfaction of some abstract, normative assembly interface.

As we will see in the next section, multiple-criteria evaluation can play a positive role in both aspects of evaluation.

Multiple-Attribute Evaluation and Beyond

We have almost reached the terminus of our argument, not because there is no more to be said, but because what must follow lies in the realm of design process, which has a significantly broader scope than the putative subject of this chapter, component evaluation. This was, of course, our objective. However, some readers may have inferred that we believe that multiple-criteria evaluation is unsuitable for, or irrelevant to, component-based design. We did not mean to imply this. While we hedge our bets on the usefulness of multiple-attribute utility, other forms of multiple-criteria evaluation appear to play a role in the science of design.

Figure 8.8 depicts a fragment of a design search space drawn from the extended case study of component-based design presented by Wallnau et al. [11]. At the risk of oversimplification, we say that each of the boxes represents a stable assembly[9]—they constitute a set of design decisions that address one or more design risks and move the design forward toward the goal of establishing that at least one assembly is feasible. Each assembly has associated with it one or more feasibility attributes (not shown), whose values are defined in strong three-value logic: *true, false,* or *unknown.* The design process terminates at a leaf when all feasibility attributes are evaluated as *true.* In this illustration, the design (search) process is mediated by a multiple-criteria evaluation function expressed as logic equations. While this is not multiple-criteria evaluation in the genus described earlier, it is a multiple-criteria process nonetheless.

There is also room for other forms of multiple-criteria evaluation. Although we did not do so in [11], we could have applied architecture-based evaluation methods to each assembly depicted in Figure 8.8. That is, each

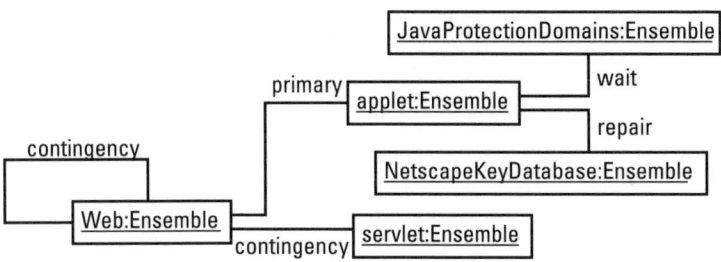

Figure 8.8 Fragment of design (assembly) search space.

---

9. In Figure 8.8, "ensembles" in this illustration are equivalent to "assemblies."

node in Figure 8.8 has associated with it a more detailed view containing a set of components and their interactions. The resultant "component and connector" views are amenable to a variety of architecture-based analysis techniques [1, 12, 13]. These techniques may offer greater insight into the performance of particular assemblies with respect to key attribute goals than could be obtained by a preference-structure-based evaluation method. The point here is to recognize component selection as being performed in the context of design selection, and to understand and accept that the use of components does not require a separate and distinct form of design evaluation, a myth we have attempted, in this chapter, to expunge from our conception of CBSE.

Summary

In exposing (and, we hope, exploding) the myth of component evaluation, we have not succeeded in simplifying matters. Instead, we have made it apparent that the selection of components involves an evaluative activity no less difficult than that which arises in the evaluation of design alternatives. We have shown that, in fact, component selection is subjunctive to assembly selection and therefore to assembly evaluation, and that assembly evaluation is bound up with both the design process and its end products. However, if we have not simplified matters, we have at least replaced a mythical conception of component evaluation with something authentic.

References

[1]   Balsamo, S., P. Inverardi, and C. Mangano, "An Approach to Performance Evaluation of Software Architectures," *Proc. Workshop on Software and Performance*, Santa Fe, CA, 1998.

[2]   Jeanrenaud, A., and P. Rmanazzi, "Software Product Evaluation Metrics: Methodological Approach," *Software Quality Management II. Building Quality into Software 2*, Vol. 776, 1995, pp. 59–69.

[3]   Kontio, J., "A Case Study in Applying a Systematic Method for COTS Selection," *Proc. 18th Int. Conf. on Software Engineering*, Berlin, Germany, IEEE Computer Society, 1996.

[4]   Min, H., "Selection of Software: The Analytic Hierarchy Process," *Int. J. of Physical Distribution and Logistics Management*, Vol. 22, No. 1, 1992, pp. 42–52.

[5] Morisio, M., and A. Tsoukias, "IusWare: A Methodology for the Evaluation and Selection of Software Products, *IEE Proc. Software Engineering*, Vol. 144, No. 3, 1997, pp. 162–174.

[6] Rowley, J. E., "Selection and Evaluation of Software," *ASLIB Proc.*, Vol. 45, 1993, pp. 79–81.

[7] Roy, B., "The Outranking Approach and the Foundations of the ELECTRE Methods," *Theory and Decision,* Vol. 31, Dordrecht, The Netherlands: Kluwer, 1991, pp. 49–73.

[8] Edwards, W., and J. R. Newman, "Multiattribute Evaluation," *Series on Quantitative Applications in the Social Sciences,* Thousand Oaks, CA: Sage Publications, 1982.

[9] Hissam, S. A., and D. Carney, "Isolating Faults in Complex COTS-Based Systems," *J. of Software Maintenance: Research and Practice*, Vol. 11, No. 4, 1999, pp. 183–199.

[10] Simon, H. A., *The Sciences of the Artificial,* 3rd ed., Cambridge, MA: The MIT Press, 1996.

[11] Wallnau, K. C., S. A. Hissam, and R. C. Seacord, *Building Systems from Commercial Components*, Reading, MA: Addison-Wesley, 2001.

[12] Bertolino, A., et al., "An Approach to Integration Testing Based on Architectural Descriptions," *Proc. 1997 Int. Conf. Engineering of Complex Computer Systems*, Lake Como, Italy, IEEE Computer Society, 1997.

[13] Kazman, R., "The Architecture Tradeoff Analysis Method," Report CMU/SEI-98-TR-009, Software Engineering Institute, Carnegie Mellon University, 1998.

9

Component Composition and Integration

Judith A. Stafford and Kurt Wallnau

Introduction

Software systems are composed hierarchically using components that might themselves be systems. These *subsystem components* might have been developed in a separate organization and might even have been developed with a specific purpose in mind unrelated to their current usage context. CBSE involves connecting sets of components to create a software system capable of performing some useful function. Component integration is the mechanical task of "wiring" components together by matching the needs and services of one component with the services and needs of others. Integration alone is not sufficient to assure the quality of many details of run-time interactions in software systems composed of assemblies of components.

Component integration and composition are not synonymous. All assemblies are potentially subsystems. There must therefore be a means of determining the properties of assemblies in order to check their run-time compatibility. *Component composition* supports this type of reasoning; it goes one step further than integration in that the result of component composition is a component assembly that can be used as part of a larger composition. Assemblies must be designed in such a way that they can live in a variety of contexts. Once a component assembly has been created it must be possible to reason about how the assembly will affect the systems in which it is used and also how it is affected by these systems.

Component composition is based on the ability to assign properties to the whole based on the properties of the parts and the relationships between the parts. Composition provides a foundation for reasoning about emergent behavior. It is an engineering task beyond the mechanics of wiring components together. In analogy, consider the incompatibility of connecting a very powerful audio amplifier to low-wattage speakers. The speakers will plug in with no problem and at low volumes will probably function acceptably, but if the volume is raised the speakers will most likely be destroyed.

Component integration is based on syntactic information such as method signatures and, when available, supplementary information supplied in a component's interface. Supplementary information will most likely include information such as a description of the function to be performed and types of exceptions thrown. While this information is certainly helpful it is not sufficient for reasoning about properties of the resulting assembly and does not support composition. Indeed, it is often the case, as in the stereo example above, that components whose interfaces are syntactically compatible, in fact, exhibit undesirable behavior when used together. Thus, composition is distinguished from integration primarily by the fact that composition also focuses on emergent assembly-level behavior, making certain that the assembly will perform as desired and that it could be used as a building block in a larger system. The constituent components must not only plug together, they must play well together.

In the previous chapter we described a method for identifying and selecting among feasible design alternatives. In this chapter we look at a different aspect of component-based software development. We describe component mismatch and the mechanisms employed by component technologies to help developers plug components together. We then introduce a new paradigm for composing software components, which we call *predictable assembly from certifiable components* (PACC) and describe *prediction-enabled component technologies* (PECTs), our approach to bridging the integration–composition gap. PECTs support building assemblies that compose software components into assemblies that predictably meet quality requirements.

Component Integration

Integrating components can be illustrated as a mechanical process of wiring components together. It is rarely the case that two components are perfectly matched so the process generally involves more than simply finding two components, which together perform the desired tasks, and then connecting their APIs. It may be necessary to create adaptors to translate data types or to manage control issues. Garlan, Allen, and Ockerbloom [1] report on a variety of difficulties they encountered when developing the Aesop system, which made use of components obtained from outside sources. Two of the difficulties were integration mismatches that prevented the plugging together of components. One mismatch was caused by the incompatibility of the event-based communication mechanisms used in two of the constituent tools; the second was caused by two tools having different assumptions about the form in which data was to be exchanged. The first mismatch was resolved by reverse engineering and the modification of one of the tools; the second was resolved by the development of a translator and the wrapping of the components. Adaptations such as these not only take a considerable amount of time and effort, but they require a great deal of knowledge about the internals of the tools being used. And, in the end the resulting system is complex, difficult to maintain, and functionally compromised.

Component-based system developers have been wiring, prototyping, tweaking, and tuning components into assemblies for years. As generally happens in industries that involve the fitting of parts together, standardization was recognized as a necessary restriction to simplify the building process. Integration mismatches have, to a large degree, been ameliorated by the introduction of component models such as EJB, CORBA, and COM. Component models provide standards for components and a framework into which components can be plugged. The component standard defines what it means to be a component in the particular model; generally speaking, the standard describes the syntax for interfaces and may specify methods that components must implement. A framework defines a set of protocols and services that supports communication between components. Component models enforce a structure on the design of component-based systems that not only makes them easier to build but also easier to maintain over time. Although the introduction of component models has enabled component-based developers to plug components together much more easily than in the past, it is still difficult to get them to play well together.

From Integration to Composition

The advent of component standards and frameworks has moved component technology many steps forward so that wiring problems are becoming a difficulty of the past. What is emerging in their place is the more important problem of predicting the emergent behavior of assemblies. The problem of reasoning about how well components will play together is the most important problem facing component-based system developers today. It is in resolving this problem that CBD will make the transition from integration to composition. The value of a component marketplace will only be realized when components can be predictably and reliably purchased and used to build larger and more complex systems by organizations that specialize in composition rather than programming.

The desire to move beyond integration to composition is hampered by the fact that component interfaces do not provide enough information to predetermine the consequences of using two components together, let alone a group of components. An interface normally provides enough information to determine if the component can be wired to some other component. For example, the CORBA IDL provides syntax for object encapsulation, which uses language-independent specification of method signatures and can be embodied by a variety of objects. What is missing is a parallel form of specification that supports reasoning about emergent properties of the assemblies in which it is used.

This current view of component interfaces has proved to be inadequate. Integration decisions based on this level of information alone have often resulted in assemblies with unexpected behavior or of unacceptable quality. The reason for this is the lack of concern with the architecture of the assembly and its effects on the behavior of individual components. In addition to the wiring problem cited in the previous section encountered by Garlan et al. [1] while developing Aesop, they experienced a variety of other serious difficulties in getting the components to work together. Various aspects of their experience are likely to resonate with anybody who has attempted to build a component-based system. As mentioned above, two of the problems prevented the components from being plugged together. The remaining problems were related to their inability to build the system as they intended because of the assumptions components made about the environment in which they would be used.

In their report, Garlan et al. [1] describe four classes of structural assumptions that came into play during the integration of their system: the nature of components (infrastructure, control model, and data model), the nature of connectors (protocols and data models), the architecture of the assemblies (constraints on interactions), and the run-time construction process (order of instantiations). By the time they had a working version of Aesop—after working around the integration mismatches and component assumptions—it was bloated, difficult to maintain, and suffered from poor performance.

Inverardi, Wolf, and Yankelevich [2] describe the use of formal architectural description and analysis to uncover what they call *behavioral mismatch* among components used to build the compressing proxy. We distinguish this type of problem, as well as most of the problems encountered by Garlan et al. [1], from component mismatch. Most of these difficulties did not prevent the plugging of the components together—what we call component mismatch—but rather prevented the system from meeting its functional and extrafunctional requirements. To make this distinction clear, we contrast the integration mismatch encountered by Garlan et al., which prevented them from plugging components together because of the use of different data formats, with the behavior of the compressing proxy, discussed in the next paragraph, which exhibited an undesirable emergent property—a potential for deadlock. In the latter case, there was no problem with wiring the components together. The use of sophisticated analysis techniques provides the means of predicting the potential for run-time failure.

The compressing proxy was designed to improve performance of Web browsers through the transparent compression and decompression of transmitted data. The mismatch allowed the proxy to deadlock—not a positive feature for an assembly designed to improve performance. Figure 9.1 contains a graphical representation of the compressing proxy. Data to be transmitted over the Web enters the proxy by way of the filter on the left. It is then fed into another filter that acts as an adaptor that supports the use of the GZIP application, which performs data compression. Careful analysis revealed the potential for deadlock because the adaptor blocked while supplying data to GZIP. The adaptor could not then receive any compressed data until all the data had been read by GZIP. GZIP was not allowed to offload zipped data over connection 3 until all the data had been read from the adaptor via connection 2. This meant that any attempt to process a file larger than the capacity of the GZIP buffer would cause the system to deadlock. Based on this finding the adaptor was replaced by a nonblocking version and the proxy functioned as intended. This is not a mismatch of components. In fact, under many circumstances the proxy will function correctly. It is a mismatch with the requirements of the system. If the requirements are changed to restrict transmission to small enough files, the potential for deadlock disappears.

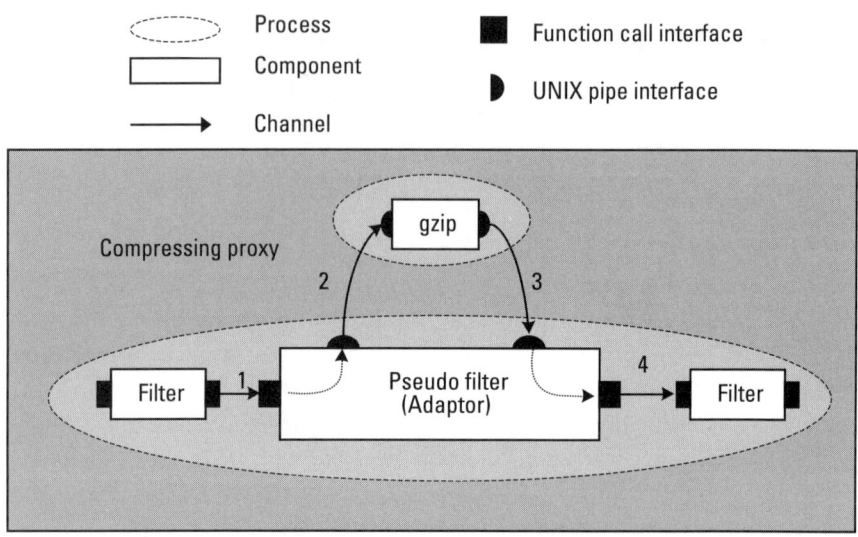

Figure 9.1 The compressing proxy. (From [3] and supplied by Alexander L. Wolf.)

The lesson learned from this and the experiences of Garlan et al. [1] is that careful analysis of the assumptions components make about the context in which they are to be used can help prevent design errors and result in building the right product faster. Garlan et al. point out:

> Architectural mismatch stems from mismatched assumptions a reusable part makes about the structure of the system it is to be part of. These assumptions often conflict with the assumptions of other parts and are almost always implicit, making them extremely difficult to analyze before building the system [1].

A component must express such assumptions as buffer size or expected data formats that it makes about any environment in which it is to be used and it must also be able to express its effects on these environments. Without an expression of behavioral properties it is not possible to encapsulate component behavior because it is not possible to encapsulate something that cannot be represented in the encapsulation mechanism. This lack of expressiveness results in component property leaks, which may in turn become sources of implicit component dependency. Unspecified, but real, assumptions may obscure the contribution that a component makes to some emergent property of the assembly.

The success of a component marketplace depends on having trustworthy claims for component properties and global analysis techniques to support reasoning about the emergent properties of assemblies before component acquisition and integration [4–7].

Predictable Assembly from Certifiable Components

We are studying approaches to ensuring that assemblies of components play together as expected and that the properties of assemblies be made explicitly available to support hierarchical system composition. Informally, compositional reasoning posits that if we know something about the properties of two components, $c1$ and $c2$, then we can define a reasoning function f such that $f(c1, c2)$ yields a property of an assembly comprising $c1$ and $c2$.

Many would argue that compositional reasoning is the holy grail of software engineering. This argument usually has as its unspoken premise that only a fully formal and rigorous reasoning function is acceptable. If we follow this premise, then progress will indeed be slow. Instead, we suggest that it is possible to adopt a more incremental approach involving many levels of formality and rigor. To begin, we suggest that three interlocking questions must be answered:

1. What types of system quality attributes are developers interested in predicting?
2. What types of analysis techniques support reasoning about these quality attributes, and what component property values do they require as input parameters?
3. How are these component properties specified, measured, and certified?

These three questions are interdependent. The types of compositional reasoning that can be accomplished ultimately depend on the types of component properties that can be measured. Conversely, it is the reasoning techniques that determine what component properties are material in the first place. Therefore, the answers to these three questions, which are mutually informing (and constraining), will provide a foundation for a sustainable improvement in predicting the properties of component assemblies and for confidence in the software components that make up these assemblies. However, answering these questions will be an ongoing process. New prediction models will require new or improved component measures, which will in turn lead to more accurate prediction, and to a demand for better or additional prediction models, more precise component measures, and so forth.

Prediction-Enabled Component Technology

A prediction-enabled component technology consists of a component model and an associated analysis model. Many analysis techniques support reasoning about emergent properties of assemblies. These techniques will influence the design of component models, depicted by the lower arc in Figure 9.2; or analysis models might be developed or adapted for application to specific component models as depicted by the upper arc in the figure. The PECT approach is based on two fundamental premises: first, that system quality attributes are emergent properties that are associated with patterns of interaction among components, and, second, that software component technology provides a means of enforcing predefined and designed interaction patterns, thus facilitating the achievement of system quality attributes by construction.

As discussed in the "Component Integration" section, software component models provide a means of composing systems from precompiled parts.

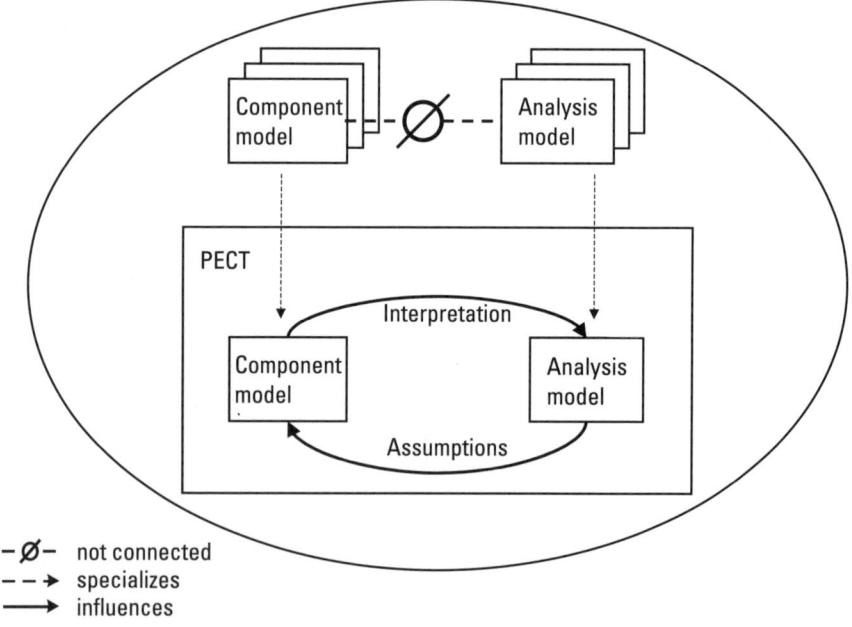

Figure 9.2 Prediction-enabled component technologies.

Component models have been developed to support integration of components that are created in isolation, perhaps in heterogeneous environments and languages. The assumption is that a component makes known, through its interface, all the information required to use (and deploy) its services [8]. However, current component models do not support reasoning about emergent system quality attributes (e.g., performance, modifiability, reliability, and safety). Instead, engineers must wait until the components have been acquired, integrated, and the system as a whole benchmarked, to determine whether a system meets its quality attribute goals.

Software architecture provides a means of analyzing system designs with respect to quality attributes. Indeed, a premise of software architecture is that emergent properties—and our ability to reason about them—adhere to particular, recurring structural patterns. These structural patterns are often referred to as architectural styles, and are usually defined as sets of component and connector types and their allowable patterns of interactions [3, 9, 10]. Thus, a synchronizing concurrent pipeline style might be appropriate for systems with stringent latency requirements, since that style supports rate monotonic analyses (RMAs) [11]. On the other hand, a three-tiered style might be appropriate for systems in which modifiability of business logic is of paramount concern.[1] Software architecture, however, as yet has had no appreciable impact on software component technology.

The objective of our work is to demonstrate how component technology can be extended to support compositional reasoning. To do this, PECT integrates ideas from research in the areas of software architecture, component certification, and software component technology. The ideas of architecture-based analysis, component certification, and architectural style are not new but their integration is.

Architecture-Based Analysis

Software architecture-based analysis provides a foundation for reasoning about system completeness and correctness early in the development process and at a high level of abstraction. To date, research in the area has focused primarily on the use of ADLs as a substrate for analysis algorithms. The analysis algorithms that have been developed for these languages have, in general, focused on correctness properties, such as liveness and safety [2, 12–14]. However, other types of analysis are also appropriate for use at the architecture level and are currently the focus of research projects. Examples

---

1. We rely on the evocative names of these styles to convey the main point.

include system understanding [15, 16], performance analysis [17, 18], and architecture-based testing [9, 19].

One still unresolved challenge within architecture technology is the bridging of the gap between architectural abstractions and implementation. Specification refinement is one approach that seeks to prove properties of the relationship between abstract and more concrete specifications, across either heterogeneous design notations [20] or homogeneous notations [21]. We are currently exploring an approach to proving properties of concrete specifications or constructive models that involves identifying mappings between analytic models and constructive models in order to produce reasoning-enabled component technologies. Analytic models capture the fundamentals of compositional reasoning techniques: assumptions of the algorithms used as well as the algorithms themselves.

Component Certification

The National Security Agency (NSA) and the National Institute of Standards and Technology (NIST) used the trusted computer security evaluation criteria (TCSEC), a.k.a., the "Orange Book"[2] as the basis for the Common Criteria,[3] which defines criteria for certifying security features of components. Their effort was not crowned with success, at least in part because it defined no means of composing criteria (features) across classes of component. The Trusted Components Initiative (TCI)[4] is a loose affiliation of researchers with a shared heritage of experience in the formal specification of interfaces. Representative of the TCI is the use of pre- and postconditions on APIs [22]. Quality attributes, such as security, performance, availability, and so forth, are beyond the reach of these assertion languages. Voas and Payne have defined rigorous mathematical models of component reliability based on statistical approaches to testing [23], but have not defined models of composing reliability measures. Commercial component vendors are not inclined to formally specify their component interfaces, and it is not certain that it would be cost effective for them to do so. Shaw observed that many features of commercial components are discovered only through use. She proposed component credentials as an open-ended, property-based interface specification [24]. A credential is a triple (attribute, value, knowledge) that asserts a component has an attribute of a particular value and that this value is known

---

2. For more information, go to http://www.radium.ncsc.mil/tpep/library/tcsec/ index.html.

3. For more information, go to http://csrc.nist.gov/cc/.

4. For more information, go to http://www.trusted-components.org/.

through some means. Credentials reflect the need to address component complexity, incomplete knowledge, and levels of confidence (or trust) in what is known about component properties, but do not go beyond notational concepts. Therefore, despite many efforts, fundamental questions remain. What does it mean to trust a component? Still more fundamental: What ends are served by certifying (or developing trust) in these properties?

Architectural Styles and Component Models

Architectural styles are sets of component types and constraints on how instantiations of those types can be interconnected. Component technology provides the means of realizing architectural-style constraints in software and, in fact, the concept of architectural style is quite amenable to a component-based interpretation [14]. In our view, a component model can play a role in assembly composition analogous to that played by structured programming languages and compilers in imperative programming—it limits the freedom of designers (programmers) so that the resulting design (program) is more readily analyzed. In one of many possible examples, the EJB specification defines component types, such as session and entity beans,[5] and constraints on how they interact with one another, with client programs, and with the run-time environment. When viewed in this way it is clear that EJB specifies an architectural style.

Prediction-enabled component technologies exploit the relationship between structural restrictions and assumptions of analysis models to compute properties of assemblies based on trusted properties of the assembly's constituent components.

Summary

In summary, component integration and composition are not synonymous. Component integration is the mechanical process of "wiring" components together, whereas composition takes this one step further to ensure that assemblies can be used as components in larger assemblies. A new paradigm for building component-based software is emerging that promises to support building the right software from components the first time and on time. We are developing a model for prediction-enabled component technologies to support this goal. Prediction-enabled component technologies exploit research in the areas of software architecture-based analysis, component

---

5. Components are denoted as *beans* in EJB.

certification, and architectural style to produce component models that are enhanced to support reasoning about both the functional and extrafunctional properties of software systems composed of components.

References

[1] Garlan, D., R. Allen, and J. Ockerbloom, "Architectural Mismatch: Why Reuse Is so Hard," *IEEE Software*, Vol. 12, No. 6, 1995, pp. 17–26.

[2] Inverardi, P., A. L. Wolf, and D. Yankelevich, "Static Checking of System Behaviors Using Derived Component Assumptions," *ACM Trans. on Software Engineering*, Vol. 9, No. 3, 2000, pp. 238–272.

[3] Shaw, M., and D. Garlan, *Software Architecture: Perspectives on an Emerging Discipline*, Upper Saddle River, NJ: Prentice-Hall, 1996.

[4] Crnkovic, I., et al.,(editors), 4th ICSE Workshop on Component-Based Software Engineering: Component Certification and System Prediction, *Software Engineering Notes*, Vol. 26, No. 6, 2001.

[5] Bachman, F., et al., "Technical Concepts of Component-Based Software Engineering," Report CMU/SEI-2000-TR-008, Software Engineering Institute, Carnegie Mellon University, 2000.

[6] Hissam, S. A., J. Stafford, and K. C. Wallnau, "Packaging Predictable Assembly," in *Proc. of First International IPIP/ACM Working Conference on Component Deployment*, Berlin, Germany, June 2002.

[7] Stafford, J., and A. L. Wolf, "Annotating Components to Support Component-Based Static Analyses of Software Systems," Report CU-CS-896-99, Boulder, CO, University of Colorado, 2000.

[8] Szyperski, C., *Component Software Beyond Object-Oriented Programming*, Reading, MA: Addison-Wesley, 1998.

[9] Garlan, D., and M. Shaw, "An Introduction to Software Architecture," *Advances in Software Engineering and Knowledge Engineering*, Vol. I, 1993.

[10] Medividovic, N., P. Oreizy, and R. N. Taylor, "Reuse of Off-the-Shelf Components in C2-style Architectures," *Proc. Int. Conf. Software Engineering*, Boston, MA, IEEE Computer Society, 1997.

[11] Klein, M., et al., *A Practitioner's Handbook for Real-Time Analysis*, Dordrecht, The Netherlands: Kluwer, 1993.

[12] Magee, J., J. Kramer, and D. Giannakopoulou, "Analysing the Behaviour of Distributed Software Architectures: A Case Study," *Proc. 6th IEEE Workshop Future Trends of Distributed Computing Systems*, Tunis, Tunisia, IEEE Computer Society, 1997.

[13] Naumovich, G., et al., "Applying Static Analysis to Software Architectures," *Proc. 6th European Software Engineering Conf.*, Lecture Notes in Computer Science, No. 1301, Springer Verlag, 1997, pp. 77–93.

[14] Wallnau, K. C., et al., "On the Relationship of Software Architecture to Software Component Technology," *Proc. 6th Workshop on Component-Oriented Programming*, Budapest, Hungry, 2001.

[15] Kramer, J., and J. Magee, "Analysing Dynamic Change in Software Architectures: A Case Study," *Proc. 4th Int. Conf. Configurable Distributed Systems*, 1998, pp. 91–100.

[16] Stafford, J., and A. L. Wolf, "Architecture-Level Dependence Analysis in Support of Software Systems," *International Journal of Software Engineering and Knowledge Engineering*, Vol. 11, No. 4, August 1998, pp. 431–453.

[17] Spitznagel, B., and D. Garlan, "Architecture-Based Performance Analysis," *Proc. Conf. Software Engineering and Knowledge Engineering*, San Francisco, CA, 1998.

[18] Balsamo, S., P. Inverardi, and C. Mangano, "An Approach to Performance Evaluation of Software Architectures," *Proc. Workshop on Software and Performance*, 1998.

[19] Vieira, M. E. R., S. Dias, and D. J. Richardson, "Analyzing Software Architectures with Argus-I," *Proc. Int. Conf. Software Engineering*, Los Angeles, CA, IEEE Computer Society, 2000.

[20] Gilham, F., R. Reimenschnider, and V. Stavridou, "Secure Interoperation of Secure Distributed Databases: An Architecture Verification Case Study," *Proc. World Congress on Formal Methods (FM'99)*, Lecture Notes on Computer Science, No. 1708, Berlin, Springer Verlag, 1999.

[21] Philips, J., and B. Rumpe, "Refinement of Information Flow Architectures," *Proc. Int. Conf. Formal Engineering Models*, Hiroshima, Japan, IEEE Computer Society, 1997.

[22] Meyer, B., *Object-Oriented Software Construction*, Upper Saddle River, NJ: Prentice Hall, 1997.

[23] Voas, J., and J. Payne, "Dependability Certification of Software Components," *J. of Software Systems*, Vol. 52, 2000, pp. 165–172.

[24] Shaw, M., "Truth vs Knowledge: The Difference Between What a Component Does and What We Know It Does," *Proc. 8th Int. Workshop on Software Specification and Design*, Schloss Velen, Germany, 1996.

10

Predicting System Trustworthiness

Jeffrey Voas

Introduction

Much of the work during the past 10 years in CBSE and CBD has dealt with functional composability (*FC*) and functional correctness. *FC* is concerned with whether $f(A) \, \xi \, f(B) = f(A \, \xi \, B)$ is true (where ξ is some mathematical operator, and $f(x)$ is the functionality of component x), that is, whether a composite system results with the desired functionality given that the system is created solely by joining A and B.

But increasingly, the software engineering community is discovering that *FC*, even if it were a solved problem (using formal methods, architectural design approaches, model checking, etc.), is still not mature enough for other serious concerns that arise in CBSE and CBD. These concerns stem from the problem of composing "ilities." Ilities are nonfunctional properties of software components that define characteristics such as security, reliability, fault tolerance, performance, availability, and safety.

The problem stems from our inability to know a priori, for example, that the security of a system composed of two components, A and B, can be determined from knowledge about the security of A and the security of B. Why? Because the security of the composite is based on more than just the security of the individual components. There are numerous reasons for this, and here, we will consider factors of component performance and calendar time.

As an example, suppose that A is an operating system and B is an intrusion detection system. Operating systems have some level of built-in authentication security, and intrusion detection systems have some definition of the types of event patterns that warn of a possible attack. Thus, the security of the composition clearly depends on the security models of the individual components. But even if A has a worthless security policy or flawed implementation, the composite can still be secure. How? By simply making the performance of A so poor that no one can log on (i.e., if the intrusion detection system is so inefficient at performing an authentication regardless of the performance of A, then in a strange way, security is actually increased). And if the implementation of A's security mechanism is so unreliable that it disallows all users access, even legitimate ones, then strangely, security is again increased. Whereas these last two examples are clearly not a desirable way to attain higher levels of system security, both do actually decrease the likelihood that a system will be successfully attacked.

And if we again use the example of A as an operating system and B as an intrusion detection system, and we assume that both A and B provide excellent security, we must still accept the fact that the security of B is also a function of calendar time. The reason for this is that new threats and ways to "break into systems" are always being discovered and made public. So even if a mathematical composition scheme such as Security(A) ξ Security(B) = Security(A ξ B) could be created, it is still the case that Security(B) is a function of the version of B that is being composed and of what new threats have arisen.

So the question then comes down to this: Which ilities, if any, are easy to compose? The answer is that none of the ilities is easy to compose and some are much harder to compose than others. Further, there are no widely accepted algorithms for doing this. We have just demonstrated this problem with respect to security. But note that the same holds true for other ilities such as reliability [1]. For reliability, consider a two-component system in which component A feeds information to B and B produces the output of the composite. Assume that both components are reliable. What can we assume about the reliability of the composite? While it is reasonable to assume that the composite system will be reliable, it must be recognized that the components (which were tested in isolation for their individual reliabilities) can suddenly behave unreliably when connected to other components, particularly if the isolated test distributions did not at all reflect the distribution of transferred information after composition. Further, some component behaviors can be termed "nonfunctional" and cannot be observed or do not manifest themselves until after the composition. Such behaviors can undermine the reliability of the composition. Finally, if one of the components is simply the wrong component, although highly reliable, the resulting system will naturally be useless.

In addition to reliability and security, one ility that at least on the surface appears to have the best possibility of successful composability is performance. But even that is problematic from a practical sense. The reason stems from the fact that even if a big-O algorithmic analysis has been performed on a component, its performance after composition depends largely on the relevant hardware and other physical resources.[1] This means that it might be necessary to take into consideration many different hardware variables in developing any certification making even minimal, worst-case claims about the performance of the component. Clearly, this introduces serious pragmatic difficulties.

Note that nonfunctional behaviors are particularly troublesome in COTS software products, for which source code is not available. Nonfunctional behaviors can include malicious code (Trojan horses, logic bombs, etc.) and any other behaviors or side effects not documented. Such behaviors can cause serious problems for system integrators and users and maintainers of systems incorporating substantial quantities of COTS software functionality.

Finally, another worrisome (and related) problem facing CBSE and CBD is the issue of "hidden interfaces." Hidden interfaces are typically channels through which application or component software is able to induce an operating system to execute undesirable tasks or to launch undesirable processes. An example of this would be an application making a request to attain higher levels of permissions than the application should be allowed. Further, hidden interfaces can also be used by rogue developers who know how to activate certain functionality at a remote site (once the software is installed) in a manner totally unknown to the owners of the site.

What Else Can Be Done?

Well, to begin, we will now stop discussing the notion of mathematically composing numerical scores representing the quantification of different ilities for components. We can instead discuss observation-based techniques

---

1. Big-O notation is a function that returns the order of magnitude of a computation, such as a linear search being $O(n^2)$.

that, although also quantitative in nature, will be used in a more qualitative manner. For example, if a piece of software fails only once after 100 tests, instead of trying to create some quantitative score based on this information, we can simply consider that fact to be the result of the testing, and not a number derived from a reliability equation.

Our interest, then, is in creating and deploying techniques that can augment traditional reliability quantification techniques. We wish also to be able to predict the behavior of the software when it is supplied with corrupted information. By doing so we gain new information about how the software will behave, information that is completely different from the information collected during operational profile-based reliability testing. By performing this analysis in addition to reliability testing, we gain a better understanding of the behavior to be expected of the software when confronted with unexpected circumstances caused by a skewed (off-nominal) environment.

When software systems fail, confusing and complex liability problems ensue for all parties that have contributed software functionality (whether COTS or custom) to the system. Potential contributors to the system failure include (1) defective software components, (2) problems with interfaces between components, (3) problems with assumptions (contractual requirements) between components, and (4) hidden interfaces and nonfunctional component behaviors that cannot be detected at the component level.

Our approach here will be to disregard particular reasons for the possible failure of a component or of the interface between components and assume the worst case (i.e., the occurrence of both possibilities). Once such an assumption is made, it is possible to predict, a priori, how the composite system will behave as a result of the failure of a particular component. Let's look briefly at several different techniques for making such predictions.

To begin, we should recognize that more and more software is delivered to system integrators in a form described as a black box. Software components are termed black boxes because they are packaged as executable objects (with licensing agreements forbidding decompilation back to source code). A worthy goal, then, is to provide a methodology for determining how well a system can perform if particular COTS components are of such poor quality that interoperability problems arise.

The technique for assessing the level of interoperability between COTS software components and custom components presented here is designated IPA [2]. IPA perturbs (i.e., corrupts) the states that propagate through the interfaces that connect COTS software components to other types of components. By corrupting data going from one component to a successor component, failure of the predecessor is approximated (simulated), and its impact on the successor can be assessed. Because many of the interoperability issues related to software problems are a result of one component's intolerance of another, our approach enables a determination of the level of intolerance when one component fails and sends "junk" information (or even a lack of information) to its successor.

Note that IPA is simply one type of software fault injection [3]. Before we explain further how IPA works, we will explain the key difference between traditional reliability testing and fault injection, because many readers may think these techniques are equivalent, and while they are complementary, they are by no means equivalent.

To begin, consider the following analogy. Consider a software program to be a dense tropical rain forest. The animals living in the forest represent different behaviors that the software can exhibit. The goal of every software quality assessment technique is then to detect as many as possible of the animals living in the forest. Software testing, then, can be thought of as the process of walking through the forest or even floating over the forest in a hot air balloon and looking for the forest's inhabitants. The lower the balloon flies and the more powerful the binoculars, the more animals that will be discovered (i.e., the better the test-case generation scheme). Likewise the more time spent walking (i.e., more test cases), the more animals will be discovered.

But the smaller the animals are and the better they are concealed by camouflage, the less likely that testing will find them. In contrast, fault injection can be thought of as sending wildly barking dogs into the forest to see what animals they can drive out. Thus, while the goals of testing and fault injection are similar, the results can be vastly different because the methods used for discovery are different.

Note that software fault injection is also a form of accelerated testing. To understand why, consider the following example. Assume that a program is tested 1 million times and that during those 1 million tests, only one input causes the program's state to become corrupted. Not much is learned from those 1 million tests about the robustness of the software to corrupted internal states, only how the software behaved for one particular corrupted state. From the other 999,999 tests, nothing is learned about the robustness of the software.

Testing the software 1 million times to gain one data point of information is unacceptably expensive. Instead, it would be preferable to test the software 1 million times, knowing on each occasion that at least one data state was corrupted, thus providing 1 million data points revealing how robust software was to the injections. This is precisely what software fault injection does. Note that in either case the software is tested 1 million times but that in the latter case, 1 million data points concerning the software's robustness are obtained. In the former, only one piece of data is obtained. (Of course, in the former situation the reliability of the software can be quantified as a result of the 1 million tests.) This demonstrates the fundamental difference between reliability testing and robustness (fault tolerance) testing. Note further that the more reliable the software is, the less robustness testing results can be obtained by traditional software testing. This is an unfortunate circumstance that can fortunately be overcome by using fault injection techniques.

Now let's return to IPA and explain briefly how the process works. Recall that our objective is to determine the impact on one component if a predecessor component were to fail and send corrupted information to the successor component. To do this, we must artificially corrupt the information produced by the predecessor component, send this to the successor, and see how the successor behaves.

To modify the information (states) that components use for intercommunication, write access to those states is required (in order to modify the data in those states). This is obtained by creating a small software routine named PERTURB that replaces, during system execution, the original output state with a different (corrupted) state. By simulating the failure of various software components, we determine whether or not these failures can be tolerated by the remainder of the system. The cos() function (a fine-grained COTS utility for which we do not have access to the source code) can be used in an illustration:

```
double cos(double x)
```

This declaration indicates that the cos() function receives a double float (contained in variable *x*) and returns a double float. Because of C's language constraints, the only output from cos() is the returned value, which is therefore all that fault injection can corrupt.

To see how this analysis works, consider an application containing the following code:

```
if (cos(a) > THRESHOLD) {
    do something
}
```

Our objective is to determine how the application will behave if cos() returns incorrect information. For this, the return value from the call is modified:

```
if (PERTURB(cos(a)) > THRESHOLD) {
    do something
      }
```

Several key issues should now be mentioned with respect to any fault injection function such as PERTURB. Firstly, the value added by having a utility such as PERTURB is, in general, dependent on how well PERTURB mimics corruptions that the utility under consideration (which in this case is cos()) could produce in the real world. Note, however, that there are interesting cases, particularly from safety-critical code, in which, although PERTURB had created corrupt states that in no way reflected how the components could behave while in real operation, the fault injection process was still able to reveal to the designers of the system certain system-level behaviors that were totally unexpected [4]. These behaviors were completely unsafe, and protection against them was essential (since it is still possible that there were unknown and actual output states from the components that could induce similar or identical system behaviors). It is also possible that other hardware components or human activities associated with the system might also be able to force the system into such hazardous states. For example, it is impossible to predict all the human errors that many systems can experience during operation, and because of that, it is also likely that we will fail to predict which system-level behaviors resulting from human error will be unpredictable. Interestingly, an analysis such as IPA can actually partially address this problem, by showing us events never before imagined.

Note that IPA need not only be used to simulate bad information leaving a component. IPA can just as easily simulate other components of the system sending bad information to a COTS component. This then simulates the results of the COTS software receiving bad information from its environment. This is particularly important information in critical systems that are very dependent on COTS functionality, because it is incorrect to assume that in a COTS-based system, all problems that arise are the results of COTS software failure.

Finally, it must be acknowledged that the exhaustive fault injection of software components is just as infeasible as the exhaustive testing of software. Thus here, we are no less restricted in terms of how much analysis can be performed than we are with reliability testing. Therefore the proper approach to maximizing the value added by such a technique is first to identify which portions (functionally speaking) of the system are the most critical, and then analyze how that critical functionality degrades when components on which it depends fail. From there, we can continue to perform more analysis on those critical components, or we can move on to other portions of the system and perform a similar analysis.

The point here is that the space of potential corruptions that can be injected is often a number of times larger than the size of the entire input domain, and therefore intelligent decisions must guide the process. But one thing of which we can be certain is that the results from this technique are viable predictors of the potential future behavior of the software because we have already seen the system behave in that manner as a result of our analysis.

In summary, IPA begins from the assumption that all software components will fail and that the interfaces between them can be defective. By simulating the failure of troublesome COTS components and defective interfaces, we can observe the system's tolerance of their misbehavior. Such an analysis is clearly prudent.

Two Additional Useful Techniques for Predicting Component Interoperability

Finally, we will consider two techniques in addition to IPA that are useful in addressing the composability of components problem.

The entire software reliability field (or what is now termed *software reliability engineering*) is currently evangelizing about techniques that make software programs behave in "reliable" ways (given specific expectations about the environments in which the software will reside). And it is reasonable to design software in the light of where it is likely to execute. After all, why overdesign a software package to handle negative integers reliably if the software will never input negative integers?

Thus, the entire notion of what is reliable software versus what is not reliable software is a function of how the software will be used in the environment in which it will be embedded. This means that component *A* embedded in environment *B* may behave far more reliably than component *A* embedded in environment *C*. This illustrates how fragile the science of quantifying software reliability really is. And, unfortunately, because the science of quantifying software reliability is so imperfect, there is even more confusion as to when a software component is truly "reliable enough" for a specific environment.

This problem is impossible to overcome, but there is yet another problem of even greater magnitude: knowing how a software component will react when it receives inputs that are outside the range of any profile that the original designers anticipated. [Note that here we are not necessarily talking about component input information that is corrupted, but instead input information that is simply outside the nominal operational (probabilistic) range within which reliability testing would normally test the component.] Such profiles can be the result of (1) an oversight on the part of the designers failing to know what the actual operational environment would be (which, of course, is very common when we are talking about generic, use-everywhere software components), and (2) unanticipated radical modifications of the environment. In each case, a priori predictions as to how reliably the software component will behave during its lifetime are no longer trustworthy. This means that all of the previous reliability quantification for the component should be disregarded and any efforts toward "design-for-reliability" of the component cannot necessarily be trusted.

Technique 1

The first technique involves the deliberate inversion of the *operational profile* originally anticipated by the system designers.[2] This technique is most beneficial when the description of the expected profile is accurate. If the defined operational profile turns out to be inaccurate, then the only benefit from doing so would be to learn about potentially dangerous output modes from the software, which might be difficult to detect by other means.

At this point, the reader may ask why we should recommend such. The answer is simple: We wish to force the software to experience unusual yet possible inputs to enable us to learn more about its output behavior. The software is forced to experience these inputs because traditional operational profile testing is highly likely to overlook them due to the low probability of their being selected. This is valuable from a component point of view, because there could well be possible behaviors delivered from a predecessor component that could never be tolerated by any successor component, no matter how robust the successor component is designed to be.

Note that this technique is indeed different from software fault injection. In fault injection, the environment is in a fixed state and the information flowing between components is corrupted. Yet in this technique, there is

---

2. The operational profile for a piece of software is simply a mathematical distrubution representing the probabilistic likelihood that any particular input vector will be fed into the software during operational usage. Therefore an operational profile contains two pieces of information: (1) the domain of the software, and (2) the likelihood that any particular element of the domain will be selected for execution during operation.

no corruption of information, but simply the selection of states flowing between components that are very rare. This is generally a result of the environment itself being in very rare mode. It is here that the fundamental difference between the two analyses lies.

Technique 2

The second technique is simply a combination of the previous technique with IPA. This is a situation in which the software is operating in an unusual input mode while being bombarded with corrupt information. This provides a unique assessment of how robust the software is when it is operating under unusual circumstances and receiving corrupt information.

Thus, knowing how trustworthy a software system built from software components will be involves far more than a simple assessment of the reliability of the component with respect to an assumed operational profile and the assumption that all of the other components with which it interacts will behave properly. It involves knowing how reliably the system can behave when its components are being stressed as a result of operating under unusual circumstances (regardless of the cause of those unusual circumstances). And it also involves knowing how robust its components are when the components are forced to experience the consequences of the failure of other subsystems.

Summarizing, reliability testing of software components, while necessary, is not sufficient. It disregards a variety of operational anomalies that can seriously disrupt the reliable and safe behavior of a component-based system due to the inherent unpredictability associated with all digital systems.

Summary

This short chapter has briefly discussed interoperability issues with respect to both software component failures and the lack of scalable composability theories for the ilities, those nonfunctional behaviors that occur when software executes.

Component failures and how they propagate present a fascinating prediction problem in software engineering. IPA is a technique geared toward addressing this problem. Hidden interfaces and nonfunctional behaviors are problematic for CBSE and CBD. Inverted and skewed operational profile testing, in conjunction with IPA, can easily increase the a priori knowledge of the system integrator who is responsible for building a component-based system from black-box components.

In our opinion, CBSE and CBD will not flourish until technologies exist that permit the successful predictability of the degree to which different software components are interoperable. Without predictability, interoperability cannot be known a priori until after a system is built. It may then be too late in its life cycle for financial recovery if it is discovered that one or more of the components is not compatible.

References

[1]   Voas, J., and J. Payne, "Dependability Certification of Software Components," *J. of Software Systems*, Vol. 52, No. 2–3, 2000, pp. 165–172.

[2]   Voas, J., "Error Propagation Analysis for COTS Systems," *IEEE Computing and Control Engineering J.*, Vol. 8, No. 6, 1997, pp. 269–272.

[3]   Voas, J., and G. McGraw, *Software Fault Injection: Inoculating Programs Against Errors*, New York: John Wiley and Sons, 1998.

[4]   Voas, J., "Discovering Unanticipated Software Output Modules," *The Annals of Software Engineering*, Vol. 11, No. 1, 2001, pp. 79–88.

Part 5:
Software Product Lines

Using software product-line architectures is a means to implement planned reuse of components within an organization. This kind of architecture supports structured assembly of product-line components. The various components can be assembled together as long as they follow the implicit rules of the planned architecture. This approach has been proven to be very successful for companies that produce many variants of products with similar functionality (e.g., TVs and VCRs). By having planned for development of many different products over a longer period of time, the software product line helps both with developing and reusing components. Components do not have to be developed bottom up with a great deal of generality; they can instead be developed with guidelines from the product-line architecture.

Chapter 11 describes how product-line architectures can be used to utilize component reuse. The reuse of components between many different products is dependent on how the architecture is set up in the beginning; the more investment put into the architecture, the more possible reuse of components that can be achieved. Creating an architecture requires decisions about how to develop the products. To choose one of the two approaches of top-down versus bottom-up development is not appropriate at all times. A mixture is often suitable and it is here where product-line architectures can help to set the stage for a development that both uses components in a bottom-up way and architectures in a top-down approach.

Chapter 12 presents the findings from using a product-line architecture within Philips for the creation of a product population of consumer electronics. Koala, the component model that was developed, is also an architectural description language used to build products from a repository of components. The chapter describes the Koala model and how it is used to build components that fit into a product-line architecture.

11

Components in Product-Line Architectures

Rob van Ommering and Jan Bosch

Introduction

Reuse of software is a long-standing dream of the software engineering community. We have seen some successes, but also many failures. In the last decade, the interest in software component technology has grown, and a vision of a global software component market solving all our reuse problems is emerging. We believe this vision to be oversimplified for (at least) two reasons:

1. We are far from a global component market yet. Success stories today only involve relatively small components in generic and mature domains.
2. There will always be a need for intraorganizational reuse of core software for companies that produce sets of related products.

This chapter is about *software product lines*: proactive, systematic, planned, and organized approaches toward software reuse for sets of products within an organization. Figure 11.1 summarizes the driving forces of such product lines. Complexity and quality are best handled with an explicit

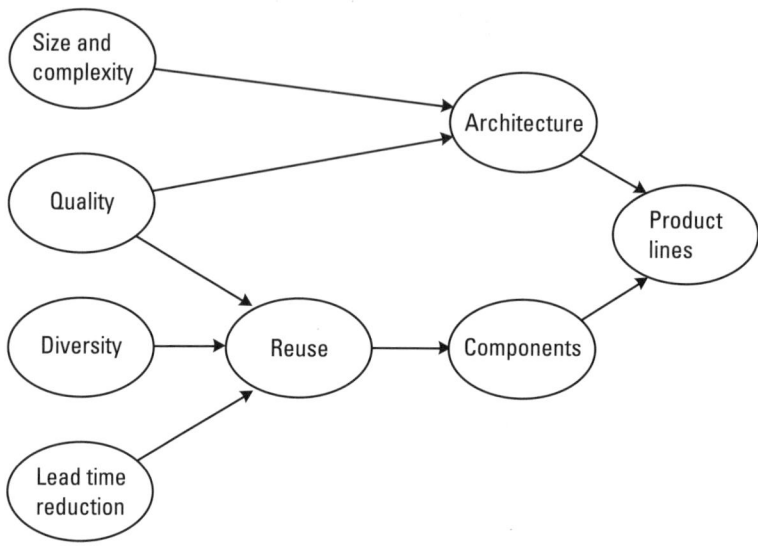

Figure 11.1 Basic arguments for software product lines.

architecture, while quality, diversity, and lead-time reduction are achieved by reuse of software components. There is a delicate balance between classical, architecture-driven top-down development for single products and the visionary bottom-up component assembly as suggested by many advocates of component technology. It depends on the required diversity of the products: For small product families, a product-line approach may resemble single-product development, but for large populations of products, it may have many elements of bottom-up component assembly.

In the first section of this chapter, we contrast single-product development with envisaged component assembly and show some shades in between. Then, we discuss various reuse approaches along two dimensions, variability and composability. In the next chapter we illustrate our findings with a case: the Koala component model as used within Philips for the creation of a product population of consumer electronics.

From Products to Components

Classical software development—for a single product—differs in many aspects from the building of applications by selecting and combining third-party components. Many companies are successful in the former, but the latter—we believe—is currently only successful in specific, limited domains. In the next sections we will be concerned with the use of components within organizations to achieve the reuse of core product software. This requires an approach that lies somewhere between that of classical single-product development and third-party component markets. We first describe the two extremes: single-product development and the notion of component markets. We then address some forms of established reuse, before turning to product lines for product families and product populations.

Developing a Single Product

We already know how to develop a single product by applying a standard software engineering process. Starting from the requirements, we define an architecture that helps us to realize the required functional and nonfunctional properties. The architecture decomposes the system into subsystems and components. We build and test the components, then the subsystems, and finally the product. Typical characteristics of this approach (see also Figure 11.2) include the following:

- It is a top-down activity (all software governed by a single architecture).
- Use of components is planned (develop only what is needed).
- All software is developed during the process.
- All development is within a single organization.

Component Markets

Let us now contrast single-product development with the building of systems from existing components, obtained from third parties. Typical characteristics include these:

- It is a bottom-up activity (no global architecture defined).
- Use of components is opportunistic (use whatever is available).
- The component software is available when starting the project.
- It results in interorganizational reuse.

	Product Lines		
Single Product	Product Family	Product Population	Component Markets
Top-down	Top-down	Partially bottom-up	Bottom-up
Planned	Planned	Planned / opportunistic	Opportunistic
Developed	Developed	Developed / available	Available
Intraorganization	Intraorganization	Intraorganization	Intraorganization

Figure 11.2 Characteristics of product lines.

This sounds ideal, but we must make some remarks here. The first is about *architecture*. During the past few years we have learned that we cannot build large, efficient, high-quality software systems without paying a lot of attention to the architecture (see, for instance, [1]). We have also learned that combining components that have not been developed under the same architecture may result in an architectural mismatch [2] (e.g., both may assume that they are running the highest priority thread) and thus a less efficient system (if functioning at all). So our component market vision only works if either there is some kind of global architecture, or if we manage to abstract sufficiently from an architecture. The success of Microsoft's Visual Basic [3] is probably due to the first: An ActiveX control must provide a large number of interfaces to be useful in Visual Basic, and it will require an undefined subset of the Win32 API, making it useless outside Visual Basic or even outside Windows. In Koala we attempt to take the other direction, as we show in the next chapter.

Our second remark is about scale. It is easy to reuse small components such as buttons and labels, but the larger components become, the more specific they tend to be for the situation for which they were originally designed. A natural friction is observed between reusability and usefulness: Small components can be very reusable but are not very useful, whereas large components are very useful but often not very reusable, as is nicely illustrated in Figure 1.1 of [4]). The solution is parameterization, but how well this works for large components is not yet well understood.

Thirdly, successful component reuse frameworks, such as Visual Basic, often require an excess of resources that are not available in many products, for example, in embedded software. A high-end television, for instance, has the computing resources of a personal computer 10 years ago; a low-end television sets time 20 years back. Still, reuse of software within a family of televisions is an important requirement if a company is to stay ahead of the competition.

Finally, many companies categorize their product software into core, key, and base. Core software is the software that provides the competitive edge: Only a few other companies are able to produce such software and sharing is not an option! Key software is software that could be obtained from others but is not for strategic reasons, whereas base software can and is obtained from others. So there will always be software that is produced by a company for itself only, but that needs to be reused in different products. The software cannot be turned into generic components—the "customer" base is not large enough. But the software cannot be made too specific either, because that would hamper the intraorganizational reuse. This is where product lines enter the picture.

Established Reuse

Before we discuss product lines, let us consider some established forms of software reuse, namely, that of mathematical or graphical libraries, operating systems, database management systems, compilers, and so forth. There is hardly any product today that is completely built from scratch—even a television contains at least an off-the-shelf real-time kernel. Even more, this form of reuse often concerns large pieces of software. Is software reuse already happening?

The answer is yes, but with many restrictions. The use of an existing software package often has a large influence on the design of the software to be developed, which may be good or bad depending on the circumstances. For example, the use of Windows results in applications based on message loops, which may not be the best architecture in all cases. As a result, the application becomes dependent on the chosen software package, and if not anticipated, it is virtually impossible to port the application to another package (operating system or library).

The most important problem is that the use of two existing packages that have not been developed together (or one on top of the other) is often virtually impossible, sometimes for simple syntactical reasons (they both define the class String), and sometimes for fundamental reasons such as that both packages implement the function "main." But to be restricted to the use of only one existing package is too limiting, and will not result in dazzling products.

Also, as we have already discussed in the previous section, existing software packages often only implement functionality that can be considered to be mature and therefore generic, while many companies rely on core software that they can only develop themselves. Note that it may take decades before certain functionality is implemented by standard software: Operating systems were researched in the 1960s and 1970s, and windowing systems in the 1970s and 1980s. It takes such a long time for people to actually agree on the concepts—a necessary prerequisite for reusable software.

The final contrast with product lines to be discussed next is the topic of *economics*. A company that sells a software package can only survive if it has many customers. Conversely, other companies usually only accept the software when there is at least a "second source" supplying the same or similar software. So the interorganizational reuse of software obeys normal economic laws. These do not usually hold within a company! We therefore believe that intraorganizational reuse should be built on different foundations. Just setting up a reuse division within an organization does not work. Instead an overall proactive approach is required: that of a product line.

Product Families and Product Lines

We define a product family as follows: A *product family* is a set of products with many commonalties and few differences. An example of a product family is a set of televisions. Variations include the kind of output device (tube, flat panel, projection), the size of the output device, the broadcasting standards that it supports, the quality of picture and sound, the user interface, and the data processing functions such as Teletext and an Electronic Programming Guide. By definition, a product family is intraorganizational, and reuse of core software within the family is a strategic issue.

We define a product line as follows: A product line is a top-down, planned, proactive approach to achieve reuse of software within a family (or population, see the next section) of products. Product lines have received quite some attention lately [5, 6]. If the product family is small and most of the variation is known in advance, then a fixed generic architecture (called *variant-free* in [7]) can be chosen that has explicit *variation points* to deal with diversity. Such variation points could be compile-time flags (using #ifdef), run-time options [using 'if (p)' where p is stored in some nonvolatile memory], plug-in components (accessed through a registry), configuration management parameters, and so forth.

This is indeed the approach advocated by many researchers in the field of product lines. Typically, an organization creates a platform first, from which products can be derived later. Having a single common architecture is a sound basis for realizing the functional and nonfunctional properties of the systems. In particular, properties such as quality, size, and performance of the code can be handled with techniques similar to those for a single product. The downside is that in certain situations it is difficult to forecast the requirements of future products, thus resulting in an architecture that becomes an obstacle for realizing new products. A second problem is that it may be virtually impossible to agree on a single architecture in a large multiple-business-line organization, with different interests and different time horizons.

Product Populations

Some organizations want to extend the reuse of software beyond the boundaries of a (small) product family. We define a product population as follows [8]: A *product population* is a set of products with many commonalities but also many differences. An example of a product population is the set of televisions, video recorders, CD and DVD players and recorders, and so forth. Such products have things in common: A TV and a VCR share a video tuner. They also have differences. A TV has a picture tube, whereas a VCR has a tape mechanism. This implies that a single generic architecture no longer suffices; instead we should create reusable components that we can combine in seemingly arbitrary ways. So are we now back at third-party component markets?

No, we are not. We are talking about core software that has to be developed by the organization itself. The functionality may not be mature enough yet to create truly generic reusable components. The relatively few customers are all within the organization, so the laws of economics of component markets do not readily apply. Finally, the products are resource constrained, ruling out many of those powerful component technologies out on the market.

Instead, again we have to adopt a product-line approach: a top-down, planned, proactive process to design and create components that can be combined in more than one way (though not freely), and that can be turned into products (without being overly generic). But the approach now has bottom-up elements (unforeseen combinations of existing components), planning is less strict (products may have different life cycles that are shifted in time), and though still intraorganizational, development will cross business line, group, or division boundaries. This has a number of consequences, of which we name two.

First, the wider the spread over the organization, the more difficult it becomes to define common architectural rules and mechanisms. It is therefore important to minimize the global architecture and to define a number of issues "regionally," that is, to be valid only in certain parts of the system. A syntactical example is that naming conventions could be reduced to the use of a prescribed prefix to avoid name clashes. Note, however, that this may increase the chance of an architectural mismatch.

Second, planning becomes an important issue. In single-product development, there is only one plan: that of the product. On the component market, companies that sell reusable components have a plan for the development of their component only, based on vague expectations of what is economically interesting on the market. In a product population, however, a product plan has to incorporate the planning of many components, and the component plan has to incorporate the planning of many products. In particular, if products belong to different parts of the organization, the component developers will face many conflicting requirements, both with respect to the functionality and to the planning.

The Lessons

What can we learn from this? Reuse within an organization requires a top-down, planned, proactive effort; in other words, a product-line approach. For product families we can define a generic architecture with explicit variation points to manage diversity. For product populations we need to create reusable components that can be combined in different ways, but without the generality and flexibility that one would expect of components on a component market because there is no economic benefit to offset the extra effort. Instead, a careful road mapping process is required to determine what functionality is needed when and in which product [9]. Also, technically the architecture must be such that there is sufficient freedom to combine components in new ways without resulting in systems that have poor quality, performance, or a large code size.

Component Approaches

In the previous section we discussed various aspects of software reuse depending on the scope of reuse. We now discuss a number of technical options for achieving reuse. We categorize them in two dimensions: *variability* and *independence*.

The variability dimension concerns the degree to which an existing piece of software can be modified when used in a product. This may range from no variation (reuse "as is"), through parameterization and inheritance, to sophisticated mechanisms such as component plug-ins. Remember that small reusable components are not very useful, and that larger components tend to become too specific. The ability to adapt a component when it is integrated into a product is therefore very important.

The second dimension is about independence, and we distinguish two cases. Suppose a product contains two pieces of software, A and B. In the first case, A is reused from somewhere else, and B is built on top of A. In the second case, A and B are developed independently (given some lightweight common architecture), and are only composed when creating the product. In the second case, A and B are independent, but in the first case, B is usually dependent on A. There are ways of decoupling B from A even in the first case, but certain techniques for reuse, such as the use of inheritance, actually induce dependence. If we deploy a class library that uses inheritance as a specialization technique, then our specialization, B, is intertwined with the class library A, and cannot be decoupled from it.

As explained before, we believe that the combination of nontrivial components that were not developed together is the major challenge that we are facing for software components, but it is not the only way to achieve reuse. Figure 11.3 shows example techniques for different points in the two-dimensional space, and we discuss each of them briefly. See [10] for an inventory of some techniques for achieving independent deployment.

Libraries

The classic technique for organizing reusable software is in the form of (functional) libraries. Examples are a mathematical library and a graphical library. Typically, software built on top of the library includes the header file(s) of the library (if programmed in C), and with that it becomes dependent on the specific library. It is possible to abstract from the library by defining a library-independent interface; POSIX is an example of this. The actual implementation can then be selected in the build process. However, in

		Independence	
		Reusable	Composable
Variability	"As is"	Libraries	Lego
	Parameterized		Koala
	Inheritance	OO Frameworks	Frameworks as components
	Plug-ins	Component frameworks	

Figure 11.3 Variability versus independence.

practice, most software built on top of libraries becomes specifically dependent on those libraries.

This is especially true for the libraries themselves. Often, a library uses
other software (in the form of libraries), but few (or none) of these libraries
allow the user to select which underlying library to use. And, as we have seen
before, if two libraries that do not depend on each other and that have been
independently developed are combined, mismatches may occur: simple ones
such as name clashes, or fundamental problems such as that both libraries
assume the ability to implement the main control loop.

Parameterization of libraries is often limited to the setting of parameters and—at the most—callback functions. Parameterization happens mainly
through callable interfaces, so that a run-time penalty is associated with the
parameterization. If source code is available, some parameters may influence
the compilation and linking process.

Object-Oriented Frameworks

An OO framework is a set of classes from which one can create an application
by specializing the various classes in the framework using implementation
inheritance. The power lies in the use of inheritance as a parameterization

mechanism. Inheritance allows the framework to abstract from specific behavior; this is added later in the form of specialized classes. But the danger also lies in the use of inheritance: The derived classes are very dependent on the framework and cannot be used in any other context.

The situation may even be worse. A new version of the same framework, with new versions of base classes, may break down existing applications. This phenomenon is known as the *fragile base class problem* (see, e.g., [4]) and is a further illustration of the strong dependencies between the applications with the underlying framework.

Also, because many OO frameworks are an application by themselves, the combination of two OO frameworks is often virtually impossible. We will come back to this later, when discussing OO frameworks as components.

Component Frameworks

We define a component framework as an application or part of an application in which components can be plugged to specialize the behavior. Component frameworks resemble OO frameworks, and indeed many component models have their roots in OO technology. The difference is in the dependencies between specialized code and generic code. Whereas OO frameworks rely on implementation inheritance, component frameworks specify the *interfaces* between the plug-ins and the underlying framework. This greatly reduces dependencies, and especially the risk of the "fragile base class problem" when the framework evolves over time.

The frameworks that exist today often have some disadvantages. First, the plug-ins are only useful in the context of the framework and cannot be independently deployed. Second, the framework itself often implements a complete application, and is thus not composable itself. We'll come back to this topic in the next section.

Figure 11.4 illustrates a component framework as developed within Philips [11]. The ground plane contains an (almost) variant-free skeleton of components. Most of these components are present in all members of the family, while the others are optional. Each component can only be used together with the other components of the ground plane—there is no independent deployment of ground plane components. The plug-in components, drawn in the third dimension, serve to implement diversity. One can create different members of the family by inserting different plug-ins. The plug-in components also have no life outside of the scope of the ground plane (there is no independent deployment in space), but it is possible to use

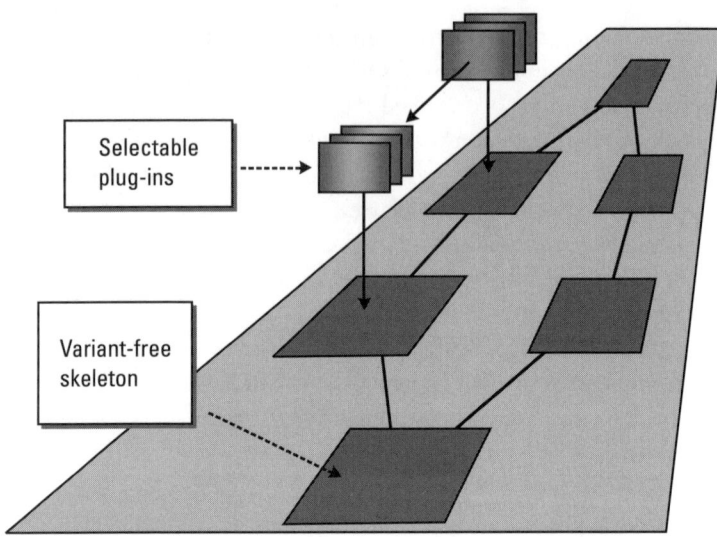

Figure 11.4 Component frameworks with plug-ins.

old plug-ins with new versions of the ground plane (there is independent deployment in time).

Lego

The archetype example for reusability is Lego, the toy bricks with the standard "click and play" interface. Indeed, Lego bricks are very composable, but they are not parameterized at all, so they are at the top of the vertical axis of Figure 11.3. This results in the following two phenomena: First, it is possible to create complicated shapes with ordinary Lego bricks, but it results in huge objects requiring thousands of bricks to make the shapes seem smooth (as can be admired in LegoLand). Because the reusable components are then very small compared with the resulting product, there is effectively not much reuse. The reuse of Lego bricks is then comparable to the reuse of statements in a programming language.

On the other hand, Lego started manufacturing specialized bricks some years ago, bricks that can only be used for one purpose (for example, the head of a pirate). With such bricks it is possible to create smooth shapes with only a few bricks. The downside is that the specialized bricks can only be used in specialized cases.

The solution should be parameterized bricks, but somehow this is mechanically inconceivable. Maybe a Lego printer, a device that can produce new plastic bricks of any shape at home, is the answer (although strictly speaking, the software equivalent of a Lego printer is a code generator, and not a parameterized component).

Koala

Koala is an architectural description language and component model for the development of embedded software for consumer electronics products. It is discussed in more detail in the next chapter; for now it suffices to say that Koala supports both parameterization and composability. Parameterization is supported in the form of special diversity interfaces; a named parameter mechanism allows for the creation of a large set of parameters with default values, thus not overloading the users of the component. Composability is obtained by making all required functionality explicit in the form of required interfaces that can be bound to selected services by third parties.

Frameworks as Components

The ultimate solution for both variability and independence lies, we believe, in the use of frameworks as components. As explained before, a framework is a large piece of software with a powerful parameterization mechanism, such as the use of implementation inheritance (in an OO framework) or component plug-ins (in a component framework). If a framework only covers a part of the application domain (a subdomain), and if frameworks can be "arbitrarily" combined (making them true components), then we can create a multitude of products by selecting and combining such framework components and specializing them toward the product to be created using inheritance or component plug-ins.

Some examples of OO frameworks used as components do exist [12], but no examples of component frameworks used as components yet. The basic mechanism for achieving composability is to make every context dependency explicit and bindable by a third party, much in the way, for instance, Koala does. Put differently, components should also be parameterized over their context dependencies. We see this happening already in the small scale; consider, for instance, a sort function that is parameterized over the compare function. We do not see this happening in the large scale yet.

Summary

We talked about variability and independence. We also talked about anticipated variation only; in practice, it is also important to be able to adapt existing components to new situations for which they were not designed. A typical solution here is to insert product specific glue code between components. Unfortunately, many binding techniques (such as the inclusion of libraries or the inheritance of base classes) do not allow the insertion of extra code or do at least require special techniques [13]. Only solutions that rely on some form of third-party binding, such as GenVoca [14], Darwin [15], and Koala [16], allow for easy insertion of glue code.

We also did not talk about code generation, another way to reuse code. We believe this approach to be very successful but in restricted domains only, such as in the generation of compilers. In a way, GenVoca, Darwin, and Koala are also code generation solutions, albeit for the code that connects hand-written components only.

Conclusion

We started this chapter with a comparison between traditional single-product development on the one hand, and third-party component markets on the other hand. We concluded that there is a large and still relatively unexploited area of potential reuse of software within an organization for a set of related products. Product lines are the answer: a planned and proactive approach for the sharing of software. For small product families, traditional techniques are still sufficient. But for larger product populations, an approach is required that combines top-down with bottom-up approaches, in other words, the best elements of single-product development and third-party component markets.

We then investigated various mechanisms that facilitate the reusability of software. We organized these along two dimensions: mechanisms for variability on the one hand, and the degree to which independently developed (large) components can be deployed on the other hand. We gave examples of techniques for various points in this two-dimensional space.

References

[1] Bass, L., P. Clements, and R. Kazman, *Software Architecture in Practice*, Reading, MA: Addison-Wesley, 1998.

[2] Garlan, D., R. Allen, and J. Ockerbloom, "Architectural Mismatch: Why Reuse Is So Hard," *IEEE Software*, Vol. 12, No. 6, 1995, pp. 17–26.

[3] Microsoft, "Microsoft Visual Basic," http://msdn.microsoft.com/vbasic.

[4] Szyperski, C., *Component Software Beyond Object-Oriented Programming*, Reading, MA: Addison-Wesley, 1998.

[5] van der Linden, F., *Proc. 2nd Int. ESPRIT ARES Workshop,* Lecture Notes in Computer Science, No. 1429, Berlin, Springer Verlag, 1998.

[6] Donohoe, P., *Proc. 1st Software Product Line Conf.,* Kluwer Int. Series in Engineering and Computer Science, No. 576, Dordrecht, The Netherlands, Kluwer, 2000.

[7] Perry, D. E., "Generic Architecture Descriptions for Product Lines," *Proc. 2nd Int. ESPRIT ARES Workshop*, Lecture Notes in Computer Science, No. 1429, Springer Verlag, 1998.

[8] van Ommering, R., "Beyond Product Families: Building a Product Population?" *Proc. 3rd Int. Workshop on Development and Evolution of Software Architectures of Product Families*, 2000, LNCS1951, Springer Verlag, pp. 187–198.

[9] van Ommering, R., "Roadmapping a Product Population Architecture," *Proc. 4th Int. Workshop on Product Family Engineering*, Berlin: Springer, Verlag, 2001.

[10] van Ommering, R., "Techniques for Independent Deployment to Build Product Populations," *Proc. WICSA2001, The Working IEEE/IFIP Conf. Software Architecture*, Amsterdam, The Netherlands, 2001.

[11] Wijnstra, J. G., "Supporting Diversity with Component Frameworks as Architectural Elements," *Proc. 22nd Int. Conf. Software Engineering*, Limerick, Ireland, IEEE Computer Society, 2000.

[12] Bosch, J., *Design & Use of Software Architectures*, Reading, MA: Addison-Wesley, 2000.

[13] Balzer, R., "An Architectural Infrastructure for Product Families," *Proc. 2nd Int. ESPRIT ARES Workshop*, Lecture Notes in Computer Science, No. 1429, Berlin, Springer Verlag, 2001.

[14] Batory, D., and S. O'Malley, "The Design and Implementation of Hierarchical Software Systems with Reusable Components," *ACM Trans. on Software Engineering and Methodology*, Vol. 1, No. 4, 1992, pp. 355–398.

[15] Magee, J., N. Dulay, and S. Eisenbach, "Specifying Distributed Software Architectures," *Proc. European Software Engineering Conf.*, Lecture Notes in Computer Science, No. 989, Berlin, Springer Verlag, 1995.

[16] van Ommering, R., "Koala, a Component Model for Consumer Electronics Product Software," *Proc. 2nd Int. ESPRIT ARES Workshop*, Lecture Notes in Computer Science, No. 1429, Berlin, Springer Verlag, 1998.

12

The Koala Component Model

Rob van Ommering

Introduction

Koala is a component model and an architectural description language that is used to build a large diversity of products (a product population) from a repository of components. Koala was designed for use in building consumer products such as televisions, video recorders, CD and DVD players and recorders, and combinations of these (e.g., a TV-VCR). In this chapter we highlight the most important features of Koala, starting with the original requirements. More information on Koala can be found in various publications listed at the end of this chapter; a good starting point is [1].

Requirements for Koala

The following three requirements were formulated for Koala at the time of its design (in 1996):

- (R1) Devise a technique with which components can be "freely" composed into products as the main approach to dealing with diversity in a product population.

- (R2) The technique must work in resource-constrained environments such as televisions and video recorders (which are typically 10 years behind on PCs in computing power).

- (R3) Make the product architectures as explicit as possible, to manage complexity.

Note that we took composability as our starting point (R1), instead of designing, for instance, a variant-free framework with variation points, as explained in the previous chapter. We expected that it would not be feasible to define such a single global architecture in our organization where new innovative products are often created by new combinations of existing assets. Requirement R2 is prominent in consumer electronics, where the "bill of material" plays a dominant role: Given the millions of products sold per year, making the product one dollar cheaper immediately shows in the company's profit and loss calculation. Requirement R3 shows that even for a single product, we needed some way to cope with complexity.

Thinking about solutions for these requirements, three auxiliary requirements were formulated:

- (R4) Permit components make as few assumptions as possible about their environment.

- (R5) Allow for parameterized components that are—when instantiated—as efficient as dedicated components.

- (R6) Allow for various ways of connecting components; more specifically, allow for adding glue code to the connection between components.

Requirement R4 is directly related to R1 and results in the introduction of required interfaces and third-party binding, as discussed in the next section. Requirement R5 is related to R2 and results in the notion of late compile-time binding, also as explained in the next section. Requirement R6 anticipates that we will not be able to construct "perfectly fitting" components, and hence need some help in connecting components.

Binding and Bind Time

Let us consider a product P that consists of a component A and a component B, and suppose that A uses B (see the left-hand side of Figure 12.1). This

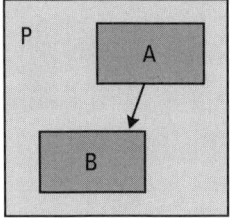 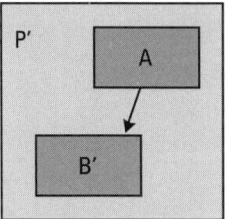

Figure 12.1 Principle of binding.

means that *A* can call a function in *B*. In traditional software development, this implies that *A* must know the name of the function in *B*. Components *A* and *B* are compiled separately, and the call of *A* is bound to the function in *B* by the linker. Although the actual binding occurs at *link time* (and some linkers indeed offer possibilities to change the binding), and can even occur at run time (if dynamically linkable libraries are used), in most cases the name of the function of *B* is hard-coded into *A*, so the actual choice for using *B* in *A* is already made at compile time.

Now let us look at this from a different point of view. We can also say that the choice of using *B* is made by the designer of component *A*, and is therefore made at component time. But this specific choice makes it difficult to create a product *P'* consisting of component *A* and a different component *B'* (see the right-hand side of Figure 12.1). We actually want the product creator to be able to make that choice, that is, at product time. How can we achieve such flexibility?

Modern component technologies often deploy run-time binding to achieve product-time binding. In such cases, component *A* implements a pointer to a function (or a pointer to a VTable of pointers to functions). This pointer is filled with the address of the function in *B* at run time by software specific to the product *P*. This third-party binding (where *P* is the third party) is sometimes also called late binding, and it is an essential technique to delay decisions in, for instance, product lines. The extra indirection introduced by the pointer provides a slight overhead in code size and performance.

Koala is to be used in resource-constrained environments (R2) where typically 90% or more of the bindings is known and fixed at product time (but different for different products). It is also not known in advance which 10% of the bindings must remain flexible, so this knowledge cannot be built into the components (R4). This has led to the following basic binding scheme:

- Components that require functions of other components use symbolic names to refer to such functions.

- Components are declared in an architectural description language, and so are products interconnecting components.

- A compiler generates a simple `#definestatement` to map symbolic names to physical names for bindings known at product time, and it generates code for run-time binding otherwise.

Our use of `#define` is sometimes called late compile-time binding: It is late in the development process, but still early in the compilation process. We can use this efficient implementation technique as long as we build closed systems, which will be for quite some years. When computing resources allow us to build open systems, we only have to change the compiler to generate run-time binding.

The remainder of this section provides a brief overview of Koala.

Koala Components

A Koala component is a piece of code that can interact with its environment through explicit interfaces only. As a consequence, a (basic) Koala component has no dependencies on other Koala components. The implementation of a Koala component is a directory with a set of C and header files that may use each other in arbitrary ways, but communication with other components is routed only through header files generated by the Koala compiler, based on the binding between components. To achieve this, the directory also contains a component definition file, describing (among other things) the interfaces of the component.

A Koala configuration is a list of components (a part list) and a list of connections between components (a net list). Configuring components *A* and *B* to work together is the task of a third party, resulting in a configuration *C*. We call this third-party binding. To be able to scale this approach to build large systems, the Koala model is recursive; any combination of components is again a component. A configuration is just a top-level component that has no interfaces at its border.

To be more precise, a component definition describes a template for instantiating a component and its subcomponents (if present), in other words, a type. Different products are described by different component definitions that—when instantiated—may aggregate subcomponents of the same type, hence we obtain reuse. A single product is even allowed to contain more than one instance of a certain component type; we call this multiple instantiation.

In that respect, a Koala component definition resembles a class in, for instance, Java, and a component instance is an object. It is not possible, however, to pass pointers to components in Koala.

Figure 12.2 shows an example of a Koala component. The small squares that contain triangles denote interfaces as explained in the next section; the tip of the triangle points in the direction of the function call. Components $C_1 \ldots C_3$ are subcomponents of C_c. The objects marked with "m" and "s" are modules and switches, respectively, as discussed in a section below.

Provides and Requires Interfaces

Connections between components are expressed in terms of interfaces. As in COM and in Java, a Koala interface is a small set of semantically related functions. An interface definition defines the prototypes and semantics of these functions, while components provide or require *instances* of interfaces.

Koala provides interfaces are much like the interfaces from COM and Java. A component may provide multiple interfaces, which is a useful way of handling evolution and diversity. Koala components also have requires interfaces, which are explicit connection points for communicating with the

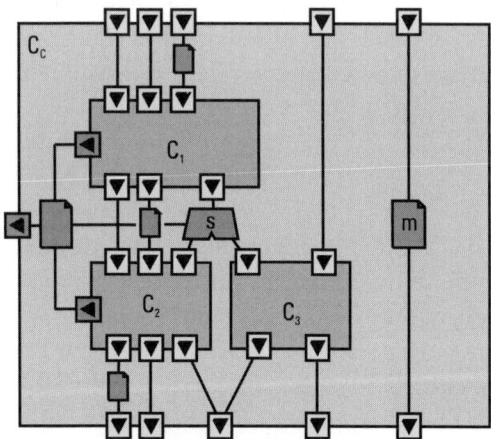

Figure 12.2 A Koala component example.

environment of the component that are bound by a third party. Such a feature is not part of COM or Java, but can easily be built on top of it, by declaring interface pointer variables within the COM or Java class, and providing a way to set these from outside. But in Koala all communication is routed through such requires interfaces, even calls to the operating system, while COM components and Java classes still have many implicit connections to the environment.

Koala interfaces can be optional. An optional requires interface need not be connected and an optional provides interface need not be implemented. This allows components to fine-tune themselves to their environment by observing what the environment can and cannot deliver. Such implicit adaptability is also a goal of COM, where `QueryInterface` is used to examine the connected component. Self-adaptable components make the task of handling diversity easier. As a side effect, the compiler can also optimize the memory usage of the application (the so-called footprint), by eliminating functionality in a component that is not used.

Binding, Gluing, and Switches

The normal way of composing components is to connect requires interfaces of one component to provides interfaces of another component. Naturally, in compound components it is also possible to connect provides interfaces of subcomponents to provides interfaces of the compound component, and similarly for requires interfaces. In all cases, it is assumed that interfaces fit. What happens if interfaces have to be connected that do not have the same type?

One feature of Koala is that it is allowed to connect a requires interface to a provides interface of a wider type. The provides interface should implement all of the functions of the required interface, but it may implement more than that. This allows for an easy evolution of functionality, though in practice it is better to support both the old interface and a new one, as one would do in COM.

Now suppose that two interfaces do not fit. In Koala it is possible to add glue code to the binding between interfaces. Simple glue code can be expressed in an expression language within Koala; more complicated code can be written in C. This allows us to easily overcome a certain category of syntactic and semantic differences. Glue code is not independently reusable code. It belongs to the compound component that performs the binding.

A special case of glue code is code that switches a binding between components. Such a mechanism to select from components can be implemented in C, but it occurs so frequently that we decided to define a special concept for this in the language: the *switch*. The compiler converts a switch internally to a set of Koala expressions, which has the advantage that it can perform certain optimizations, such as reducing the switch to a straight binding if the switch is set to a position that is known at compile time.

The "normal" binding, the glue module, and the switch are examples of connectors. The Koala language defines no other connectors. But other kinds of connection can easily be made as special-purpose components. We created, for example, a set of generic components that implement remote procedure call services, for use in products with multiple processors. These services are instantiated by hand for different interface types—in principle, this can be automated.

Diversity Interfaces

Koala components can be parameterized through diversity interfaces. Koala has no specific construct for this. They are just requires interfaces that can be bound using any Koala binding technique, although the use of Koala expressions is preferred for optimization reasons. The mechanism allows us to define component-specific sets of parameters. Note that in many software systems, either low-level components know about product diversity parameters, or at the product level low-level component parameters must be given a value. In Koala, low-level parameters of subcomponents can be calculated in terms of higher level parameters of compound components.

The use of optional interfaces also implies a diversity mechanism. Components can observe what is connected to their interfaces, and thus decide to adapt themselves to their environment. A more thorough treatment of various ways of handling diversity can be found in [2].

Product-Line Architecture

The Koala model is a relatively simple model that allows us to combine different components as long as the provided services can be made to match the required services. The most important prerequisite to combine components is that both should obey the Koala model. For newly developed components, this requires a trivial effort; they must satisfy the naming conventions so that the Koala compiler can generate the appropriate #define statements. For legacy components, encapsulation into a Koala component is straightforward (using a special construct that circumvents the default naming conventions), albeit the creation of bindable requires interfaces may be a problem if source code is not available.

But even for Koala components, architectural mismatches are still possible, so we defined a set of simple architectural rules for preventing gross mismatches. We discuss three of these here: initialization, multithreading, and notifications.

All components should provide an initialization interface. The general rule is that functions in this interface must be called before any of the other interfaces can be accessed. Components that do not control hardware provide a simple initialization interface IInit, with a single function Init. Components that do control hardware provide a more complicated interface, IPower, that has an Init function to initialize the software component, but also a Turn-on and Turn-off function to control the hardware power of the specific device. Different devices may be on or off, depending on the power state of the system as a whole.

A particular point of attention is that most components need functionality of other components during initialization. In principle, components designers must specify what outcalls they make in the implementation of the Init function, and it is the task of the system designer to satisfy these requirements. In practice, we define a number of legal outcalls during initialization, mostly concerning access to the computing infrastructure, such as creating semaphores and accessing nonvolatile memory.

Our second rule concerns multithreading. Control software for consumer electronics typically contains a large number of relatively small and independent activities, for example, a control loop to measure and control the image quality. Some of these activities are hard in real time (a TV may not catch fire), some are relatively hard (you do not want to miss Teletext data, but nothing disastrous happens if you do), and some are relatively soft. A real-time kernel with preemptive scheduling is used to separate the high-frequency tasks from the low-frequency tasks. However, two problems remain:

1. Consumer products are resource constrained. They do not have ample memory and processing cycles, and this severely constrains the number of threads that can be created.

2. Reusable components cannot make too many assumptions about the execution architecture of products, because these may be different for different products.

The first problem is solved with a technique called *thread sharing*. In our software, autonomous activities use *pumps*, message queues with a function to process messages and a logical thread to activate the pump function. We also have *pump engines*, which essentially are physical threads controlling pumps and which solve the second problem. Pumps are allocated to pump engines at the product level, where a single pump engine may serve multiple pumps. This is again a form of late binding, as are many techniques in product-line engineering. More information on our execution architecture can be found in [3].

Our third rule concerns notifications. Given the large number of asynchronous activities, many components need the ability to report the occurrence of "spontaneous" events. An example in the TV domain is if a broadcast stops; the software must then mute the sound and blank the picture. Another example is a frequency search for a next station. This will typically take seconds, up to 1 minute, and is therefore not implemented as an indivisible action. Instead, the search action is started and a notification is raised when a station has been found (or not).

In the majority of our products, each notification is connected to a single client (which may be different in different products). We therefore model notifications as outcalls through optional requires interfaces, and rely on Koala interface binding as a notification subscription mechanism. Whenever we encounter a situation with multiple clients, we insert a small component to broadcast the notification. Only if we foresee that for a specific component, all products will define multiple clients that are interested in notifications following specific requests, will we build an explicit subscription mechanism into the component.

We have now discussed three basic rules in our architecture. Let us now highlight some of the modular architecture of our products. The overall architecture is separated into three layers, as is illustrated in Figure 12.3:

1. A computing platform layer, abstracting from computing hardware;

2. An A/V/data platform layer, abstracting from audio, video, and data processing hardware;

3. An applications and services layer.

Components from the second layer can use the components from the first layer, and components from the third layer can use components from both the first and the second layer. Each layer contains a set of subsystems that cover one specific subdomain. Figure 12.3 lists nine of them described briefly below:

- *infra* implements most of the computing infrastructure—some would call this the operating system;

- *uims* implements a user interface management system to build applications (*apps*);

- *tvplf* is a "TV platform," abstracting from hardware peculiarities;

- *tvsvc* is a set of hardware-independent services in the TV domain;

- *txt* and *epg* are Teletext and Electronic Programming Guide, respectively;

- *fact* and *deal* are special software for the factory and the dealer.

Each subsystem contains many components, ranging from basic components dealing with only one aspect of the subdomain to compound components implementing the full subdomain for one specific category of products. We elaborate on this in the next section.

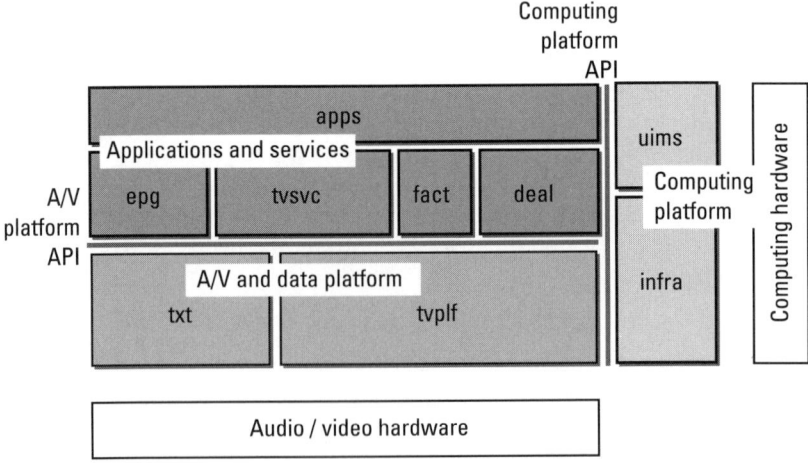

Figure 12.3 Layers and subsystems in the product-line architecture.

Creating Products

Koala components are stored in a repository. The repository is a set of packages, where each package is a set of component and interface definitions, some of which are public, some of which are private. Each package is developed by a single team and at a single location. The package is published as a source tree and as a ZIP file on an intranet, for downloading by others. A "home page" makes the repository look like a single conceptual directory structure.

Creating a product is simple. A subset of packages is downloaded into a private directory structure. Then, a top-level component definition is created that instantiates and binds components from the repository, preferably compound components (subsystems). If existing compound components do not satisfy the product requirements, new compound components can be created from basic components. If existing basic components do not satisfy the requirements, new basic components can be created. A software development environment consisting of an off-the-shelf software development environment (SDE) extended with the Koala compiler allows the required configuration to be built.

The previous paragraph describes an idealized bottom-up approach for product generation. In practice, development of basic and compound components occurs in parallel with the development of products using these components. This requires careful planning—a topic already discussed previously in this chapter (see also [4]).

Managing Versions and Variants

The management of versions and variants of components and products is traditionally the domain of configuration management (CM) systems. We believe that diversity in a product line should not be handled by a CM system, for the following two reasons:

1. It keeps diversity outside the scope of the architects (at least in practice), whereas we feel that diversity should be one of the main architectural issues.

2. CM systems can only handle compile-time variation, whereas we expect that more and more diversity will be handled at run time in the (near) future.

This leads to the following approach:

1. We use a CM system to maintain the full-version (revision) history of all our software assets, including source code and documentation.
2. We use the CM system for temporary branches with a short lifetime (e.g., when one developer corrects an error while another adds a feature).
3. We also use branches in the CM system for safeguarding a product in its final testing phase from changes to the code made on behalf of other products only.
4. We use Koala for all permanent diversity in the product family or population.

The large scale of our development and the fact that it is distributed give rise to a second level of version and variant handling, namely, at the level of packages. We have already seen that each package is the responsibility of a single team at a single location; each package is also maintained in its own CM system. This package-specific CM system maintains the full-version history of all files in the package; users of a package only see formal releases of that package (which are numbered sequentially). It is the responsibility of the package development teams to ensure consistency within a package, so that users only have to worry about consistency among packages.

Most variation is handled within a package, by having different compound Koala components for different ranges of products. Occasionally we find it useful to define two different packages to implement the same functionality for different parts of the product population. We currently have, for instance, two disjoint implementations of a TV platform, one for our older hardware and one for our newer hardware.

More information on handling variants can be found in [2]. More information on the relation with configuration management can be found in [5].

Subtyping

We have already shown how Koala allows us to connect "wider" provides interfaces to "narrower" requires interfaces, as long as all required functions are indeed implemented. In object-oriented terminology, an interface definition can be seen as a type, more specifically as an abstract base class.

Providing an interface is equivalent to inheriting the virtual functions from that abstract base class and implementing them. This allows us to formalize the notion of "wider" interfaces, because it coincides with the notion of subtyping in OO: A wider interface is a subtype of a narrower interface.

Compatibility checks between components are thus reduced to type and subtype checks on the interfaces. We can also see components as classes and use the same notion of subtyping there. In a nutshell, a component is a subtype of another component if it provides more and requires less. The "provides more" part will look familiar to the reader, as a class that inherits from more abstract base classes. The "requires less" part may come as a surprise. Consider, however, a function with input and output parameters. It can be substituted by a function with fewer input parameters and more output parameters (ignoring some syntactic problems).

We use subtyping at the component level mainly for ensuring that new versions of a component are backward compatible with old versions. It is sufficient for this if the new component is a subtype of the old component. We can also use subtyping to achieve substitutability: A component *A* can be replaced by a component *B* if *B* is a subtype of *A*. There are, however, no direct constructs for replacing components by other components in the Koala language.

We can also use subtyping at the level of packages, where a subtype of a package provides more and requires less. Note that packages may require component definitions from other packages and will usually require interface definitions from other packages. A full treatment of this is outside the scope of this document.

Conclusion

We introduced the Koala component model as used for the creation of a family of television products. We highlighted some of the features against the background sketched in previous sections, stressing the importance of variability, composability, and adaptability.

Koala is currently in use by a few hundred software engineers for the creation of a family of televisions. Experience shows that it is very easy to create derivative products by selecting components, binding them, adding glue code, and so forth. The technology is not difficult—it can be learned in a few days.

As far as we know, Koala is the only large-scale industrial application of an architectural description language. Because code is generated from the

ADL, the architectural descriptions are by definition consistent with the implementation. We use the ADL as a design tool, as a communication tool, and also as a means to check properties of the system. The latter is an especially interesting area for future research.

Koala does not have special features to achieve nonfunctional attributes such as quality, reliability, safety, and security. Nor does it prevent engineers from achieving those either. In fact, the encapsulation and parameterization facilities offered by Koala allow developers to use components without changing them, resulting in stable components that in the long term will increase their quality.

The products that are created with Koala consist in large part of software especially written for Koala. Some parts concern legacy software that was also written at Philips but not for Koala. At the moment, the only third-party component in the TVs is the real-time kernel. In set-top boxes it is more common to have third-party software, usually in the form of large middleware stacks such as OpenTV.

References

[1]   van Ommering, R., F. van der Linden, and J. Kramer, "The Koala Component Model for Consumer Electronics Software," *IEEE Computer,* Vol. 33, Issue 3, pp. 78–85.

[2]   van Ommering R., "Mechanisms for Handling Diversity in a Product Population," *Proc. Int. 4th Software Architecture Workshop,* Limerick, Ireland, 2000, http://www.extra.research.philips.com/SAE/papers.

[3]   van Ommering, R., "A Composable Software Architecture for Consumer Electronics Products," *XOOTIC Magazine,* Vol. 7, No. 3, 2000, pp. 37–47.

[4]   van Ommering, R., "Roadmapping a Product Population Architecture," *Proc. 4th Int. Workshop on Product Family Engineering,* Bilbao, Spain, 2001.

[5]   van Ommering, R., "Configuration Management in Component Based Product Populations," *Proc. 10th Int. Workshop on Software Configuration Management,* Toronto, Canada, 2001, http://www.ics.uci.edu/~andre/scm10.

Part 6:
Real-Time Software Components

Real-time systems are computer systems in which the correctness of the systems depends not only on the logical correctness of the computations performed but also on time factors. In such systems it is essential that the timing constraints are always met. Real-time systems must satisfy, under all conditions, requirements of timeliness (meeting deadlines, i.e., finishing certain tasks within specified time limits), simultaneous processing (more than one event may occur simultaneously, all deadlines must be met), predictability (predictable reactions to all possible events), and dependability (including characteristics such as reliability, integrity, privacy, safety, and security). In many cases, real-time systems are safety critical (i.e., their failure may result in injury, loss of life, or major environmental damage). Very often, real-time systems must strictly satisfy requirements with respect to restricted use of memory, CPU performance and energy.

It is clear that these specific requirements have a strong impact on real-time system design procedures, not only at the application level but with respect to entire system architectures and infrastructures. Standard component models and technologies cannot be guaranteed to meet these requirements and can only be used in such systems to a limited degree. Different concepts of system design, in component composition reasoning, in reusing components, and so on, must be applied. The concept of a component-based approach is as attractive for real-time systems development as for other software systems, and a component-based concept has been used successfully in certain domains. The chapters in this part address questions relating to component-based development of real-time, embedded and safety critical systems.

Chapter 13 presents an introduction to real-time systems by describing their main principles and introducing the basic terminology of real-time systems. The basic requirements of real-time systems for infrastructural components such as operating systems, databases, and so on, are then discussed. Some successful examples of CBD models are presented. Finally a process for designing component-based real-time systems is described, using a top-down approach, identifying components at the design phase, specifying their properties, selecting preexisting components, reasoning about the composition of the components, and analyzing the system. This chapter shows that it is possible to apply the CBD concept even to dependable real-time systems.

Chapter 14 presents arguments for the reuse and reverification of components in safety-critical real-time systems. The arguments for reuse of software (components) are usually arguments for rapid prototyping, arguments for outsourcing, and arguments for greater reliability. In the latter case, it is assumed that the verification of the components can be eliminated or reduced and that the reliability of the component has been demonstrated in previous applications. Expensive and catastrophic experiences have shown, however, that it is not always so simple. The authors approach this problem by presenting a framework for determining when components in real-time systems can be reused immediately, when complete retesting is necessary, or when only parts of the systems need additional verification. As an alternative to complete reverification, the possibility of decreasing the testing effort is attractive, and essential in the case of safety-critical real-time systems.

Chapter 15 investigates a practical approach to developing real-time applications in an environment consisting of COTS components with minimal support for real-time use. They concentrate on resource management and scheduling techniques to reduce the unpredictability inherent in these types of components. Instead of modifying the COTS components, they provide solutions sitting on the COTS components. They also discuss the limitations and real-time features of modern general-purpose operating systems and in particular present a characterization of Windows NT from the perspective of real-time constraints. They find that the unpredictable part of Windows NT can be minimized by the use of a user-level scheduling scheme. The chapter concludes with guidelines and recommendations of use to real-time system designers building applications using Windows NT.

13

Components in Real-Time Systems

Damir Isovic and Christer Norström

Introduction

The development of complex embedded systems is an expanding field. More and more applications are being based on the use of embedded computers. Examples include highly complex systems such as medical control equipment, mobile phones, and vehicle control systems. Most of such embedded systems can also be characterized as *real-time systems* (i.e., systems in which the correctness of the system depends not only on the logical result of the computations it performs but also on time factors) [1]. Embedded real-time systems contain a computer as part of a larger system and interact directly with external devices. They must usually meet stringent specifications for safety, reliability, limited hardware capacity, and so on. The increased complexity of embedded real-time systems leads to increasing demands with respect to requirements engineering, high-level design, early error detection, productivity, integration, verification, and maintenance. This calls for methods, models, and tools that permit a controlled and structured working procedure during the complete life cycle of the system [2]. When applying CBSE methodology in the development of real-time systems, an important factor is reusability of real-time components. Designing reusable real-time components is more complex and more expensive than designing

239

nonreusable non-real-time components [3, 4]. This complexity arises from several aspects of real-time systems not relevant in non-real-time systems. In real-time applications, components must collaborate in meeting timing constraints. Furthermore, to keep production costs down, embedded systems resources must usually be limited, but they must perform within tight deadlines. They must also often run continuously for long periods of time without maintenance.

In this chapter we present some issues related to the use of component technology in the development of real-time systems. First we give a short but comprehensive introduction to real-time systems, providing some background and defining the basic terminology. After this introduction, we will present that which is required of infrastructural components such as operating systems, databases, and the communication protocol when employed in real-time systems. The main requirement is predictability in the time domain (e.g., knowledge of the maximum response time for each system service used). Thereafter, we will state the demands on domain-specific component models for embedded real-time systems such as the port-based object model and the IEC 61131 standard [5, 6]. From a real-time perspective, the demands on a component can be divided into communication, synchronization, and timing requirements.

Given a system composed of a set of well-tested real-time components, we face the composability problem. Besides guaranteeing the functional behavior of a specific component, the composition must also guarantee that the communication, synchronization, and timing properties of the components and the system are retained. The composability problem with respect to timing properties, which we refer to as *timing analysis*, can thus be divided into (1) verifying that the timing properties of each component in the composed system still hold, and (2) *schedulability analysis* (i.e., system-wide temporal attributes, such as end-to-end deadlines, can be fulfilled). This timing analysis must be included in a design procedure. We present one such method that focuses especially on enabling high-level analysis on the architectural design level. This analysis is important to avoid costly redesign late in the development due to the detection in the integration test phase that the system as developed does not fulfill the timing requirements.

Furthermore, we propose a method for composing components and show how the resulting compositions could be handled when designing real-time systems. This is followed by a description of how an existing real-time development environment can be extended to support our design method. Finally, we provide guidelines about what one should be aware of when reusing and updating on-line real-time components.

Characteristics and Challenges of Real-Time Systems

Real-time systems are computing systems in which the meeting of timing constraints is essential to correctness. Real-time systems are usually used to control or interact with a physical system, and the timing constraints are imposed by the environment. As a consequence, the correct behavior of these systems depends not only on the result of the computation but also on the time at which the results are produced [1]. If the system delivers the correct answer, but after a certain deadline, it could be regarded as having failed. Many applications involving the external world are inherently of a real-time nature. Examples include aircraft and car control systems, chemical plants, automated factories, medical intensive care devices, and numerous others. Most of these systems interact directly or indirectly with electronic and mechanical devices. Sensors provide the system concerned with information about the state of its external environment. For example, medical monitoring devices, such as ECGs, use sensors to monitor patient and machine status. Air speed, attitude, and altitude sensors in aircraft provide information for the proper execution of flight control plans.

Real-time systems can be constructed of sequential programs, but typically they are built of concurrent programs, called *tasks*. Tasks are usually divided into *periodic* and *nonperiodic* tasks. Periodic tasks consist of an infinite sequence of identical activities, called *instances*, which are invoked within regular time periods. Nonperiodic tasks are invoked by the occurrence of an event, for example, a stimulus that may be generated by processes external to the system (e.g., an interrupt from a device).

When a processor is to execute a set of concurrent tasks, the operation of the CPU must be assigned to the various tasks according to a predefined criterion called a *scheduling policy*. Various algorithms are currently available for scheduling of real-time systems. They fall into two categories [1]: *off-line* and *on-line* scheduling. In off-line scheduling, the scheduler has complete knowledge of the task set and its constraints. Scheduling decisions are based on fixed parameters that are assigned to tasks before their activation. The off-line-generated schedule is stored and dispatched subsequently during run time of the system. On the other hand, on-line scheduling algorithms make their scheduling decisions during run time.

A typical timing constraint on a real-time task is the *deadline*. A deadline is the maximum time within which the task must complete its execution with respect to an event. Depending on the consequences that could result from a missed deadline, real-time systems are divided into two classes, *hard* and *soft* real-time systems. In hard real-time systems, all task deadlines must be met, whereas in soft real-time systems, meeting deadlines is desirable but not essential. In hard real-time systems, late data is bad data. Soft real-time systems are constrained only by average timing constraints (e.g., handling input data from the keyboard).

As mentioned earlier, many real-time systems are safety critical and the design of such systems must focus on demands for predictability, flexibility, and reliability. When applying CBSE methodology in the development of real-time systems, another important factor is the reusability of real-time components. Designing reusable real-time components is more complex than designing nonreusable, non-real-time components [3]. This complexity arises from several aspects of real time not relevant in non-real-time systems. In real-time applications, components must collaborate to meet timing constraints, also referred to as end-to-end transaction deadlines [7]. Furthermore, to keep production costs down, embedded systems resources are usually limited but they must perform within tight deadlines. They must often run continuously for long periods of time without maintenance.

Concurrent real-time systems are extremely complex to specify and develop because the performance of many independent operations may be required at the same time. When systems are large, these interactions make it difficult for developers to appreciate the implications of their design decisions. It is often impossible to predict with certainty when particular events will occur and what their order of occurrence and their duration will be. Real-time systems, however, must respond to events within a specified, predictable time limit. Similarly, hardware and software failures are usually unpredictable, but real-time software must be able to handle them in a predictable manner.

The load on a real-time system from its external environment is another source of complexity. This often requires the development of a priority-driven system that postpones less important tasks during heavy system loading. To be able to contend with this, real-time components must be designed to handle exceptional situations.

Real-time system developers must ensure that they are using the most efficient target resources available. Hence, common CBSE technologies (such as JavaBeans, CORBA, and COM) are seldom used, due to their excessive processing and memory requirements and unpredictable timing characteristics, which is unacceptable in the class of application we consider. They have, however, one desirable property which is flexibility, but predictability and flexibility have often been considered to be contradictory requirements, particularly from the scheduling perspective. Increased flexibility leads to lower predictability. Hence, a model for hard real-time systems cannot support flexibility to the same extent as the above-mentioned infrastructures.

Further, the development of standard real-time components that can be run on different hardware platforms is complicated by the components having different timing characteristics on different platforms. Thus a component must be adapted and reverified for each hardware platform to which it is ported, especially in safety-critical systems. Hence, we need to perform a timing analysis for each platform to which the system is ported.

Timing analysis is performed at two levels, the task level and the system level. At the task level the worst-case execution time (WCET) for each task is analyzed or estimated. The analysis can be performed in two ways, either via measurement or by static analysis of the code. If the execution time is measured, we can never be sure that we have determined the worst case. On the other hand if we use analysis, we must derive a safe value for the execution time. The estimated execution time must be greater than or equal to the real worst case and in the theory provided, the estimate can be excessive. The challenge here is thus to derive a value as close as possible to the real worst-case execution time. Puschner and Koza give a good introduction to this problem in their seminal paper [8] and the state of the art can be found in a special issue of real-time systems devoted to timing analysis [9].

At the system level we conduct analyses to determine if the system composed fulfills the timing requirements. Several different mature analysis methods exist, for example, analysis for priority-based systems and pre-run-time scheduling techniques [10, 11]. Both kinds of analysis have been proven to be useful in industrial applications [12, 13].

When designing a system, we can assign time budgets to the tasks that are not implemented by intelligent guesses based on experience. By doing this, we gain two positive effects. First, the system-level timing analysis can be performed before implementation, thus providing a tool for estimating the performance of the system. Second, the time budgets can be used as an implementation requirement. By applying this approach, we make the design process less ad hoc with respect to real-time performance. In traditional system design, timing problems are first recognized when the complete system or subsystem has been implemented. If a timing problem is then detected, ad hoc optimization will begin, this most surely making the system more difficult to maintain.

Real-Time Component Models

In this section we will try to make a distinction between infrastructure components such as real-time operating systems, databases, communication protocols, and user-interface subsystems, and application-specific component models that are normally specific to a particular application area and used to program the specific functionality. Examples of application-specific component models are IEC 61131 for industrial control [6], and the port-based objects approach that has been developed for designing embedded control systems, especially for robotics [5].

Infrastructure Components

A desirable feature in all system development, including the development of real-time systems, is the possibility of reusing standard components. However, using any particular operating system or database system for a real-time application is not always feasible, because many such systems are designed to maximize the average throughput of the system but do not guarantee temporal predictability. Therefore, to guarantee predictability, we must use either specific COTS developed for real-time systems or an appropriate subset of the functionality provided by the COTS.

The main characteristic of a standard real-time operating system (RTOS), for example, is temporal predictability, which means that each system service has a known upper limit to execution time [14]. We also need to know the upper limit to the interrupt latency provided by the RTOS. If the RTOS supports predictability, we can perform an analysis of our application's temporal behavior by using schedulability analysis. However, predictability is not enough, the RTOS must also be efficient with respect to memory and CPU usage to be useful in a cost-sensitive system. Other real-time components such as a database must of course also satisfy predictability and efficiency requirements.

Assume instead that we wish, if possible, to use a standard operating system in a real-time application. Consider the use of Windows NT in a real-time application. Because Windows NT was not developed for real-time application, we must use it carefully. In Chapter 15 and in [15], Ramamritham et al. discuss the features of Windows NT that should not be used if predictability is of importance. One of the weaknesses identified was that priority inversion could easily occur if real-time threads invoke routines in the Windows API. To achieve predictability when using Windows NT, the system must be designed in such a way that the real-time threads do not use all of the CPU and I/O capacity. Some resources must be reserved for functionality without real-time priority, especially functionality that handles interactive I/O.

A current research project, VEST [16], at Virginia State University is the study of how an RTOS for embedded real-time systems can be built from components when limited resources are available. VEST aims at the construction of the operating system (OS) part of an embedded real-time system with small resource requirements. System development begins with the design of an infrastructure that can be saved in a library and used again. The infrastructure consists of microcomponents such as interrupt handlers, indirection tables, dispatchers, plug and unplug primitives, proxies for state mapping, and so forth. It constitutes a framework for composing a system consisting of components. Configuration tools permit the user to create an embedded real-time system by composing components into a system and by mapping passive components into run-time structures (tasks).

After the system is composed, dependency checks are invoked to establish certain properties of the composed system. If the property requirements are satisfied and the system needs no further refinement, the user can invoke analysis tools to perform timing and reliability analyses. Note that components in VEST are passive (a collection of code fragments, functions, and objects) and are mapped into run-time structures (tasks). Each component can be composed from subcomponents. For example, a task management component can consist of components such as create task, delete task, and set task priority. Components have real-time properties such as WCET, deadline, and precedence and exclusion constraints, which enable timing analysis of the composed system.

In addition to temporal properties, each component has explicit memory needs and power supply requirements for efficient use in an embedded system. Selecting and designing the appropriate component(s) is a fairly complicated process, because both real-time and non-real-time aspects of a component must be considered and appropriate configuration support must be available. Dependency checks proposed in VEST [16] provide configuration support and demonstrate the effectiveness of the VEST approach.

Due to their complexity, dependency checks are separated into four types:

- *Factual:* Component-by-component dependency checks (WCET, memory, importance, deadline, etc.), intercomponent: pair-wise component checks (interface requirements, version compatibility, a component is included in another, etc.);
- *Aspects:* Checks of issues that affect the performance or semantics of components (real-time, concurrency synchronization and reliability issues);

- *General:* Checks of global properties of the system (the system should not be subject to deadlocks, hierarchical locking rules must be followed, etc.).

Using well-defined dependency checks is very important because they minimize possible errors in the system composition.

Application-Specific Component Models

In addition to infrastructure components, domain-specific component models, which in fact have been used for many years for certain domains, must be considered. Here, the objective is to make use of components with well-defined temporal behavior and resource demands that can be easily composed to constitute a system. The basic idea is to have a component library that the application engineer can use when developing an application. Components for an industrial control system can be different kinds of controllers, alarm functions, algorithms, etc. The application engineer should also be able to design new components for the particular application and thereby achieve a uniform handling of components both purchased and developed in-house.

We first present a standard IEC 61131-3 [6] for programming industrial control and thereafter a component-based system for robotics designated *port-based objects* (PBOs). As will be seen, these models are quite similar to the pipe-and-filters model presented in Chapter 3. The main difference is that in the IEC 61131 and PBO models, the pipe can accommodate only one data item, which means that if the data have not already been processed when new data arrive, they will be overwritten.

Examples of Component Models

IEC 61131 is a standard for programmable control systems and a set of associated tools, for example, debuggers, test tools, and programming languages. The part of IEC 61131 related to components is referred to as IEC 61131-3 [6] and is concerned with the programming of an application. IEC 61131-3 structures an application hierarchically and provides mechanisms for executing an application and providing support for communication between the different components. The model is shown in Figure 13.1.

A configuration in IEC 61131-3 encapsulates all software for an application. In a distributed system several configurations allocated to different nodes may communicate with each other. A configuration consists of one or

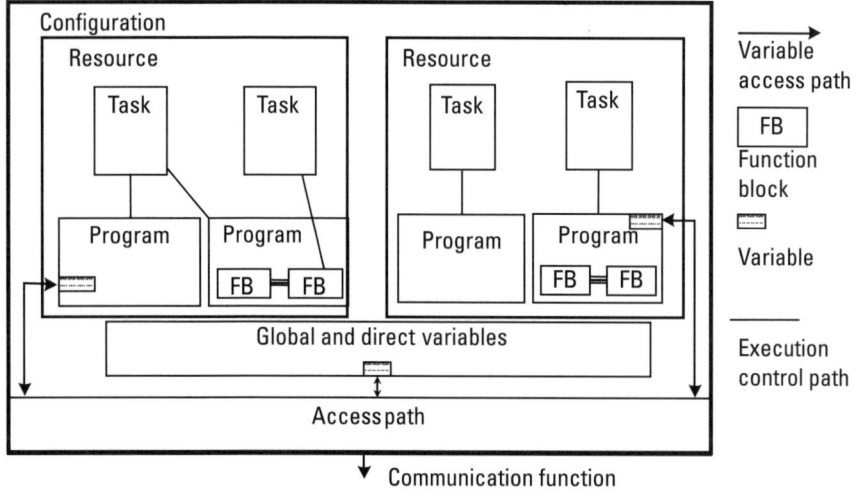

Figure 13.1 The IEC 61131-3 application structure.

several resources that provide the computational mechanisms. A program is written in any of the languages proposed in the standard, for example, instruction lists, assembly languages, structured text, a high-level language similar to Pascal, *ladder diagrams,* or *function block diagrams* (FBDs). Ladder diagrams and FBDs are graphical programming languages, FBD being the most relevant for CBD of embedded systems. The data flow is specified in IEC 61131-3 function blocks by connecting in-ports and out-ports. Out-ports contain the result from a computation based on input and the current state of the function block. Figure 13.2 presents a simple function block diagram representing a feedback control loop.

Real-time tasks can also be associated with a function block. Tasks can either be periodic or event driven. For periodic execution of a function block

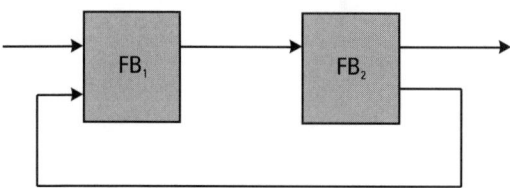

Figure 13.2 A feedback control loop with two function blocks (FB).

a period of time must be specified. In implementations of IEC 61131-3, the RTOS checks that the function block is periodically invoked. Event-triggered blocks are also supervised by the RTOS, which monitors that the CPU load does not exceed a certain threshold for a longer period of time than specified. Communication between function blocks within the same program is straightforward, whereas communication between function blocks in different programs requires support by special mechanisms.

The PBO approach was developed at the Advanced Manipulators Laboratory at Carnegie Mellon University [5]. The model is based on the development of domain-specific components that maximize usability, flexibility, and predictable temporal behavior. Independent tasks are the bases for the PBO model. Independent tasks are not permitted to communicate with other components, and components are thus loosely coupled and consequently, at least in theory, easy to reuse. Although no system can consist of independent components only, minimization of synchronization and communication among components is a desirable design goal. The data flow is specified by connecting in- and out-ports of different components, as in IEC 61131-3. Whenever a PBO needs data for its computation, it reads the most recent information from its in-ports, irrespective of its producer. When PBO components wish to make information available to other components in a system, they store data at their out-ports. A parameterization interface is provided to make PBO components more flexible and reusable. Several different application-specific behaviors can be implemented by one single component through a parameterization interface. In addition to the data interface and the parameterization interface named above, each PBO has an I/O interface. A PBO is shown in Figure 13.3. The PBOs are by their nature periodic and

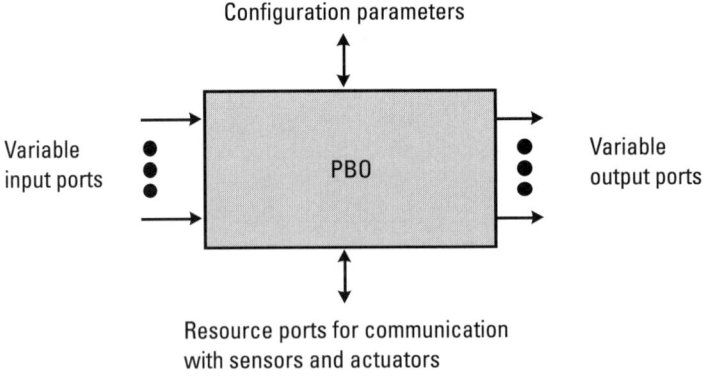

Figure 13.3 A PBO.

the system can be analyzed using traditional schedulability analysis [5]. As can be seen in this figure, the PBO model is quite simple and domain-specific.

Designing Component-Based Real-Time Systems

In this section we present a method for system development using real-time components. This method is an extension of [12], which is also in use in developing real-time systems within a Swedish automobile manufacturing company. It is a standard top-down development process to which timing and other real-time specific constraints have been added and precisely defined (or more correctly, have been predicted) at design time. The idea is to implement the same principles, but also take into consideration features of existing components that might be used in the system. This means that the system is designed not only in accordance with the system requirements, but also with respect to existing components.

This concept assumes that a library of well-defined real-time components is available. The component model used is an extension of the earlier described PBO model. The extension includes temporal attributes such as WCET, release time, and deadline, and synchronization constraints such as mutual exclusion and precedence relationships (see [17]). The development process requires a system specification, obtained by analyzing the customer's requirements. We assume that the specification is consistent and correct in order to simplify the presentation of the method.

The development process with real-time components is divided into several stages, as depicted in Figure 13.4. Development starts with the system specification, which is the input to top-level design. At the top level of design, which includes the decomposition of the system into components, the designer browses through the component library and designs the system, making selections from the possible component candidates.

The detailed design will show which components are suitable for integration. To select components, both real- and non-real-time aspects must be considered. In the architecture analysis, different architecture analysis methods are used for analyzing the extendibility of the design, the maintenance of the design, and so forth. The scheduling and interface check will show if the selected components are appropriate for the system, if adaptation of components is required, or if new components must be developed.

The process of component selection and scheduling may need to be repeated several times to refine the design and determine the most appropriate

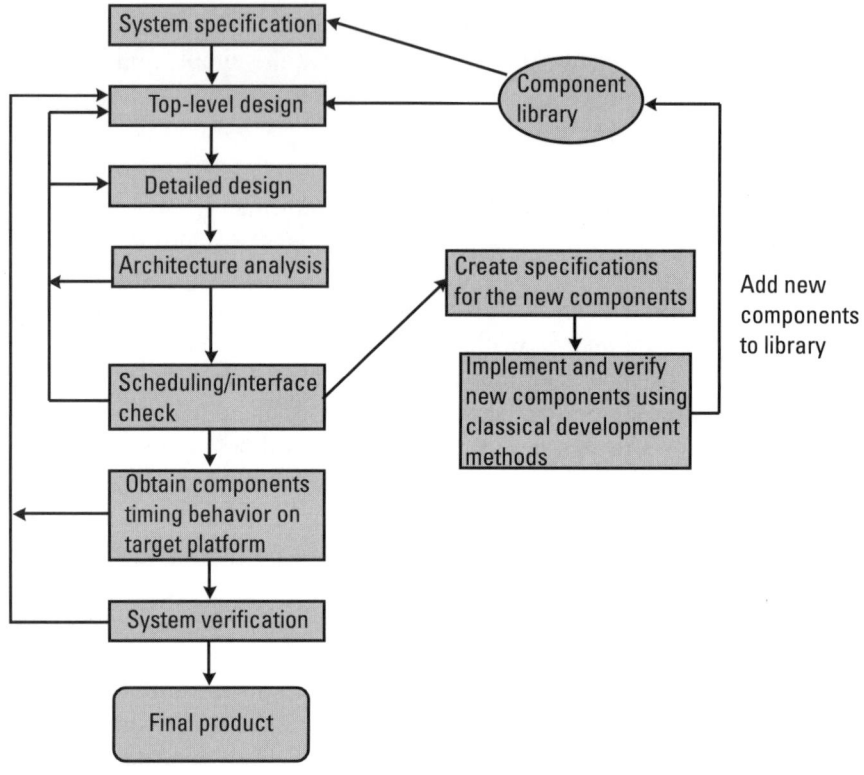

Figure 13.4 Design model for real-time components.

components. When a new component must be developed, it should be (when developed and tested) entered into the component library. When the system finally meets the specified requirements, the timing behavior of the different components must be tested on the target platform to verify that they meet the timing constraints defined in the design phase. A detailed description of these steps is given below.

Top-Level Design

The first stage of the development process involves decomposition of the system into manageable components. We need to determine the interfaces between them and to specify the functionality and safety issues associated with each component. Parallel with the decomposition, we browse the component library to identify a set of candidate components (i.e., components which might be useful in our design).

Detailed Design

At this stage a detailed component design is performed by selecting components to be used from the candidate set. In a perfect world, we could design our system only using the library components. In a more realistic scenario, we must identify missing components that we need according to our design but which are not available in the component library. Once we have identified all of the components to be used, we can start by assigning attributes to them, such as time budgets, periods, release times, precedence constraints, deadlines, and mutual exclusion.

A standard method of performing the detailed design is to use the WCET specified for every task, which specifies the upper limit of the time needed to execute a task. Instead of relying on WCET values for components at this stage, a time budget is assigned to each component. A component is required to complete its execution within its time budget. This approach has also been adopted in [17] and shown to be useful in practice. Experienced engineers are often needed to make correct assignments of time budgets. The time budget is thus an implementation requirement in addition to the functional requirements of a component.

Architecture Analysis

At this stage it is time to check that the system under development satisfies extrafunctional requirements such as maintainability, reusability, modifiability, and testability. Different approaches to performing an analysis for this purpose include scenario-based methods, simulation-based methods, mathematical model-based methods, and experience-based methods [18]. For instance, in addition to experience-based methods, we can apply the scenario-based Software Architecture Analysis Method (SAAM) [19, 20]. If the analysis shows that the design satisfies the extrafunctional requirements, the next step is to analyze the design's temporal requirements. If not, an architectural transformation of the design must be performed.

Scheduling

At this point we must check that the temporal requirements of the system can be satisfied, assuming time budgets assigned in the detailed design stage.

In other words, we need to make a schedulability analysis of the system based on the temporal requirements of each component. A scheduler that can handle the relevant timing attributes has been presented in [17], but other approaches such as a fixed priority schedulability analysis can also be used [21].

The scheduler in [17] takes a set of components with assigned timing attributes and attempts to create a static schedule. If scheduling fails, changes are necessary. It may be sufficient to revise the detailed design by reengineering the temporal requirements or by simply replacing components with others from the candidate set. An alternative is to return to the top-level design and either to select other components from the library or to specify new components.

During the scheduling we must check that the system is properly integrated. Component interfaces are checked to ensure that input ports are connected and that their types match. If the specified system passes this test, the schedules and the infrastructure for communication between components will be generated.

The benefit of this analysis is an increase in the confidence that design will fulfill the requirements. Further, the detection of any flaws or bugs at this stage will permit a system redesign that is relatively inexpensive compared with that necessary if such shortcomings are first recognized during the integration test when all code is available. This approach avoids the possible necessity of desperate optimization toward the end of a project, which most often has serious effects on the maintainability of the system.

WCET Verification

Performing a worst-case analysis can either be based on measurements or on a static analysis of the source code. Because no static analysis tools are available on the market, we use dynamic verification by running the code on the target platform. This must be done even if the component supplier provides a specification of the WCET, unless the specification is for an identical platform. We can verify the WCET by running test cases developed by the component designer and measuring the execution time. The longest time measured is accepted as the component WCET.

Obtaining the WCET for a component is quite a complicated process, especially if the source code is not available for the performance of the analysis. For this reason, correct information about the WCET from the component supplier is essential. Giving the WCET as a number does not provide sufficient information. What is more interesting in the test cases is the execution time behavior shown as a function of input parameters as in Figure 13.5. The execution time shows different values for the different input subdomains.

Producing such a graph can also be a difficult and time-consuming process. In many cases, however, the component developer can derive WCET test cases by combining source code analysis with the test execution. For example, the developer can find that the execution time is independent of input parameters within an input range (this is possible for many "simple" processors used in embedded systems but not for others). The exact values of the execution time are not as important as the maximum value within input intervals, as depicted in Figure 13.6. When a component is instantiated, the WCET test cases are chosen from the appropriate input subdomain. The timing behavior depends on how the component is instantiated. Further reading about this method is available in [22]. This approach has been tested successfully on a real industrial system [23].

Implementation of New Components

New components—that is, those not already in the library—must be implemented. The designer of the component has two requirements, the functional requirements and the assigned time budget. A standard development process for the development of software components is used, with the exception that the time budget must be considered. It may happen that some of the new components fail to meet their assigned time budgets. The designer can either add these to the library for possible reuse in other projects or redesign them.

One approach when redesigning a component is to apply a negotiation strategy, which means that we can move execution time to the component

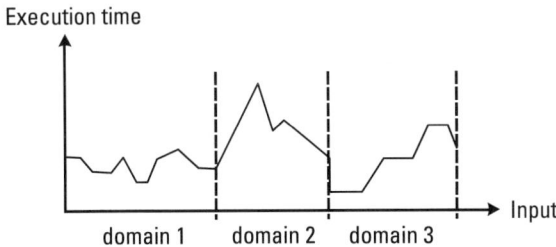

Figure 13.5 An execution time graph.

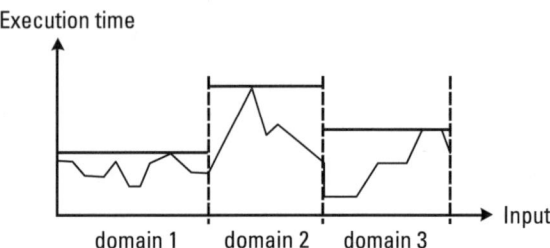

Figure 13.6 Maximum execution time per subdomain.

from other components that do not use the complete time budget, or from the components considered that are not yet implemented. This negotiation strategy has been successfully used in a concrete project applying this approach [12]. To perform the implementation and the verification, the target platform must be available.

System Build and Test

Finally, we build the system using old and new components. We must now verify the functional and temporal properties of the system obtained. If the verification test fails, we must return to the relevant stage of the development process and correct the error. Using this approach together with the static scheduler has shown that the system test has been successful since the scheduler has already integrated the system, despite the unavailability of some code. This is because all synchronization and communication between the components was fully specified in the design and checked by the static scheduler [10].

Component Library

The component library an important part of any CBSE system, because it contains binaries of components and their descriptions. When selecting components, we examine the attributes available in the library. A component library containing real-time components should provide the following in addition to component identification, functional description, interface, component binary, and test cases:

- *Memory requirements.* This is important information to have when designing memory-restricted systems and when performing trade-off analyses;

- *WCET test cases.* These are test cases that indicate the WCET of the component's WCET for a particular processor family. Information about the WCET for previously used targets should be stored to give a sense of the component's processor requirements.

- *Dependencies.* This describes dependencies on other components.

- *Environment assumptions.* These are assumptions about the environment in which the component operates, for example, the processor family.

Composition of Components

As mentioned earlier a component consists of one or more tasks. Several components can be composed into a more complex one. This is achieved by defining an interface for the new component and connecting the input and output ports of its building blocks, as shown in Figure 13.7.

This new kind of component is also stored in the component library, in much the same way as the other components. However, two aspects are different: the timing information and the component binary. The WCET of a composed component cannot be computed because its parts may be executing with different periods. Instead we propose that end-to-end deadlines should be specified for the input to and output from the component. End-to-end deadlines are set such that the system requirements are fulfilled in the same way as the time budgets are set. These deadlines should be the input to a tool that can derive constraints on periods and deadlines for the subcomponents. This possibility remains the subject of research and cannot be considered feasible today.

Furthermore, we specify virtual timing attributes (period, release time, and deadline) of the composed component, which are used to compute the timing attributes of subcomponents. For example, if the virtual period is set to P, then the period of a subcomponent A should be $f_A \times P$ and the period of B is $f_B \times P$, where f_A and f_B are constants for the composed component, which are stored in the component library. This enables the specification of timing attributes at the proper abstraction level. The binary of the composed component is not stored in the component library. Instead references to the subcomponents are stored, to permit the retrieval of the correct set of binaries.

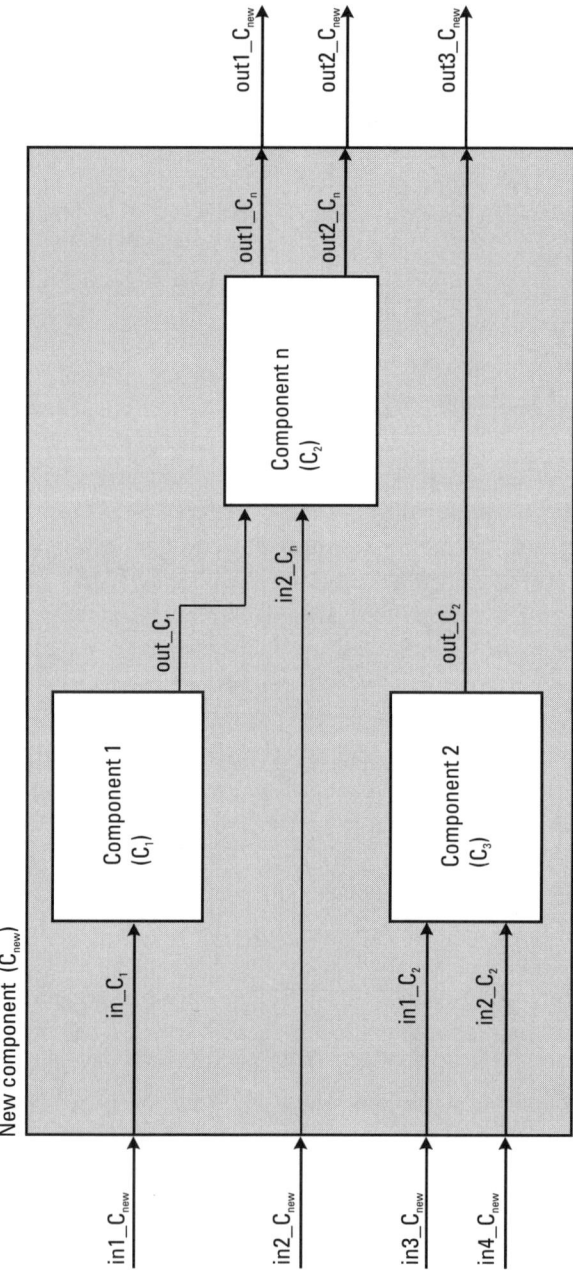

Figure 13.7 Composition of components.

Example: Real-Time Components in Rubus OS

Only a few real-time operating systems are currently available that have some concept of components. The Rubus operating system [24] is one of these. In this section we describe the main features of Rubus, and then present certain extensions that make it suitable for use in our development process. The scheduling theory behind this framework is explained in [17].

Rubus

Rubus is a hybrid operating system, in the sense that it supports both preemptive static scheduling and fixed priority scheduling. That which is referred to as the red part of Rubus deals only with hard real-time requirements and that referred to as the blue part, only with soft real-time requirements. Here we focus on the red part only.

Each task in the red part is periodic and has a set of input and output ports, which are used for unbuffered communication with other tasks. This set also defines the interface of a task. A task provides the thread of execution for a component and the interface to other components in the system via the ports. In Figure 13.8 we can see an example of the appearance of a task/component interface.

Each task has an entry function that has input and output ports as arguments. The values of the input ports are guaranteed not to change during the execution of the current instance of the task, in order to avoid inconsistency problems. The entry function is reinvoked periodically by the kernel.

The timing requirements of the task are shown in Figure 13.8. The timing requirements are specified by release-time, deadline, WCET, and period. Remember here that the WCET is a static attribute that is based on

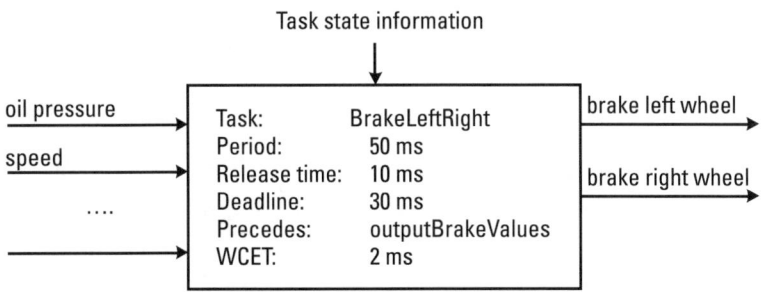

Figure 13.8 A task and its interfaces in the red part of Rubus.

the component code, while the release time and deadline are requirements derived from the process controlled and defined for the task. In addition to the timing requirements, it is also possible to specify the ordering of tasks using precedence relations and mutual exclusion. For example, the task depicted in Figure 13.9 is required to execute before the OutputBrakeValues task (i.e., task BrakeLeftRight precedes task OutputBrakeValues). A system is composed of a set of components/tasks the input and output ports of which have been connected, as depicted in Figure 13.9.

When the design of a system is completed, a pre-run-time scheduler is run to check that the temporal requirements are satisfied. If the scheduler demonstrates this, it then generates a schedule for the design, which is later used by the red kernel to execute the system.

Extensions for CBSE

Rubus and its supporting tools have certain deficiencies that make them currently unsuitable for CBD. First, there is no support for creating composite components (i.e., components that are built of other components). Second, a tool is needed to manage the components available and their associated source files, so that components can be fetched from a library and instantiated into new designs. Further, there is a lack of real-time tools such as WCET analysis and allocation of tasks to nodes.

Support for composition of components can easily be incorporated into Rubus, because only a front-end tool is needed to translate component specifications to task descriptions. For composition of components, the front-end tool should be able to perform these tasks:

1. Assign a name to the new component.
2. Specify input and output ports of the composition.
3. Connect input and output ports to the tasks/components within the component (see Figure 13.10).

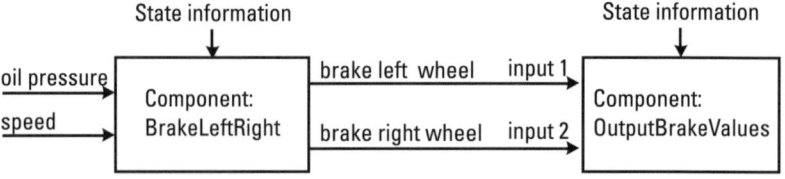

Figure 13.9 A composed system in the red model of Rubus.

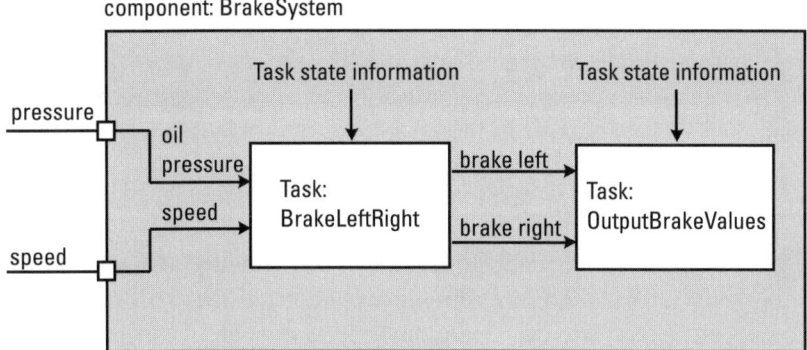

Figure 13.10 Composition of components in Rubus.

4. Generate task descriptions and port connections for the task within the component.

Reuse of Real-Time Components

Design for reuse means that a component from a current project should require a minimum of modification for use in a future project. Abstraction is extremely valuable for reuse. When designing components for reuse, designers should attempt to anticipate as many future applications as possible. Reuse is more successful if designers concentrate on abstract rather than existing uses. The objective should be to minimize the difference between the component's selected and ideal degrees of abstraction. The smaller the variance from the ideal level of abstraction, the more frequently a component will be reused.

Designers of reusable components must consider other important factors, in addition to anticipating future design contexts and future reuses. They must consider:

- What users need and do not need to know about a reusable design, or how to emphasize relevant information and conceal that which is irrelevant;

- What is expected from potential users, and what their expectations are about the reusable design;

- That it is desirable, although difficult, to implement binary components, to allow users to instantiate only relevant parts of components. For example, if a user wants to use only some of the available ports of a component, then only the relevant parts should be instantiated.

No designer can actually anticipate all future design contexts or when and in which environment the component will be reused. This means that a reusable component should depend as little as possible on its environment and be able to perform sufficient self-checking. In other words, it should be as independent as possible because frequency of reuse and utility increase with independence. Thus independence should be another main area of concern when designing reusable components.

An interesting observation about efficient reuse of real-time components, made by engineers at Siemens [25], is that, as a rule of thumb, the overhead cost of developing a reusable component, including design plus documentation, is recovered after the fifth reuse. Similar experience at ABB [26] shows that reusable components are exposed to changes more often than nonreusable parts of software at the beginning of their lives, until they reach a stable state.

Designing reusable components for embedded real-time systems is even more complicated due to memory and execution time restrictions. Furthermore, real-time components must be much more carefully tested because of their safety-critical nature.

These examples show that it is not easy to achieve efficient reuse, and that the development of reusable components requires a systematic approach in design planning and extensive development and support of a more complex maintenance process.

On-Line Upgrades of Components

A method for on-line upgrades of software in safety-critical real-time systems has been presented in [27]. It can also be applied to component-based systems when replacing components.

Replacing a component in a safety-critical system can result in catastrophic consequences if the new component is faulty. Complete testing of new components is often not economically feasible or even possible (e.g., shutting down a process plant with high demands on availability can result in enormous financial losses). It is often not sufficient to simulate the behavior of the system including the new component. The real target must be used for this purpose. However, testing in the real system means that it must be shut down, and there is also a potential risk that the new component could endanger human life or vital systems.

To overcome these problems, Sha [27] has proposed that the new component be monitored to check that its output is within valid ranges. If it is not, then the original component will resume control of the system. It is assumed that the old component is reliable, but not as effective as the new component in some respects; for example, the new component may provide much improved control performance. This technology has been shown to be useful for control applications.

A similar approach can be found in [21] where a component wrapper invokes a specific component version depending on the input values. The timing constraints related to the wrapper execution time must be taken into consideration, and such a system must support version management of components.

In this development model we assume that a static schedule is used at run time to dispatch the tasks, and since the schedule is static the flexibility is restricted. However, in some cases it is possible to perform on-line upgrades. On-line upgrades of the system require that the WCET of the new component be less or equal to the time budget of the component it replaces. It must also have the same interface and temporal properties (e.g., period and deadline). If this is not feasible, a new schedule must be generated and we must close down the system to upgrade it. Using the fault-tolerance method discussed earlier, we can still do this safely with a short downtime.

Summary

In this chapter we presented certain issues related to the use of component technology in the development of real-time systems. We pointed out the challenges introduced by using real-time components, such as guaranteeing the temporal behavior not only of the real-time components but also of the entire composed system.

When designing real-time systems with components, the design process must be changed to include timing analysis and especially to permit high-level analysis on an architectural design level. We presented a method for the development of reliable real-time systems using the component-based approach. The method emphasizes the temporal constraints that are estimated in the early design phase of the systems and are matched with the characteristics of existing real-time components. We outlined the information needed when reusing binary components, saved in a real-time component library.

Furthermore, we proposed a method for composing components and how the resulting compositions could be handled when designing real-time systems. We also provided guidelines about what one should be aware of when reusing and updating on-line real-time components.

References

[1] Stankovic, J., and K. Ramamritham, *Tutorial on Hard Real-Time Systems,* Los Alamitos, CA: IEEE Computer Society Press, 1998.

[2] Kalansky, D., and J. Ready, "Distinctions Between Requirements Specification and Design of Real-Time Systems," *Proc. TRI-Ada'88,* ACM Press, 1988.

[3] Douglas, B. P., *Real-Time UML—Developing Efficient Objects for Embedded Systems,* Reading, MA: Addison-Wesley-Longman, 1998.

[4] Basil, V. R., and H. D. Rombach, "Support for Comprehensive Reuse," *Software Engineering,* Vol. 6, No. 5, 1991, pp. 303–316.

[5] Stewart, D. B., R. A. Volpe, and P. K. Khosla, "Design of Dynamically Reconfigurable Real-Time Software Using Port-Based Objects," *IEEE Trans. on Software Engineering,* Vol. 23, No. 12, 1997, pp. 759–776.

[6] IEC, *Application and Implementation of IEC 61131-3,* Geneva: IEC, 1995.

[7] Cornwell, P., and A. Wellings, "Transaction Integration for Reusable Hard Real-Time Components," *Proc. High-Assurance Systems Engineering Workshop,* Niagra, Canada, IEEE Computer Society Press, 1996.

[8] Puschner, P., and Koza C., "Calculating the Maximum Execution Time of Real-Time Programs, *J. of Real-Time Systems,* Vol. 1, No. 2, 1989, pp. 159–176.

[9] Stankovic, J., W. A. Halang, and K.-F. Man, *Special Issue on Real-Time Systems on Worst-Case Execution Time Analysis,* Dordrecht, The Netherlands: Kluwer, 2000.

[10] Audsley, N. C., et al., Fixed Priority Pre-emptive Scheduling: An Historical Perspective, *J. of Time-Critical Computing Systems,* Vol. 8, Nos. 2/3, 1995, pp. 173–198.

[11] Jand, X., and D. L. Parnas, "Scheduling Processes with Release Times, Deadlines, Precedence and Exclusion Relations," *IEEE Trans. on Software Engineering,* Vol. 16, No. 3, 1990, pp. 360–369.

[12] Norström, C., et al., "Experiences from Introducing State-of-the-art Real-Time Techniques in the Automotive Industry," *Proc. 8th Annual IEEE Int. Conf. and Workshop on the Engineering of Computer Based Systems—ECBS01,* Washington, D.C., IEEE Computer Society Press, 2001.

[13] Casparsson, L., et al., "Volcano: A Revolution in On-Board Communications," Volvo Technology Report 98-12-10, Volvo, Sweden, 1998.

[14] Buttazzo, G., *Hard Real-Time Computing Systems: Predictable Scheduling Algorithms and Applications*, Dordrecht, The Netherlands: Kluwer, 1997.

[15] Ramamritham, K., "Using Windows NT for Real-time Applications: Experimental Observations and Recommendations," *Proc. 4th Real-Time Technology and Applications Symp.*, Denver, CO, IEEE Computer Society, 1998.

[16] Stankovic, J., "VEST: A Toolset for Constructing and Analyzing Component Based Operating Systems for Embedded and Real-Time Systems," Report CS-2000-19, Department of Computer Science, University of Virginia, 2000.

[17] Eriksson, C., et al., An Overview of RTT: A Design Framework for Real-Time Systems, *J. of Parallel and Distributed Computing*, Vol. 36, Issue 1, 1996, pp. 66–80.

[18] Bosch, J., *Design & Use of Software Architectures*, Reading, MA: Addison-Wesley, 2000.

[19] Kazman, R., et al., "SAAM: A Method for Analyzing the Properties of Software Architectures," *Proc. 16th Int. Conf. on Software Engineering*, 1994.

[20] Kazman, R., et al., Scenario-Based Analysis of Software Architecture, *IEEE Software*, Vol. 13, Issue 6, 1996, pp. 47–55.

[21] Cook, J. E., and J. A. Dage, "Highly Reliable Upgrading of Components," *Proc. 21st Int. Conf. on Software Engineering*, Los Angeles, CA, 1999.

[22] Lindgren, M., H. Hansson, and H. Thane, "Using Measurements to Derive the Worst-Case Execution Time," *Proc. 7th Int. Conf. on Real-Time Computing Systems and Applications—RTCSA 2000*, Cheiu Island, South Korea, IEEE Computer Society, 2000.

[23] Lindgren, M., and C. Norström, "Using Simulation to Verify Real-Time Properties," Report MRTC 00/27, MRTC, Mälardalen University, Västerås, Sweden, 2000.

[24] Articus, "Rubus OS Reference Manual," Articus Systems, 1996.

[25] Mrva, M., "Reuse Factors in Embedded Systems Design," Munich: High-Level Design Techniques Department, Siemens AG, 1997.

[26] Crnkovic, I., and M. Larsson, "A Case Study: Demands on Component-Based Development," *Proc. 22nd Int. Conf. Software Engineering*, Limerick, Ireland, ACM Press, 2000.

[27] Sha, L., "Dependable System Upgrade," *Proc. 20th Real-Time Systems Symp.*, Madrid, Spain, IEEE Computer Society, 1998.

14

Testing Reusable Software Components in Safety-Critical Real-Time Systems

Henrik Thane and Anders Wall

Introduction

In this chapter we will discuss how dynamic verification (i.e., testing) of real-time software relates to component reuse in safety-critical real-time systems. Experience with software reuse has shown that retesting cannot be eliminated in general. For safety-critical systems, this is a significant problem because testing is the single most expensive and time-consuming activity during system development.

The arguments for reuse of software in general, and software components in particular, are usually arguments for rapid prototyping (reusing code), arguments for outsourcing, and arguments for greater reliability, all of which are to be achieved at lower cost. In the case of reliability, it is assumed that testing of the components can be eliminated and that the reliability of the component can be "inherited" from previous uses. Expensive and catastrophic experiences with Ariane 5 and Therac 25 have shown, however, that this is not necessarily so: The explosion of the Ariane carrier rocket [1, 2], and the accidents due to excessive dosages administered by the Therac 25 radiotherapy apparatus [3] were all due to misconceptions, or disregard, of changes in the target environment from earlier uses of the software (in Ariane 4 and Therac 20). The assumed proven reliability of the components had no relevance in the new environments in which they were reused. The belief in the reliability of the components meant, in the cases of Ariane 5 and Therac 25, that retesting was neglected.

One lesson learned from these accidents is that if components are to be reused, testing cannot be eliminated. However, testing and maintenance are the two most resource-consuming activities in software development projects, especially in those that are safety critical. We will address this problem by presenting a framework for determining when components in real-time systems can be reused immediately, when complete retesting is necessary, or when only parts of the system need additional testing.

The framework deals with testing on the component level. The complete system must always be minutely tested even when reusing components that have been proven correct in previous applications. However, if component testing, as part of the total verification process, can be reduced, time and money will be saved.

There is no single, commonly accepted definition of a component in the software engineering community. Therefore we must specify what we consider a component to be. We refer to a component as being an encapsulation of services implemented in software and other subcomponents. The data processed by a component and the data it produces are specified in its data interface. The execution of a component is controlled by a *task,* which specifies the temporal constraints associated with the particular component. Tasks are connected to a component through the component's control interface. For a more exhaustive description of our component model, we refer to [4]. Components usually have contracts that specify the environment where they are defined to execute. Typically a contract specifies pre- and postconditions for services provided by a component, as well as invariants on, variables and infrastructure in which the component will execute [5]. In the cases of the Therac 25 and the Ariane 5 accidents, the contracts were not sufficiently defined or not adequately enforced. To remedy this shortcoming, we propose in this chapter the inclusion of evidence based on operational experiences of previous uses of a component in the contract description. This additional information gives us the opportunity to deem whether a component can be reused immediately or needs to be retested.

Reuse and Exhaustive Testing

We introduce here our approach in a comprehensible and simple manner. The concept is further expanded in succeeding sections of this chapter to encompass systems with real-time characteristics. The basic idea is to provide evidence, based on the component's contracts and the experience accumulated, that a component can be reused immediately, that only parts can be reused, or that it cannot be reused. We are only considering testing of the component's behavior in isolation. The complete system must also be verified according to the specification. This is very important because a reused component may interact with components with which it was not initially designed to interact. As a consequence of such a reuse, failures may reveal themselves that were tolerated (masked) by the initial system, but are unacceptable in the new context.

For example, assume that we have designed, exhaustively tested, and debugged a component for cellular telephones, *dual-band,* with an input domain *I* corresponding to a set of ranges of integer inputs, *I(dual-band)* = [0,1027] × [*G*, ... , *P*], and an output range *O, O(dual-band)* = [345, 640] (see Figure 14.1). It is consequently believed that the behavior the component is correct after testing all possible inputs.

Assume now that we reuse this component in a different environment, a new telephone design, where the input domain is different. That is, the component interacts with the same components, using the same infrastructure, but with inputs different from previous uses (see Figure 14.2). A system's

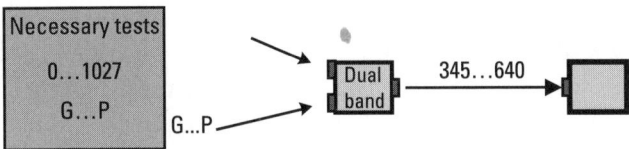

Figure 14.1 The dual-band component in its first use.

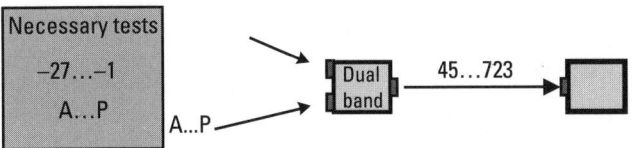

Figure 14.2 The dual-band component in the new environment.

infrastructure consists of the operating system, the hardware architecture, and other parts necessary for executing the system's implementation.

This reuse of the component warrants no confidence in the correctness of the component because there are new possible inputs, and therefore possibly incorrect outputs. Consequently, we should exhaustively test the component with those new inputs with which it was not tested previously $I(dual\text{-}band) = [0,1027] \times [A, \ldots, E] \cup [-27, -1] \times [A, \ldots, P]$.

If we should subsequently reuse the dual-band component in a third telephone for which the input domain overlaps those domains tested for the previous uses, the component may be reused without further testing as shown in Figure 14.3.

To record each component's history we can, by means of defensive programming, define the intervals of input for which the component has been tested. These defensive mechanisms, for example, pre- and postconditions, may be implemented in the component itself. If the component is later used in a different environment with a different input domain, the defensive mechanisms will detect this. If the new inputs give correct results we can expand the input domain experienced by changing the pre- and postconditions to encompass the new environment (see Figure 14.4).

As illustrated in Figure 14.5, the pre- and postconditions would be released and indicate a change in the new environment. If the new input domain is successfully verified, the pre- and postconditions can be updated to reflect the new domain experienced.

For components for which exhaustive testing is feasible, the above is sufficient, but for most systems in practice exhaustive testing is not possible, due to the size of the state space to explore. We could for such systems make use of probabilistic testing such that the reliability of the component could be estimated with a certain confidence. The estimated reliability of a software component is defined as the probability of the component functioning correctly, according to the specification, over a given period of time under a given set of operating conditions [6]. The confidence indicates how much we

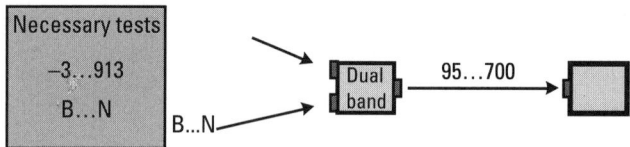

Figure 14.3 The third reuse of the dual-band component with an overlapping input domain.

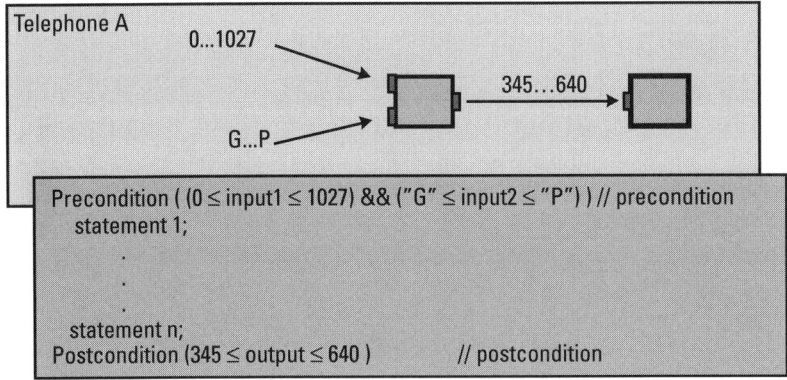

Figure 14.4 A component with pre- and postconditions.

can trust the estimated reliability. However, due to data storage issues, we need an external database containing the individual test cases executed because we cannot store them in the component itself.

So far, we have made use of a rather simplistic approach where only changes in the inputs and outputs have been considered. However, it is likely that a component will be reused in an infrastructure for which it was not initially designed. Components must therefore be reverified in some cases, even if the new input domains are completely within the verified domains. These matters are discussed later in this chapter.

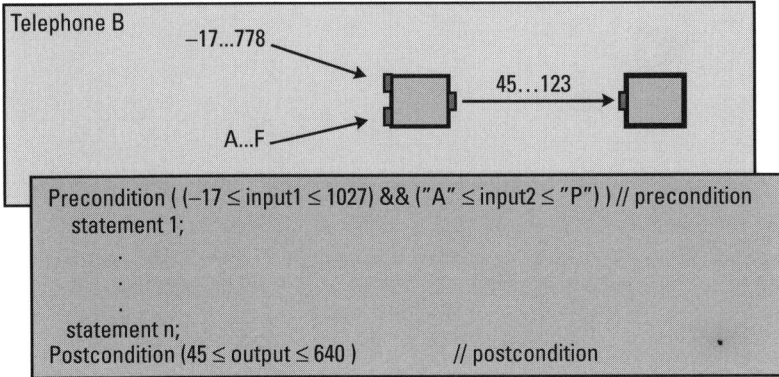

Figure 14.5 A new environment would violate the pre- and postconditions unless they are updated.

Reuse and Statistical Evidence

To elaborate on the approach in the previous section, we now consider components for which we have gathered statistical evidence regarding reliability through testing. Assume that we have tested a dual-band component with an input domain $I = [0,1027]$, nonexhaustively to a measured reliability of R with confidence C (Figure 14.6). If the component is reused in an environment in which the reliability requirement is lower than that in the original application (Figure 14.7), it is possible to reuse the component immediately.

If we are now to reuse the component in an application with the same I but with a need for greater reliability, as shown in Figure 14.8, we must test the component further until it is demonstrated statistically that the component has the required reliability.

If, however, the reused component's input domain differs from the previous one (although with a lower reliability than that previously ascertained), we must test these unexplored inputs until the required level of reliability is achieved (see Figure 14.9).

Component Reuse, Statistical Evidence, and Failure Behavior

When we test a component we always test the component with certain fault hypotheses in mind (i.e., we always look for certain types of faults). Depending on the architecture of the system, we can assume different degrees, and classes, of failure behavior. Certain types of failures are extremely improbable (impossible) in some systems, but are very likely to occur in others. If we are

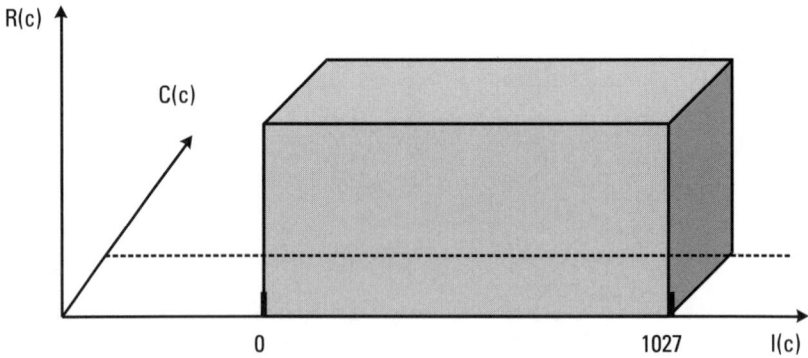

Figure 14.6 A graph representing the reliability and the confidence for an input domain.

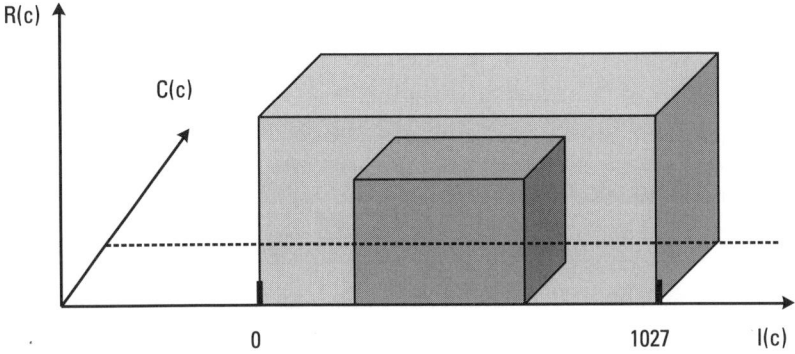

Figure 14.7 A component reused in a context with lower reliability requirements.

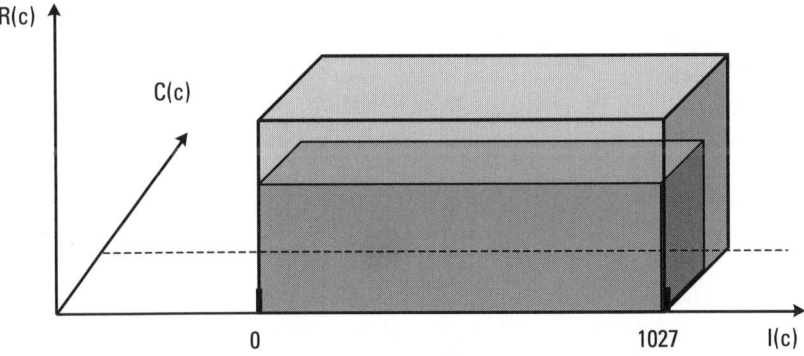

Figure 14.8 The component must be run for a longer time to reach the desired reliability.

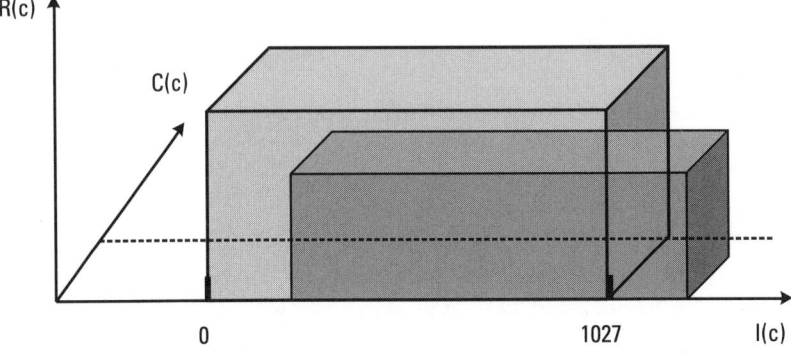

Figure 14.9 Previously experienced reliability cannot be utilized if input domains are outside historical use of the component.

aware of the system's possible failure behavior, we can reduce the testing effort because certain failures can be excluded and need not be searched for.

We define a failure as the inability of a system or component to perform its intended function as defined by the specification. A failure is a consequence of a *fault*, (i.e., a defect within the system or component), a bug, that has been executed. When a fault in a computer program is executed an *error* arises [7]. Finally, if the error propagates and becomes externally visible for an observer of a system or component, a failure occurs.

Components can fail in different ways and the ways in which they fail can be categorized as failure modes. The assumptions on how they fail are named *fault hypotheses*. We present failure modes ranging from failure behavior that sequential programs or single tasks can experience, to failure behavior that is only significant in multitasking real-time systems, where more than one task is competing for the same resources (e.g., processing power and memory). Failure modes are defined through their effects, as perceived by the component user.

We begin by defining the weakest assumption, namely, byzantine and arbitrary failure behavior:

> *Byzantine and arbitrary failures.* This failure mode is characterized by a nonassumption, meaning that there is absolutely no restriction with respect to which effects the component user may perceive. The failure mode has therefore been called *malicious* or *fail-uncontrolled.* This failure mode includes two-faced behavior: A component can output "X is true" to one component user, and "X is false" to another component user.

In the following sections we will gradually extend the list of failure behaviors. A system's failure behaviors constitute a partially ordered set in which real-time systems may exhibit sequential failure behavior and concurrent real-time systems may exhibit both sequential failure behavior and timing failure behavior.

Sequential Systems

Components in sequential programs exhibit the least number of possible failure behaviors among the classes of systems discussed in this chapter. We introduce *sequential failure behaviors* in the following list [7]:

- *Control failures,* for example, selecting the wrong branch in an if–then–else statement;

- *Value failures,* for example, assigning an incorrect value to a correct (intended) variable;

- *Addressing failures,* for example, assigning a correct (intended) value to an incorrect variable;

- *Termination failures,* for example, a loop statement failing to complete because the termination condition is never satisfied;

- *Input failures,* for example, receiving an (undetected) erroneous value from a sensor.

As an example of how the failure behavior for a sequential system may vary, consider a system that eliminates the possibility of a function erroneously overwriting the memory space used by other functions (i.e., addressing failures). Using hardware with memory management units (MMU), we can eliminate an entire class of failures and can, therefore, during testing, eliminate the search for them. On the other hand, when reusing the same component in a platform with no MMU support, the confidence regarding correct behavior is very low, because we have no evidence that the component will function. To increase our confidence, we must test the component with respect to addressing failures. In contrast, if the component has been proven in a system with no MMU support, the component may be reused immediately, because the failure semantics of the previous use are more pessimistic than in the new context (see Figure 14.10).

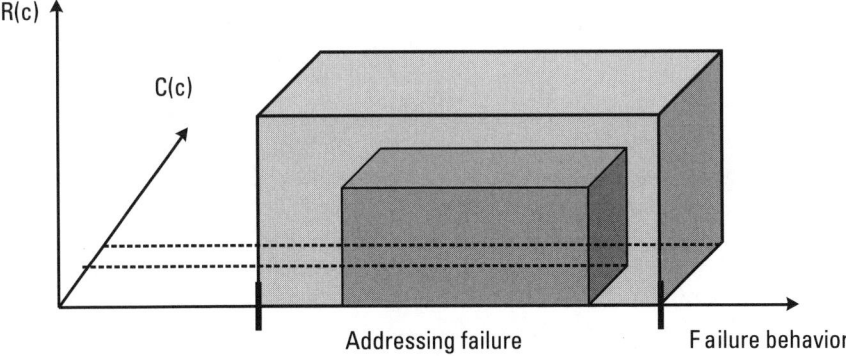

Figure 14.10 The confidence in the measured reliability is decreased when new failure behaviors can develop.

Real-Time Systems

We now add time to sequential programs. Real-time systems are character-ized by the required *temporal correctness*, that is, correct operation at the cor-rect time. Data, correct in itself, but delivered too late or too early is incorrect. Consequently, the reliability and confidence of a component will be negatively affected if the temporal behavior of a component is altered.

The usual temporal constraints for a sequential program are execution times, deadlines, period times, jitter constraints (variations in execution time, variations in the time span from sampling to actuation), and so forth. We now introduce timing failure behavior:

> *Timing failure behavior:* This failure mode yields a correct result (value), although the procurement of the result is time-wise incorrect. For exam-ple, if deadline violations, starting a task too early, an incorrect period of time, too much jitter, too many interrupts (interarrival time is too short between consecutive interrupt occurrences) occur.

A typical instance of the degrading of confidence in the temporal cor-rectness of a component may occur when a component is reused on another hardware platform. For example, if the new system executes on different hardware, the execution time may change (e.g., due to a slower CPU), and as a consequence the deadline may be violated.

We next provide examples of reuse in real-time systems with respect to three typical cases: deadline requirements, response time requirements, and periodicity requirements. The first two cases are discussed in the context of changing the execution time for a component by running it on a different CPU. The third case relates to possible effects of changing the period time (the frequency), of a component in a control system.

- *Deadline requirements.* If we reuse a component with only a dead-line requirement in a new environment in which the execution time is shorter, the component can be reused without retesting (see Figure 14.11).

- *Response time requirements.* If the component is reused on a faster CPU and we have an end-to-end deadline, the reuse may result in a response time that is too short (e.g., an airbag in a car deflated too soon after initial inflation at crash). On the contrary, a slower CPU might prolong the response time. In this case it is not easy to decide whether or not retesting can be ignored. However, if tolerances are

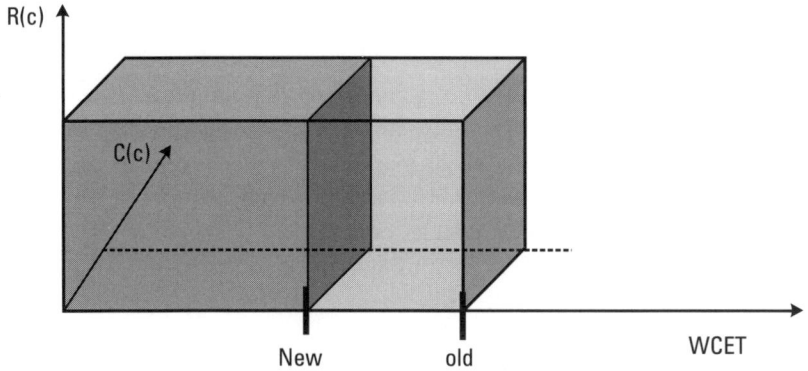

Figure 14.11 The deadline requirement is still fulfilled because the new execution time is shorter.

specified in terms of response times (end-to-end deadlines), it might be possible to argue that a component can be reused in a new environment provided the tolerances are not violated (see Figure 14.12).

- *Periodicity/frequency requirements.* If the component is a periodic controller in a control system, and we change the periodicity of its activation, the controlled system might become unstable, typically if we decrease the frequency of the component's activation. However, if we reuse the component and run it with a higher frequency, retesting may be ignored if the resulting system remains schedulable (i.e., the component still meets its deadline).

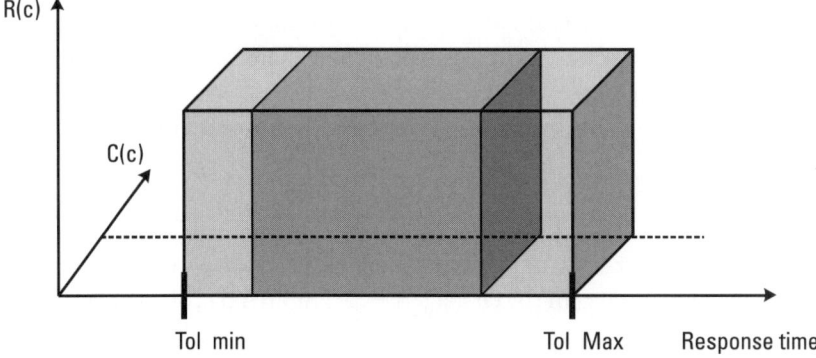

Figure 14.12 The response time for the reused component is within the tolerance.

Concurrent Real-Time Systems

If we now add concurrency (the running of several components simultaneously), either on the same CPU or on different CPUs, we must consider synchronization. Synchronization of component execution is used in concurrent real-time systems for several reasons, two of which are to resolve mutual exclusion or to resolve precedence relations.

Mutual exclusion solves the problem of protecting critical resources from being accessed by multiple components simultaneously. As an example consider writing data in a database. To keep the data consistent, only one component is allowed to write at a time. Multiple simultaneous readers, however, present no problem.

The precedence relation defines the order in which two components must execute. Typically, control systems consist of a component sampling process values and other components performing calculations based on the sampled values. In such a case, the sampling component might be required to execute before any of the calculating components.

Depending on the RTOS used, we can either make necessary synchronizations between tasks off-line if the RTOS is time triggered and supports offsets, or if we can synchronize tasks on-line using primitives such as semaphores. In the off-line case we guarantee precedence and mutual exclusion relations by separating tasks time-wise, using offsets.

Communication between tasks in real-time systems can be achieved in many ways. We can make use of shared memory, which is guarded by semaphores, or time synchronization, or we can, via the operating system, send messages or signals between tasks. Depending on the relation between the communicating tasks with respect to periodicity, the communication can vary between totally synchronous communications to totally asynchronous communication. That is, if task i sends data to task j, and both tasks have equal periodicity, $T_j = T_i$, we can make use of one shared memory buffer only. However, if $T_j > T_i$ or $T_j < T_i$, the issue becomes more complicated. Either we make use of overwriting semantics (state-based communication), using just a few buffers, or we record all data that have been sent by the higher frequency task so that it can be processed by the lower frequency task when it is activated. There are several approaches to solving this problem [8–10].

Continuing the list of possible failure behaviors we can now add three more items inherited from the characteristics exhibited by concurrent systems:

1. *Ordering failures,* for example, violations of precedence relations or mutual exclusion relations;

2. *Synchronization failures,* that is, ordering failures but also deadlocks;

3. *Interleaving failures,* for example, unwanted side effects caused by nonreentrant code, and shared data, in preemptively scheduled systems.

Synchronization is discussed later with respect to changes in the system's infrastructure, which includes the operating system and the synchronization mechanisms it provides.

- *Original environment: off-line synchronized.* Reusing a component that in its original environment resolved synchronization by separation in time in a system that also resolves synchronization by separation in time without retesting is acceptable if the new system is schedulable. If, however, the same component is reused in an environment that uses semaphores for synchronization, the system must be reverified. This is because we can make no assumptions about synchronization failures because the original component is only tested for ordering failures, which is a more relaxed assumption than synchronization failures. For example, deadlocks are impossible in off-line scheduled, time-synchronized systems.

- *Original environment: on-line synchronized.* Reusing a component that has been using on-line synchronization (semaphores) in an environment that resolved synchronization by separation in time is warranted as long as the system is schedulable. Reusing the component in an on-line synchronization environment does not warrant the omission of retesting even though the system is proven schedulable because the coupling between components in an on-line synchronized system is much tighter than in an off-line synchronized system. We cannot, for example, guarantee that the other components in the new environment are correct with respect to synchronization.

Note that reuse across synchronization paradigms in general requires rewriting code that results in a behavior that has not been tested.

The failure modes listed for sequential systems, real-time systems, and concurrent systems build up a hierarchy in which byzantine failures are based on the weakest assumption (a nonassumption) regarding the behavior of the components and the infrastructure, and sequential failures are based on the strongest assumptions. Consequently, byzantine failures are the most severe and sequential failures the least severe failure mode. The byzantine failure mode includes all failures classified as timing failures, which in turn include synchronization and other failures.

Summary

In this chapter we have presented a framework for arguments with respect to the reuse and retesting of components in safety-critical real-time systems. The arguments for reuse of software (components) are usually arguments for rapid prototyping (reusing code), arguments for outsourcing, and arguments for greater reliability. In the latter case, it is assumed that testing of the components can be eliminated and that the reliability of the component can be "inherited" from previous uses. Expensive and catastrophic experiences have shown, however, that this is not necessarily so (e.g., Ariane 5, and Therac 25 [1–3]). In this framework, we formally described component contracts in terms of temporal constraints specified in the design phase (the design task model) and the temporal attributes available in the implementation (the infrastructure). Furthermore, the input–output domain for a component is specified in the contract. By relating the input–output domain, fault hypotheses, probabilistic reliability levels, and the temporal behavior of the component, we can determine if a component can be reused without retesting or not. It is of great significance that we can determine how much of, and which subsets, of, say, input–output domains, need additional *testing* based on reliability requirements in the environment in which the reuse is intended. Faced with complete retesting, the possibility of decreasing the testing effort is attractive. Decreasing the cost for testing is especially attractive when developing safety-critical real-time systems where testing is a major activity.

References

[1]   Le Lann, G., "An Analysis of the Ariane 5 Flight 501 Failure—A System Engineering Perspective," *Proc. 4th Int. Conf. Engineering of Computer-Based Systems*, Boston, MA: IEEE Computer Society, 1997.

[2]   Inquiry Board, "ARIANE 5—Flight 501 Failure," http://wxtnu.inria.fr/actualirdsfra .htrnl.

[3]   Leveson, N., and C. Turner, "An Investigation of the Therac-25 Accidents," *IEEE Computer*, Vol. 26, No. 7, 1993, pp. 18–41.

[4] Wall, A., and C. Norström, "A Component Model for Embedded Real-Time Software Product Lines," *Proc. 4th IFAC Conf. Fieldbus Systems and Their Applications*, Nancy, France, 2001.

[5] Meyer, B., "Applying Design by Contracts," *IEEE Computer*, Vol. 25, No. 10, 1992, pp. 41–50.

[6] Storey, N., *Safety-Critical Computer Systems*, Reading, MA: Addison-Wesley-Longman, 1996.

[7] Clarke, S. J., and J. A. McDermid, "Software Fault Trees and Weakest Preconditions: A Comparison and Analysis," *Software Engineering J.*, Vol. 8, No. 4, 1993, pp. 255–236.

[8] Chen, J., and A. Burns, "Asynchronous Data Sharing in Multiprocessor Real-Time Systems Using Process Consensus," *Proc. 10th Euromicro Workshop on Real-Time Systems*, Madrid, Spain, IEEE Computer Society, 1998.

[9] Eriksson, C., et al., "An Overview of RTT: A Design Framework for Real-Time Systems," *J. Parallel and Distributed Computing*, Vol. 36, 1996, pp. 66–80.

[10] Kopetz, H., and J. Reisinger, "The Non-Blocking Write Protocol NBW: A Solution to a Real-Time Synchronization Problem," *Proc. 14th Real-Time Systems Symp.*, Orlando, FL, IEEE Computer Society, 1993.

15

Providing Real-Time Services for COTS Components

Oscar Javier Gonzalez Gomez, Krithi Ramamritham, Chia Shen, and Gerhard Fohler

Introduction

In an ideal situation, a real-time operating system should be used for supporting a real-time application. However, market forces and the acceptance of COTS OSs in industrial applications have generated a need for achieving real-time functionality. A COTS OS is preferred in many real-time systems and applications to avoid the overhead of either the installation of other kernels and facilities beyond those provided in the standard OSs or the usage of some other APIs running parallel with these.

This chapter describes how to build real-time systems using commercially available off-the-shelf components, focusing on operating systems and scheduling algorithms. In our experiment we use two COTS, one large—the operating system, Windows NT, which does not provide genuine real-time services—and a small one—the video player application. We build a third component that bounds the unpredictability of the underlying component, Windows NT, to provide soft real-time services to the application component.

Specifically, a characterization of Windows NT is presented from the perspective of real-time constraints. We have also analyzed Windows 2000 in a separate study and obtained results similar to those presented here. In our study, we systematically develop guidelines and recommendations that will be useful to real-time system designers building applications using Windows NT. The observations are validated by the use of Windows NT for a prototype application involving real-time control, which includes multimedia information processing. A key result of this study is that the unpredictability of NT can be *bounded* by the use of a user level-scheduling scheme [1].

Although the benefits of using Windows NT are many, there are certain limitations to its use in real-time applications. The reasons for these limitations can be found in a few key Windows NT kernel policies and mechanisms. In this chapter, we study the source of these limitations from the perspective of real-time constraints and systematically develop guidelines and recommendations that will be useful in the development of predictable communication services. A key element of our study is to address the following two questions:

1. *What type of applications can use Windows NT as is?* Because Windows NT was not designed with predictability in mind, it is neither advisable nor feasible to use NT for hard real-time applications. However, we show that when used judiciously, Windows NT may be useful for applications that (a) can tolerate occasional deadline misses, and (b) have delay/response time requirements in the tens to hundreds of milliseconds range such as those described in [2–4].

2. *Can the unpredictable parts of Windows NT be "masked"?* One of the results of our study is that we provide guidelines and insights needed to overcome some of the limitations of Windows NT without having to make changes in the operating system. This knowledge enables us to develop techniques to support the needs of tasks having a variety of real-time and non-real-time requirements.

We begin this chapter with an overview of the capabilities of Windows NT that are potentially useful to real-time system builders. We then critically evaluate their performance characteristics via a series of experiments. The experiments and the observations derived from them are summarized in the "Real-Time Features of Windows NT" section of this chapter. We then use these observations to build a prototype of an application involving real-time control, which includes multimedia information processing. The "Windows

NT in a Real-Time Setting" section in this chapter describes the components of the prototype along with the resulting assessment of NT's suitability for such real-time applications. This section also contains a set of guidelines and recommendations that emerged from the experimental evaluation of NT for real-time uses. Finally, a conclusion summarizes the chapter.

Windows NT as an RTOS

To determine the shortcomings of Windows NT, it is important to have some understanding of its architecture. The original design of NT was based on a microkernel, common to many real-time operating systems (e.g., RT-Mach, VxWorks, QNX). For performance reasons, the architecture has evolved from the original design and a limited number of real-time features have been incorporated. Because NT's use of threads and 32 possible priority levels can be helpful in constructing real-time applications, we will discuss these first.

Each process belongs in one of the following priority classes: IDLE, NORMAL, HIGH, and REAL_TIME. By default, the priority class of a process is NORMAL. Processes that monitor the system, such as screen savers or applications that periodically update a display, are in the priority class IDLE. A process in the HIGH priority class takes precedence over a process in the NORMAL priority class. The REAL_TIME priority class is available as support for real-time applications.

Windows NT assigns a scheduling *base priority* to each thread. This *base priority* is determined by the combination of the priority *class* of its process and the priority level of the thread. A thread can be on any of the following seven priority levels: IDLE, LOWEST, BELOW_NORMAL, NORMAL, ABOVE_NORMAL, HIGHEST, and TIME_CRITICAL. The *base priorities* range from zero (lowest priority) to 31 (highest priority). The base priority for the REAL_TIME class includes levels 16 to 31. Levels 17 to 21 and 27 to 30 are currently not used by the scheduler. Base priority levels from 0 to 15 are reserved by the dynamic classes as shown in Figure 15.1.

Given this priority structure, Windows NT performs *priority-based preemptive scheduling* (i.e., the highest priority active task is chosen for execution), possibly interrupting the execution of another task. When two threads have the same *base priority*, a time-sharing approach is used. REAL_TIME priority class threads have nondegradable priorities, while NORMAL and HIGH priorities threads can be delayed by the NT scheduler. For this reason the latter priority classes are commonly referred to as *dynamic* classes.

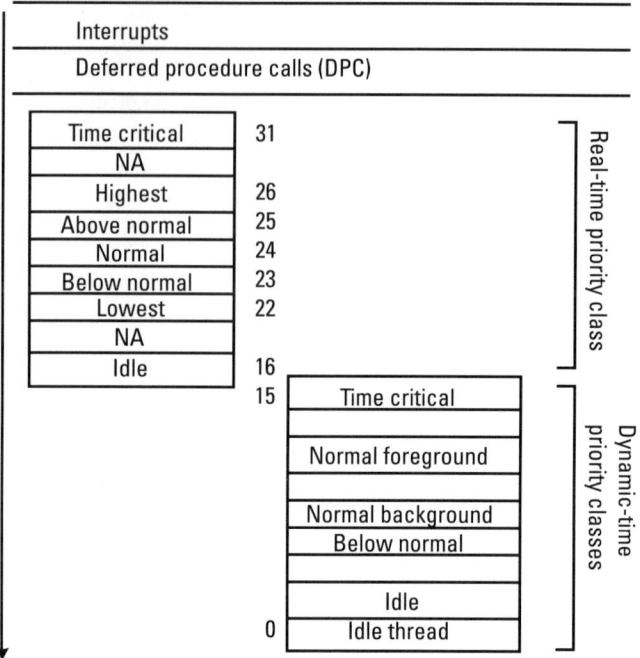

Figure 15.1 Windows NT priority structure.

However, at a fundamental level, Windows NT was designed as a general-purpose OS and many of the policies/mechanisms are geared toward optimizing the average case, this being at odds with the high predictability requirements of many real-time environments. We next discuss some of the limitations in Windows NT—due mainly to the lack of provision for various services/mechanisms to take into account the priority of an event/object—which may contribute to unpredictable delays in user applications [4–6].

The priority levels of interrupts are always higher than that of a user-level thread, including threads in the real-time class. When an interrupt occurs, the trap handler saves the machine's state and calls the interrupt dispatcher. The interrupt dispatcher makes the system execute an interrupt service routine (ISR). Only critical processing is performed in the ISR and the bulk of the processing is performed in a deferred procedure call (DPC).

DPCs are queued in the system DPC queue, in a first-in, first-out (FIFO) manner. While this separation of ISR and DPC ensures quick response to any further interrupts, it has the disadvantage that the priority structure at the interrupt level is not maintained in the DPC queues. A DPC is not preemptable by another DPC, but can be preempted by an (unimportant) interrupt. As a consequence, the interrupt handling and the DPC mechanisms introduce unpredictable delays both for interrupt processing and for real-time computations. More generally, the lack of provision for avoiding priority inversions is the primary problem for real-time applications. Windows CE, another operating system from Microsoft, designed for embedded communication and entertainment applications, supports priority inheritance (see the "Windows NT in a Real-Time Setting" section in this chapter).

Threads executing in kernel mode are not preemptable by user-level threads and execute with dispatching temporarily disabled, but interrupts can occur during the execution of the kernel. Because kernel-level threads can mask some or all interrupts by raising the CPU's current interrupt request levels (IRQL), the responsiveness at any point in time to an interrupt depends on the mask set by kernel entities at that time, and the execution time of the corresponding kernel entities. Also, because only kernel level threads are permitted to mask and unmask **interrupts,** even an unimportant interrupt can adversely affect a real-time priority **user-level** thread. All of these factors do not bode well for real-time processing. Unpredictability also occurs because some system calls (e.g., some GUI calls) are synchronous and are executed by system processes, running at a non-real-time class priority.

Given these, the natural question to ask is this: What are the conditions under which NT can, in fact, be used for real-time applications? This is what we intend to explore in the remainder of this chapter, by first studying the behavior of the real-time-related NT components and then by using them in a prototype real-time application.

Real-Time Features of Windows NT

In this section we report the results of experiments conducted to evaluate the real-time features of Windows NT Workstation 4.0.

Empirical Characterization of NT Features That Affect Real-Time Activities

The first set of experiments was targeted toward the behavior of threads at REALTIME priority class and their effect on the I/O subsystem and vice versa. To this end, we used two threads with the same thread priority in the REALTIME class, one performing I/O and another, a CPU-intensive thread, performing a continuous FOR loop. The following three experiments were conducted:

- *Experiment 1.* To study the effect on keyboard and mouse I/O, the I/O thread was made to read from the keyboard/mouse. When the CPU-intensive thread was running, no I/O activity was observed. After the CPU-intensive thread completed running, all the keyboard inputs were processed. This showed that the CPU-intensive real-time thread essentially shuts out keyboard/mouse I/O even when this I/O is from/to a real-time thread.

- *Experiment 2.* To study the effect on disk I/O, the I/O thread was made to write a file with 40,000 64-bit values. The time stamps for the I/O and CPU-intensive activities were found to be interleaved, indicating time sharing between the two threads. This showed that a CPU-intensive real-time thread did not shut out disk I/O.

- *Experiment 3.* To study the effect on network I/O, the I/O thread was made to read data from a remote server using Windows Sockets API. Here again, the time stamps for the two activities were found to be interleaved, this indicating time sharing between the two threads. This showed that a CPU-intensive real-time thread has no adverse impact on network I/O.

To explain these observations, we must explain how NT handles I/O—beyond the use of DPCs. In the Windows NT I/O subsystem, I/O requests pass through several stages of processing:

1. The I/O manager sends the request in the form of an I/O request packet (IRP) to the device driver. The driver starts the I/O operation.
2. The device completes the I/O operation and interrupts. The device driver then services the interrupt. (This involves execution of ISR and queuing of a DPC.)
3. The I/O manager completes the I/O request.

In the third step of I/O processing, the system writes the data from the I/O operation into the address space of the thread which requested the I/O. In this step, two mechanisms are used (for more details see [7]):

1. *Buffered I/O.* Used for slower I/O devices in which the data is first transferred into the system memory area and an asynchronous procedure call (APC) is queued to copy this data into the local area of the user thread.

2. *Direct I/O.* Used for faster devices such as the disk. The data is transferred directly into the local address space of the user thread, which is locked by the system.

In experiment 1, because the keyboard and mouse I/O are performed as buffered I/O, the execution of APCs responsible for copying the data into the address space of the user thread address space was not possible until the CPU-intensive thread was completed. This is because the input from the keyboard/mouse is actually processed by threads in the kernel that are not running with real-time priority. Because there is no priority inheritance, the threads processing the input do not execute until the CPU-intensive thread completes.

On the other hand, for experiments 2 and 3, because the disk and network I/O are performed as direct I/O, the system locks the buffer space of the corresponding thread into the memory. This ensures that the I/O is performed even if a CPU-intensive real-time thread of the same priority is running, which is possible due to time sharing between threads of the same priority.

One way to counter the lack of complete predictability while using Windows NT is to have user-level control over the scheduling and execution of real-time activities. Hence, we next describe the overheads inherent in Windows NT's API calls. We subsequently examine the hidden overheads due to the execution of various system-level activities in NT.

To perform such user-level scheduling of real-time threads, which we consider to be a necessary approach to running real-time applications on Windows NT, it is a prerequisite that the time taken for the completion of various process/thread related API calls be determined. We measured these times experimentally and the values obtained are listed in Table 15.1. The times listed (in microseconds) fall within the 90th percentile, that is, 90% of the 1,000 observations had values that were equal to or less than the reported number. We report these times and not worst case (or average) times because of our interest in soft real-time and not hard real-time (or time-sharing) applications.

The next set of experiments was performed to identify the system activities taking place in the background and the worst-case processor time

Table 15.1

Time Taken for System Operations*

Win32API Function Name	Time (μs)
CreateProcess()	2,600
SetPriorityClass()—from normal to real-time priority class	240
SetPriorityClass()—for all other combinations	125
SetThreadPriority()—for a thread to set its own priority	9
SetThreadPriority()—for a thread to set priority of another thread of the same process	10
QueryPerformanceCounter()—to obtain the current time stamp	6

*The platform used was a PC equipped with a 233-MHz Pentium processor, 64 MB of RAM, and 256 KB of cache. Where communication is called for, the network used was a 10-Mb Ethernet. Each PC uses a 3Com3C590 combo Ethernet card connected via a department-wide network. Events were timed and the time taken for various activities was determined using NT's QueryPerformanceCounter.

needed to perform these activities. This is necessary to determine the unpredictability introduced by system-related activities—activities over which users may have no control. The schedule constructed must be designed to take these system activities into account to achieve predictability. To this end, we observed the system with no other application running and logged the activity every second for a continuous period of 30 min. The following were (individually) observed in at least one of the logs:

- Process *system* had 23 threads, thread 1 getting a maximum of 53 ms.

- Process *csrss* had 10 threads, thread 4 getting a maximum of 50 ms.

- Process *services* had 18 threads, thread 15 getting a maximum of 50 ms.

- Process *perfmon* had 2 threads, thread 1 getting a maximum of 53 ms.

Other threads of these processes occupied negligible processor time. Even though the preceding time periods were not observed within the same second, the observations mean that system activities can take at most a total of 153 ms in a 1-sec interval (discounting the time process *perfmon* takes because this is a performance monitor we instantiated, not a system activity).

Note that when user processes are running in the system, they may generate some system activity such as page-faults.

Observations and Recommendations

It might appear from our experimental results that Windows NT is unsuitable for real-time applications because of Windows NT's hidden and unpredictable system activities, priority hierarchy for I/O and system interrupts, and handling of I/O. Because Windows NT was not designed with predictability in mind, it is neither advisable nor feasible to use Windows NT for hard real-time applications. However, we show in the next section that when used judiciously, Windows NT may be useful for applications that (1) can tolerate occasional missed deadlines and (2) have delay/response time requirements in the tens to hundreds of millisecond range such as those described in the following.

Next, we provide the guidelines and insights needed to overcome some of the limitations of Windows NT without having to make changes in the operating system. This knowledge enables us to develop techniques to support the needs of tasks having a variety of real-time and non-real-time requirements. These observations indicate that the following principles should be practiced when Windows NT is used for real-time applications:

- The potential blocking time due to Windows NT system activity must be taken into consideration when accounting for the delays incurred by an application thread. If processes or threads are performing network or disk I/O, the effect of system-wide FIFO DPC queues may lead to unbounded response times, even for real-time threads. If the duration of I/O activity in a given period can be characterized, it may be possible to compute the response times conservatively.

- One should not depend on the Windows NT scheduler to achieve correct "fair sharing" behavior in cases where screen, keyboard, and mouse interactions are at the same level of priority as the other real-time CPU-intensive tasks.

To achieve more predictability for real-time tasks in general, and to achieve responsiveness to operator/human inputs in particular, a real-time system designer must avoid a real-time thread monopoly of the CPU and I/O. Some computation and I/O time must remain available for execution of such important but non-real-time Windows NT tasks as servicing the inter-active I/O activities. These non-real-time Windows NT tasks are not under our (user-level) control, but there will be adverse effects on the intended real-time tasks if they are not executed on time.

To accomplish this goal, one approach is to use periodic execution with user-level-controlled cooperative preemptions, that is, to design all threads in the real-time class as periodic tasks using a heartbeat timer mechanism described in the next section, such that real-time threads voluntarily relin-quish CPU time to permit the completion of interactive I/O operations.

It is also good practice for real-time applications to lock pages in the memory. With this done, we are ensured that real-time threads are not inac-tive for a longer time, because Windows NT may unlock pages of inactive threads.

In the next section, we show how an industrial application can be designed making use of the above insights and recommendations. This appli-cation has many time constraints that, while important to meet and in some ways soft, make the application suitable for use with Windows NT.

Windows NT in a Real-Time Setting

To understand Windows NT better, we developed a real-time industrial con-trol scenario involving multimedia information. In particular, the focus was on the *operator's workstation* in an industrial control setting [4]. The software running in the workstation has the following components:

- *Operator input.* The operator inputs control messages and actuator settings. An input must be recognized, processed, and sent to a remote destination through the network. The control message is processed at the remote node and the necessary control action is taken. After this, an acknowledgment will be returned to the opera-tor station.

- *Incoming sensor data.* Data arrives from sensors at regular intervals and must be stored in a ring buffer in the main memory. A con-sumer process reads a single record from the buffer, performs some computation, and displays the result on the screen in a graphical for-mat.

- *Incoming video streams.* Also executing at the operator workstation is one video process responsible for retrieving streaming video from the network and displaying it on the screen. It is reasonable to assume that such software will most likely be a commercial product. In fact, in our experimental setup this is a single COTS product. Thus we have one COTS product being used on top of another. As distinct from Windows NT where we have some control over the scheduling of activities and the load applied, we must use this COTS product, the RealVideo player, as is. Fortunately, as we will see, our setup placed much less demand on the RealVideo player and any constraints it imposed had no perceivable effects on the rest of the real-time activities, given our adherence to the principles outlined at the end of the previous section.

Design of the Real-Time Application

The following general principles were followed in designing the prototype application:

- *Efficiency through threads.* For reasons of efficiency we attempted to use threads wherever possible, and processes elsewhere.
- *Achieving periodicity.* Some of the processing, for example, sensor data processing, is periodic. We achieved this periodicity by implementing a heartbeat timer. This is a process running with the highest real-time priority. It periodically sets events for which different processes or threads are waiting. Each time an event is set, the corresponding thread or process can execute one periodic instance and then once again wait for the event to be set. The heartbeat timer uses Windows NT's *multimedia timers* to suspend itself until it is time to signal the next event.

In addition to designing the operator workstation, we needed to model the entity with which the operator interacts. This entity may correspond, for example, to the local controller on the factory work floor, which actually carries out the operator's instructions, monitors the local state, and sends state information back to the operator. Such an entity was modeled as a *remote server*. UDP was used for communicating between operator station and the remote server. The source of the video stream was just another node on the network to which the operator workstation is connected.

The software architecture of the prototype is shown in Figure 15.2. Besides the *heartbeat timer* at each node, the main entities at the remote server are as follows:

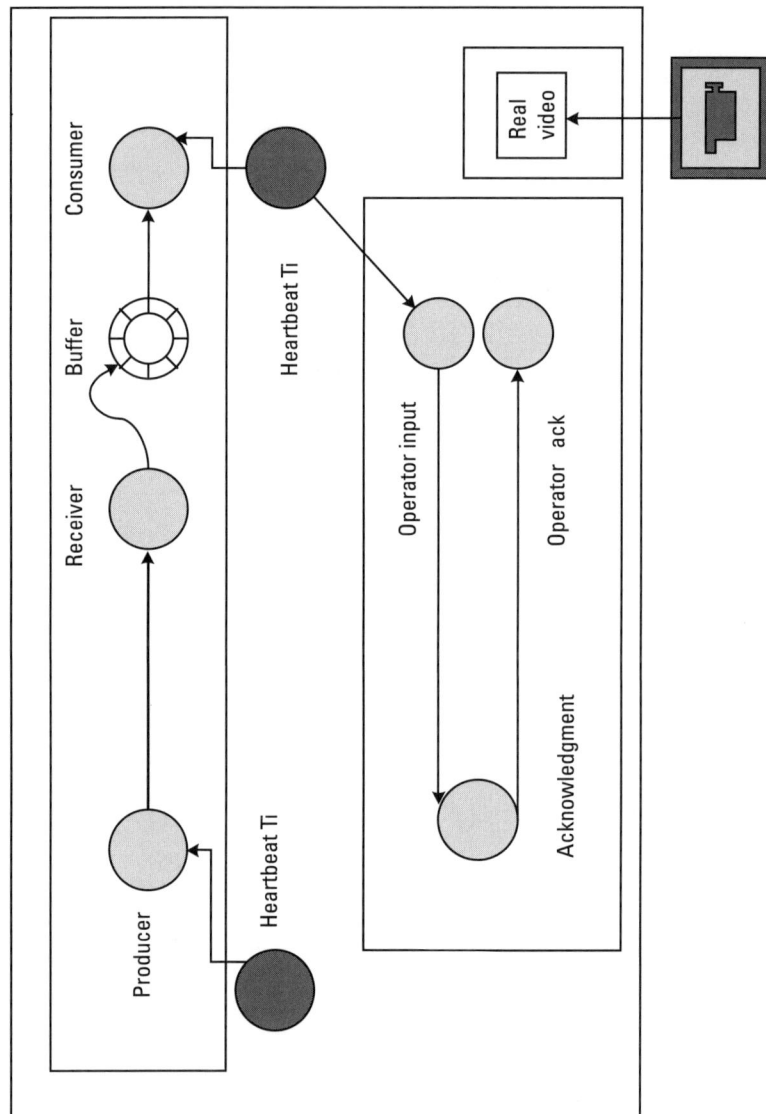

Figure 15.2 Software architecture of industrial control prototype.

- *Producer.* This periodically generates sensor data and sends it to the operator workstation.

- *Acknowledgment.* This entity waits for operator input data from the operator workstation. In our setting, this entity acknowledges a command by sending the same data back to another thread on the operator workstation.

The main entities at the operator workstation are as follows:

- *Receiver.* This is a periodic process that receives sensor data from the remote server. It then stores the same data in a circular buffer.

- *Consumer.* This is a periodic process with the same period as the receiver. It reads sensor data from the circular buffer and stores it in memory. A precedence relation exists between the receiver and consumer, enforced by using an event that the receiver must set to permit the consumer to proceed. The buffer management protocol has the following retrieval semantics: The consumer always receives the most recent data. Many consumers will require this type of semantics. For example, the operator is interested in the most recent speed measured within a turbine. However, the implemented buffer data structure is general enough to accommodate a wide variety of retrieval semantics.

- *Operator input.* This entity waits for the operator to provide commands and sends them to the remote server. To avoid being affected by NT's inability to handle mouse/keyboard processing and screen displays in a timely fashion, all of the operator interactions with the system were simulated via memory reads/writes. Specifically, operator input was implemented by reading 1K bytes of information from a specified memory location. At the end of this section, we discuss approaches to the accommodation of such operator interactions and experiment with one possible approach.

- *Operator ack.* This entity waits for acknowledgments sent by the remote server in response to operator input messages. It stores the received acknowledgments in memory.

Experimental Results

Of particular interest to us are the timing properties of the three types of processes—video display, sensor data processing, and operator command processing—as a function of the priority level at the operator side, the offered load, and the size of data sent by the operator. As for the workload tested, we have experimented with a real workload characterizing a typical operator workstation that experiences periodic sensor data input in 1K byte sizes, sends out sporadic operator commands not more often than every 100 ms, and displays one video window.

The quality of the video output was used as an indicator of the effect on the video player's performance. We saw, however, no perceivable differences in the quality of the video output as we experimented with different parameters. Similarly, in all cases, the processing of sensor data (by the receiver–consumer pair) was not affected. This pair was found to execute at the specified frequency with almost no jitter. So we focus on the round-trip time (RTT) as seen by the operator input process.

In this set of experiments, operator input and receiver–consumer entities run at the same frequency. Results clearly indicate that:

- The round-trip delay for the operator input varies much more if the operator input processes have NORMAL priority. There is significantly less variance if HIGH or REAL_TIME priorities are used.

- Even though the average round-trip delay is very similar in all cases, the average decreases as priority increases. For example, for an operator input period of 50 ms, the average round-trip delay ranges from 3.356 ms, corresponding to NORMAL priority, to 2.428 ms for REAL_TIME priority.

- The maximum value also tends to decrease with increasing priority.

- The most dramatic change is in the variance. For example, for a 50-ms operator input period, it decreases from 19.721 (normal) to 5.879 (high) to 0.242 (real time). This augurs well for predictability.

These results indicate that even with all the processes running, the system has enough processing power to handle all tasks. The large variance at NORMAL priority, therefore, can be at least partially attributed to the Real-Video player as well as system activities that are running at a higher priority. As the process priority is increased, this effect diminishes, resulting in lower variance. The real-time processes in the prototype are typically not computationally intensive, but have strict delay requirements. System activities on the other hand can suffer some amount of jitter. As such, it makes sense to elevate the priority of these real-time processes to ensure that their delay requirements can be met.

To exercise the system even further, we experimented with different message lengths (corresponding to differing amounts of operator input) and a higher rate of operator input (needless to say, operator input every 10 ms is humanly impossible, but helps stress the system).

In the experiments discussed thus far, the threads in the operator and remote processes were on the same priority level (NORMAL) and therefore ran in a time-shared fashion. With a view to improving the responsiveness to operator threads, we experimented with an alternative approach in which the priority of the operator input and acknowledgment was raised to HIGHEST as soon as the operator input thread was given a ticket to run, thereby giving them a priority higher than the sensor data threads. This ensures that the operator input and acknowledgment are processed with a higher priority than the sensor data threads. No effect on the timeliness of sensor data threads was observed.

The maximum delay was considerably lower when we increased the priority of the operator thread from NORMAL to the HIGHEST level. In fact, because the maximum was greater than the period when NORMAL priority level was used, some of the messages missed their deadlines. Even though the mean delays do not differ by much, the variance becomes very small when the operator thread's priority is increased to HIGHEST. For example, for a 1.5-K message size, an order of magnitude improvement is seen. These experiments suggest that by systematic manipulation of thread priorities, better and more predictable response times can be achieved.

Finally, because no deadlines were missed even with the period set to 10 ms for both operator and sensor, we decided to evaluate the effect of keyboard/screen I/O from the operator thread. To this end, we made the operator thread display the acknowledgment from the remote server on the operator's screen. This experiment was performed with a message size of 1K and as described earlier, the whole message is returned as the acknowledgment and is then displayed to the operator. The results indicate that when the period is set to 10 or 20 ms, because screen I/O is handled at lower priorities, many of the deadlines are missed and this has a cascading effect. However, increasing the period of the operator thread to 100 ms alleviates these problems. At this period, even with screen I/O, no deadlines are missed and the variance in the round-trip delay is low. These results are very encouraging in that, given human response times, operator interactions are likely to occur at relatively low frequencies (i.e., longer periods) and it should therefore be possible to accommodate them in many situations.

An alternative to assigning or requiring higher periods for operator threads is to permit controlled preemption of different real-time threads so that operator interactions can take place.

Summary of Results

The prototype implementation models a simple multimedia operator workstation for factory operations. The prototype is parameterized, so different configurations and workloads can be tested. In particular, the frequency of the operator input as well as the receiver–consumer pair are tunable parameters, as is the message size.

A simple heartbeat timer mechanism along with events was used to emulate periodic processes. This heartbeat timer is an ideal candidate for implementing metalevel scheduling functionality in Windows NT. Even without using specialized scheduling, it was observed that using HIGH or REAL_TIME priority alone significantly reduces the variability in response times, without any observable degradation in system performance. This suggests that as long as the application tasks do not monopolize the CPU for long duration and there is sufficient CPU capacity, using these priority assignments may be sufficient to meet the performance requirements of these processes—even when I/O is involved. However, if the periodic workload per process is high, or if a process is a COTS application whose workload varies, it will be necessary to impose some additional controls on the amount of time allocated to a task. Our findings indicate that a scheduling approach combined with an admission control policy is needed to meet timeliness requirements with higher loads.

Conclusion

In this chapter, we have presented evidence that it is possible to use Windows NT for certain types of real-time applications. By measuring the delays involved in Windows NT's real-time functions we have gained a number of insights regarding the feasibility of Windows NT for real-time applications. By building a prototype application that models a simple multimedia operator workstation, we have also demonstrated how to use these insights in the design of such real-time applications. With the use of real-time priorities, we have shown that it is possible to improve the stability of certain real-time tasks.

Windows NT is very platform dependent only with respect to the handling of I/O interrupts. A designer must be aware of the effect of the system-wide FIFO DPC queue on any user thread. This queue has priority over all user-level threads. This may lead to unbounded delays if a badly designed driver is used. This is the part of Windows NT about which general analytical or quantitative statements for all potential platforms can be made. A user needs to know what devices and what drivers he or she is using and what performance characteristics a particular driver will induce in the system. It is possible to characterize various I/O activities and their contributions to the DPC queue, and some pessimistic bounds can be placed on the response time for real-time threads. Soft real-time applications that can tolerate occasional delays due to factors such as system-wide DPC queues can be realized using Windows NT.

To achieve more predictability for real-time tasks in general in Windows NT, and to achieve responsiveness to operator/human inputs in particular, we offer the following key recommendation to a real-time system designer using Windows NT.

Design the system such that real-time threads do not monopolize the CPU and I/O at all times. Some computation and I/O time must remain available for executing important but non-real-time Windows NT activities, such as those servicing interactive I/O. These non-real-time Windows NT tasks are not under our (user-level) control; if they are not executed on time, the intended real-time tasks may suffer adverse effects. To this end, we experimented with one approach in this chapter: facilitating periodic execution with user-level controlled cooperative preemption. All threads in the real-time class were designed to execute periodically using a heartbeat timer mechanism such that real-time threads voluntarily gave up CPU time to permit the completion of interactive I/O operations. We had mentioned earlier that one way to counter the lack of explicit support in Windows NT for scheduling real-time activities is the use of user-level scheduling.

We have investigated the suitability of Windows NT and MidART's user-level scheduler [2] for slot-based scheduling. In a first step, we replaced the MidART user-level scheduler with another scheduler with a modular interface, providing for a variety of scheduling schemes to be included. We then implemented a slot-based scheduling scheme and tested the variation in slot lengths. This experiment also demonstrates another attempt to use COTS components, in particular, using one COTS component to supersede another. Our results indicate, not surprisingly, that whereas slots lengths are adhered to whenever the lengths are in the tens of milliseconds range or when the system is not heavily loaded, wide fluctuations in the slot lengths are observed otherwise.

This observation is consistent with our observation from the industrial plant application—that leaving enough free time is one way to achieve higher predictability for real-time applications built using Windows NT.

References

[1]   Ramamritham, K., et al., "Using Windows NT for Real-Time Applications: Experimental Observations and Recommendations," *Proc. 4th Real-Time Technology and Applications Symp.*, Denver, CO, IEEE Computer Society, 1998.

[2]   Gonzalez, O., et al., "Implementation and Performance of MidART," *Proc. IEEE Workshop on Middleware for Distributed Real-Time Systems and Services*, San Francisco, CA, IEEE Computer Society, 1997.

[3]   Mizunuma, I., C. Shen, and M. Takegaki, "Middleware for Distributed Industrial Real-Time Systems on ATM Networks," *Proc. 17th IEEE Real-Time Systems Symp.*, Washington, D.C., IEEE Computer Society, 1996.

[4]   Shen, C., and I. Mizunuma, "RT-CRM: Real-Time Channel-Based Reflective Memory," *IEEE Trans. on Computers*, Vol. 49, No. 11, 2000, pp. 1202–1214.

[5]   Timmerman, M., "Windows NT as Real-Time OS," *Real Time Magazine*, Vol. 1, 1997.

[6]   VenturCom, "Real-Time Extension 4.1 for Windows NT," http://www.venturcom.com.

[7]   Custer, H., *Inside Windows NT*, Redmond, WA: Microsoft Press, 1993.

Part 7:
Case Studies—CBD in Industrial Applications

During recent years, component-based software has been used frequently in the development of desktop applications. A comparable approach in the area of industrial and embedded real-time systems, with the reuse of tested and robust parts of previous applications, is of increasing interest. However, additional requirements such as low-power design and real-time constraints make it difficult to use the component frameworks that are well-known in the desktop area. Either they must be used in a very strict and limited way, or new models must be developed.

In the previous part related to real-time components, we were exposed to an academic approach to the building of real-time component-based systems. This part extends this approach to using components in industrial applications by presenting four different industrial case studies. Experience gained using de facto standard component models and using in-house developed models are presented here.

Chapter 16 discusses the requirements of embedded omnipresent devices (e.g., cell phones, personal digital assistants, and home or industrial automation devices) with a focus on resource constraints. These requirements impact on the component model, the composition environment, and the run-time environment. The problems of component-based software development for embedded real-time systems are discussed and the requirements of a component framework for this domain are derived. The chapter concludes with a presentation of a CBD of an embedded real-time system. The example presented is based on the synchronous approach to the design of reactive systems.

Chapter 17 presents the current state of practice in architecting component-based, industrial automation platforms tuned for both reuse within and reuse across application domains. After a brief introduction to industrial automation systems, the motivation for building a platform that can be used to create industrial automation systems is explained. The chapter describes ABB's next-generation automation system architecture. The platform that implements the base of the architecture is also presented. The chapter particularly elaborates on an architectural approach that introduces AspectObjects and Aspects together with flexible structuring hierarchies as the fundamental concepts. In addition, it discusses the different dimensions of component-based reuse achieved by the architectural approach presented.

Chapter 18 describes an object model with a framework supporting component-based system development and application integration. The object model is very similar to the one presented in Chapter 17 with the notion of AspectObjects. The framework has been used to develop a number of different components, such as components for document handling, workflow functionality, and general database integration. These components are presented more in detail together with a framework that is implemented in a product designated *Information Organizer*. The case study covers the architecture and a number of tools that enable the arrangement and structuring of information. The framework presented provides support for different levels of reuse, ranging from smaller components to complete applications. The basic concept in implementing Information Organizer is, as far as possible, to follow standards and de facto standards, which are defined with respect to both concept and implementation. The de facto standards used and how they are applied are described in more detail.

Chapter 19 discusses the component model *Object Modeler* (OM) developed for Dassault Systèmes. The rationale behind the introduction of component technology at Dassault Systèmes is interesting. The objective was not primarily to sell isolated OM components, nor to sell the OM component framework, nor to make their component model a standard. The primary objective of Dassault Systèmes was to find a way to develop its software under the best conditions and to provide its customers with powerful adaptability facilities. Actually, Dassault Systèmes sells a family of highly customizable applications. The customers are not informed of the topology of the architecture of these applications. Applications are customized by extending existing components or adding new components.

This chapter presents the OM component model and explains how components are used to build applications. The use of different architectures, such as logical, physical, and packaging architectures, are discussed in connection with the component model. The second part of the chapter describes the lessons learned during the years during which the model was elaborated and used. Essentially, the design of a powerful component model is shown to be a complex task that involves many facets of technology in ways that are not always obvious.

16

Component-Based Embedded Systems

Peter O. Müller, Christian M. Stich, and Christian Zeidler

Introduction

Embedded systems are facing their own software crisis because plummeting hardware costs are leading to rapid growth in new application domains and increased demands for application interconnectivity between, for example, smart cell phones, personal digital assistants, and home or industrial automation devices. This in turn leads to increased demands for more complex software built in ever-shorter time frames. Embedded real-time systems like those used in industrial field devices must be correct and deterministic, because they must always react the same way to the same inputs.

Traditionally such systems are still developed in an assembler or in C.

Today's monolithic, platform-dependent embedded systems are difficult to port, upgrade, and customize, and offer limited opportunities for reuse, even within a single application domain. Component technology offers an opportunity to increase productivity by providing natural units for reuse (components and architectures), by raising the level of abstraction for system construction, and by separating services from their configurations to facilitate evolution.

Within this chapter we provide a short introduction to the application domain and then present the foundation of programming embedded systems. A case study presents the first results from modeling embedded systems with components. We also derive and postulate requirements for component-based embedded system programming and describe the goals of the pervasive component systems (PECOS) project [1] under which all the investigations were made. We conclude with an outlook and description of future activities.

Problem Domain

ABB's Instruments Business Unit develops a large number of different industrial field devices (e.g., temperature, pressure, and flow sensors and actuators and positioners). As field device hardware becomes more and more common and affordable, the software determines the competitiveness of embedded products. Today's field devices have to provide increasing functionality in their areas of responsibility. The market demands the following additional functionality in ever-shorter time cycles:

- Local and remote human/machine interface;
- Automation processes;
- Remote control options via a fieldbus.

These requirements mean that software dominates the development and maintenance costs of field devices.

The state of the art in software engineering for embedded systems is far behind other application areas. Software for embedded systems is typically monolithic and platform dependent. CBSE would bring a number of advantages to the embedded systems world such as fast development times, the ability to secure investments through reuse of existing components, and the ability for domain experts to interactively compose sophisticated embedded systems software.

Visual techniques have been proven to be very effective in specific domains such as GUI software composition. Composition of embedded systems software still has a long way to go to reach that level. At the very least, users would benefit greatly from the effective use of visual techniques for providing feedback in the development process (during the design, composition, installation, and run-time validation processes). Unfortunately CBSE cannot yet be easily applied to embedded systems development today for a number of reasons.

To date, mainstream IT players have not paid much attention to the relatively small but quickly growing, embedded systems market and consequently have not provided it with suitable technologies or off-the-shelf software (such as operating systems or suitable component models). From a technical point of view, these choices were justified by considering the major characteristics of embedded devices, such as limited system resources (CPU power, memory, etc.), human/machine interface functionality, the typically harsh environmental conditions, and the fact that the development and target systems were not the same.

The rapidly changing market makes investment in CBSE for embedded systems not only viable but also essential for the business success of technology appliers and providers. The key for industries to benefit from the increasingly powerful and less expensive hardware is the ability to develop and port embedded software more quickly and at acceptable costs. Vendors of embedded devices would benefit by being able to offer scalable product families, whose functionality could be tailored by flexible composition of reusable building blocks. These families are differentiated by the performance of the hardware and the provided functionality, but are based on reuse of many identical software components. All of this requires that the embedded systems software be modular and composed of loosely coupled, largely self-sufficient, and independently deployable software components.

However, today's embedded device software is monolithic software developed specifically for each product (e.g., field device type). Monolithic software prevents companies from serving the field device market with value-added features in a cost-efficient way. The same functions needed by different field devices are implemented repeatedly at different development locations in different ways (e.g., fieldbus drivers, nonvolatile memory manager, fast Fourier transformation algorithm).

In addition, functions and modules are implemented for a specific environment with no standardized interface (e.g., interrupt driven, port I/O). These systems are hard to maintain, upgrade, and customize, and they are almost impossible to port to other platforms.

Implications for Component Technology

While component technology promises an escape from monolithic software that is expensive and hard to maintain for general-purpose IT solutions, the question remains of whether it can do the same for programming of embedded devices. Moreover, it is unlikely that state-of-the-art component technology like COM, CORBA, JavaBeans/EJB, and component technology as it is currently discussed in the literature (e.g., [2, 3]) can be applied as it is to field devices.

In the following sections, aspects of component technology are discussed in the context of the requirements for field devices. We discuss the major issues of Szyperski's component definition in Chapter 1 of [2], in the context of embedded systems.

Contractually Specified Interfaces

State-of-the-art component technologies specify interfaces as pure collection of methods (events and attributes are finally modeled as interface methods as well). However, for embedded software and especially embedded real-time software, nonfunctional specifications such as memory consumption of a component, WCET of a method, and expected power consumption of a component under a certain execution schedule are an equally important part of the contract. The currently progressing UML profile for scheduling, performance, and time [4] may provide a specification means, which completes the first step toward expressive interface declarations. As discussed in Chapter 13, specifying the WCET of function blocks will allow us to verify that the overall schedule of all function blocks can be met.

Component interfaces are usually implemented as object interfaces supporting polymorphism by late binding. Whereas late binding allows us to connect components that are completely unaware of each other beside the connecting interface, this flexibility comes with a performance penalty. A component model for embedded devices should allow for procedural interfaces and object interfaces with and without polymorphism. Procedural interfaces can be used for stateless component instances and component singletons. Object interfaces without polymorphism can be applied if the target component implementation can be determined at design time. Such optimization reduces overhead at run time.

Semantic specifications, like pre- and postconditions, are of great value for the software quality especially if they are checked during run time. However, for embedded devices these additional run-time checks may turn out not to be feasible if microcontroller resources are limited. Alternatively, design-time checking using a composition environment, which either simulates or calculates the correctness of connected components with given pre- and postconditions, could be a viable method. But today there are only a few investigations of design-time checks in progress and most of them are not related to any component model.

Unit of Composition and Independent Deployment

"Components are for composition" [2]. State-of-the-art component technologies allow for component composition at design time and at run time. Both [2] and [3] take the position that components are binary units of deployment that should be deployable to a component system at run time. To fulfill these requirements, support from the component model (e.g., late binding), support from the run-time environment (e.g., life-cycle management, dynamic loading, garbage collection, or reference counting), and dynamic communication mechanisms such as the JavaBeans' events or COM connection points are needed.

Having the limited resources of field devices in mind, we argue that such a run-time infrastructure is too expensive in terms of processing power. Embedded devices of the discussed class cannot afford the overhead of garbage collection or reference counting, the overhead of late binding for every interface method especially for fine-grained components, and the memory overhead required for the infrastructure itself and for each component needed to support the infrastructure. Therefore, complete stripping of this functionality or sensible degradation is required.

Because embedded devices as discussed in this chapter have a static software configuration, design-time composition should be sufficient. Limiting component composition and deployment to design time allows composition tools to generate monolithic firmware for the device from the component-based design. This concept of generative components allows us to adapt component implementations. For example, depending on the storage class of a parameter, the parameter value can be put into ROM for constant parameters or into RAM for dynamic and nonvolatile parameters. For nonvolatile parameters, an appropriate interaction code with the persistent storage for saving and loading the parameter can be generated.

In addition, design-time composition allows for optimization. In a static component composition known at design time, connections between components could be translated into direct function calls instead of using dynamic event notifications. Such optimizations probably require components to be available in source language or at least introspection abilities at design time. Composition tools are required that can inspect and adapt such components. On the other hand, source code components can provide support for composition tools in the form of metainformation and scripts to be executed by the composition tool.

Finally, design-time composition could be the instance of specific adaptation of components and generated code toward specific microcontroller families and RTOS APIs [5].

Explicit Context Dependencies

Besides other interfaces and components that are required for a component to work, context dependencies also include the required run-time environment such as CPU, real-time operating system, and component implementation language (with respect to the binary interface). From the viewpoint of state-of-the-art component technology, this run-time environment can become quite basic for embedded devices due to the resource and real-time constraints.

Besides JavaBeans, component models provide programming language independence by a binary object model or by different language bindings. We argue that abandoning programming language independence in favor of higher performance is acceptable for embedded devices.

In the case of source language components as discussed in an earlier section, the composition support in the form of metainformation and scripts to be executed in the composition environment appears as an additional context dependency.

Component Granularity

According to [3], coarse-grained components up to complete server applications promise better reusability (megaprogramming), which stands in contrast to what the Business Component Factory approach [6] states. Both statements are right to some extent. Heavyweight components contain, of course, much functionality that could be reused, but not even exclusively within resource-sensitive real-time applications will they be reused if the ratio of used against not used features is too small. But this scenario is most likely for coarse-grained components.

Addressing large-scale distributed applications, state-of-the-art component technology often includes object request broker functionality (DCOM, CORBA, RMI). However, communication capabilities of field devices are restricted (bandwidth) and specified by standards [7, 8] in order to achieve interoperability of the devices within a system. This means that those distributed components are out of scope for this class of embedded devices. Consequently, component technology could only be applied for building the firmware of one field device.

Limiting the use of component technology to one device and the smaller application size of embedded devices will lead to more fine-grained components compared with business applications. Finding the right component size to support optimal component reuse is a critical design decision that can only be decided in the context of the embedded device's application and its architecture (see also the "Architecture" section in this chapter).

Some papers (e.g., [9]) present real-time operating systems, protocol stacks, and embedded databases as typical components. Such components build up the infrastructure or run-time environment. Most often, they are commercial components that have hardly been formally specified according to a component model for embedded devices. An open issue is how to integrate them into a component model for embedded devices and to which part such infrastructure components should be wrapped into an abstraction layer (see also the section on "Portability and Platform Independence" in this chapter).

Nevertheless, we want to put the focus on components as building blocks of the application of the embedded device. In this context, architectural styles and the ability to describe architecture and how components should fit into it gain increasing importance.

Reuse

Black-box component reuse seems to be the best solution because it hides component implementation completely from the client. Source language components require parts of their implementation to be opened, leading to gray-box or even white-box reuse. According to [2], gray-box and white-box reuse very likely prevents the substitution of the reused component by other components. However, establishing clear conventions about the available knowledge of the implementation and the allowed changes of the implementation should help to overcome this problem. If this knowledge can be captured completely in architectural styles (e.g., component connectors) or in composition scripts belonging to the component, one could reach gray-box reuse from the composition environment's point of view but black-box reuse from the component user's point of view. Only the composition environment would be allowed to use knowledge about the component's implementation.

Architecture and Frameworks

Defining components alone will not lead to reuse.[1] In addition, a common architecture for a family of embedded devices is needed that guides the usage of components and their interaction. Such an architecture can be captured in a framework for the device family consisting of, for example, standardized interfaces, container components, and architectural styles (component connectors). The framework also defines the primary dimensions of independent extensibility [2], that is, the points where the framework is open for new, independently developed components. In our example an architecture for field devices is discussed in a later section as the basis for such a framework.

Location Transparency

As mentioned in the "Component Granularity" section of this chapter, we deal with the construction of the firmware for one embedded device. Therefore, location transparency is not an issue. For embedded devices as discussed in this chapter, component technology is not intended to be used as or in conjunction with communication middleware such as CORBA, DCOM, or RMI.

Portability and Platform Independence

The demand for reusable software components leads directly to the requirement of platform independence and portability because software components as abstractions of application functions will have a longer lifetime than the hardware and the microcontroller used. But that leads directly to an either conceptually provided abstraction layer in terms of programming standards or an implementation-based solution such as a virtual machine.

We argue that source-level portability will be sufficient (or, better yet, *must* be sufficient). Source-level portability requires agreement on the implementation language (e.g., ANSI C or C++). Microcontroller-specific language extensions provided by many compilers for the embedded domain prevent source-level portability, require manual porting effort, and finally lead to a version explosion of the component. Source-level portability also requires agreement with the available libraries such as the ANSI C run-time library, operating system API, hardware access, and device drivers. One way

---

1. We are fully aware that reuse is a major topic of software process and organizational issues. But due to this chapter's scope we restrict the discussion to technology issues.

to achieve this is to provide proper abstractions, for example, for the RTOS APIs, which are specified according to the component model used.

Binary platform independence as provided, for example, by the Java platform is not a requirement for the discussed class of field devices. However, this may change in the future if run-time component composition and deployment become a requirement. Also, from a development productivity perspective, it would be very desirable to have a Java platform available.

Component Wiring

Component wiring experiences an emphasized role. Once the components are present, efficient and flexible composition of new applications out of existing components becomes the first priority. Therefore, composing an application in a drag-and-drop manner, while preserving the consistency of the new composed application pops-up is one of the most challenging tasks. On one hand, it requires an advanced component model and at the same time support for expression of architectural styles in order to provide a prescription about how to construct according to given domain rules. On the other hand, it gives us the ability to optimize component interactions by means of source code adaptation or interweaving of component glue code. For performance reasons, we argue that component glue code must be generated in the implementation language (e.g., C or C++). Script languages known from state-of-the-art component technologies used as glue code, will not be affordable.

Embedded Systems with Synchronous Components

Synchronous Approach

Synchronous languages [10] have been developed to simplify the programming of reactive systems. They were born from the recognition that broadcasting was the way to handle communication in reactive systems, making it possible to handle together concurrency, determinism, and response time control. They are based on the synchrony hypothesis, which makes the following abstractions:

- The computer is infinitely fast.
- Each reaction is instantaneous[2] and atomic, dividing time into sequences of discrete instants.
- A system's reaction to input appears in the same instant as the input.

A real system can behave synchronously if it is fast enough. It must always finish its computations before events are recognized. This requires the minimum interevent time as well as the WCET. The synchrony hypothesis is a generalization of the synchronous model used for digital circuits in which each reaction must be finished in one clock cycle.

Tools for reactive systems do not develop in the same way as tools for desktop systems. One reason for this is that high-level reasoning and programming tools promoted by computer scientists were considered to be quite useless by many control engineers, whose main problem was (and still is) to pack code in small ROM for cheap microprocessors [11].

Synchronous Software Components

On the basis of the synchrony hypothesis, we can define components that can easily be composed to larger systems. Because the components communicate through signals being sent as broadcast, the components are not required to make any assumptions about each other. They work independently in the same way as software ICs [12]. Usually synchronous software components consist of a reactive part and a transformational part. The reactive part is usually specified in a synchronous language. The transformational part is optional and consists of data-type specifications and several data-handling functions [13].

In the synchronous programming language Esterel [13], for example, all reactive parts of all synchronous software components are assembled in a single program. The Esterel compiler translates this program into a finite-state machine, called a reactive kernel. All transformational parts together form the data processing layer. In our approach the reactive part is developed in C or C++. Reasons for this include the following:

- Wide acceptance of C/C++ as an implementation language. Synchronous languages such as Esterel are not very common, so a large training effort is necessary.

- In terms of memory usage, as described in [11], current Esterel compilers generate much more code in comparison with a handwritten C component.

---

2. A statement starts in some instant t, remains active for a while, and may terminate in some instant $t' \geq t$. A statement is instantaneous if $t' = t$ [11].

- As mentioned, the reactive parts of all components in Esterel are assembled to one single Esterel program. This is a drawback if binary components should be used to protect knowledge.

In a C or C++ implementation where input I occurs at $t(n)$ it must be asserted that output O occurs at time $t'(n) > t(n)$ with the constraint $t'(n) < t(n+1)$ for the reactive system to behave properly. An additional bounded delay such that $t'(n) - t(n) < \delta$ for all n may be additionally required [11]. The favorable case is when the maximum delay can be computed for a given implementation. In that case, if the delay is small enough, synchronous behavior is assured. Otherwise the implementation must be improved.

Case Study Description

In our example we refer to implementation of industrial field devices. An analysis of different existing field devices revealed seven main components with different variations (up to 14). The potential business impact by domain reuse differs from (1) very high (e.g., fieldbus function blocks[3]) to (2) more or less small (process application) according to the reuse over device families or over device generations. These identified components are illustrated in Figure 16.1. The two main functional blocks of the field device are the analog output function block (AO) and the transducer block. They are mainly responsible for the current state, converting and scaling of parameters, and the closed-loop control of the motor. One block in Figure 16.1 is the Profibus PA Mapper block, which acts as wrapper for the bus communication.

The market for embedded systems has been analyzed for two trends: (1) A 32-bit microcontroller will soon overtake the 16-bit microcontroller, and (2) the availability of the EC++ [14] compiler is increasing constantly. Based on these trends, our case study device has been defined as an electric actuator[4] with a Motorola 32-bit microcontroller and the Profibus fieldbus system. (Today about 1 million Profibus devices are used in process

---

3. Function blocks represent the basic automation functions of a fieldbus device. Each function block processes input parameters according to a specified algorithm and an internal set of control parameters. They produce output parameters that are available for use within the same function block application or by other function block applications.

4. An actuator transmits a torque to a valve for a defined output movement.

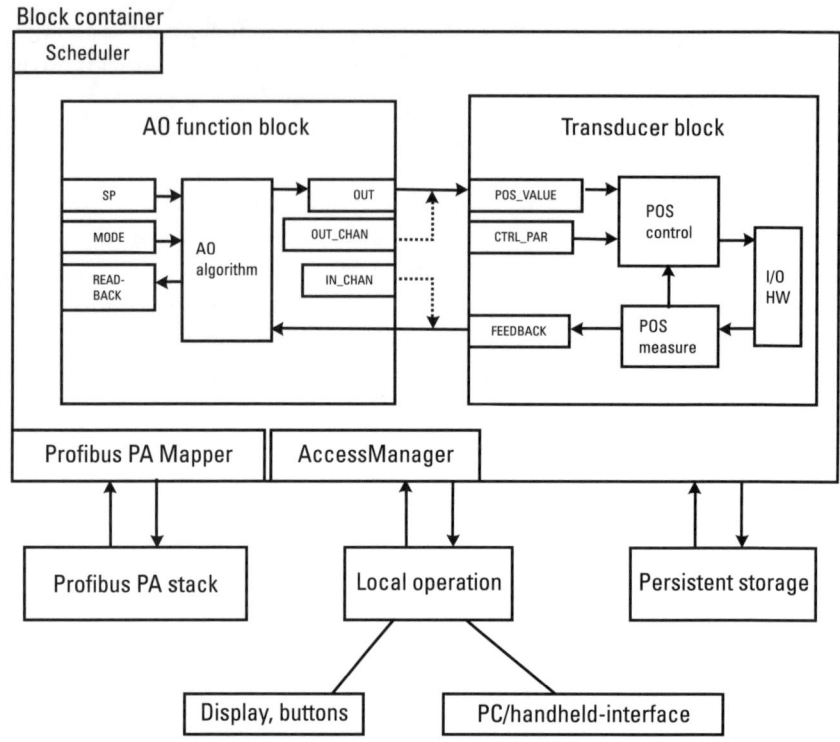

Figure 16.1 Architecture of field device.

engineering.) The implementation will be done with C++ and Java to get a meaningfulness evaluation about these main embedded languages for the future.

According to the requirements of the selected domain the basics of the synchrony hypothesis to define components, which can easily be composed to systems, are applied. The component interaction for the selected domain requires most often a horizontal and vertical channel for the interaction with other components as well as the interaction with the operating system and system hardware. Therefore the separation in application interfaces and platform interfaces must be evaluated.

Architecture

In this section an architecture for reactive control systems is presented that directly supports the synchronous approach. Figure 16.2(a) shows a typical

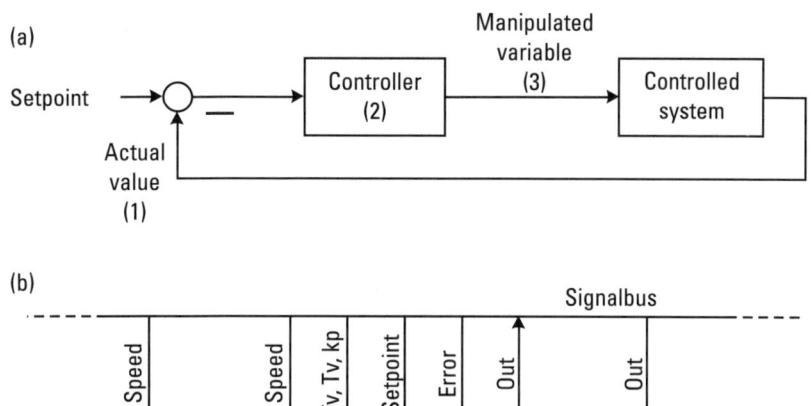

Figure 16.2 Typical layout of a control application: (a) a control layout and (b) software components building the control loop.

control layout. The setpoint is the desired value typically coming from a superior control system. The controller realizes a control strategy to achieve its desired behavior. Figure 16.2(b) displays the software components building the control loop. In this case controller (2) uses a PID closed-loop control algorithm to achieve its goal. It reads the actual speed and calculates the speed error. Based on timing and amplification parameters (T_n, T_v, k_p), the error, and the actual setpoint, a new output value is calculated. This value is used from the actuator to manipulate the controlled system.

Signals available on the signal-bus (see the "Signal Bus" section in this chapter) are public and can be used from all components connected to the bus (broadcast). A component can either be the sink or the source of a signal.

In addition to a traditional interface, a controller has interfaces to the process (including sensors and actuators). A modern real-time computer interacts with the environment in a number of other ways, including interfaces with a plant operator, mass storage (database), and computer network. A detailed view of these interfaces is presented in a unified diagram shown in Figure 16.3.

In practice, a number of real-time systems exist that do not represent a complete system in the sense of Figure 16.3, but nevertheless fit very well into this concept. For our domain, the field devices, all of the interfaces listed exist.

Dynamic Behavior

To behave as a reactive kernel, a control application must fulfill several requirements as shown in Figure 16.2(b). As explained in the section about synchronous software components, all outputs O emitted from component C must occur within a specified *reaction time*.

The following condition must be valid: $T_{tot} \geq T$ whereby $T = \Sigma^m_1 \, n_m \times t_m$. The sum of all component reaction times t_m must be shorter than the specified total execution time T_{tot}. The term n 1 indicates that a component is executed more than once in a cycle. For an application to be composed of three components, we assume that the execution time of $C_1 = \frac{1}{2}C_2 = 2C_3 = 10$ ms and C_1 must be executed twice. Let's further assume that $T = 100$ ms. For the given execution times $T_{tot} = 2 \times 10$ ms + 20 ms + 5 ms = 45 ms. This means that the CPU has a load of 45%. The execution time includes the time for the reactive part and the data handling part of the components. The engineering environment must ensure that the real-time computer can perform the schedule of the components.

For the scheduling of components, a simple round-robin scheduler can be used. In [15] the strategy pattern is used to decouple real-time specific constraints and the application service to which they apply. This allows one to adapt the real-time related aspects in a system-specific manner.

Active Components

The example from Figure 16.3 covers only part of the components typically available in an embedded real-time computer. It covers only components of which the transformational part is short enough to be executed each time the component gets execution time. This is not always possible.

Active components typically have their own thread[5] of control. Examples for such components include communication handlers or mass storage handlers. References [16] and [17] present a solution for PBOs. For each PBO a local table of the used variables is available. The variables corresponding to input ports are updated prior to execution of each cycle of a periodic PBO. During its execution, a PBO may update the state variable corresponding to output ports at any time. These values are updated in the global table after the PBO completes its processing for that cycle or event.

In our approach only active components need a local signal table. In this case, the execute method of a component copies the required input

---

5. Most real-time systems do not know the term *thread*. They use the term *task* instead, but the meaning is very similar.

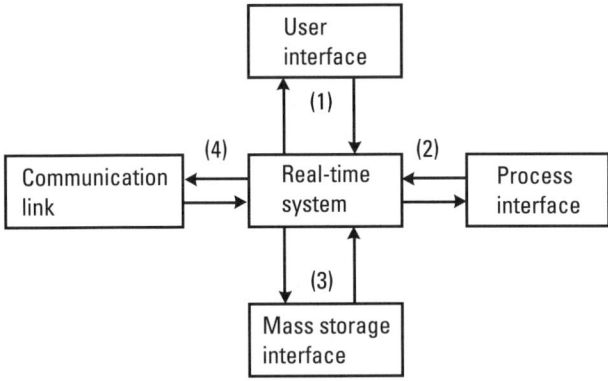

Figure 16.3 Real-time computer systems with example interfaces. (1) 216-character LCD display, (2) RS422 link to a frequency converter, (3) E2PROM, and (4) Ethernet.

signal values in a local buffer and copies updated output signals to the signal bus. For this action some kind of synchronization inside the component is necessary.

Intercomponent Communication

Signal Bus

The signal bus is the communication backbone in our approach. Data available on the bus can be used from all components. The engineering environment must make sure that there is only one source per signal. In contrast to the synchronous approach, signals are not like events that can be associated with data; in our definition signals simply represent data items. Access to the signal bus is open to the general public. This means that there is no access control on this level (read and write access). Each signal on the bus represents a data type. Data types are not limited in general. Depending on the type of application, different sets of types may be necessary. For our application the types used are based on the data types specified in the fieldbus specs of Profibus [7] and Fieldbus Foundation [8]. A typical type looks like this:

```
typedef struct{
    unsigned short status; /* current status */
    unsigned float; /* value */
} t_analogValue;
```

Signals can have different requirements in relation to persistency. Supported levels include these:

- *Persistent.* Variables marked as persistent are stored frequently (counters, etc.) or on user request ("save settings") using the mass storage interface shown in Figure 16.3.
- *RAM.* The state of variables in this group is lost when the system is restarted.
- *ROM.* Variables in this group are read only.

The idea behind the last group is simply to save RAM. For all three types of signals default values can be specified.

Events

Events represent the more functionally oriented way in which intercomponent communication occurs. An event can be based on message queues or can be a simple method or function call. Events can have parameters and several nonfunctional properties. Properties can be evaluated in the engineering environment during system construction time. A mandatory property is the execution time. The execution time can be specified as infinite if the call is blocking.

Object Manager

The Object Manager is simply the owner of the signal bus. It must provide at least the following functionality:

- Provide definitions of the signal types;
- Reserve memory for the signals on the signal bus;
- Initialize the signals on the signal bus;
- Provide an event interface for accessing the signal bus from the outside world.

This means that the Object Manager acts as wrapper using the mediator pattern. Tasks that it handles include security and type conversions. For security tasks, access restrictions may be dependent on the system state or user rights. Consider these examples: (1) If state-dependent, the setpoint only is evaluated if the computer is in the *Regular Operation* state. (2) If user-dependent, the serial number of the device can only be updated if the user belongs to the group *Service Staff.*

The Object Manager also handles type conversions. A component can specify the data type of a requested signal. Several benefits accrue from performing type conversion in the Object Manager. Figure 16.4 shows two components accessing signals from the Object Manager. For communication components like Profibus in this example, mapping of types is an important issue because most of the communication links use their own proprietary data types. The GUI handler is connected this way mainly to make sure that signals are only changed by those who are authorized.

By discussing the realization of those components identified during the case study analysis, we have discovered a significant lack of support for the development of component-based systems in general, not just component-based embedded systems. Our view on these deficiencies is presented in the next section.

Prerequisites of Effective Development

Our scenario depicts just a few of the aspects essential to field device realization, which are used to implement the framework outlined in this section. Because building of frameworks is difficult [18] we have tried to spend as much time as possible in obtaining in-depth knowledge about the problem domain and analyzing code from the domain to find patterns that solve typical problems.

The framework has a better chance of being successful when several iterations are made. Therefore we have started to develop a series of prototypes that utilize different architectural styles. A more detailed description of the first example case study can be found in [19]. The second presented in this section gave us additional insights, which we summarize together with those gained before.

The scenario in the case study presented gives us an indication of what kinds of functionality and abilities a component model should be provided with from the point of view of the application domain. To name just one, a component should be able to handle resource constraints and their implications for the component technology.

Coping with the resource limitations is one domain-specific problem. Another one is to support development of real-time application assembled out of components. This is a challenge in itself and has been a topic of investigation for many years. The most prominent approaches are RoseRT by

Rational [20] and Rhapsody by Ilogix [17]. Both of them apply the event-based programming style and support implementation based on state automata, but do not consider reuse or component orientation to be their major drivers. Composition of applications out of components and active reuse support by appropriate repository implementation is not offered adequately either. For more details of state-of-the-art tools such as Rhapsody or Ros-eRT, see the appropriate section in this chapter.

To use CBSE successfully, and to achieve a reduction of development cost and time by reuse of established and proven components, it is not enough to solve only problems related to field devices. An overall approach for the development of component-based embedded software is needed. We believe this approach must comprise several main features, depicted in Figure 16.5, which we have categorized in five groups and describe next.

In a first outline the identified groups should concentrate on the following issues:

Component Model

- Addresses nonfunctional properties and constraints such as WCET and memory consumption;
- Allows us to specify efficient functional interfaces (e.g., procedural interfaces);
- Allows us to specify architectural styles that describe component connections and containment relations;
- Allows for code generation and controlled component adaptation when architectural styles are applied to components (source language or generative components);

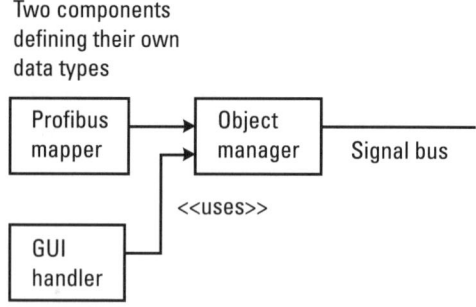

Figure 16.4 Two components defining their own data types.

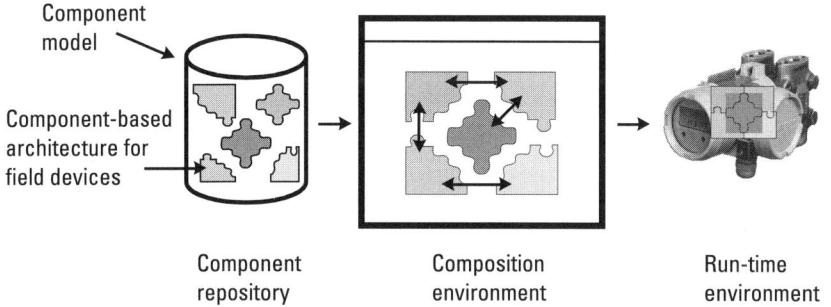

Component model

Component-based architecture for field devices

Component repository

Composition environment

Run-time environment

Figure 16.5 Component technology for embedded devices.

Component-Based Architecture for Field Devices

- Expresses a framework for field devices as standard interfaces, components, and architectural styles based on field bus architecture;
- Expresses compile-time optimization abilities, which could be applied during target code preparation.

Component Repository

- Allows for storage and retrieval of components during analysis, design, implementation, and composition;
- Stores components and architectural styles according to the component model including interface descriptions, nonfunctional properties, implementation (potentially for different microcontrollers), support scripts for composition environment, and test cases;
- Supports component versioning.

Composition Environment

- Supports composition techniques (visual or script based);
- Checks composition rules attached to architectural styles in order to verify that a component configuration meets their constraints;
- Performs component adaptation and code generation for the application;

- Supports definition of composition rules, which in a subsequent step could be compiled to architectural styles description.

Run-Time Environment

- Provides an efficient implementation model for components;
- Addresses the constraints for field devices: low available memory, implementation possibly necessary in C or optimized C++;
- Supports the approach for compiling a component-based design into optimized firmware for the embedded device, thus eliminating the run-time environment except for the RTOS;
- Allows for a hardware- and RTOS-independent implementation of components (e.g., by an RTOS abstraction layer).

Based on these five categories, which make up the major ingredients for component-based system (CBS) development, we investigate a vision of a software development process taking these considerations into account [13].

Summary

To bring the advantages of CBSE to embedded systems, special domain characteristics must be taken into account. To manage the development of the components, a comprehensive systematic approach to embedded software is needed. We divided this component-based software development process into five categories in which the requirements of field devices are concentrated.

To build a case study for a usable CBSE system for field devices, the ability to retain the special needs and requirements of the field devices in each step is necessary. We have begun exploration of these needs in a case study and drafted first component models, which enables us to reason about the specified constraints of the components and their composition.

References

[1]   PECOS, "PECOS Project Web Site," http://www.pecos-project.org.

[2] Szyperski, C., *Component Software Beyond Object-Oriented Programming*, Reading, MA: Addison-Wesley, 1998.

[3] Griffel, F., *Componentware: Konzepte und Techniken eines Softwareparadigmas*, Berlin: dPunkt-Verlag, 1998.

[4] OMG, "UML Profile for Scheduling, Performance, and Time—Request for Proposal," Report ad/99-03-13, OMG, 1999.

[5] Maurice, S. F., and J. Larmour, "Source Level Configuration in Embedded Systems," *Proc. Embedded Systems Conf.*, San Jose, CA, CMP, Inc., 1999.

[6] Sims, O., and P. Herzum, *Business Component Factory*, New York: John Wiley and Sons, 2000.

[7] PNO, "Profibus PA: Draft Profile for Process Control Devices, General Requirements," Report V 3.0, PNO, 1999.

[8] Fieldbus Foundation, "FF Specification," Report V 1.1, Fieldbus Foundation, 1999.

[9] Rhodes, A., "Component Based Development for Embedded Systems," 1999.

[10] Halbwachs, N., *Synchronous Programming of Reactive Systems*, Dordrecht, The Netherlands: Kluwer, 1993.

[11] "The Esterel v5 Language Primer," Centre de Mathematiques Appliquees, Ecole des Mines and Inria, 2000.

[12] Naegele, A., and M. Gunzert, "Component-Based Development and Verification of Safety Critical Software for a Brake-by-Wire System with Synchronous Software Components," *Proc. Symp. on Parallel and Distributed Systems Engineering*, Los Angeles, CA, IEEE Computer Society, 1999.

[13] Berry, G., "The Esterel v5.91 System Manual," Centre de Mathematiques Appliquees, 2000.

[14] Caravan, "Embedded C++ Specification," http://www.caravan.net/ec2plus.

[15] Schmidt, D. C., "Real-Time Constraints as Strategies," www.cs.wustl.edu/~schmidt.

[16] Stewart, D. B., "Designing Software for Real-Time Applications," *Proc. Embedded Systems Conf.*, San Jose, CA, CMP, Inc., 1999.

[17] Ilogix, "Rhapsody," http://www.ilogix.com.

[18] Bushmann, F., et al., "Framework-Based Software Architectures for Process Automation Systems," *Proc. 9th IFAC Symp. on Automation in Mining, Mineral and Metal Processing—MMM'98*, Braunschweig, Germany, 1998.

[19] Müller, P. O., C. Stich, and C. Zeidler, "Components [CIRCLEAT] Work: Component Technology for Embedded Systems," *Proc. 27th Euromicro Conf. and Workshop on Component-Based Software Engineering*, Warsaw, Poland, IEEE Computer Society, 2001.

[20] Rational, "RoseRT," http://www.rational.com/products/rosert/index.jsp.

17

Architectural Support for Reuse: A Case Study in Industrial Automation

Otto Preiss and Martin Naedele

Introduction

This chapter presents the current state of practice in architecting component-based industrial automation platforms tuned for both reuse within and reuse across application domains. By definition, such a platform must support the system family concept (i.e., it must provide basic capabilities to aid product-line development). After a brief introduction to industrial automation systems and the motivation for a platform approach to building such systems, the chapter describes ABB's next generation of automation system architecture, which is called the Aspect Integrator Platform (AIP) and is the basis for the design of automation systems such as open control systems for continuous and batch-type processes, traditional supervisory control and data acquisition systems, and others.

The chapter elaborates on an architectural approach that introduces AspectObjects and Aspects together with flexible structuring hierarchies as the fundamental concepts in accomplishing a unified object approach to information representation. In addition, it discusses the different dimensions of component-based reuse achieved by the architectural approach presented.

It supports the observation that reuse payoff correlates with domain effort, in that the valuable assets of reuse are the domain-specific infrastructures and conceptual components (sometimes also called business objects), both preferably realized by means of technological components, that is, software components.

Industrial Automation Systems

For historical reasons, different types of monitoring and process control applications led to highly specialized, independent, and incompatible hardware and software system solutions. However, the growing demand for open systems blurred these borders. It is recognized that a flexible combination of basic hardware and software components, communications infrastructure, and application components would lead to the ability to build the majority of monitoring and controlling applications. Furthermore, by integrating information from different business processes, through the interoperation of the dedicated systems that exist thus far, more complex tasks than controlling an individual piece of process equipment can be automated. For example, if a procurement system were interoperating with a manufacturing process control system, the latter could notify the procurement system that the reservoir of an ingredient had reached a certain level so that a new supply of this ingredient could be ordered automatically.

Frequently, the possible control hierarchy of a technical process is represented by a layered structure, in which the layers are referred to as levels or enterprise levels. They represent the different levels of control of an enterprise whose business value depends on the control of a technical process (e.g., a manufacturing process or a utility with its gas, water, or electricity distribution). Each level has a predefined set of control tasks that are typically supported by some kind of computer systems and which may or may not involve human interaction. A pyramid of layers is often used to depict the organization of such levels (see Figure 17.1). Their meaning is as follows:

1. *Enterprise management level.* This level comprises systems and their applications that deal with enterprise-wide control activities. These tasks are usually subsumed under the term enterprise resource planning (ERP). They include human resources, supply chain management, administrative order processing, and finance and accounting.

2. *Production or manufacturing management level.* This level comprises systems and applications for production planning. They support

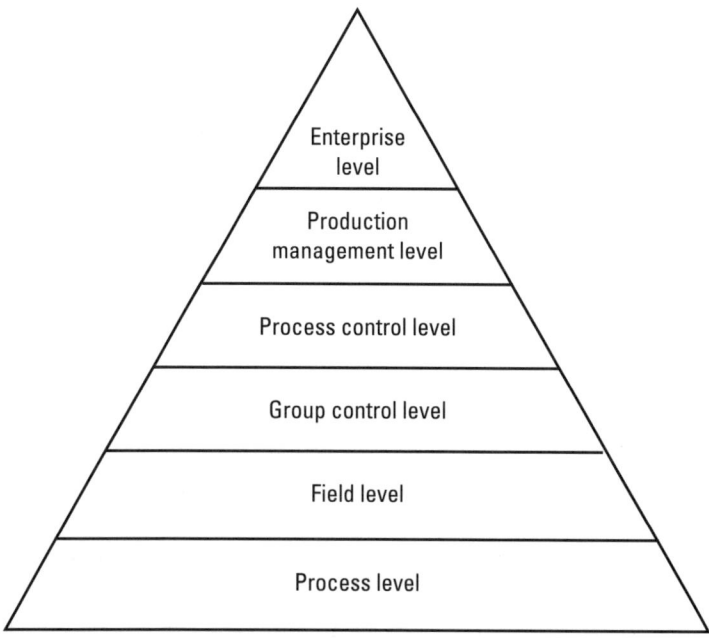

Figure 17.1 The six-layer model of a technical process.

the managerial/administrative tasks in preparing for the next batch of work. The so-called manufacturing execution system is an important representative for a system on this level.

3. *Process control level.* This level comprises the operator stations and processing systems with their applications for plant-wide remote supervision and control (manually or automatically) and hence overview of the entire process to be controlled. It provides human/machine interface applications for different types of supervision and control activities, such as process state visualization, alarm processing, process event handling, and batch preparation. As discussed later, an open control system is mainly concerned with this level and its interfaces to the levels below and above. Consequently the AIP presented in this chapter belongs to this level.

4. *Group control level.* This level comprises the controller devices and applications that typically control a group of related process level devices (e.g., those pertaining to a manufacturing robot) in a closed-loop fashion.

5. *Field level (or single control level).* This level contains sensors, actuators, drives, and so forth. The level comprises the interfacing equipment of a control system to the physical process. Typically, one would find the different input/output modules and platforms on this level.

6. *Process level.* This level contains the process equipment to be controlled, for example, a valve in a water pipeline, a boiler, or a high-voltage switch in a power transmission network.

While real-time performance, safety, and environmental capabilities are increasingly important for the products and systems toward the bottom of the pyramid, large-scale information processing and presentation capabilities are gaining in importance toward the top. The types of systems involved span from embedded systems with limited computing resources at the lowest levels to full-fledged information processing systems with abundant computing power at the upper levels.

Automation applications can now involve a single system on single level or multiple systems on multiple levels. Abstractly speaking, the complexity and information requirement of the control task at hand determines whether the control loop is closed at lower or higher levels and with or without human intervention. Although a homogeneous IT integration of all levels seems to be desirable, current practice remains focused on the provision of dedicated, homogeneous IT systems for subsets of these levels and of open interfaces to interact with the systems on other levels.

In the context of industrial automation, the term *automation system* is used to denote a set of systems that collaborate to perform some sort of automated activity. It is for this loose definition that the term is heavily overloaded and that vendors sell almost all process control-related systems as industrial automation systems nowadays. The automation system architecture discussed in the remainder of this chapter was essentially conceived as an Open Control System (OCS) architecture. An OCS is a general-purpose process control system platform that is used to build applications for the control of continuous or batch-type industrial processes in various vertical market domains. These can be anything from a manufacturing process for chocolate bars, to the continuous monitoring and remote control of an oil refinery plant, to a group of robot cells to assemble and paint cars. The basic end-user functionality of an OCS is process data acquisition, process visualization for operators, process alarm- and event handling, and local and remote control.

The predicate *open* indicates that building control applications are not confined to a vendor-specific solution, but allows for some degree of flexibility with respect to the choice of hardware and software components. A user of an OCS associates with the term *open* some basic capabilities of a control system platform, such as portability, scalability, extendibility, exchangeability, and interoperability. In the context of software systems, an OCS would fall into the category of distributed, reactive, command-and-control type systems. Depending on the particular application domain, it is a safety-critical and/or soft real-time application. A common demand on all of these types of systems and their applications is a high degree of dependability.

The AIP, discussed in the remainder of this chapter, is a generic framework for the realization of applications on the process control level, which includes the means to interface the levels immediately below and above. The AIP is intended to be used by applications in different vertical market domains. As such, the AIP is the heart of the process control level—no more and no less.

The Motivation for a Platform

A current buzzword in the industrial automation world is *Industrial IT*. It is the all-encompassing term used when people refer to an envisioned seamless link between front-end business processes and plant control processes (i.e., the link over all the control levels discussed earlier). In practice, the integrated computerized support for such a seamless link is based on a collection of different systems. A process automation system—this name is often used as the more fashionable term for open control system—is only one type of system in that collection.

Because the basic functionality of process automation systems (or automation systems for short) is of a similar nature across vertical market domains (recall the discussion of OCS above), building generic platforms has always been a primary concern, but has been practiced with mixed success. An automation system platform in this context is the application-independent infrastructure of a distributed automation system, that is, it consists of both the basic hardware infrastructure as well as the software infrastructure. According to Figure 17.1, it covers the application-neutral components for the process control level, and often also includes the group control level and field level. Hence, the hardware infrastructure is the equipment for process interfacing, instrumentation, data communications, control logic execution (e.g., programmable logic controllers), and operator workstations. The software infrastructure consists not only of operating systems, communication stacks, I/O preprocessing, run-time infrastructure to support distributed processing, and the above-mentioned basic functionality, but also the application development environment.

The motivations for a large global company active in many vertical market areas to invest in the development of a "single" platform are manifold. Here are some of the more obvious objectives:

- Avoidance of parallel developments in different business segments;
- Harmonization of the diversity of "legacy" automation platforms acquired through company mergers or resulting from previous parallel developments;
- Adoption of product-line business strategies (i.e., pursuing a system family concept both within and across vertical market segments).

Inherent in all of these motivations is the implicit expectation of a reuse payoff. Although the different approaches to software-related reuse have changed over time, systematic software reuse is still the most attractive way to shorten development time, save costs, and improve quality. CBSE is the software community's current attempt to encourage large-scale software reuse. However, the success of reuse depends on a number of equally important factors [1]: organizational issues, component and system architectures, a more or less stable market environment, existing domain and technology standards, and sustained managerial support.

In describing a substantial case study, the following sections are representative of the current state of practice in dealing with only one of these success factors, namely, the consideration of component and system architectures required.

To be able to derive new products efficiently using a component-based approach (i.e., by sharing components), the product structures must be similar. There must be a standard set of basic components with agreed-on responsibilities, performance, coordination mechanisms, and so forth. The agreements regarding such a structure, a basic set of components, and the properties that must hold for all future developed components (and products) can be considered the platform architecture. Because these characteristics are exactly those of a product line, an industrial automation platform is an obvious candidate for a software product-line architecture, in which "a collection of systems share a managed set of features constructed from a common set of core software assets" [2].

The automation system architecture described below employs a component-based reuse strategy, as opposed to a generative reuse approach. For a good treatment of component-based reuse versus generative reuse, we refer the interested reader to [3]. Component-based reuse is accomplished on two levels: on the platform infrastructure and related services level, and on the application domain-specific level. However, because the degree of reuse payoff primarily correlates with the effort invested in domain-related work, a platform architecture alone does not guarantee the success of, but merely supports reuse efforts.

The Aspect Integrator Platform

The generic and fundamental functionality to be provided by an OCS is as follows:

- Acquisition and presentation of information relating to the process history;

- Acquisition and presentation of information relating to the current status of the process;

- Provision of real-time facilities to control the process;

- Presentation of information to predict and influence the future of the process.

This functionality must be provided in a very reliable manner, to mention just one quality requirement.

Hence, the main task of an OCS is the reliable presentation of information that pertains to domain objects and that reflects their past, current, and future. In addition to the standard set of architectural challenges, this leaves the architect of an OCS with three fundamental technical problems:

1. How do we cope with the diversity of information pertaining to objects of interest in the domain? The fact that the underlying mechanism must satisfy objects of various domains intensifies this problem.

2. How do we provide user-type specific navigation to representations of domain objects and context-related information?

3. How do we accomplish information acquisition and integration in the distributed configurations of today's control systems?

The architecture presented, designated Aspect Integrator Platform, employs specific approaches to these problems. Objects with aspects are the architectural means to deal with the first question above. An extendable set of tree structures based on the concepts introduced in the IEC1346 standard[1] [4] is used to cope with question 2. A selection of predominantly off-the-shelf technologies [e.g., Microsoft COM-based OLE for Process Control (OPC) [5]] provides a technical basis for dealing with question 3.

An OCS architecture and its embodiment as a run-time infrastructure relegates the development complexity to the infrastructure developer and thereby reduces the effort required for application development. On a high level, the AIP is an object-structuring and programming model, a run-time infrastructure, an application development environment, and a set of generic control system applications.

The AspectObject Paradigm and Object Organization

The process control community separates the process into domain objects. Thus, a natural model for information representation is an object-oriented model. Domain objects can be associated with rather diverse (and often orthogonal) information aspects, that is, data and behavior of different concerns. The AIP introduces the notion of an AspectObject to represent a domain object that has Aspects to denote explicit, stakeholder-specific information concerns. Note that information not only refers to data but also to concepts that encapsulate behavior (e.g., a control algorithm pertaining to an AspectObject). Hence, objects and aspects are the fundamental concepts in the architecture of the AIP to accomplish a unified high-level object approach. In fact, an AspectObject can be understood as a conceptual object in the problem domain, similar to those that are typically identified in conceptual modeling. However, besides the terminology and the fact that aspects are first-class design concepts that are applicable to different kinds of objects, there is no commonality between the AspectObject approach presented in this article and Aspect-Oriented Programming (AOP) [6]. For an illustrative

---

1. The IEC 1346-1 standard defines three structures to designate an object. The structures are compositional by nature, that is, "part-of" relationships, and divided into a function-oriented structure, a product-oriented structure, and a location oriented structure.

example of the AspectObject model, see Figure 17.2, in which a Valve Aspect-Object models a valve domain object and its five relevant aspects.

As mentioned above, flexible object structures are used to organize objects for navigational purposes hierarchically. An AspectObject may appear as a node in an arbitrary number of structures, typically three structures. As an example consider the diary in Figure 17.3. A valve (FIC201 Valve) is part of three structures. The functional structure identifies it as part of the milk supply function. The location structure identifies it as part of an unambiguously defined location "B2.R3" (building B2 and processing area R3). Finally, the valve is also part of a batch structure. In the example, it is part of a defined batch procedure for mixing the milk for a product named BananaMilk100.

As opposed to other realizations of reference structures, in which reference holders will not normally be notified of changes in the object they reference (unless an explicit callback is programmed), the AspectObject structure employs a central reference management that automatically informs reference holders of changes in the contents of referenced objects. Applications can build on this feature and adapt a reactive programming style.

The Architecture of the Aspect Integrator Platform

In this section, the architecture of the AIP is described in more detail. Further details can be found in [7]. The explanation of the architecture is structured according to the "4+1 views approach" [8] referring to the logical view, the physical view, the development view, the process view, and the scenario

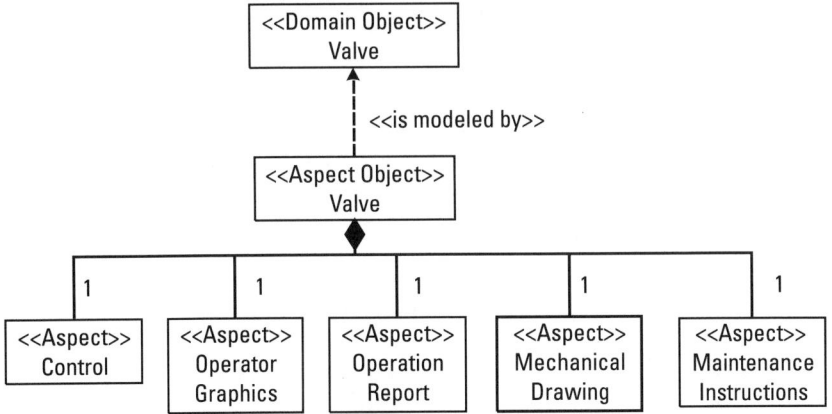

Figure 17.2 Model objects and their aspects.

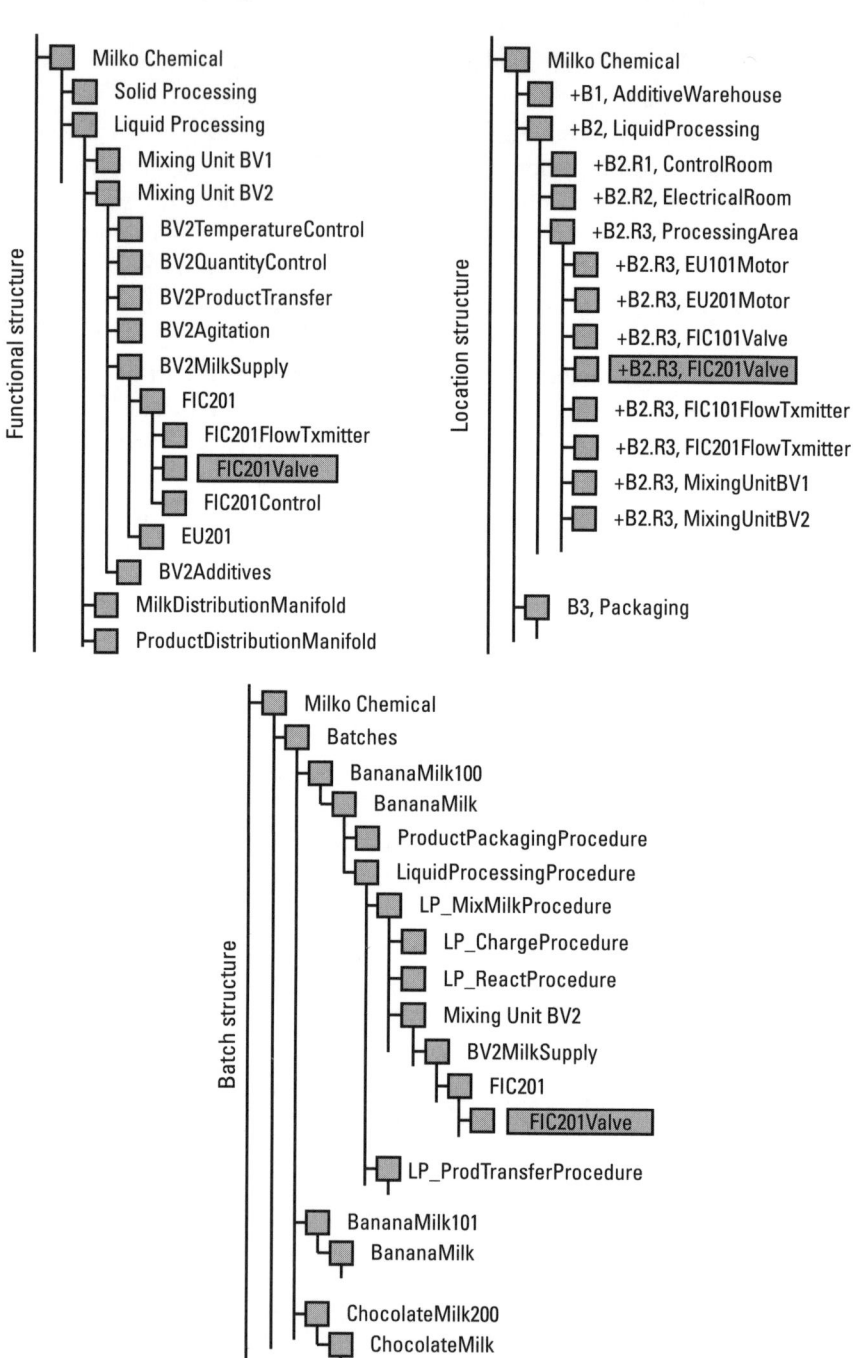

Figure 17.3 An AspectObject (FIC210 Valve) present in three structures.

view. Because the scenario view (the "+1"), which essentially models some important use cases, is redundant for the other views, we omit it here for brevity. Nevertheless, in the analysis and conception phase of an architecture, it serves as the focal point for developing the other views as well as for testing the consistency between views.

Logical View

As explained in the previous section, the concepts of objects and aspects are fundamental for an understanding of the AIP architecture. The logical view explains and puts into context the various elements that constitute the Aspect-Object paradigm. Figure 17.4 shows the logical elements and their relationships, discussed in the following sections.

AspectObject

The model element of a domain object is designated AspectObject in ABB nomenclature to express the fact that its attributes, which refer to the application domain, are separated into so-called Aspects. Except for some framework-internal, administrative attributes, AspectObjects do not carry data but serve only as reference keys and mediators between the domain Aspects.

In an AIP-based system, AspectObjects represent all the concrete and abstract concepts relevant within the system context and to the system functionality, for example, machines, plant, hosts, devices, controllers, and algorithms.

An AspectObject has a globally unique identifier, GUID (the Microsoft name for a universally unique identifier, UUID, defined by The Open Group) and the basic property that it can be part of an arbitrary number of hierarchical structures. Its position in a structure determines its Aspects, that is, its associated data attributes and their initialization and modification behavior. Hence, it resembles a configurable inheritance mechanism. Aspects, Aspect Types, and even Object Types (all explained below) inherit this basic ability due to the fact that they are technically AspectObjects themselves, and thus first-class objects in specific system configuration structures.

Object Type

Each AspectObject in an AIP-based application is of a certain type, a so-called *Object Type*. As has been explained above, an Object Type is also an AspectObject. Therefore, it can be created and modified at run time, effecting corresponding changes in all AspectObjects of this Object Type. An

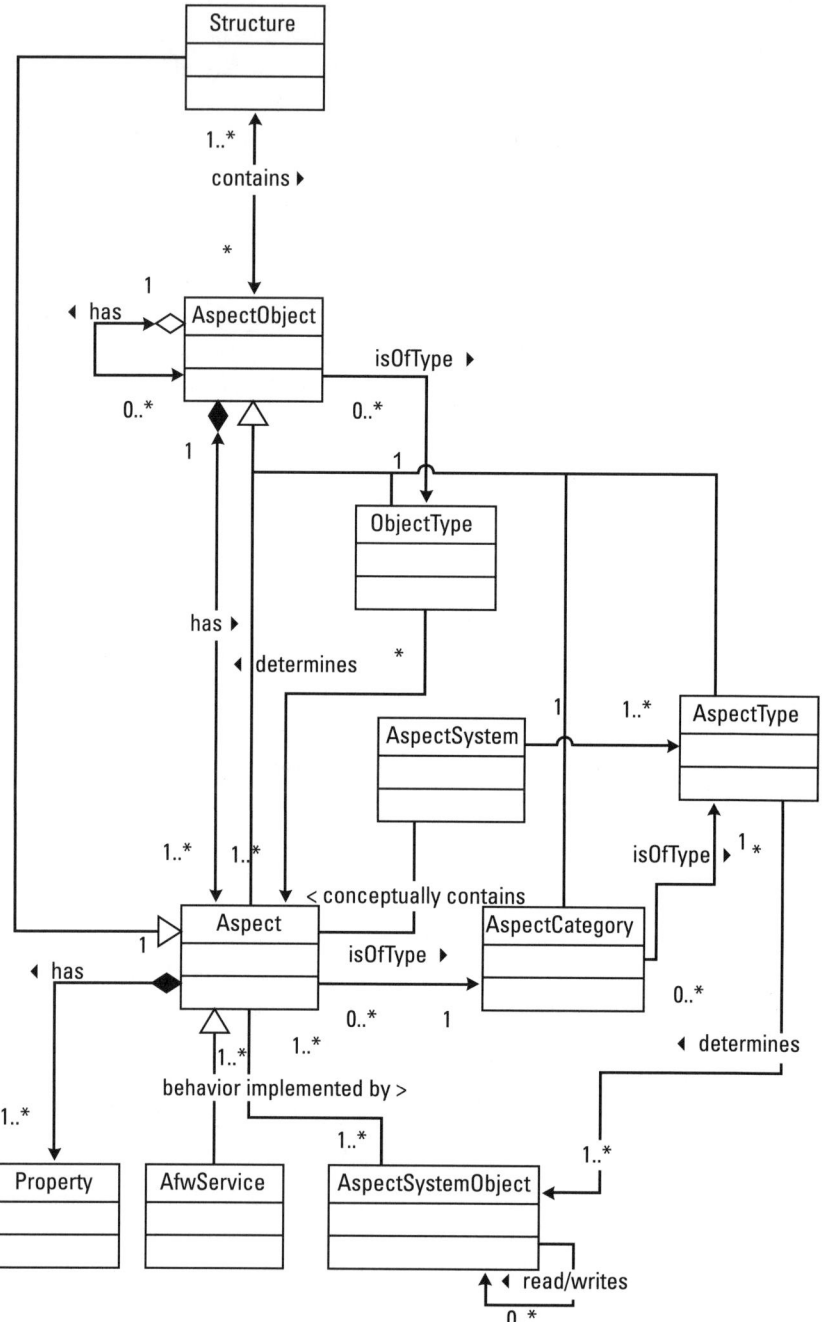

Figure 17.4 Elements of the AIP logical view.

Object Type determines which Aspect Types (see below) are associated with an AspectObject and also how Aspects and their properties are initialized and modified at AspectObject instance creation and modification, respectively. Because an AspectObject comes into being through the creation of a node in any of the hierarchical structures, the initialization/modification configuration is referred to as an inheritance setting, because the Aspect initialization would normally propagate from the parent node.

Because Object Types are AspectObjects themselves, they are also located in hierarchical structures that provide inheritance features.

While specific AspectObjects are presumably created for each individual AIP-based application project, domain-specific libraries of Object Types (such as the valve Object Type of the "FIC210 Valve" instance in Figure 17.3) constitute one of the main domain-specific reuse mechanisms in the AIP architecture; Aspect Types, as we will see, constitute the other. For example, libraries for steel mills, power distribution substations, and so on, can be developed and harvested.

Aspect

Each AspectObject has a number of Aspects. An Aspect encapsulates a subset of the data and corresponding behavior. It relates to a common context or purpose. Figure 17.2 above provided an illustrative example. Which Aspects of an AspectObject should be accessible in a certain context is configurable. The Aspect Category (discussed below under Aspect Type) defines the type of an Aspect. So-called *AspectSystemObjects* (see below) implement the data and behavior of an Aspect. A container for data, in the form of a binary large object (Blob), is associated with each Aspect and is one means of storing its data within certain size constraints. Only the Aspect can interpret the data in its Blob. An Aspect, being an AspectObject itself, is directly accessible from anywhere in the system via its GUID. However, in most cases it will be located via the AspectObject that owns it.

Aspect Type

Each Aspect conforms to a certain *Aspect Type*. As any type definition does, the Aspect Type defines the properties for a set of Aspects. With respect to the Aspect behavior, it references the possibly multiple AspectSystemObjects that implement the different behaviors of an Aspect (operational user interface, configuration user interface, data persistence strategy, context menu entry, etc.). The notion of an Aspect Category has been introduced to permit the definition of variations of Aspect Types. An Aspect Category behaves in exactly the same way but defines certain different static parameters. They can be used for the sorting or classification of Aspects. For instance, an Aspect Type "Web Page Reference," whose behavior is to start a browser and display a selected Web page, could be of Aspect Category "Manufacturer Documentation Web Page" to denote the fact that all Aspects of this category relate to manufacturer-provided on-line documentation for a certain AspectObject.

Aspect System

An *Aspect System* is a collection of Aspect Types for a certain context or purpose (e.g., a maintenance Aspect System may consist of a maintenance manual Aspect Type), a maintenance work log Aspect Type, and an Aspect Type to encapsulate access to a third-party maintenance management application (e.g., scheduling, work order). The Aspect Types of an Aspect System should be applicable to multiple Object Types. After Object Types, Aspect Types organized in Aspect Systems are the second most important vector for domain-related reuse in AIP-based applications.

AspectSystemObject

An Aspect contains data associated with an AspectObject. To work with this data (create, view, modify them)—realized in classical object-oriented design by methods—some Aspect-specific software is needed. The (binary) software component, which provides the behavior for a particular Aspect, is an *AspectSystemObject* (ASO). Technically, an ASO is a Microsoft COM [9] component following specific rules (see the "Development View" section of this chapter). An Aspect System itself is purely conceptual. It comes into existence only through the fact that a set of ASOs for the Aspect Types of the Aspect System is registered with the AIP infrastructure.

The basic set of ASOs distributed with the AIP contains functionality for alarming and event handling, historical data management and trending, viewing Web/HTML pages, viewing PDFs, wrapping Win32 applications, and wrapping Microsoft ActiveX components. The latter technology is easily configured to encapsulate applications such as Microsoft Word and Microsoft Excel. An ASO can have (but does not need) a user interface. More than one ASO can cooperate to implement one Aspect Type, as described previously. The implementation code of an ASO can make use of the AIP infrastructure functionality to navigate to and access other ASOs of other Aspects. For instance, an ASO being part of a service personnel support Aspect System provides the graphical representation of the list of all documents relating to a particular Object Type used in the system. It might therefore need access to the ASO of the computer-aided design (CAD) tool Aspect to inquire about the CAD-related documents and their file location.

Aspect Framework Services

Aspect Framework Services (*AfwServices*) can be considered as Aspects of the AIP infrastructure. They provide GUI-less, continuously running infrastructure functionality, such as security access control, object locking, or name lookup. An AfwService is basically a normal Aspect whose ASOs execute in the server layer. One important framework service is the provision of an infrastructure for consistency management (e.g., callback events). In this way, Aspects can react to changes in other Aspects on which they depend. This holds for both changes in content and changes in their position in Structures (see below).

More details can be found in the discussion of the physical view of the architecture.

Structures

The AIP provides *structures* as an important concept for ordering Aspect-Objects in an AIP-based application. Structures are graphs (trees in the most simple case) whose nodes are the AspectObjects in the system. The important idea here is that each AspectObject may be referenced by multiple structures and the AspectObject knows about these references. Figure 17.5 shows an example in which the AspectObject *Maier* (representing a human resource) is both a child of the AspectObject *CHCRC* (an organizational unit of a company) of the hierarchy formed by the Structure "OrgUnitStructure" and of the AspectObject *Gamma* (a concrete development project) in the hierarchy formed by the structure *ProjectStructure*.

Abstractly speaking, structures can be used to model objects and their relations with is-a, has-a, is part of, or similar semantics, depending on the application. Speaking in concrete terms, a structure is used as a hierarchical organization of AspectObjects that describes the dependencies between (primarily) domain concepts in a certain navigation context. Because an Aspect-Object can exist in multiple structures, multidirectional navigation starting from the object is possible. If the problem domain is broken down into structures so that each structure represents one meaningful context and notion of relatedness between concepts (e.g., a manufacturing machine is part of a control system, located at a certain place, has a certain function in the purpose of the whole plant, is from a certain manufacturer, etc.) then this paradigm of multiple connected structures provides a powerful information navigation mechanism.

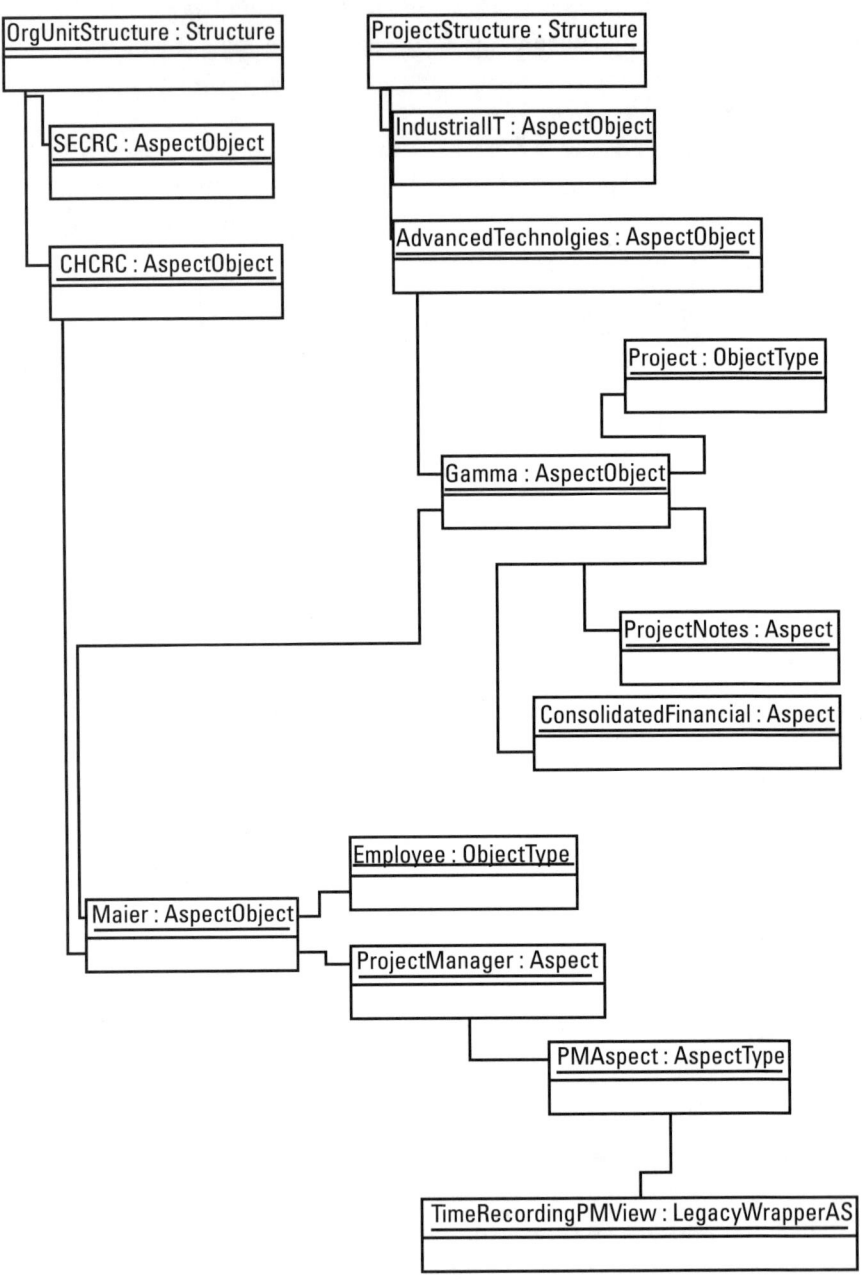

Figure 17.5 AspectObjects organized in structures.

Note that membership of an AspectObject in a certain structure is represented by a corresponding structure Aspect. If an AspectObject is a member of several structures it will have several Structure Aspects.

Physical View

This section describes how AIP-based applications consisting of AspectObjects, Aspect Systems, and the AIP infrastructure can be distributed to multiple hosts within a local-area network (LAN). As will be seen, the most important qualities that must be addressed by an OCS architecture are:

- Reliability in the sense of fault tolerance, that is, avoidance of single points of failure;

- Scalability and thus a means of load-balancing;

- Application relocation; the ability to move transparently a single combined workplace/server configuration to a complex, distributed multiserver topology without any changes in the AspectObjects and AspectSystemObjects.

An AIP application is a client/server system with a variable number of clients and servers. The minimum system consists of one host on which both the server-side and the client-side applications are running. Process control applications are often required to support the concurrent access of multiple operators to the same control system. Hence, a need arises for multiple concurrent client applications (called workplaces) at different hosts. Several workplaces can access the services running at one single server host. However, for improved scalability and reliability, system topologies with multiple servers are often desirable. Servers and clients require Windows 2000 as the operating system.

Figure 17.6 shows an example of a topology consisting of two workplace hosts, one combined workplace/server host and three server hosts. Four controllers are connected to the servers via the controller network. Further elements of the figure are explained below.

Application and Data Distribution

In addition to the AIP run-time infrastructure, the binary code [Dynamic LinkLibrary (DLLs)] for all Object Types, Aspect Types, and AspectSystemObjects required must be distributed to all workplace and server machines. If any Aspect System accesses a third-party application (e.g., a CAD system),

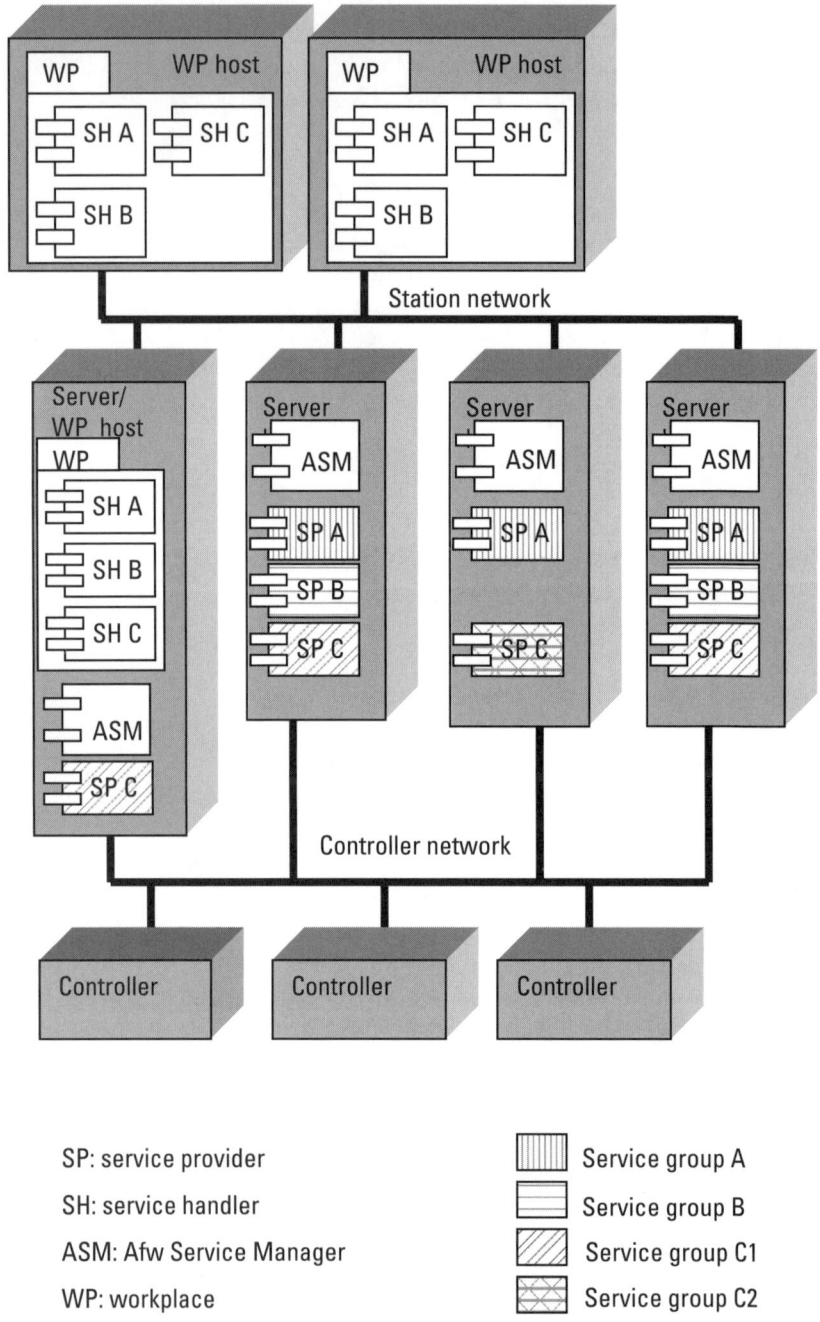

SP: service provider   Service group A

SH: service handler   Service group B

ASM: Afw Service Manager   Service group C1

WP: workplace   Service group C2

Figure 17.6 Example of system topology with multiple AfwServices and server groups.

the respective client application must also be installed locally at each workplace host.

The core of the AIP is the *Aspect Directory*, a distributed database of names, GUIDs, and administrative data for AspectObject and Aspect instances. In essence, it manages associations of AspectObjects, Aspects, and Structures. The Aspect Directory identifies Aspects and AspectObjects via GUIDs. The Aspect Directory is realized as an Aspect Framework Service.

An instance of an AIP-based application together with its data is designated a system. Multiple systems can coexist on a host, each with its own run-time data structures and persistent data. AspectObjects and Aspects in different systems are completely independent, both conceptually and at run time. Each system has its own Aspect Directory instance.

Data associated with an Aspect can be stored at two places: either in a Blob (as defined earlier) in the Aspect Directory itself, together with the other information about the Aspect, or locally at the workplace host. The first method is recommended for small amounts of data, the latter is especially relevant if the Aspect System makes use of a third-party application that uses the file system for persistent data storage (e.g., Microsoft Word). In the case of local data storage, the problem arises that the data files must be distributed to all workplace machines so that each workplace has a continuous, consistent, and identical system. The AIP offers support for that purpose through the file set distribution service explained below.

Services

As mentioned above, the AIP infrastructure offers various services (aspect framework services) that AspectSystemObjects can use to achieve location transparency and reliability. The services are controlled by the *AfwService-Manager,* which is implemented as a Windows 2000 service, and part of the AIP run time. Currently, the AIP offers the following services:

- *Aspect Directory.* This is the basic service of the platform. It realizes the functionality of the AspectObject concept, the structures and bidirectional references between Aspects and AspectObjects.

- *Structure and name service.* This service is closely connected to the Aspect Directory. It permits querying the Aspect Directory not only via COM references, but also via complex query strings describing paths in single or multiple Structures in the system.

- *File set distribution (FSD) service.* The FSD service addresses the issue of replicating locally stored and changed files, for example, persistent data edited with third-party applications, to all workplaces and servers in the system. FSD supports preload and on-demand replication and checks for modifications, automatic registration of DLLs, and replication priorities.

- *OPC data access server.* Permits access to ASOs using the OPC protocol [5]. More specifically, it provides access to those COM/OLE properties of ASOs that are declared for export.

- *System message service.* This AfwService provides system-wide central logging, storage, and viewing of multiple-language, prioritized messages generated by the AIP-based application.

Further AfwServices such as lock service and time services are available but are not discussed here.

Service Groups

To improve fault tolerance, an AfwService can be distributed over multiple service providers that execute at different server hosts but provide the same functionality (see Figure 17.6). A set of mutually redundant providers is named a *Service Group.* The providers in a Service Group are responsible for replicating state information between them. A client finds a provider in a number of ways: (1) via a broadcast to a Service Group, (2) via a list of preferred workplace server mappings, or (3) via an explicitly configured provider for a relevant AspectObject. However, the clients are responsible for recognizing failure of a provider and for application-transparent switchover to another within the Service Group. Figure 17.6 shows three AfwServices, A, B, and C, in four Service Groups. The Service Group for AfwService A contains three providers; that for B contains two providers. For AfwService C there are two Service Groups (C1 and C2) with two providers each. Therefore, there is only simple redundancy for C, but the configuration of two groups permits better load balancing.

Development View

The development view of an architecture presents how the elements of the logical view are arranged in terms of actual programming artifacts. Because programming-level information is not within the scope of our discussion of the architecture of the AIP in this case study, this section only briefly discusses the different notions of components used in the AIP and how they are mapped to software technology.

The AIP architecture distinguishes between conceptual and technological components. The conceptual components—AspectObjects and Aspects—are manipulated, that is, created, modified, deleted, inside an AIP-based application itself. The conceptual components are used to build the application in terms of concepts known to the user and system engineer, who is not necessarily a software developer. A conceptual component is internally basically a data structure containing references to other conceptual and technological components.

The technological components of the AIP are mostly the Aspect-SystemObjects described above. As mentioned previously, an ASO is a Microsoft COM [9, 10] component following certain additional, AIP-specific conventions with regard to the COM interfaces that it must implement. Both Aspects and AfwServices are implemented by means of ASOs. In addition to ASOs, the AIP contains a number of other COM components that together implement the basic platform infrastructure. Hence, this infrastructure can also be considered a valuable high-level business object for reuse.

Microsoft's wire protocol called DCOM is not used for communication between distributed parts of an AIP-based application. A proprietary, socket-based protocol has been developed, because DCOM lacked features that were needed (e.g., with respect to redundancy and fault tolerance).

The AIP-based infrastructure and the ASO programming conventions offer APIs for use with Microsoft Visual C++ and for more restricted use with Microsoft Visual Basic and scripting languages. The AIP is delivered with add-ons for Microsoft Visual Studio for the creation of AspectSystem-Objects, which generate a large part of the AIP-specific COM conventions and thus help to deal with the complexity of the development of ASOs.

Process View

Client and server tasks (AfwServices) in an AIP-based application communicate via sockets. The implementation of an ASO must permit multiple concurrent accesses to the data of an Aspect. As an alternative, the locking service provides infrastructure support for this purpose. Concurrency issues on the implementation level are mostly relevant with respect to the Object Manager and are discussed in [11]. Because ASOs map to COM components and the AIP infrastructure is also realized with COM components, the Microsoft COM and Windows 2000 conventions with respect to operating system processes and threads apply.

Developing a Domain-Specific Application

In [1], Jacobson et al. have introduced the distinction between an application system and a component system. In essence, application systems are built from reusable sets of components[2] and are the result of a reuse-based business. Reusable components are organized into component systems. This emphasizes the fact that reusing a single component is usually insufficient. Obtaining meaningful and useful behavior requires the reuse of a set of components, which in turn may have several relationships with each other. For example, in the AIP, a set of components pertaining to an Aspect System must be reused to obtain the alarm handling functionality. In Chapter 7 of their book, Jacobson et al. also suggest a four-layer representation of the static organization of software. While the top layer represents application systems with possible variants, all other layers contain component systems according to the definition above. The semantics of the layers is that systems on the same layer may interact and systems across layers have static dependencies. In Figure 17.7, we classify the AIP concepts introduced in the previous sections by showing their association with these four layers. To aid the understanding of the figure, we briefly summarize the definitions of the layers given by Jacobson and his colleagues:

- *The application system layer* contains several application systems, each of which offers a coherent set of use cases to some end users. Application systems may interoperate. This can be realized directly by means of their interfaces or indirectly by means of some services from underlying component systems.

- *The business-specific layer* contains several component systems that are specific to the business. In our case, the term *business* refers to the OCS type of business and to the OCS business that is specific to a vertical market domain. Typically, this layer offers components that are used by the application engineer.

- *The middleware layer* contains several component systems that are independent of particular types of business. Among others, this layer can include GUI builders, interfaces to database management systems, OCS-foreign COM/Object Linking and Embedding (OLE) components (spreadsheets, etc.). Because this layer offers

---

2. In their basic definition a component can be any work product that has been engineered for reuse. This includes any type of model element, templates, documents, COM components, and so forth.

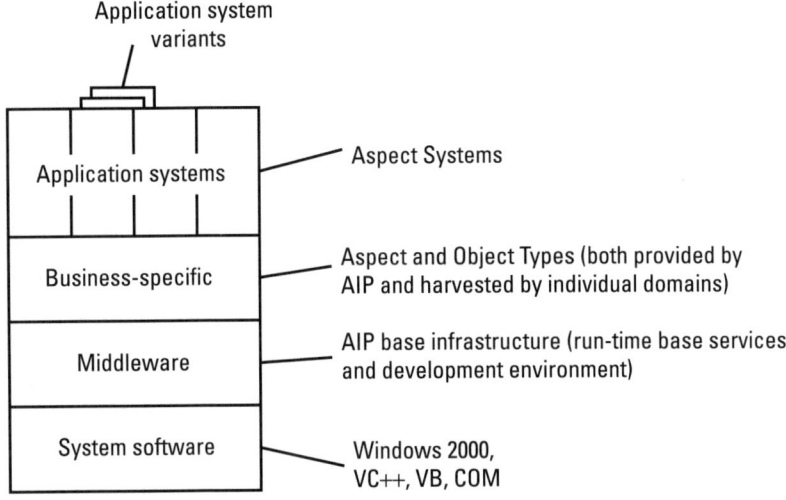

Figure 17.7 AIP concepts assigned to the architectural layers as defined by Jacobson et al. [1].

components for the development of business-specific component and application systems, we also consider the AIP development environment as middleware.

- *The system software layer* contains the basic computing and networking software such as operating systems and TCP/IP stacks. The software is usually platform dependent, but the use of platform-independent software is increasing. The boundaries between the middleware and system software layer are indistinct.

Within the well-known phases of software development, the development of an AIP-based application (such as that described in [12]) requires the following activities:

1. *Requirements and possibly even domain engineering.* The requirements of a particular customer project must be captured, or, if an application family is envisioned, the features and feature variability of an entire application domain must be analyzed. The result is a requirements specification with a set of required applications and their features. This activity is not supported by the AIP. However, a mapping of aspect systems to applications is expected.

2. *Analysis and design.* This includes definition of the different kinds of AspectObjects (Object Types), that is, the selection of the domain objects to be modeled, and definition of the various Aspect Types and their association with Object Types. This activity is supported by business-specific component systems. These are reusable generic Aspect and Object Types as provided by the AIP as well as those Aspect and Object Types specific to a vertical market domain. The latter assumes that such a specific component system has been developed. This phase also includes design of the physical topology and distribution of client/server applications and services.

3. *Implementation.* AspectObject structures must be defined and AspectObjects within them instantiated. New Aspect Types (i.e., development of AspectSystemObjects in the form of COM components) must be implemented. Inheritance settings must be configured and, in general, the utilization of component and application system variability determined for customizing applications (e.g., a foreseen variability point of an Aspect System, which provides function plan programming according to the IEC61131-3 standard [13] is the code section that allows programming of a custom control logic). The implementation activity is supported by the AIP through business-specific component systems in the form of reusable ASOs, entire application systems (i.e., Aspect Systems) with defined variability points, and the development environment.

Deployment and testing activities are not discussed here.

Reuse in AIP-Based Applications

To make explicit the various components of reuse, Figure 17.8 gives a more detailed view of the different levels of reuse for AIP-based applications and the supportive means ("enablers") provided by the AIP. The dark gray parts are reusable artifacts supplied with the AIP, whereas the light gray parts represent the reusable assets that are potentially harvested for certain application domains. The different levels correspond with layers depicted in Figure 17.7. The system and middleware layer have been collapsed into the base level while the business-specific layer has been expanded to an Aspect and Object Type level, respectively. The reuse levels discussed are, therefore, base, Aspect Types, Object Types, and experience.

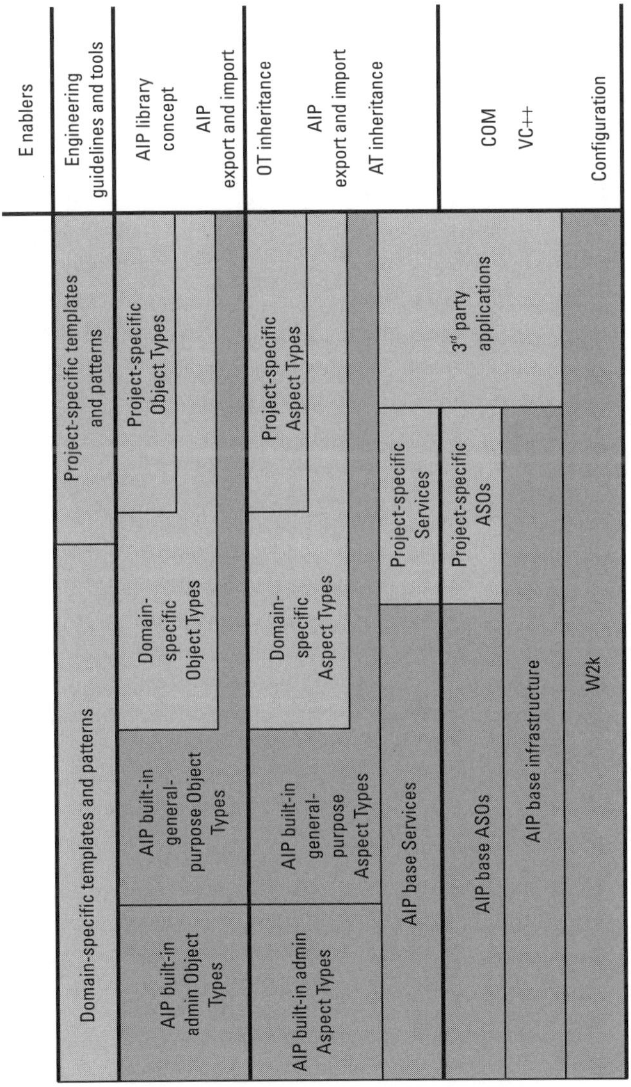

Enablers

Engineering guidelines and tools

AIP library concept

AIP export and import

OT inheritance

AIP export and import

AT inheritance

COM

VC++

Configuration

Domain-specific templates and patterns

Project-specific templates and patterns

AIP built-in admin Object Types

AIP built-in general-purpose Object Types

Domain-specific Object Types

Project-specific Object Types

AIP built-in admin Aspect Types

AIP built-in general-purpose Aspect Types

Domain-specific Aspect Types

Project-specific Aspect Types

AIP base Services

Project-specific Services

AIP base ASOs

Project-specific ASOs

AIP base infrastructure

3rd party applications

W2k

Figure. 17.8 AIP reuse hierarchy.

The AIP reuse base level consists of the Windows 2000 operating system, the AIP basic run-time infrastructure, and the AspectSystemObjects, a collection of COM objects. All of the levels discussed earlier use these by means of either configuration or low-level programming.

The Aspect Type level includes client Aspect types and Services. The AIP is delivered with Aspect Types used for internal configuration and a set of Aspect Types with more generic functionality. In addition, the users of the platform can realize their own Aspect Types—in the figure, a two-level hierarchy of domain-specific and product/customer/project-specific Aspect Types is shown symbolically. Aspect Types can be developed via implementation of ASOs, thus reusing from the lower level, or they can be realized via inheritance from existing Aspect Types. Of course, exchange of Aspect Types between projects requires the export/import facilities provided by the AIP. Both newly implemented and refined Aspect Types may access the base-level infrastructure and will often encapsulate non-AIP applications such as CAD or office applications.

The Object Type and Aspect Type levels are similar. The latter is on a higher level, because Object Types are specified in terms of Aspect Types. In addition to inheritance and export/import, the AIP provides a versioning facility for libraries of Object Types.

Whereas the three lower levels are concerned with the building blocks, the top level refers to the building of the final applications. AIP engineering tools support the assembly of applications from these building blocks. Except for certain examples, the know-how for the most effective and efficient building of systems is not delivered with the AIP. It is expected that platform users will codify their experience in domain- and project-specific design guidelines.

Some Words of Caution

While the development of a platform seems an attractive means of supporting the architecture and technology issues of a successful reuse business, some words about possible risks are justified:

- If an enterprise (and thus its business segments) merely relies on a platform as the reuse "silver bullet" and does not have a reuse-driven process or product-line practice with a top-down and planned approach to reuse, the potential payoff is restricted to "low-level reuse" (platform services and technology). An opportunistic reuse of domain-specific components, that is, components that were created during application system development without the explicit engineering for reuse, will not succeed.

- Requirements management (i.e., requirements elicitation, prioritization, and trade-offs across products, domains, and organizational units) is extremely complex.

- Bugs in a released version of platform components and delays in the platform development can have a major financial impact on even a large organization because it may have negative effects on many lines of business simultaneously. However, with the incorporation of COTS components such as operating systems or database management systems in their products, companies are already facing similar risks today and have learned to cope with them.

Summary

After an introduction to industrial automation systems and the rationale for building such systems in a platform fashion, this chapter presented the software architecture of the Aspect Integrator Platform in the "4+1 view" style [8]. The AIP is an object structuring and programming model, a run-time infrastructure, an application development environment, and a set of generic control system applications for building open control systems. Because automation system platforms strive for reuse within and across vertical market domains, we emphasized those aspects of the architecture that encourage reuse.

Because the control system domain is inherently domain-object-centric, the AIP introduces the notion of AspectObjects with Aspects as the fundamental modeling constructs. AspectObjects and Aspects are used for the information representation of domain objects and its partitioning into crosscutting information concerns.

The discussion in this chapter showed that component-based reuse is not primarily a software component technology issue but requires component systems in the form of coherent sets of business objects and infrastructure objects. In the AIP these are the Object Types and Aspect Systems and framework services, respectively. Only these higher level components, which we called conceptual components, are useful artifacts for reuse. They are the result of a large domain and not technology-related efforts. However, technological software components (in the AIP the AspectSystemObjects realized as COM components) provide a valuable packaging entity for realizing and deploying conceptual components.

In the AIP, the run-time infrastructure and its services, the conceptual components (Aspect Types, Object Types), and Aspect Systems (application systems with well-defined variability) are the most valuable assets for reuse. However, with the exception of the run-time infrastructure and some generic Object and Aspect Types, the reuse business requires substantial domain effort; that is, investments in the various business segments is required to harvest conceptual component libraries and to run a reuse-oriented process with appropriate tool support. This is why ABB has launched several activities to coordinate and support domain-specific reuse efforts on the basis of AIP.

References

[1] Jacobson, I., M. L. Griss, and P. Jonsson, *Software Reuse, Architecture, Process and Organization for Business Success*, Reading, MA: Addison-Wesley and ACM Press, 1997.

[2] Bass, L., P. Clements, and R. Kazman, *Software Architecture in Practice*, Reading, MA: Addison-Wesley, 1998.

[3] Biggerstaff, T. J., "A Perspective of Generative Reuse," *Annals of Software Engineering*, Vol. 5, 1998, pp. 169–226.

[4] IEC, "Industrial Systems, Installations and Equipment and Industrial Products—Structuring Principles and Reference Designations, Part 1: Basic Rules," International Standard IEC 1346-1, International Electrotechnical Commission, 1996.

[5] OPC, "OLE for Process Control," Report v1.0, OPC Standards Collection, OPC Foundation, 1998.

[6] Kiczalez, G., et al., "Aspect-Oriented Programming," *ACM Computing Surveys*, Vol. 28, 1996, p. 154.

[7] Andersson, J., "Aspect Integrator Platform Architecture," Internal Technical Report 3BSE012770, ABB Automation, Västerås, Sweden, 2001.

[8] Kruchten, P., "The 4+1 View Model of Architecture," *IEEE Software*, Vol. 12, No. 6, 1995, pp. 42–50.

[9] Microsoft, "The Component Object Model Specification," Report v0.99, Microsoft Standards, Redmond, WA: Microsoft, 1996.

[10] Box, D., *Essential COM*, Reading, MA: Addison-Wesley, 1998.

[11] Hollender, M., "Aspect Integrator Platform Programmer's Guide," Internal Technical Report 3BSE023959 R0101/-2, ABB Automation, Västerås, Sweden, 2001.

[12] Naedele, M., C. Vetter, and T. Werner, "A Framework for the Management of Virtual Enterprises," *Proc. 5th World Multiconference on Systemics, Cybernetics and Informatics—SCI 2001*, Orlando, FL, 2001.

[13] IEC, "Programmable Controllers, Part 3, Programming Languages," Report IEC 1131-3, Geneva: IEC, 1992.

18

A Framework for Integrating Business Applications

Erik Gyllenswärd and Mladen Kap

Introduction

A challenge to the software industry today is to encourage reuse of not only components but also complete applications and information. This chapter describes an object model and a framework providing a solution to this problem by supporting component-based system development, application integration, and the ability to organize and structure all information in a company or organization in a uniform and simple manner, thus making it readily available to different categories of users. The framework is implemented in the product *Information Organizer*.

The basic concept in implementing Information Organizer is to exploit the reuse approach as far as possible and to follow standards and de facto standards, which are defined with respect to both concept and implementation. A number of component-based patterns have been implemented to support the development of new applications such as patterns for document handling, workflow functionality, and general database integration. Some of these patterns are described in more detail, focusing on how Information Organizer and its concepts have been used in the development.

Motivation

All information of importance, irrespective of its source, is to be made available to different categories of users, both in the workshop and in the office. This is to ensure that all concerned have access to correct information to enable them to perform their work most effectively. An employee in a manufacturing industry will find assembled together all information regarding, for example, a pump: drawings, specification, installation instructions, manuals, operating instructions, invoices, and production logs. The same applies with respect to an employee in a governmental office with, for example, an issue management system. All information relating to an issue must be easily accessible, and the employee should be able to present and obtain information from different issue management systems in a uniform manner.

Companies frequently develop various information systems at different periods in company history that contain information that, in pursuit of efficiency, must be reused. Rewriting all existing systems to make the information uniformly available is not likely to be practically or economically acceptable. Another method for accessing and interrelating associated information in different systems is called for—a common specification model, regardless of the origin of the information, and reuse of existing application-specific tools to access and manipulate the information in a familiar manner, as shown in Figure 18.1. A concept and support for integrating existing information systems in a simple manner and on the appropriate level is required. Satisfying these requirements and providing the possibility of building new functionality using existing components and applications makes possible a greater degree of reuse than can be achieved using existing component-based technologies.

A number of software vendors have recognized this. For example, Microsoft has made available the *Active Directory* [1] as a tool for sharing information between different applications. The term *directory-enabled applications* is most often used to describe an application built in such a way that it can make use of information available via the Active Directory. Almost all new applications developed by Microsoft (for example, Exchange 2000) are directory-enabled. The ABB concepts of Aspects and AspectObjects, described in Chapter 17, are other examples of this approach and are mainly intended to be used in the automation industry, whereas Information Organizer is mainly intended to be used in the office automation domain. The two concepts are quite similar due to the fact that they both are based on the same standard, IEC1346 [2] but their implementations are completely different.

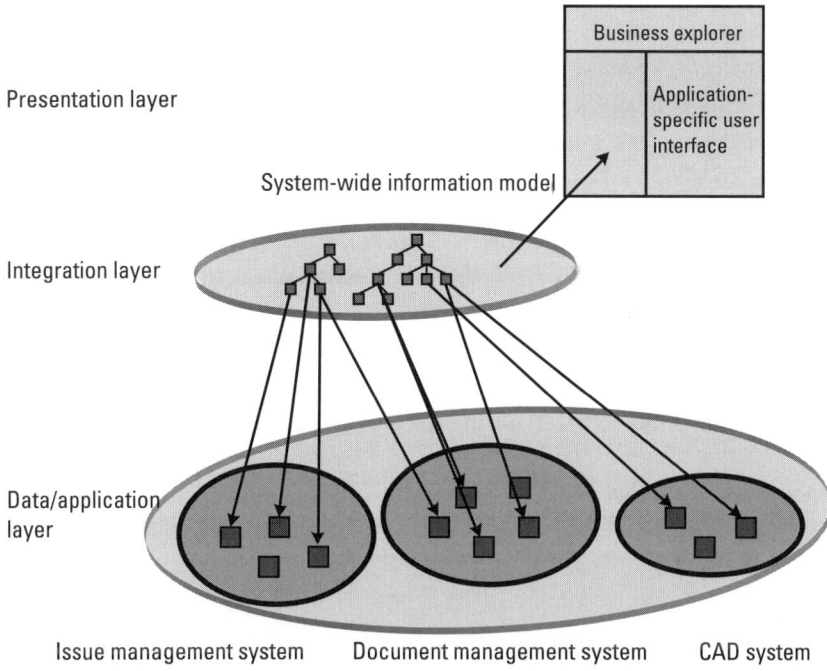

Presentation layer

Integration layer

Data/application layer

Issue management system   Document management system   CAD system

Figure 18.1 Information Organizer, an architecture for application integration.

Compfab [3], the producer of Information Organizer, has further developed the concept of directory-enabled applications by adding a number of important properties defined in standards such as IEC1346, OMG [4, 5], and research projects such as IT4 [6]. The two most important of these properties are the possibility of holding together all aspects belonging to an object, regardless of which application provides the feature, and a powerful relation model that makes it possible to create a high-level information model covering a number of applications (see the "BOM" section in this chapter). The relation model makes it possible for an object to be included in many structures at the same time, for example, an organizational structure and a functional structure, and for structures to be removed from a system or for new structures to be added at any time during the lifetime of the system. The relation model is largely obtained from the OMG relation model but is implemented on top of the Active Directory. The concept has been implemented in a framework with associated tools for simple navigation and presentation of structures and objects.

The architecture has been adapted to exploit the functionality supplied with Microsoft Windows 2000 as exemplified by the use of the Active Directory and a close integration with the development environment (see the "Practical Experience" section in this chapter). Information Organizer makes reuse possible in two different ways. First, in the more traditional way, it functions as a framework for building component-based applications with the possible advantage of a shortened development time. Second, it serves as a framework for integration and presentation of existing applications by offering a model and a number of tools.

Information Organizer: Support for Building Integrated Systems

The architecture of Information Organizer is a three-layer architecture, consisting of a user interface layer, a business layer, and a data layer. Software components mainly from Microsoft are used throughout the implementation.

Information Organizer Basic Parts

Information Organizer consists of two basic parts: a BOM and a BOF.

A BOM can represent in a uniform way different entities of importance to the user. BOM defines five basic concepts: objects, aspects, roles, relations, and views. Objects represent quite large-grained entities and can be described as empty containers; business logic is added in the form of aspects. An object can perform a number of roles. One or more aspects implement a role. A relation connects roles in two different objects. The concept of views provides means to restrict access to a system and all its information.

BOM is implemented with the help of the Microsoft Active Directory and thus builds on the concept of directory-enabled applications. Features such as a powerful relation model and a concept to keep all parts of an object together have been added to this to create a powerful model for integration and reuse. BOM is based on the COM technology defined by Microsoft.

A BOF is provided as assistance to application programmers in building components and applications and integrating existing applications. BOF implements the BOM concept, thus providing an implementation of objects, aspects, relations, views, and roles. It also contains tools for creating instances of these, finding them in a distributed environment and communicating with them. BOF can be described as a toolbox with a number of tools and software components common to different applications for effective reuse.

The primary user interface for a user of the system is a standard browser, Microsoft Internet Explorer. The system is largely based on the concept of thin clients, even if fat clients are used with respect to certain functions and applications (see Figure 18.2). An advantage with thin clients is that no code need be installed and maintained on the client machine. The system handles integration of legacy applications built without the Internet being taken into consideration. These applications must then be installed in each client machine. The level of integration is discussed later in the section on modeling and integration. The system also provides support for access to information via wireless application protocol (WAP).

BOM

The BOM provides support for the presentation and arrangement of all the information in a system. The basic concepts of BOM introduced earlier are explained next:

- *Objects.* BOM objects represent complex real entities that are of interest in one or several applications. Examples of such are organizations, departments, issues, steps in a workflow, pumps, and valves. A BOM object is most often an object with little functionality implemented. A BOM object offers a uniform way to assemble related information that is most often defined in different applications. For

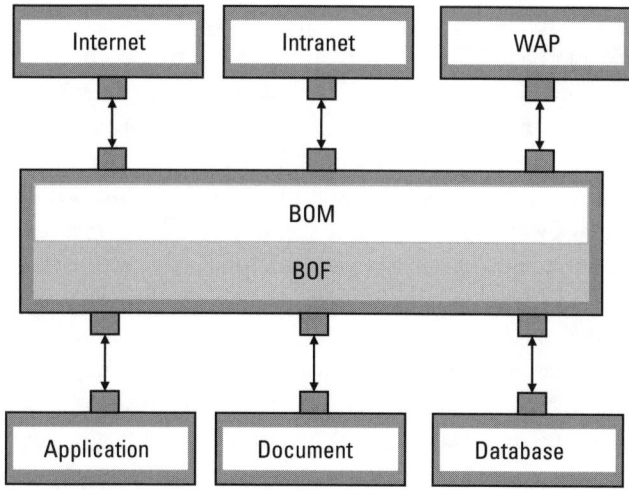

Figure 18.2 Uniform presentation of heterogeneous information systems.

an issue, examples of related information can include mail, documents, reports, notes, persons dealing with issues, and video sequences.

- *Aspects.* Instead of attempting to permit an object itself to represent all of its behavior, part of its behavior is delegated to different aspects. This means that new aspects can be added to the object at any time during its entire life without this necessarily affecting other aspects or the object itself. BOM objects and aspects offer the possibility of working with components of applications in a simple manner due to the fact that new business logic can be added to the object when the object is ready for a new role. Aspects are typed and added to objects as instances. Aspects can either contain all business logic themselves or be used to associate existing applications or parts of existing applications with an object and thereby facilitate their reuse. An aspect used to associate an existing application has no own business logic and can therefore only be an instance of a generic aspect type. Examples of aspects include process dialogues (to present and access, for example, a pump), Excel sheets, PowerPoint presentations, CAD drawings, and invoices.

- *Relations.* Objects seldom exist independently but are related to other objects to provide certain functionality. BOM offers a relation model with both generic relations and typed relations, that is, relations with a strong semantic significance. New relation types can be defined in the system during its service life. Many relations can be associated with an object. The relations are used to build both hierarchic structures and net structures. New relation instances can be associated with an object at any time. This means that new relations can be associated with an object even if the object cannot utilize them, because the object is not aware of the relation and not implemented in such a way that the relation can be used. These relations can, however, be useful because an external user understands them and can interpret their semantic significance. An "external user" can be another application or person browsing information with a graphic tool. Relations and aspects often occur in pairs because aspects provide the semantics that can interpret and utilize the relation. By extracting the relations and locating them outside the object, an architecture is obtained that is adaptable in a changing world as new types of relation and instances are added to the system, without affecting the existing functionality. However, this introduces a risk because relations that are expected to be present can be removed without the object being informed.

- *Roles.* A role defines a certain function that can be offered by an object. The function is provided as a number of interfaces. One or more aspects implement a role. The term *role* is similar to that of interface in a component model such as Microsoft COM. A relation type associates two roles. A generic relation can associate any type of object because all objects are of the generic type.

- *Views.* Views make possible the arrangement of objects, aspects, and relations to limit the extent to which they are accessible to different categories of users. This is necessary, partly because certain information is classified but also to reduce the volume of information presented to make it easier for the user to understand. Initially, a system most often contains a number of predefined views. A selected object will remain in focus when the view is changed. This characteristic can be used to navigate between different views. Views can be added in the same dynamic manner as objects, aspects, and relations.

We can illustrate the relationship between the basic concepts specified above by an example. Figure 18.3 shows an object representing an issue in an issue management system. An issue management system can have the following views: a personal view, which shows all the persons dealing with issues and the issues for which they are responsible; a process view, which shows an existing workflow and where in a workflow an issue is located; and an organizational view, which shows the organization and all its employees. In the personal view, issue A and a relation to a user of that issue are shown. In the personal view, the object has also an aspect *A-Note,* which indicates that personal notes can be added to an issue and that these are only visible in the personal view. One role can be the ability to participate in a workflow. To be able to fulfill that role, the issue has been allocated an aspect, *A-Workflow,* and a relation that indicates where in the workflow concerned the issue is located. When the issue is processed, this relation will move to the next step. The aspect *A-Document* is visible in both the organizational view and the process view. A user of the system who is interested in where in the workflow an issue is located can either proceed via the process view and browse forward to the issue in which he is interested or enter via another view (e.g., the personal view), find the object, select the object, and then change view. The issue will then be in focus but visible in the process view with the relevant relations and aspects. The organizational view shows how the organization is

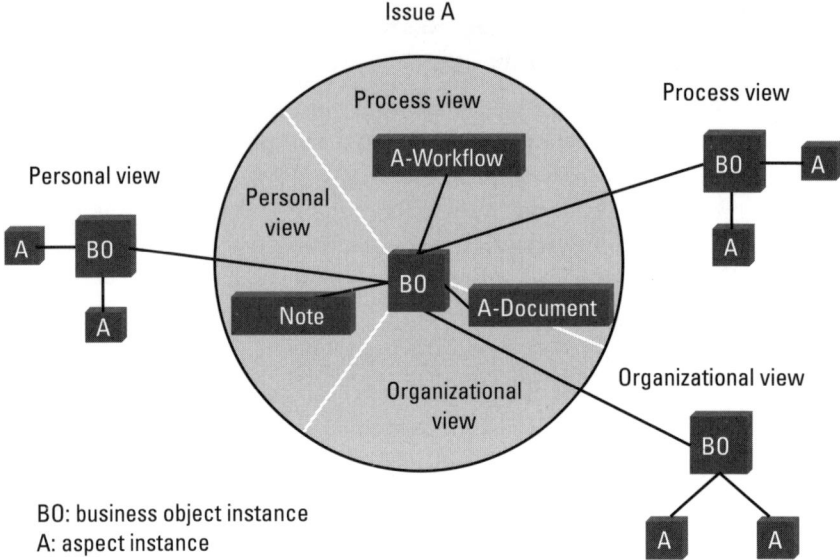

Figure 18.3 An issue object and its views, aspects, and relations.

structured and, for each organizational unit such as a department, the issues associated with the department concerned.

BOF

The BOF provides a set of tools for building business objects. Here are some of these tools and functions:

- An implementation of a generic aspect type, object type, and relation type.
- A configuration environment with tools and models for the simple creation of new instances of existing types and the easy configuration of new types. New views and roles can also be defined.
- A development environment that makes possible the programmatic addition of new components in the form of objects and aspects. The development environment of BOF is completely integrated with Microsoft Visual Studio, which permits the programming of objects and aspects, simply and in an optional language. The BOF also makes available an API for creating new relations and views.

- A run-time environment that makes it possible to execute components locally on a client machine or centrally on one or more server machines. The BOF also provides services for finding and calling components over both the Internet and intranets.

Modeling and Integration

Information Organizer provides a framework not only for building with components but also for integrating external systems and applications. Aspects are used to associate information and business logic originating from these different systems and applications with an object. Objects, views, and relations are used to model the activity in a way that can be said to be system and application independent. It is important to stress that this model is a high-level model that often spans several applications and systems and is independent of the manner in which the different external systems model their part of the entire activity.

The aspects represent information that is included in the integrated system. The aspects can integrate information on different levels. At least three levels of integration can be identified: application level, business logic level, and data level. On the application level, the application does not provide an API to its internal parts. When the application is referred to from an aspect, the application will be activated and the user will enter at the top level and is required to navigate to that part of the application at which the object concerned is located. Consider an external database application such as a document and issue management system. By using Information Organizer it is possible to create views and define structures that are not present in the integrated system. Figure 18.3 shows such an example: a personal view showing all issues per individual. If the system is integrated on the application level, the complete external application will be invoked when one issue is to be studied and the user must use application tools to navigate to the correct issue.

To be able to integrate on the level of business logic, the application must be componentized or provide an API permitting access to its different parts. That is, when called, the application could itself receive a number of input parameters that describe the part in which the user is actually interested and, with the help of this information, navigate to the part concerned. The input parameters very much depend on the application to be integrated and are often stored in the aspect instance. The aspect can be seen as a gateway between the framework and the integrated application. The complexity of the aspect implementation very much depends on the level of integration but also on which kind of application is to be integrated. If the application is COM based, it is very likely to be easier because the framework itself is COM based. A well-integrated application must provide all methods required by the BOF interface to manipulate the data that the application's own dialogues use (i.e., its own business logic).

Integration at the data level means that data is accessed directly without invoking the business logic (code), which the integrated system itself makes available for the presentation and processing of data. In many applications, this is an appropriate level of integration. It can be used to present information from many different systems but to change data, system dialogues already available should be used. The relational database connector is an example of a number of cooperating components providing support for the integration of applications on this level. By using the connector, information stored in a relational database can be easily integrated. If data is stored in some other data source, a specific connector for that particular data source must be implemented. In practice, this level has been found to be very useful because a rapid integration can be performed and BOF features such as security can be applied to each row in the database because they are represented as business objects.

Integration at the data level is most often a suitable level of ambition at which to begin. The level of ambition can be raised subsequently and integration can then be performed on the business logic level.

Structure of Aspects and Objects

In BOF, both aspects and objects are components with the same structure. A BOF object can in most cases be characterized as a relatively empty container and new functionality is added by the implementation of new aspects and their attachment to an instance of a generic object type. Much of the following discussion will therefore be focused on aspects, even if most of what can be said about aspects also applies to objects.

Both objects and aspects have a three-layered implementation architecture, a user interface part, a logic part, and a data part as shown in Figure 18.4. The user interface consists of a number of services. As a default, the BOF makes available a number of services that have more of a management character. Figure 18.4 shows examples of these services, the deletion of a component, the presentation of properties, and the definition of new services. New user-defined services such as a Web camera and a Word document describing the Web camera can be easily attached as in this figure. They are presented in the menu with the text Camera and Help. The services can be activated by selection from the menu.

To this point, we have discussed the left-hand side of Figure 18.4. A number of default services and new services, very loosely coupled to the aspect, can be attached to a generic aspect type. Neither the Web camera nor the Word document is aware that it is attached to an aspect. The existing implementation is sufficient in this situation. If more logic is to be associated with a component, or changes are to be made in the existing logic, an ActiveX component with a number of predefined interfaces should be implemented. For an aspect, the COM interface called IbofAspect must be implemented. This interface defines methods that enable the aspect to play an active role in the BOF. Examples of relevant methods include AfterCreate, Initialize, BeforeDelete, OnActivate, OnChange, OnDeactivate, and GetName. The framework will call these methods during the lifetime of an aspect.

A programmer can add new interfaces with user-defined business logic. These methods thus define user-defined business logic. MyService (presented in the menu of Figure 18.4) is an example of such method.

Each component has its data storage in Active Directory, which can be accessed via the interface IbofIADS. The BOF allocates data in the Active Directory for each component and saves important information such as name and the date of the component creation. The BOF provides binary data storage in the Active Directory that enables a programmer to store her own data easily in the Active Directory. Relevant data can also be saved in some other data storage as indicated in Figure 18.4. Word documents, for example, will naturally save their data in a file and not in the Active Directory.

Up to now, new services have been added to an instance by using dialogues provided by the service *Services*. If services are to be added to a type, the IbofServiceProvider interface must be implemented. A service can either be implemented as a thin, fat, or ultra-thin client. A fat client is often implemented in Visual Basic and communicates over an intranet. A thin client is implemented with technologies suitable for Intranet. An ultra-thin client is a WAP client.

Patterns Constructed Using the BOF

A pattern is a recurring solution to a recurring problem (see Chapter 1 and [7, 8]). An implementation of a pattern consists most often of a number of

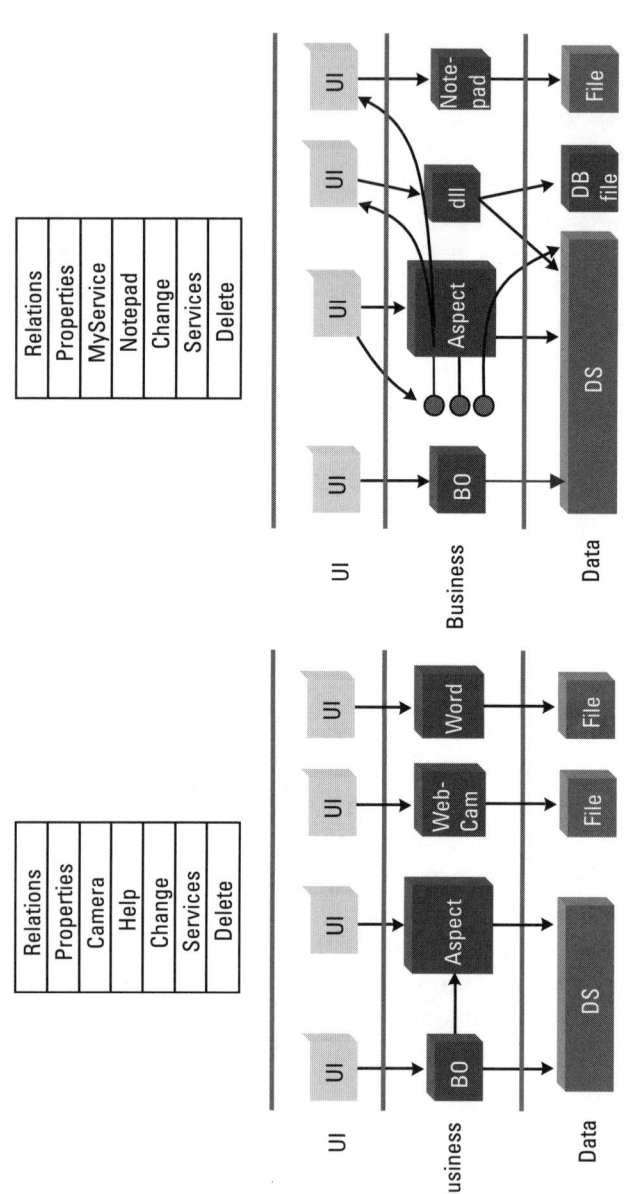

DS: Data storage
UI: User interface
BO: Business object
Dll: Dynamic linked library

Figure 18.4 Components have a three-layered implementation architecture.

interacting components in the form of objects and aspects that are connected by a number of relations. A number of patterns have been identified and implemented with the help of BOF and used in practice in developing a document and issue management system [3]:

- *Business process support* (BPS) is an example of a pattern that provides general support in building workflow applications. A feature of BPS, thanks to its component-based implementation, is its ability to provide workflow functionality that extends beyond application limits.

- *Document management support* (DMS) provides support for the handling of and generation of documents over the Internet. It provides the ability to create documents from different templates. When a document is generated from a template, information is obtained from objects with which the document is associated. For example, when the object is an issue, the issue text and the person dealing with the issue can be obtained and included in the document. If the object is a motorcar, the chassis number and registration number can be obtained if available in the system. With this function, information need only be inserted at one place in the system. The system supports the locking of a document by the user who is currently working with the document. DMS is integrated with an archive system so that documents can be easily filed. DMS is componentized so that its functionality can be coupled to any other object, for example, documents related to an issue or a pump.

- *Relational database connector* (RDC) provides a function by means of which, with the assistance of XML, external relational databases can be defined and imported. To import a database means that all the database objects are represented in Information Organizer but the data itself remains in the database. The RDC also provides support for building dialogues, which can present information from one or more data sources, and support for simple navigation between different lines in a database. All such navigation is performed with the help of URLs. In an imported database, all rows are represented as BOF objects, which in turn means that they acquire all of the properties that characterize a BOF object, such as strong security and the ability to maintain the cohesion of all aspects of an object.

BPS

The BPS pattern implements support for a general workflow functionality, partly as support for configuring a workflow and partly as run-time support that enables any object to follow a workflow. A possible way to model an issue was described earlier when BOM was discussed. In the following, using this example, the components required to create a workflow and to permit an issue to follow the workflow concerned are considered. The following component types are defined:

- *BpsProcessor aspect type.* Any object can become a step in a workflow by creating an instance of this aspect type and attaching it to the object. A number of dialogues have been defined to create user-defined actions. These actions, together with the existing system-defined actions, define what is to be performed in each step.

- *BpsProcessFlow relation type.* A workflow is built by connecting two objects with a relation of the type BpsProcessFlow.

- *BpsTarget aspect type.* If an instance of this aspect type is attached to an object, the object can participate in a workflow. This means that all types of objects can participate in a workflow even if they were not initially designed to do so. In addition to attaching the aspect to the object, the object must be associated with a step in a workflow and a new relation type is required for this.

- *BpsSession relation type.* This relation type associates an object in a workflow and defines where in the workflow the object is located.

- *BpsProcess object type.* This defines the start node for a workflow. Two aspects are attached to this object, one of BpsFactory type and one of BpsRecycler type. A relation of the BpsProcessEntry type points out the first step and a relation of the BpsProcessExit type points out the last step.

Figure 18.5 shows a simple workflow consisting of three steps. The workflow is reached primarily via the process view. Two users are involved with the system, each being responsible for one issue. Issue A is in step 2 and Issue B is in step 3 of the workflow. When the processing of an object in one step is completed, the object is moved to the next step. The activities in each step and the transport from one step to the next can be initiated by a graphic user dialogue or programmatically, by another object/aspect or application in the system. If BPS is combined with RDS, it is easy to integrate external

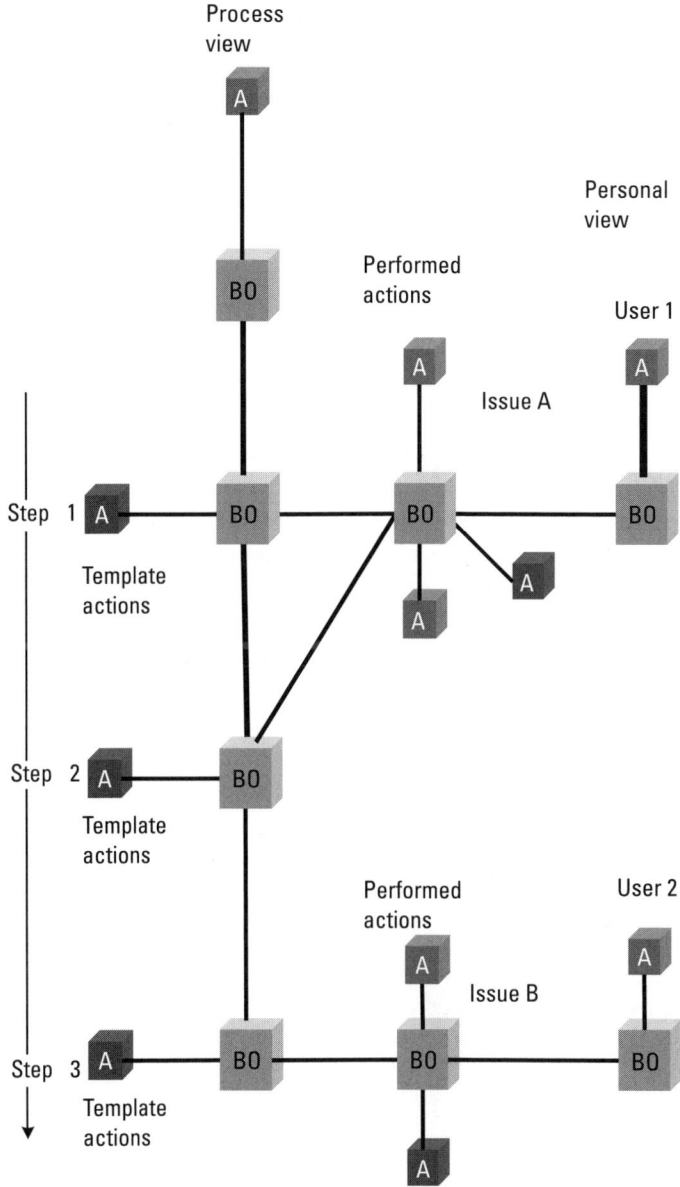

BO: instances of different business object types
A: instances of different aspect types

Figure 18.5 Using BOF components to build a workflow application.

database systems and represent them as BOF objects. Thus workflow functionality can be obtained for systems without this functionality and the interaction in the same workflow of objects originating in different systems can be obtained. This demonstrates the strength of the component-based approach.

Practical Experience

The following describes some of the lessons learned from practical experience gained from the development of Information Organizer and the document and issue management system Arch Issue [3]. The overall and certainly the most important lesson learned is that CBD can be highly profitable. For organizations with limited resources undertaking relatively ambitious development projects, it is the only viable—and therefore practically mandatory—approach. With a very limited investment, Compfab was able to build a functionally comprehensive framework for its intended purpose that, in addition, is secure, scalable, and reliable. This would not have been possible without total commitment to the reuse of not only platform components, but also architectural and design patterns, as well as "best practices" known for the platform [9–17]. Examples of platform components are the Microsoft Active Directory, Internet Information Server, and Internet Explorer. The decision to use the Active Directory was successful because the Active Directory is scalable up to millions of objects, is fully integrated with Microsoft authority and security, has redundancy, has a query language, is well tested, and is the heart of every Microsoft installation.

Microsoft Active Document Technology is one example of the many important design patterns available for use. It not only provides a run-time and design-time environment but also a large number of components and knowledge of how to build user interface components. The word "build" is used to emphasize that a significant part of the development time was spent in learning the full capabilities and impacts of existing technologies and components on functionality and features targeted in the resulting framework. Development of custom functions for the framework actually occupied a smaller part of the total project time. Our impression is that this is one of the main reasons why verbal commitments to CBD often fall short in practice.

Experience from the application of the framework to real-world problems only reinforced most of the conclusions arrived at from experience from the development of the framework itself. In general, integrating modern, well-componentized applications is easy and straightforward, providing the application is designed to run on the same platform at which the framework is targeted (or provides "proxies" for accessing it when running on other platforms).

Integrating monolithic applications with poor or no defined application programming interfaces is difficult and cumbersome—sometimes to such a degree that the original motivation for integrating the application becomes highly questionable. For example, if an order management application encapsulates orders, customers, responsible personnel, and so on, into well-defined components, and another invoice management application that is monolithic and provides access to its logical parts only through the proprietary user interface, there is no way to automate management of relations between logically related objects in these two applications, even at the user interface level.

Unfortunately, many database-centered applications that exist today are precisely of that kind. Fortunately, many of these applications have very little business logic and provide some kind of standard mechanism for accessing data directly (usually SQL). From the integration perspective, a viable solution is to provide a generic front-end "connector" that understands the target application's data (relational database concepts in this case) and provides components capable of encapsulating data from external databases for management, navigation, access, and manipulation purposes.

Because such a connector has no business logic whatsoever, it is unable to replace the original application entirely, but it can usually provide 60% to 80% of the original application functionality without any extension, in our experience. It also does not make the target application any more component-based internally, but it makes it component-based externally (providing the application is of singleton character). Because it is generic, it is also highly reusable because it can solve integration problems for many target applications with similar problems. Two additional benefits are that connector components, which are fully integrated into the framework, offer a range of functions much more extensive than that of the original application, and that they represent a solid base for beginning the migration of the original application to a truly component-based architecture, should the organization depending on the application decide to do so.

Summary

Reuse by integration of applications and information and reuse by CBD are two equally important ways to improve software development. Information Organizer emphasizes this and provides an object model, a framework, and a number of components to encourage the building of integrated solutions. By taking the concept of directory-enabled applications defined by Microsoft further by adding a number of important properties defined in standards such as IEC1346 (defining the concept of aspects, which relates all relevant information to an object), OMG (defining a powerful relation model), and IT4 (defining a way to build integrated industrial applications), a strong and powerful environment based on a standard concept to build integrated systems has been achieved.

The total commitment to reuse not only platform components (mainly from Windows 2000), but also architectural and design patterns and known "best practices" for the platform has been vital to the success of building not only the product itself (Information Organizer) but also components and applications based on Information Organizer.

References

[1] King, R. R., *Mastering Active Directory*, Network Press, San Francisco, CA, Sybex, 1999.

[2] IEC, Industrial Systems, Installations and Equipment and Industrial Products—Structuring Principles and Reference Designations, Part1: Basic Rules," International Standard IEC 1346-1, International Electrotechnical Commission, 1996.

[3] Compfab, Västerås, Sweden, http://www.compfab.se.

[4] OMG, "The Common Object Request Broker: Architecture And Specification," Report v2.4, OMG Standards Collection, OMG, 2000, http://omg.org.

[5] OMG, "CORBA Services: Common Object Services Specification," Object Management Group, 1997, http://omg.org.

[6] ABB, *Knowledge-Based Real-Time Control Systems IT4 Project: Phase II*, Studentlitteratur, Västerås, Sweden, 1991.

[7] Gamma, E., et al., *Design Patterns, Elements of Reusable Object-Oriented Software*, Reading, MA: Addison-Wesley, 1995.

[8] Bushmann, F., et al., *Pattern-Oriented Software Architecture—A System of Patterns*, New York: John Wiley & Sons, 1996.

[9] Microsoft, "DCOM Technical Overview," http://msdn.microsoft.com.

[10] Microsoft, "DCOM: A Business Overview," http://msdn.microsoft.com.

[11] Microsoft, "Microsoft Component Services: A Technology Overview," http://msdn.microsoft.com.

[12] Microsoft, "Integrating Web and Client/Server Computing with Microsoft Windows DNA," http://msdn.microsoft.com.

[13] Microsoft, "Reengineering Application Development," http://msdn.microsoft.com.

[14] Stearns, D., "Migrating Existing Information Systems to Component Architectures," *MSDN Magazine*, Vol. 4, 1996.

[15] Booch, G., *The Visual Modeling of Software Architecture for the Enterprise*, Rational Software Corporation, 1998, http://www.rational.com.

[16] Rauch, S., "Windows DNA: Building Windows Applications for the Internet Age," http://msdn.microsoft.com.

[17] Ambler, S., "A Realistic Look at Object-Oriented Reuse," *Software Development Magazine*, Vol. 1, 1998.

19

Industrial Experience with Dassault Système Component Model

Jacky Estublier, Jean-Marie Favre, and Rémy Sanlaville

Introduction

Dassault Systèmes (DS) is one of the major European software developers. Its main software product, CATIA, alone has more than 5 million lines of code and is the world leader for CAD/CAM with more than 19,000 clients and 180,000 workplaces. CATIA version 5 is a very interesting case study because, on the one hand, 1,000 DS engineers are developing software, with a commercial release every 4 months, and on the other hand, many CATIA customers around the world are also developing large amounts of code for extending and adapting CATIA to their specific needs.

CATIA has been purchased by companies with important know-how in their respective domains, Boeing, for example, which knows how to build aircraft. DS customers must be capable of adapting CATIA and integrating their own functions into existing DS applications. These extensions may constitute a significant part of the software; Boeing alone is said to have developed more lines for CATIA adaptation and extension of CATIA than DS has itself.

Some customers act as partners and use their know-how to use, build, and sell applications based on CATIA. Whatever role a company plays with respect to DS, partner or client, each company considers its own CATIA extensions a fundamental part of its assets. The source code of CATIA applications and of customer extensions must not be made accessible to others. Furthermore, due to the large amount of code involved, customer extensions should not affect the stability of CATIA. Conversely, changes in CATIA should have minimal impacts on customer code.

In the mid-1990's, and even now, no technology was capable of supporting a software product development with this adaptability requirement. After studying early versions of COM and CORBA, DS decided to define and implement its own component model, called the *Object Modeler* (OM).

The rationale behind the introduction of component technology at DS is interesting. The DS objective was not primarily to sell isolated OM components, nor to sell the OM component framework, nor to make their component model a standard. The primary objective was to find a way to develop its software under the best conditions, and to provide its customers with powerful adaptability facilities. DS now sells a family of highly customizable applications. The customers are not informed of the topology of the architecture of these applications; the applications are extended by extending existing components or adding new components.

The OM Component Model

The OM component model evolved significantly over a number of years, often under pressure from the developer, both for functional and technical reasons. We present here a simplified description of DS' component model, which for years has supported all DS software development, including CATIA Version 5.

From an external point of view, the OM is quite similar to COM [1]. However it also provides a rich set of original features, both at the conceptual and implementation levels. This chapter focuses on the component model rather than on the component infrastructure (see Chapter 4). We emphasize the concepts rather than their technical realization and execution. This does not mean that technical aspects and associated tools are not important. On the contrary, they are of fundamental importance and the success of DS is also due to the constant attention given to performance and technical issues.

The component model is presented below, using a structure similar to the one used in Chapter 4: Components are presented first from an external point of view. Then we describe how components are linked to build an application system. Finally, the concepts provided to implement a component from elementary pieces of code are presented.

Defining an OM Component

From an external point of view OM components provide functionality through a set of *interfaces* as shown in Figure 19.1(a). An interface is a set of method signatures. A component may support more than one interface, just as in most other component models. The interfaces play the role of ports as described in Chapter 4.

Using OM Components to Build Applications

In practice, there is no boundary between traditional development and CBD. DS applications are hybrids and contain OM components and traditional software entities. In particular, an OM component can be called by another component, by a C++ class, by a Java class, by a Visual Basic script, and so forth.

As illustrated in Figure 19.1(b), OM components can only be manipulated through the interfaces they provide. The client does not have knowledge of the component implementation. This independence is very important because it makes possible the changing of the implementation of a component used in an application without otherwise impacting the application.

As in COM, the connections between OM components, or between traditional entities and OM components, are deeply buried in the code. Typically, when a component, or another software entity, wants to use a component, it calls the *QueryInterface* method, which returns a pointer to the requested interface; this is very similar to COM. In other words, while a component explicitly defines the interface it provides, it does not make explicit the interfaces it requires. For example, there is no concept similar to

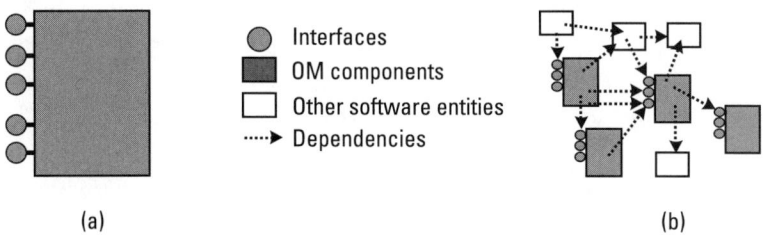

(a)   (b)

Figure 19.1 (a) External view of OM components and (b) heterogeneous application.

CCM receptacle [2]. There is no concept of connections or connectors declared outside the code.

As a result, there is no clear picture of the architecture of an application built from OM components. DS follows a *component-programming approach:* in which applications are built by programmers using existing components. Connecting components is seen as a programming task. This contrasts with the *component-assembly approach* exemplified by JavaBeans [3] or CCM [2] in which new applications can be built by connecting existing components either by means of a high-level declarative language or interactively.

The lack of support for explicit connections and assembly facilities is mainly due to the fact that DS does not aim to sell components, but extensible applications. The problem is not to provide clients with the means to assemble their own applications, but to extend an application provided with its own components.

Implementing OM Components

Most features of the OM component model are therefore dedicated to easing the implementation and extension of components. As shown below, the OM model provides more facilities at this level than other component models described in Chapter 4. The following is a simplified description of the DS component model.

Implementations

Although many component models assume that a single team within a single organization develops a component, DS components are typically developed by different teams in different companies. A component cannot therefore be implemented as a single piece of code. Components are in fact a collection of elementary pieces of code, called *implementations,* each one implementing a set of interfaces as illustrated in Figure 19.2.

Extensions

There are two kinds of implementations: *base implementations* and *extensions.* A component is defined by a base implementation to which different extensions can be attached by an extension relation (not shown in the figure). The extension mechanism enables the behavior of an existing application provided by DS to be extended by the addition of *extensions* to some of its components. This mechanism has two advantageous properties: (1) It does not change the identity of the component being extended, which contrasts with OO inheritance; and (2) it does not change the code of the component being extended,

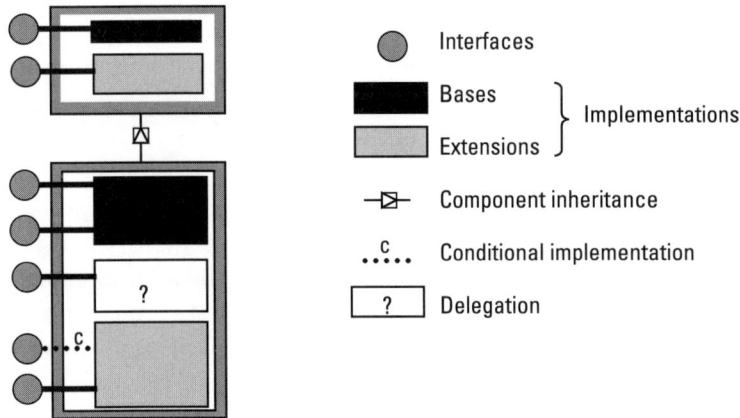

Figure 19.2 Component implementation.

which contrasts with COM. In COM, aggregation also seeks to extend a component by adding an interface implemented by another component. Unfortunately, in COM, changes in the source code of both components are required (for the correct interpretation of the QueryInterface method).

The extension mechanism permits the addition of new interfaces to a component, without overriding the definition of existing interfaces. Inheritance in OO languages makes possible the definition of a new class with a new name by adding functionality to a superclass. Both classes can then coexist in future applications. If the goal is to substitute the original class with the subclass in an existing application, all references to the original class should be changed in the source code and the application must be recompiled.

In CATIA version 5, real-world objects are represented as components. For instance, a Beam can be represented by an OM component. A team at DS may develop the Beam basic behavior, and other DS teams develop advanced functionalities to be sold independently. A team in a company may develop extensions related to Beam aerodynamics, while a team in another company may work on Beam vibration behavior. Finally the major advantage of the OM component model is that it enables the assembly of some of, or all of, these facets without making any change in CATIA applications.

Component Inheritance

The OM component model provides the notion of single *inheritance*, with respect to both components and interfaces. Extensive experience with the development of a large number of similar components reveals the importance of this concept. When one component inherits from another, it inherits all its interfaces and all its implementations.

Conditional Interfaces

The implementation relationship linking a component with an interface can be combined with a condition. When a client requests an interface, the interface will be returned to the client only if this expression evaluates to true. For instance, depending on the point of view, a Beam can be seen in 2D as a rectangle or in 3D. 2D interfaces are available depending on the point of view.

Delegation

A component can have some of its functionality performed by another implementation simply by *delegating* the implementation of some interfaces to the other implementation. The declaration of the component indicates the implemented interfaces, but without providing the corresponding implementation. The association between that interface and an implementation is performed by the application itself at run time (this can be done by clients of this component), for each component instance individually.

Discussion

The features presented above constitute the concepts of the OM component model. DS did not develop a new language to express these concepts. Instead, to realize an OM component, these concepts are implemented in terms of programming entities. The OM can be seen as a layer superimposed on the C++ language. Interfaces and implementations are represented as C++ classes and most OM constructions are indeed represented as code patterns and macros in C++ source code.

For maximum efficiency, the developer can select from various realizations of the same concept; for example, the concept of extension can be refined in *code extension, data extension, cache extension,* and so forth. Consider the following file in which an extension is realized. This file contains, before the C++ class itself, the following macros:

```
#include "TIE_CATIData.h"
CATImplementClass (MyDataExtension, DataExtension,
CATBaseUnknown, MyComponent);
TIE_CATIData (MyDataExtension);
```

The CATImplementClass macro expresses that C++ class MyDataExtension is a data extension that inherits from CATBaseUnknown and that extends component MyComponent. The TIE_CATIData macro expresses that MyDataExtension implements interface CATIData using a TIE pattern.

Different Kinds of Architecture

Following ANSI/IEEE Std 1471-2000 [4] and Hofmeister et al. [5] and Kruchten [6], different architectures can be considered in CATIA Version 5. The architecture in terms of OM components represents only one view, designated the *logical architecture* because OM components are logical units.

Small development projects typically consider only the logical architecture. In particular, a unit of composition (a logical unit) can also be considered a unit of development, a unit of business, a unit of deployment, and so on [7]. In practice, this is an oversimplification. When software expands, many other architectures are of concern. Without going into details, it is worth mentioning that DS has developed and uses not only a logical component model (the OM component model described above), but also a number of other models to organize the huge quantity of software entities.

We should mention the *physical architecture* that represents how source code is organized in terms of files and directories, and eventually how code objects are stored in DLLs. Figure 19.3 shows that the logical and physical architectures are orthogonal. The *packaging architecture* describes how applications are packaged and sold, based on the concepts of products, configuration, and media. A *product* is a consistent set of frameworks, a *configuration* is a collection of products that collectively fulfill a set of needs, and *media*, such as a CD-ROM, are a physical means of storing a set of products and configurations.

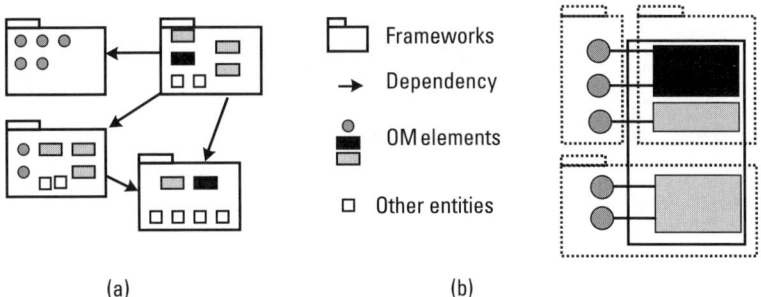

Frameworks

→ Dependency

OM elements

□ Other entities

(a)   (b)

Figure 19.3 Logical and physical architectures: (a) physical architecture and (b) OM components versus frameworks.

Lessons Learned

The DS OM case study is interesting because it shows the whole story, from needs to design, implementation, use, and enhancements. It shows the issues and potential pitfalls when designing and using a component model on a very large scale. Despite several problems, the DS experience is a success. Today, at DS, CATIA version 5, consists of more than 50,000 C++ classes and 8,000 components.

The major lesson we have learned is that there is a large gap between a component model on paper and its actual use for large-scale industrial development. This is especially worrying, because the component model is a critical element for the success (or failure) of your system development. The following is a summary of the main lessons that can be drawn from the DS experience. Most of these lessons may also apply in other industrial contexts.

Framework Evolution

What does the term *good component framework* mean? Our answer is that it is a framework that satisfies development and maintenance needs. It must provide powerful concepts and mechanisms for building efficient and reliable applications. More important, it must be easily mastered and understood by developers in their day-to-day practice.

Definition Versus Use

It is incorrect to believe that if a concept is simple, its use will also be simple, as illustrated by "goto" and pointers. In component technology we can mention the AddRef and Release features of COM [1], used to count the references to a component instance in order to control deallocation. Experience shows that it is extremely difficult, in a large development, to ensure that all AddRef and Release statements have been properly executed, which may result in unwelcome errors. Without considerable experience with a feature, its darker side effects can be very difficult to forecast. The cost of using a dangerous feature in a large development and the migration cost of eliminating that feature are extremely high and can be fatal to a project. Thus in-house design and development of a component model is very risky!

Evolution

DS's component model followed an incremental process. The concept of extension was its starting point and concepts such as delegation, conditional adhesion, or inheritance were added as solutions to practical problems.

Similarly, different implementations of the same concepts were developed as an answer to performance or stability issues. The fact that the model evolved permanently while CATIA software was in development required the coexistence of different concepts and constructs, which created problems.

The interaction between concepts creates a number of combinations that are inherently complex and may have unclear semantics. In the case of DS, experience showed that some recurring bugs are the side effects of specific (mis)use of concepts. A bug may be due to faulty implementation of the concept, to an undefined semantic hole in semantics when the concept is used in that way, or to inherent complexity. In the last two cases, it is the component model that is faulty. At DS, once identified, a list of "anti-patterns" was established, documented and a *troubleshooter* tool realized to automatically detect anti-patterns in the code.

Training

Practice shows that it is not a simple task to conduct the development process using a component model; it takes time to become a competent component programmer. Both the component model and its best practice must be taught. Initially, for productivity reasons, and because DS engineers are very skilled, it was not considered necessary to teach the component model, so blind cut and paste of existing pieces of code became common. DS therefore decided to create specific training courses explaining how to use the component model correctly.

Architecture and Components from an Industrial Perspective

Researchers working with software architecture and CBSE are very active [4, 8, 9]. An important contribution of the software architecture community was to consider connectors as first-class citizens and to promote the formal description of behavior. In CBSE and ADL domains, many definitions of what a component is and what it is not have been published. We feel uncomfortable with these definitions because none covers the different facets of component technology, at least as experienced in the DS context.

Connectors

Until now, the notion of connector has not found its way into industry. Considering procedure calls or other elementary relationships as connectors is obviously possible, but this has no large practical benefit. The match between more complex connectors and the code is not necessarily direct and software engineers do not consider this notion as essential. DS engineers do not feel they need this concept.

Behavior

CATIA is a huge software project, evolving rapidly with a high level of concurrent development. Even if all the world's software engineers developing OM components had the skill to describe formally the behavior of each component, behavioral analysis would probably be intractable at this scale. Therefore, DS has never attempted to specify formally the behavior of components nor a fortiori of the whole system; conversely, DS is very interested in impact analysis.

Architecture

What exactly is the architecture of a system? This question has provoked many definitive answers from many authors. In the case of DS, as well as in claims from other authors [4–6], many architectures appear, each one dedicated to a task or to a life-cycle need. In this short chapter, we have discussed logical architecture (with components and extensions), physical architecture (with frameworks and modules), and packaging architecture (with solutions and media), but not cooperative architecture (with workspaces). These architectures obviously coexist and fulfill a different purpose.

Components

Because different kinds of architecture should be considered, and because components are often defined as an architectural unit, what are components? In the views of different authors, components are seen as units of design, reuse, development, deployment, packaging, and so forth. Many authors even consider the component to be all of these simultaneously. Unfortunately, this is not compatible with the DS reality, at least. Are there as many component concepts as architectures?

Summary

This chapter has shown the issues raised when DS designed their proprietary component model. The first part describes the component model, which offers services not found in other industrial component models. The second part describes the lessons learned during the years when the model was elaborated on and used. Essentially, the design of a powerful component model is shown to be a complex task that involves many facets of technology, for which the use is not so obvious. The model has been improved progressively over the years both conceptually and technically through enhancements and adjustments.

Among the practical difficulties experienced, we can mention that very large systems must live with inconsistencies produced by unexpected uses and misuses of the technology proposed. On the one hand, training is needed, and on the other hand, tools for tracking invalid constructions are required.

The last major lesson is that very large software must be managed by different people, at different points in time, and with different perspectives. A different architecture, with different goals, concepts, and tools in each of these perspectives can be seen. It is an oversimplification to see the component concept as unique and capable of supporting all of the different facets.

As Robert Balzer claims, "Elevating system development from module to the architecture level requires a corresponding elevation in our tools.... While we have a long history and mature technology for the former, we have just begun to recreate these capabilities at the software architecture level" [10]. We have still to invent the CBSE environments of the future.

References

[1] Box, D., *Essential COM*, Reading, MA: Addison-Wesley, 1998.

[2] OMG, "CORBA Components," Report orbos/99-02-01, OMG, 1998, http://omg.org.

[3] Sun Microsystems, "JavaBeans 1.01 Specification," http://java.sun.com/beans.

[4] IEEE Architecture Working Group, "IEEE Recommended Practice for Architectural Description of Software-Intensive Systems," IEEE Std. 1471-2000, Piscataway, NJ: IEEE, 2000.

[5] Hofmeister, C., R. Nord, and D. Soni, *Applied Software Architecture*, Reading, MA: Addison-Wesley, 2000.

[6] Kruchten, P., "The 4+1 View Model of Architecture," *IEEE Software*, Vol. 12, No. 6, 1995, pp. 42–50.

[7] Szyperski, C., and Pfister, C., "Why Objects Are Not Enough," *Proc. Int. Component Users Conf.*, Munich, Germany, SIG Publisher, 1996.

[8] Shaw, M., and D. Garlan, *Software Architecture: Perspectives on an Emerging Discipline*, Upper Saddle River, NJ: Prentice-Hall, 1996.

[9] Garlan, D., and D. E. Perry, "Introduction to the Special Issue on Software Architecture," *IEEE Transaction on Software Engineering*, Vol. 21, No. 4, 1995, pp. 269–274.

[10] Balzer, R., "Instrumenting, Monitoring, & Debugging Software Architectures," Report from Information Sciences Institute, http://www.isi.edu/software-sciences/papers/ instrumenting-software-architectures.doc.

Contributors

About the Editors

Ivica Crnkovic, Mälardalen University, Department of Computer Engineering, Västerås, Sweden

Ivica Crnkovic is a professor of software engineering at Mälardalen University. He is the administrative leader of the computer science laboratory and the scientific leader of the industrial IT research group of the same department. His research interests include component-based software engineering, software configuration management, software development environments and tools, and software engineering in general. Professor Crnkovic is the author of more than 30 refereed articles and papers on software engineering topics. He has co-organized several workshops and conferences related to software engineering (particularly component-based software engineering). He participated in several projects organized by the Association of Swedish Engineering Industries.

From 1985 to 1998, Professor Crnkovic worked at ABB, Sweden, where he was responsible for software development environments and tools. He was a project leader and manager of a group developing software configuration management and other software development environment tools and methods for distributed development and maintenance of real-time systems. From 1980 to 1984, he worked for the Rade Koncar company in Zagreb, Croatia.

Professor Crnkovic received an M.Sc. in electrical engineering in 1979, an M.Sc. in theoretical physics in 1984, and a Ph.D. in computer science in 1991, all from the University of Zagreb.

He can be reached at ivica.crnkovic@mdh.se or http://www.idt.mdh .se/~icc.

Magnus Larsson, Mälardalen University, Department of Computer Engineering, Västerås, Sweden; ABB Automation Technology Products AB, Sweden

Magnus Larsson has been employed by ABB Automation Technology Products AB since 1993, working on several software development projects, both as a developer and as a project manager. He received his B.Sc. in computer engineering from Mälardalen University in 1993 and an M.Sc. in computer science from Uppsala University, Sweden, in 1995. Mr. Larsson's current research interests are component-based software engineering and software configuration management. His licentiate thesis, "Applying Configuration Management Techniques to Component-Based Systems," which he presented in 2000, includes selected topics from these fields.

During his years at ABB, Mr. Larsson has participated in the development of object management facility (OMF), a distributed object-oriented middleware, which was awarded second prize in the 1997 OMG/Object Worlds competition for the best use of object technology. Mr. Larsson has also developed bridges between ABB's proprietary object request broker OMF and COM/CORBA. In 1998 Mr. Larsson worked with Digital Equipment on a project that investigated the use of DCOM in real-time applications. Since 1999, he has been a committee member of the configuration management group working for the Association of Swedish Engineering Industries.

Mr. Larsson can be reached at Magnus.Larsson@mdh.se or http://www .idt.mdh.se/~mlo.

About the Authors

Martin Blom, Karlstad University, Department of Computer Science, Sweden

Martin Blom is the director of the software engineering undergraduate program at Karlstad University, where he received an M.Sc. in 1999. His research interests include software development in general, and semantic aspects of software development in particular.

Mr. Blom can be reached at martin.blom@kau.se or http://www.cs
.kau.se/~martin.

Jan Bosch, University of Groningen, Department of Mathematics and Computing Science, The Netherlands

Professor Jan Bosch is a professor of software engineering at the University of Groningen, where he heads the software engineering research group. Professor Bosch holds an M.Sc. from the University of Twente, the Netherlands, and a Ph.D. from Lund University, Sweden. His research activities include software architecture design, software product lines, object-oriented frameworks and component-oriented programming. He is the author of *Design and Use of Software Architectures: Adopting and Evolving a Product Line Approach* (published by Pearson Education) and the coeditor of three volumes in the Springer LNCS series, and has authored or coauthored more than 50 refereed journal and conference publications. Professor Bosch has organized numerous workshops, served on program committees of many conferences, and is a member of the steering groups and the program committee cochairman of several conferences.

He can be reached at Jan.Bosch@cs.rug.nl or http://www.cs.rug
.nl/~bosch.

Benneth Christiansson, Karlstad University, Department of Information Technology, Sweden

Benneth Christiansson is a Ph.D. student at Karlstad University, from which he also obtained a licentiate in philosophy (Ph.Lic.). His main subject is component-based systems development, with a particular emphasis on working methods.

Mr. Christiansson can be reached at benneth.christiansson@kau.se.

Jacky Estublier, Domaine Universitaire Grenoble, Department LSR, France

Dr. Jacky Estublier is a senior researcher (DR CNRS) at Grenoble University, where he leads the research group Tools and Environments for Industrial Software Engineering: Adèle. His research originated in the field of software configuration management. He developed the Adèle Software Configuration Management when he explored virtually all areas of software configuration management and developed a process support system. His subsequent research areas evolved toward federations of commercial tools and component-based frameworks. Currently, his team develops an open, large spectrum, component framework that extends CCM in different directions (product-line support, hierarchical model, open containers, dynamic connection, and large-scale deployment). He has authored more than 100 research papers and has been a program committee member of many conferences, often acting as chairman.

Dr. Estublier can be reached at jacky@imag.fr or http://www-adele .imag.fr.

Jean-Marie Favre, University of Grenoble 1, Laboratoire LSR-IMAG, France

Jean-Marie Favre is an assistant professor at the University of Grenoble 1, where he received a Ph.D. in 1994. His current research interests include reverse-engineering, component-based software, and component-based reverse-engineering.

Dr. Favre can be reached at jmfavre@imag.fr or http://www-adele .imag.fr/~jmfavre.

Gerhard Fohler, Mälardalen University, Department of Computer Engineering, Sweden

Gerhard Fohler is a professor at Mälardalen University and the director of the SALSART predictably flexible real-time systems laboratory in the Department of Computer Engineering. He received a Ph.D. from the Vienna University of Technology in 1994, for research into flexibility of off-line scheduling.

Professor Fohler can be reached at gerhard.fohler@mdh.se or http:// www.idt.mdh.se/personal/gfr.

Oscar Javier Gonzalez Gomez, Bell Laboratories, Services Management Department, Holmdel, New Jersey

Oscar Javier Gonzalez Gomez is a member of the technical staff at Bell Laboratories. He received a Ph.D. from the University of Massachusetts at Amherst in 2001. He is actively involved in the definition of software processes that reduce the development effort required to make Lucent Technologies' network element applications highly available, scalable, and easily maintainable.

Dr. Gonzalez Gomez can be reached at ogonzale@research.bell-labs.com.

Jilles van Gurp, University of Groningen, Department of Mathematics and Computing Science, The Netherlands

Jilles van Gurp is a Ph.D. student at the University of Groningen. He obtained his M.Sc. at the University of Utrecht, the Netherlands. Mr. van Gurp has published papers about framework design, software product lines, and software development issues, including variability and design erosion.

He can be reached at jilles@cs.rug.nl or http://www.xs4all.nl/~jgurp.

Erik Gyllensward, Mälardalen University, Department of Computer Engineering, Västerås, Sweden; Compfab AB, Sweden

Erik Gyllenswärd is the president of Compfab AB, and a researcher at Mälardalen University. He received his M.Sc. from Linköping Technical University, Sweden, in 1983 and his Ph.Lic. from the Royal Institute of Technology (KTH), Stockholm, Sweden, in 1994. Mr. Gyllenswärd worked for ABB from 1983 to 2000 as a system architect and manager. He also lectured and has been engaged in research at Mälardalen University and at KTH. He is the owner of Compfab AB, the company he founded in 2000. His fields of competence include distributed object-orientated architectures, middleware technologies, application integration, information management systems, and componentware.

Mr. Gyllenswärd can be reached at erik.gyllensward@compfab.se or http://www.compfab.se.

Brahim Hnich, Uppsala University, Information Science Department, Sweden

Brahim Hnich is a Ph.D. student at Uppsala University and a lecturer at the University of Gaevle high school, Sweden. He earned his B.Sc. in 1997 from Bilkent University, Ankara, Turkey. His research interests include combinatorial optimization problems, artificial intelligence, constraint programming, and automated software engineering.

Mr. Hnich can be reached at Brahim.Hnich@dis.uu.se or http://www.dis.uu.se/~brahim.

Shui-Ming Ho, University of Manchester, Department of Computer Science, England

Shui-Ming Ho is a Ph.D. student at the University of Manchester, where he also received an M.Sc. His research interests are formal methods for frameworks in component-based software development. Shui-Ming Ho would like to acknowledge that his work has been supported by the Engineering and Physical Sciences Research Council, United Kingdom.

Mr. Ho can be reached at sho@cs.man.ac.uk.

Damir Isovic, Mälardalen University, Department of Computer Engineering, Sweden

Damir Isovic is a lecturer and a Ph.D. student at Mälardalen University, where he also received an M.Sc. and a Ph.Lic. His research interests include real-time systems and scheduling theory, with a specific emphasis on combining flexibility and reliability in the design of schedule and real-time components.

Mr. Isovic can be reached at damir.isovic@mdh.se or http://www.idt.mdh.se/salsart/.

Lars Jakobsson, Karlstad University, Department of Information Technology, Sweden

Mr. Jakobsson is the director of the information systems undergraduate program and a Ph.D. student at Karlstad University. His research is focused on describing software components for compatibility verification.

He can be reached at Lars.Jakobsson@kau.se or http://www.cs.kau.se/~lars/.

Torsten Jonsson, Uppsala University, Information Science Department, Sweden

Torsten Jonsson is a Ph.D. student at Uppsala University. He received a B.A. in systems analysis from Uppsala University in 1984. His research topic concerns programming methods based on formal compositional and visual techniques.

Mr. Jonsson can be reached at tjo@hig.se.

Kung-Kiu Lau, University of Manchester, Department of Computer Science, Manchester, England

Kung-Kiu Lau holds a B.Sc. and a Ph.D. from the University of Leeds, United Kingdom. He is currently a senior lecturer in the Department of Computer Science at the University of Manchester, England. His main research interests are component-based software development and formal program development in computational logic. He is the editor of a book series on component-based software development, published by World Scientific.

Dr. Lau can be reached at kung-kiu@cs.man.ac.uk or http://www.cs.man.ac.uk/~kung-kiu.

Mladen Kap, Mälardalen University, Department of Computer Engineering, Västerås, Sweden; Compfab AB, Sweden

Mladen Kap is a development leader at Compfab AB and a researcher at Mälardalen University. He graduated from the University of Zagreb, Croatia, in 1975, and received an M.Sc. from the University of London in 1977. His fields of competence cover distributed component-based development, middleware technologies, and application integration.

Mr. Kap can be reached at mladen.kap@mdh.se or www.compfab.se.

Zeynep Kiziltan, Uppsala University, Information Science Department, Sweden

Zeynep Kiziltan is a Ph.D. student in computer science at Uppsala University, where she obtained an M.Sc. in 2000. Her research interests include combinatorial optimization problems, artificial intelligence, constraint programming, and automated software engineering.

Ms. Kiziltan can be reached at Zeynep.Kiziltan@dis.uu.se or http://www.dis.uu.se/~zeykiz.

Frank Lüders, Mälardalen University, Department of Computer Engineering, Västerås, Sweden

Frank Lüders is an industrial Ph.D. student, employed jointly by Mälardalen University and ABB Automation Products AB. Mr. Lüders received an M.Sc. from the Technical University of Denmark in 1997. His research interests include software engineering, software architecture, and distributed real-time systems.

He can be reached at frank.luders@mdh.se.

Peter O. Müller, ABB AG, Corporate Research, Germany

Peter O. Müller has an M.Sc. in telecommunications engineering and is currently working as a research employee at ABB Corporate Research in Germany. His research interests include distributed middleware and Internet connectivity for real-time systems.

Mr. Müller can be reached at peter.o.muller@de.abb.com.

Martin Naedele, ABB Corporate Research Ltd., Department of Information Technologies, Switzerland

Martin Naedele is a member of the research staff at ABB Corporate Research. He received an M.Sc. from Ruhr-University in 1997 and a Ph.D. from the Swiss Federal Institute of Technology (ETH), Zurich, in 2000. His research interests include embedded systems, fault-tolerant real-time computing, software engineering, component software, and IT security.

Dr. Naedele can be reached at martin.naedele@ch.abb.com.

Eivind J. Nordby, Karlstad University, Department of Computer Science, Sweden

Eivind J. Nordby is a senior lecturer at Karlstad University. He received an M.Sc. in computer science in 1979. His current research interests include semantic aspects of software development, software quality, and object-orientation. He is currently participating in the research project, "Improved Software Quality Through Semantic Descriptions." Mr. Nordby also served as manager of the Department of Computer Science at Karlstad.

He can be reached at eivind.nordby@kau.se or http://www.cs.kau .se/~eivind.

Christer Norström, Mälardalen University, Department of Computer Engineering, Sweden

Christer Norström is a manager at ABB Technology Partners/Robotics, Västerås, Sweden. He is also a part-time senior lecturer at Mälardalen University, and is one of the founding members of the Department of Computer Engineering. He has presented numerous courses on real-time system for industry in Sweden and in Europe. His research interests include the design of real-time systems, reliability and safety methods, software engineering, and architectures for real-time systems. He is also interested in technology transfer from academia to industry, which he manifested through several successful transfers to the automotive industry. Dr. Norström received a Ph.D. from KTH in 1997 and became a docent there in 2001. He won the student body award for best teacher at Mälardalan University.

Dr. Norström can be reached at christer.norstrom@mdh.se.

Rob van Ommering, Philips NatLab, the Netherlands

Rob van Ommering is a principal research scientist at Philips Research Laboratories, Eindhoven, the Netherlands. He graduated from the Technical University of Eindhoven in 1982. Since then, his research has embraced robotics; computer vision; machine learning; formal specification techniques; and formalization, visualization, and verification of software architectures. His current interests are in aspects of software architecture, with an emphasis on component technology and component-based architectures, particularly product families and populations of resource-constrained consumer products.

As such, he is actively involved in the definition of software architectures, and the Philips' range of analog and digital video products.

Mr. van Ommering can be reached at Rob.van.Ommering@philips .com.

Otto Preiss, ABB Corporate Research Ltd., Department of Information Technologies, Switzerland

Otto Preiss is a member of the research staff at ABB Corporate Research Ltd. He holds a B.Sc. from FH Aargau, Switzerland, and an M.Sc. from the University of Colorado at Boulder. He has worked in the area of distributed systems, primarily in the application domains of data acquisition and process control for power systems. Mr. Preiss has held different positions in development, engineering, commissioning, and product management enterprises. Before joining ABB Corporate Research in 1998, he was the head of the ABB Power Automation R&D department for product and system development of substation automation and protection systems. He is currently a registered Ph.D. candidate at the Swiss Federal Institute of Technology, Lausanne, Switzerland, with research focused on component-based software engineering and software architecture.

Mr. Preiss can be reached at otto.preiss@ch.abb.com or http://icapeople .epfl.ch/opreiss

Krithi Ramamritham, Indian Institute of Technology, Computer Science and Engineering, India

Professor Krithi Ramamritham received a Ph.D. from the University of Utah. He then joined the University of Massachusetts, and now holds a visiting position at the Indian Institute of Technology, Bombay, as the Verifone chair professor. He was a Science and Engineering Research Council (United Kingdom) visiting fellow at the University of Newcastle upon Tyne, United Kingdom, and has held visiting positions at the Technical University of Vienna, Austria, and at the Indian Institute of Technology, Madras. Professor Ramamritham's interests span the areas of real-time systems, transaction processing in database systems, real-time databases systems, mobile computing, e-commerce, intelligent Internet, and the Web. He has been chairman of many conferences. His editorial board contributions include *IEEE Transactions on Parallel and Distributed Systems* and the *Real-Time Systems Journal.* He has coauthored two IEEE tutorial texts on real-time systems.

Professor Ramamritham can be reached at krithi@cse.iitb.ac.in.

Rémy Sanlaville, Dassault Systèmes Research Lab, LSR-IMAG Research Lab, France

Rémy Sanlaville is a Ph.D. student at the University of Grenoble, France. He is a member of the Adèle team and has been working for Dassault Systèmes for 3 years. His current research interests include large-scale software, software architecture, component-based software engineering and reverse engineering.

Mr. Sanlaville can be reached at Remy.Sanlaville@imag.fr or http://www-adele .imag.fr/~sanlavil.

Chia Shen, Cambridge Research Lab, Mitsubishi Electric Research Labs, Cambridge, Massachusetts

Dr. Chia Shen is an associate director and senior research scientist at the MERL Cambridge Research Laboratory, Cambridge, Massachusetts. She received a Ph.D. from the University of Massachusetts, Amherst, in 1992. Dr. Shen's research interest has been in distributed real-time and multimedia systems.

She can be reached at shen@merl.com or http://www.merl.com/people/shen.

Judith A. Stafford, Software Engineering Institute, Carnegie Mellon University, Pittsburgh, Pennsylvania

Judith Stafford is a senior member of the technical staff at the Software Engineering Institute (SEI), Carnegie Mellon University. For several years, Dr. Stafford has worked in the areas of software architecture, compositional reasoning, and component-based systems. She currently coleads the Predictable Assembly from Certifiable Components project at the SEI.

Dr. Stafford can be reached at jas@sei.cmu.edu or http://www.sei.cmu .edu/staff/jas.

Christian M. Stich, ABB, Corporate Research, Ladenburg/Mannheim, Germany

Christian M. Stich is a scientist at ABB Corporate Research in Ladenburg/Mannheim. He received an M.Sc. from the University of Applied Science, Harz, Germany. His competences are in embedded systems, microcontrollers, DSPs, field devices, and real-time operating systems.

Mr. Stich can be reached at christian.stich@de.abb.com.

Henrik Thane, Mälardalen University, Department of Computer Engineering, Sweden

Dr. Henrik Thane is a senior lecturer at Mälardalen University. He received an M.Sc. in computer science from Uppsala University, Sweden, in 1995, a technical licentiate in mechatronics from KTH, Stockholm, in 1997, and a Ph.D. in mechatronics in 2000. His research interests include the design and verification of safety-critical systems; monitoring, testing and debugging of distributed real-time systems; and real-time operating system design, and scheduling.

Dr. Thane can be reached at henrik.thane@mdh.se.

Jeffrey Voas, Cigital, Dulles, Virgina

Jeffrey Voas is the chief scientist at Cigital. He is a senior member of the IEEE, he received a Ph.D. from the College of William & Mary in 1990, and was named the 1999 Young Engineer of the Year by the District of Columbia Council of Engineering and Architectural Societies. Dr. Voas was a corecipient of the IEEE's Reliability Engineer of the Year award in 2000, and he received a Third Millennium Medal from the IEEE in 2000. In 2000, he also received a Meritorious Service award from the IEEE Computer Society. Dr. Voas was the general and program chair for several conferences. He has coauthored two books: *Software Assessment: Reliability, Safety, Testability* (Wiley, 1995) and *Software Fault Injection: Inoculating Programs Against Errors*(Wiley, 1998).

Dr. Voas can be reached at voas@cigital.com or http://www.cigital .com/research/jmv.html.

Anders Wall, Mälardalen University, Department of Computer Engineering, Västerås, Sweden

Anders Wall is a Ph.D. student at Mälardalen University. He received an M.Sc. in 1994, and a Ph.Lic. from Uppsala University, Sweden, in 2000. His research interests include the design of real-time systems, software architectures, product-line architectures, and component-based software engineering for real-time systems and formal methods for real-time systems.

Mr. Wall can be reached at anders.wall@mdh.se.

Kurt Wallnau, Software Engineering Institute (SEI), Dynamic Systems Program, Pittsburgh, Pennsylvania

Kurt Wallnau has 15 years of software development experience in industry, defense, and research. His principal interests are commercial off-the-shelf (COTS) software integration and component-based software engineering. Mr. Wallnau's most recent tour at the SEI, Carnegie Mellon University, began in 1994. His primary areas of investigation at the SEI have been the techniques and technologies of COTS software integration and component-based software engineering. He co-organized the 1998 International Conference on Software Engineering (ICSE) workshop on component-based software engineering and he is co-organizing the follow-up workshop, also affiliated with the 2001 ICSE. Mr. Wallnau has published several articles in the area of COTS and component-based software engineering. He is the coauthor of *Building Systems from Commercial Components* (Addison-Wesley, 2002), and he currently coleads the Predictable Assembly from the Certifiable Components project.

Mr. Wallnau can be reached at kcw@sei.cmu.edu or http://www.sei .cmu.edu/staff/kcw.

Christian Zeidler, ABB, Corporate Research, Germany

Christian Zeidler received a Ph.D. in computer science from the University of Karlsruhe, Germany, in 1994. Within the context of DOCASE he has investigated metaprogramming-based dynamic configuration management of object-oriented distributed applications. Since 1994 he has been working for ABB Corporate Research in different positions, including the department leader for industrial IT. Dr. Zeidler's fields of IT competence cover distributed systems/application, middleware technologies, application integration, and componentware with a strong software engineering perspective. He is a member of the German Computer Society and the leader of the object-oriented software development group. He is also ABB's corporate research representative for all OMG-related activities.

Dr. Zeidler can be reached at zeidler@decrc.abb.de.

Index

For further information on these and other Artech House titles, including previously considered out-of-print books now available through our In-Print-Forever® (IPF®) program, contact:

Artech House	Artech House
685 Canton Street	46 Gillingham Street
Norwood, MA 02062	London SW1V 1AH UK
Phone: 781-769-9750	Phone: +44 (0)20 7596-8750
Fax: 781-769-6334	Fax: +44 (0)20 7630-0166
e-mail: artech@artechhouse.com	e-mail: artech-uk@artechhouse.com

Find us on the World Wide Web at:
www.artechhouse.com